AN INTRODUCTION TO AKKADIAN LITERATURE

An Introduction to Akkadian Literature

Contexts and Content

ALAN LENZI

EISENBRAUNS | University Park, Pennsylvania

Library of Congress Cataloging-in-Publication Data

Names: Lenzi, Alan, author.
Title: An introduction to Akkadian literature : contexts and content / Alan Lenzi.
Description: University Park, Pennsylvania : Eisenbrauns, [2019] | Includes biblio-
    graphical references and index.
Summary: "A short introduction to the study of Akkadian literature from ancient Baby-
    lonia and Assyria, encompassing some two thousand years of literary history of the
    ancient Middle East"—Provided by publisher.
Identifiers: LCCN 2019026488 | ISBN 9781575067292 (paperback)
Subjects: LCSH: Assyro-Babylonian literature—History and criticism.
Classification: LCC PJ3601.L46 2019 | DDC 892/.1—dc23
LC record available at https://lccn.loc.gov/2019026488

Published by The Pennsylvania State University Press,
University Park, PA 16802–1003

Eisenbrauns is an imprint of The Pennsylvania State University Press.

The Pennsylvania State University Press is a member of the Association of University
Presses.

It is the policy of The Pennsylvania State University Press to use acid-free paper. Publications on uncoated stock satisfy the minimum requirements of American National
Standard for Information Sciences—Permanence of Paper for Printed Library Material, ANSI Z39.48–1992.

I dedicate this book to my parents,

Alan and Sharon Lenzi,

who taught me the value of hard work.

CONTENTS

ILLUSTRATIONS

Figures

Maps

ACKNOWLEDGMENTS

I wish to thank Daniel Selden, professor of comparative literature at University of California–Santa Cruz, for inviting me to write a survey of Akkadian literature. What started out as an essay turned into a book. Without his invitation and encouragement, I would likely never have undertaken the task, which was more difficult and more enjoyable than I would have ever guessed. I also wish to thank University of the Pacific in Stockton, California, where I have taught for the last thirteen years. A summer research grant freed me from teaching and gave me the time to write the lion's share of what follows, and an internal grant covered the costs associated with the licensing of images in the book. I also extend my thanks to the interlibrary loan staff at the university library, especially Monica Schutzman, who patiently provided essential research support. Finally, I offer heart-felt thanks to those who read preliminary versions of this book in 2015 and 2016, including Benjamin Foster, Christopher Hays, and Daniel Selden; to my student Ziadelyn Mercado, who read chapters with me as I revised in the fall semester of 2017; to the two anonymous academic reviewers, who read the penultimate version of the book in the late summer of 2018; to Jeffrey Cooley, who commented on the Conclusion; and to Jim Eisenbraun and James Spinti, who shepherded the book through the publication process. The final version of the book is better for all of the suggestions, criticisms, and insights I received from these generous individuals. I alone, of course, bear sole responsibility for any errors, infelicities, or misjudgments.

Alan Lenzi
February 2019

ABBREVIATIONS

Chronological Periods/Linguistic Designations (see p. 3):

OB	Old Babylonian
MB	Middle Babylonian
SB	Standard Babylonian
NB	Neo-Babylonian
LB	Late Babylonian
OA	Old Assyrian
MA	Middle Assyrian
NA	Neo-Assyrian

Secondary Literature Abbreviations

AbB	*Altbabylonische Briefe in Umschrift und Übersetzung.* Edited by Fritz R. Kraus. Leiden: Brill, 1964–
ActAnt	Acta Antiqua Academiae Scientiarum Hungaricae
ADOG	Abhandlungen der Deutsche Orient-Gesellschaft
AEPHE.PH	*Annuaire de l'École Pratique des Hautes Études Section des Sciences Historiques et Philosophiques*
AfO	*Archiv für Orientforschung*
AfOB	Archiv für Orientforschung: Beiheft
AHAW	Abhandlungen der Heidelberger Akademie der Wissenschaften
AIL	Ancient Israel and Its Literature
AION	*Annali dell'Istituto Orientale di Napoli*
ALASP	Abhandlungen zur Literatur Alt-Syrien-Palästinas und Mesopotamiens
AMD	Ancient Magic and Divination
ANEM	Ancient Near East Monographs/Monografías sobre el Antiguo Cercano Oriente

ANES	*Ancient Near Eastern Studies*
ANESSup	Ancient Near Eastern Studies Supplement Series
AnOr	Analecta Orientalia
AnSt	*Anatolian Studies*
AOAT	Alter Orient und Altes Testament
AoF	Altorientalische Forschungen
AOS	American Oriental Series
Aramazd	*Aramazd: Armenian Journal of Near Eastern Studies*
ArOr	*Archív orientální*
AS	Assyriological Studies
Asdiwal	*Asdiwal: Revue genevoise d'anthropologie et d'histoire des religions*
ASJ	*Acta Sumerologica*
AuOr	*Aula Orientalis*
AuOrSup	Aula Orientalis Supplementa
BaF	Baghdader Forschungen
BAM	Die babylonisch-assyrische Medizin in Texten und Untersuchungen
BAW	Bibliothek der alten Welt
BBVO	Berliner Beiträge zum Vorderen Orient Texte
Bib	*Biblica*
BibSem	The Biblical Seminar
BJS	Brown Judaic Studies
BO	Bibliotheca Orientalis
BPOA	Biblioteca del Proximo Oriente Antiguo
BSAH	Blackwell Sourcebooks in Ancient History
BSR	*Bulletin for the Study of Religion*
BZAW	Beihefte zur Zeitschrift für die Alttestamentliche Wissenschaft
CAH	Cambridge Ancient History
CANE	*Civilizations of the Ancient Near East*. Edited by Jack M. Sasson. 4 vols. New York, 1995. Repr. in 2 vols. Peabody, MA: Hendrickson, 2006
CBET	Contributions to Biblical Exegesis and Theology
CBQMS	Catholic Biblical Quarterly Monograph Series
CDOG	Colloquien der Deutschen Orient-Gesellschaft
CHANE	Culture and History of the Ancient Near East
CM	Cuneiform Monographs
CNIP	Carsten Niebuhr Institute Publications
ConBOT	Coniectanea Biblica: Old Testament Series
CThM	Calwer theologische Monographien

CUSAS	Cornell University Studies in Assyriology and Sumerology
DSD	*Dead Sea Discoveries*
EPHE.PH	École Pratique des Hautes Études Section des Sciences Historiques et Philosophiques
FAOS	Frieburger altorientalische Studien
GAAL	Göttinger Arbeitshefte zur altorientalischen Literatur
GMTR	Guides to the Mesopotamian Textual Record
HBM	Hebrew Bible Monographs
HdO	Handbuch der Orientalistik
HR	*History of Religions*
HSAO	Heidelberger Studien zum Alten Orient
HSM	Harvard Semitic Monographs
HSS	Harvard Semitic Studies
IOS	Israel Oriental Studies
JANER	*Journal of Ancient Near Eastern Religions*
JANESCU	*Journal of the Ancient Near Eastern Society of Columbia University*
JAOS	*Journal of the American Oriental Society*
JCS	*Journal of Cuneiform Studies*
JEOL	*Jaarbericht van het Vooraziatisch-Egyptisch Gezelschap (Genootschap) Ex oriente lux*
JHS	*Journal of Hellenic Studies*
JNES	*Journal of Near Eastern Studies*
JRAS	*Journal of the Royal Asiatic Society*
LAOS	Leipziger Altorientalische Studien
LHBOTS	Library of the Hebrew Bible/Old Testament Studies
LSAWS	*Linguistic Studies in Ancient West Semitic*
MC	Mesopotamian Civilizations
Mesopotamia	Mesopotamia: Copenhagen Studies in Assyriology
MIOF	*Mitteilungen des Instituts für Orientforschung*
MVAG	Mitteilungen der Vorderasiatisch-Aegyptischen Gesellschaft
NABU	*Nouvelles assyriologiques brèves et utilitaires*
OAC	Orientis Antiqui Collectio
OBC	Orientalia Biblica et Christiana
OBO	Orbis Biblicus et Orientalis
OCuT	Oxford Editions of Cuneiform Texts
OEANE	*The Oxford Encyclopedia of Archaeology in the Near East.* Edited by Eric M. Meyers. 5 vols. New York: Oxford University Press, 1997

OHCC	*The Oxford Handbook of Cuneiform Cultures.* Edited by Karen Radner and Eleanor Robson. New York: Oxford University Press, 2011
OIP	Oriental Institute Publications
OIS	Oriental Institute Seminars
OLA	Orientalia Lovaniensia Analecta
OLP	*Orientalia Lovaniensia Periodica*
Or	*Orientalia* (NS)
ORA	Orientalische Religionen in der Antike
OrAnt	*Oriens Antiquus*
PIHANS	Publications de l'Institut historique-archéologique néerlandais de Stamboul
RA	*Revue d'assyriologie et d'archéologie orientale*
RANE	Records of the Ancient Near East
RC	*Religion Compass*
ResOr	Res Orientales
RIMA	Royal Inscriptions of Mesopotamia Assyrian Periods
RIMB	Royal Inscriptions of Mesopotamia Babylonian Periods
RIME	Royal Inscriptions of Mesopotamia Early Periods
RIMS	Royal Inscriptions of Mesopotamia Supplements
RINAP	Royal Inscriptions of the Neo-Assyrian Period
RlA	*Reallexikon der Assyriologie.* Edited by Erich Ebeling et al. Berlin: de Gruyter, 1928–.
RSO	*Rivista degli studi orientali*
SAA	State Archives of Assyria
SAAB	*State Archives of Assyrian Bulletin*
SAACT	State Archives of Assyria Cuneiform Texts
SAALT	State Archives of Assyria Literary Texts
SAAS	State Archives of Assyria Studies
SANE	Sources of the Ancient Near East
SANER	Studies in Ancient Near Eastern Records
SAOC	Studies in Ancient Oriental Civilizations
SEL	*Studia epigrafici e linguistici sul Vicino Oriente antico*
SHANE	Studies in the History of the Ancient Near East
SHR	Studies in the History of Religions (supplements to *Numen*)
SSN	Studia Semitica Neerlandica
StOr	Studia Orientalia
StPohlSM	Studia Pohl Series Maior
StSem	Studi semitici
SymS	Symposium Series

TAPS	Transactions of the American Philosophical Society
TCS	Texts from Cuneiform Sources
TSAJ	Texte und Studien zum antiken Judentum
TUAT	*Texte aus der Umwelt des Alten Testaments*. Edited by Otto Kaiser. Gütersloh: Mohn, 1984–
VAB	Vorderasiatische Bibliothek
VS	Vorderasiatische Schriftdenkmäler der (Königlichen) Museen zu Berlin
WAW	Writings from the Ancient World
WMANT	Wissenschaftliche Monographien zum Alten und Neuen Testament
WO	*Die Welt des Orients*
WZKM	*Wiener Zeitschrift für die Kunde des Morgenlandes*
ZA	*Zeitschrift für Assyriologie*
ZABR	*Zeitschrift für altorientalische und biblische Rechtsgeschichte*

Other Abbreviations

Akk.	Akkadian
ca	circa
ed(s).	edition, edited by, editor(s)
enl.	enlarged
ETCSL	Electronic Text Corpus of Sumerian Literature (http://etcsl.orinst.ox.ac.uk/)
fig(s).	figure(s)
MS(S)	manuscript(s)
ORACC	Open Richly Annotated Cuneiform Corpus (http://oracc.museum.upenn.edu/index.html)
pers. comm.	personal communication
pl(s).	plate(s)
PN	Proper Name
repr.	reprinted
rev.	revised
SEAL	Sources of Early Akkadian Literature (http://www.seal.uni-leipzig.de/)
Sum.	Sumerian
supp.	supplement

PROLOGUE

> Shumma izbu is difficult to interpret. The first time that I come before
> the king, my lord, I shall (personally) show, with this tablet that I am
> sending to the king, my lord, how the omen is written. Really, [the one]
> who has [not] had (the meaning) pointed out to him cannot possibly
> understand it.[1]

So wrote a seventh-century BCE scholar named Balasi to his employer, the
Assyrian king. Although Balasi's words were limited to the difficulty of interpreting an omen in the divination text series dealing with malformed births
(called Shumma izbu), they could just as easily apply to the contemporary difficulty of reading ancient Akkadian literature in general: without a guide, the
material is difficult to understand. The present book aims to be your guide.

The book is written for two different kinds of readers. The first are students
or general readers who wish to obtain an introductory knowledge of Akkadian
literature with a relatively small investment of time. For those of you in this
group, the main text of the book (without reference to the footnotes) will be
sufficient to get a sense of the issues that you face when reading Akkadian
literature and, in the second part of the book, to become acquainted with the
contents of a wide selection of works from the corpus. The other readership is
the nonspecialist scholar and advanced student in the humanities and historical
disciplines, ranging across fields such as Assyriology, Egyptology, biblical studies, comparative literature, and history of religions, who require more detail than
the main text provides. For those of you in this group, I offer extensive notes

---

1. Parpola 1993, no. 60, rev. 1–14. Parpola uses brackets to indicate words that had to be restored
on the broken tablet and parentheses around words supplied for sense. I have changed his spelling
of the Akkadian word *šumma* to *shumma* for the sake of clarity. For the use of special characters in
Akkadian, see page 19, below.

and bibliography that will initiate you into the recondite world of Assyriology, pointing you to text editions, criticism, and more. However you self-identify, the footnotes add a layer of depth to specific discussions in the main text and document the scholarly resources consulted and available so that those of you wanting to move to the next level (on a specific point or within the field as a whole) will have a good idea about how to get there.[2] Perhaps along the way I will convince a few souls from both groups who are not already headed into Assyriology to wander into the field and lend a hand to a task much too large (but so very interesting!) for the few scholars working in it.

For all readers, my ultimate goal in this survey is to describe and to commend an ancient body of writing to you that is both fascinating and enriching. Imagine a scribe 3,700 years ago explaining to his readers the origins of humanity (see Atram-hasis, 80, below) or a poet musing on the meaning of human suffering many centuries before the composition of the biblical book of Job (see Ludlul bel nemeqi, 175, below). Akkadian literature offers you this and much, much more. Though their histories and cultures are foreign to us—both stubbornly and delightfully so—the ancient Mesopotamian scribes responsible for the corpus surveyed here asked questions and expressed concerns that are somehow still familiar. Their literary and religious sensibilities differed markedly from our own, but as fellow human beings we can recognize—with a little effort—the artistry of their literary creations and the pathos of their religious expressions.

Assurbanipal, one of the few kings in ancient Mesopotamia who claimed to be literate, boasted in one of his royal inscriptions that he "read cunningly written text in Sumerian, dark Akkadian, the interpretation of which is difficult . . . (and) examined stone inscriptions from before the flood, which are sealed, stopped up, mixed up."[3] The latter inscriptions were understood to be very ancient literature *for him* in his own time. His boasting of reading such ancient documents, as the broader context makes clear, was intended to boost his image as a wise, knowledgeable king, who sat among scholars discussing the most difficult treatises of the day. In other words, he was establishing his scholarly *bona fides*. To attain knowledge and to earn respect among one's peers are not bad reasons for learning something, including learning something about Akkadian literature. But perhaps we should go beyond Assurbanipal's example—Assyrian kings were not known for proclaiming their introspection— and look a little deeper into ourselves for why we take an interest in this ancient material.

---

2. Despite what may look like an extensive bibliography, I have cited only a fraction of what exists in the secondary literature. It is hoped that what is cited will give the reader a point of entry into the broader body of scholarship.

3. Livingstone 2007, 100.

Why study this arcane literary corpus? What is there to gain, collectively and individually, from looking to the past and reading these long-dead voices? As challenging as these questions are, I submit that their answer is relatively straightforward and, in part, rooted in the same reason we read other kinds of literature: we want to understand ourselves.[4] I encourage you then to ask yourself as you engage in the cross-cultural, cross-temporal activity of reading ancient Akkadian literature: How does this literature affect me, my understanding of the society I live in, my place in it, and my broader outlook on the world? Although such questions have a peculiarly contemporary orientation, we fool ourselves if we believe our interest in the ancient world is simply a dispassionate antiquarianism or a rationalistic quest for knowledge. Part of understanding Akkadian literature is coming to terms with why you and I have any interest in it at all.

---

4. See Waxler 2014 for this important function of literature in general, though his point of view is limited to a narrower idea of (contemporary) literature than is used in this book.

INTRODUCTION

Akkadian: Linguistic, Geographical, and Chronological Parameters

"Akkadian" is the modern linguistic term for the ancient East Semitic dialects inscribed on clay tablets in cuneiform scripts used primarily in ancient Babylonia and Assyria (Mesopotamia) but also in regions peripheral to Mesopotamia proper (e.g., Syria, Elam) from roughly the middle of the third millennium BCE to around the turn of the eras.[1] Although derived from an ancient Babylonian word, "Akkadian" does not correspond to any ancient designation for the various dialects of the language considered as a whole. Akkadian exists today only in written documents.[2]

As a Semitic language, Akkadian is related to several other ancient languages such as Biblical Hebrew, Phoenician, and various dialects of Aramaic, as well as Ugaritic and Amorite. It is also related to a number of modern Semitic languages, including Arabic, Modern Israeli Hebrew, Neo-Aramaic, Amharic, and Tigrinya. Although influenced at one time or another by some of the ancient Semitic languages listed above (e.g., Amorite in the second millennium and

---

1. For other introductions and overviews published in the last few decades, see Reiner 1978; Röllig 1987; Reiner 1991; Bottéro 1995; Edzard 2004; Foster 2005, 2007, 2009. An introduction by Streck and Wasserman will appear in *Handbook of Ancient Mesopotamia* ("Akkadian Literature," forthcoming). They are also preparing monographs on various Babylonian and Assyrian works of literature as part of their on-going Sources of Early Akkadian Literature (SEAL) project. For grammatical or linguistic introductions to the language, see, e.g., Buccellati 1996; Huehnergard and Woods 2004; and various contributions in Weniger 2011, 330–424.

2. The fact that our knowledge of Akkadian dialects is derived completely from written evidence has important ramifications. As Michalowski notes, "in Assyriology we are used to collapsing broad diachronic and synchronic spans with a single linguistic label such as 'Sumerian' and 'Akkadian'. Since Sumerian [though his comments also apply to Akkadian] is known to us solely through the medium of writing it is extremely difficult to disentangle linguistic features of written language from anything else. . . . The vernaculars must have had more differentiation than we can detect in the written tradition, as there is simply not enough change in the language of the texts over a long span of time" (2005, 187).

Aramaic in the first), <u>non-Semitic languages</u> have also had an impact on Akkadian. Chief among these non-Semitic influences is Sumerian, the other major language of ancient Mesopotamia. Sumerian lent its ever-evolving cuneiform script to Akkadian and had a restrictive effect on Akkadian phonology.[3] It also contributed to Akkadian vocabulary and probably steered Akkadian prose to adopt Sumerian's preference for verb-final word order.[4] As some literary texts in Akkadian have predecessors in Sumerian, the latter also shaped the Akkadian literary corpus and aesthetics. "The two traditions are so closely connected," Benjamin Foster writes, "that one can speak of a hybrid Sumero-Akkadian literary culture, even in the Late period."[5]

The Akkadian language has a long and rich history.[6] <u>Its first attestation may occur in proper names on tablets from Shuruppak (Fara) and Tell Abu Salabikh in the mid-third millennium BCE.[7] Its last datable attestation exists on a Late Babylonian astronomical ephemeride from the first century CE.</u>[8] At the start of the second millennium BCE we may distinguish two major Akkadian dialects, Babylonian and Assyrian, centered in distinct geographic regions. The Babylonian dialect, termed *akkadû*, "Akkadian," in distinction to Sumerian, flourished in the southern part of the land, that is, in Babylonia, an area bounded by the Tigris and Euphrates Rivers and extending from just north of modern Baghdad southward to the Persian Gulf. The Assyrian dialect, called *aššurû*, "Assyrian," by its users, was concentrated in the north, that is, in Assyria, a land centered along the middle Tigris but extending from around modern Mosul downstream to the hills of Jebel Hamrin, some 210 km from modern Baghdad to the south.[9]

Akkadian, however, was not limited to Mesopotamia. Already in the third millennium we find evidence for its use in Syrian and Elamite cities (e.g., Mari

---

3. On the cuneiform script, see the accessible introduction by Walker 1987a and the more advanced discussion in essays by Michalowski, Cooper, and Gragg in Daniels and Bright 1996, 33–72. For Sumerian's influence on Akkadian phonology, see Zólyomi 2011.

4. For Sumerian's contribution to Akkadian vocabulary, see Lieberman 1977. Other non-Semitic languages that contributed to Akkadian vocabulary include Hurrian, Egyptian, Old Persian, and Greek. For an overview of Akkadian vocabulary (number of lexemes [16,526 on one count], loanwords, etc.), see Streck 2014. Lexica are mentioned below. Not everyone agrees about Sumerian's influence on Akkadian word order. See the discussion with literature in Michalowski 2005, 182–83.

5. For a general statement with literature, see Foster 2005, 44, whence comes the quotation. The influence was reciprocal. For an overview of Sumerian literature, see Rubio 2009.

6. George 2007a provides a historical survey with extensive literature.

7. See Kouwenberg 2011, 330–31 for a brief discussion with literature.

8. Its editors date it to 79/80 CE (Hunger and de Jong 2014). Some scholars suggest the so-called Graeco-Babyloniaca tablets (which exhibit Akkadian and Sumerian written with the Greek alphabet) push the use of Akkadian even farther into the Common Era (see Geller 1997; differently A. Westenholz 2007; for a recent treatment of the material with extensive secondary literature, see Oelsner 2014).

9. For a succinct geographic survey of Assyria, see Saggs 1984, 2–6; for Babylonia, see Oates 1986, 11–13.

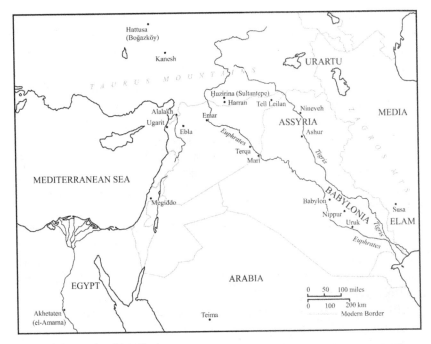

MAP I. The Ancient Near East.

and Susa, respectively) as a result of Sargonic conquests and administration.[10]
It was during the mid- and late second millennium that the language was
exported far beyond the land between the rivers to places including el-Amarna
in Egypt, Ugarit along the Syrian coast, and the Hittite capital Hattusa, 150 km
east of the modern Turkish capital Ankara, among others. The Akkadian dialects
in these distant locales are considered "peripheral," showing several linguistic
peculiarities that would take us too far afield to describe here.

Scholars generally combine geographical and chronological terms to refer
to the various Akkadian dialects that arose during the language's long history.[11]
Thus, Old Akkadian, also known as Sargonic Akkadian, designates the Akkadian dialect used during Sargon's Akkadian Empire (2334–2154 BCE), and pre-
Sargonic Akkadian refers to the various archaic forms of the language used at
sites from the mid-third millennium (e.g., Mari and Kish).[12] The Babylonian
dialects break down into Archaic Old Babylonian (Ur III, 2112–2004 BCE),

10. See Van De Mieroop 2007, 74.

11. For brief sketches of these linguistic divisions, see George 2007a; von Soden 1995, 296–302.

12. The absolute chronology used in this book follows J. A. Brinkman's, presented as an appendix in Oppenheim and Reiner 1977, 335–48. Scholars continue to debate and refine absolute dates
prior to the first millennium.

Old Babylonian (2000–1500 BCE; abbreviated OB), Middle Babylonian (1500–1000 BCE; MB), Neo-Babylonian (1000–600 BCE; NB), and Late Babylonian (600 BCE–100 CE; LB). Assyrian follows suit, with Old Assyrian (2000–1500 BCE; OA), Middle Assyrian (1500–1000 BCE; MA), and Neo-Assyrian (1000–600 BCE; NA).[13] There are a few exceptions to this rule, including the various peripheral dialects of the language reflected in archives found outside Mesopotamia (e.g., el-Amarna and Hattusa, mentioned above) and the so-called literary "dialects" or styles. The latter include the hymno-epic "dialect" of some OB literary texts and Standard Babylonian (SB; in German, *das Jungbabylonisch*), which designates the literary style of Akkadian used from the latter part of the second millennium on.[14] Since all of these dialects are Akkadian, their literatures will be considered together in this survey.

The periodization/categorization sketched above should not give the impression of linguistic uniformity within each period or tight compartmentalization. It is, rather, a scholarly convenience since within each period (the timeframes of which are simplified) and within each dialect there are linguistic variations, and this to differing degrees.[15] The *historical* periodization of the field, including studies related to literary history, largely follows the lines set out by the broad *linguistic* periodization given above.[16]

Specifying the time period from which a tablet comes archaeologically does not automatically determine the linguistic dialect of the text inscribed upon it. This may be the case *sometimes*—as in the treaties used in the Neo-Assyrian period, almost of all of which are written in the Neo-Assyrian dialect of Akkadian—but not always. A narrative poem, for example, may be attested in manuscripts from several different periods within the first millennium and yet they all may bear witness to a text in the same Standard Babylonian literary dialect

---

13. These time periods may also refer to the evolution of the cuneiform script used to write the language.

14. As George explains, some OB literary texts are written with "an elevated register of the poetic language," which "is not a true dialect but literary Old Babylonian embellished with archaizing features" (2007a, 46). Von Soden coined the term and described the dialect in two articles (1931, 1933), which Groneberg 1971 elaborated upon. C. Hess 2010 reflects on the origins of the "dialect." Lambert 2013, 34–44 provides a critical assessment of its applicability to Enuma Elish, which von Soden dated to the OB period (disputed by Lambert) and thus included in his study. Izre'el and Cohen 2004 offer a grammar of what they call Literary Old Babylonian, a term they use for a more circumscribed corpus than what "hymno-epic" usually designates (p. 2). Wasserman 2003b looks at stylistic features of OB literary texts. Metzler 2002, although focused on understanding verbal usage, is a resource of much broader value in the study of OB literary texts. See Groneberg 1987 for a description of Standard Babylonian's distinctive features (in SB hymns).

15. The same could be said of the cuneiform script used to record the Akkadian texts, which underwent significant evolution and regional development.

16. Van De Mieroop 2007; Kuhrt 1995 are standard historical overviews of the ancient Near East—the latter includes Egypt. Foster 2009, 142–64 provides a more concise historical overview that emphasizes specifics important to Akkadian literary history.

(minor linguistic variations notwithstanding) since that was the dialect of choice for such poems. There is also the problem of copied tablets and "heirlooms," whose archaeological context may not match the inscribed text's time of origin. A tablet found, for example, in a Middle Babylonian historical context may in fact have been copied from an Old Babylonian original and thus attest a dialect of the language (and script) that is older than the inscribed tablet itself. A similar problem occurs with what I have called heirloom tablets. An archive of tablets may hold (or have acquired) tablets written centuries earlier than the time period in which the archive actually flourished. Such tablets and the dialect of Akkadian inscribed on them could be centuries older than the archaeological context would indicate for the archive as a whole. When a tablet has no archaeological provenance, which is all too often the case, scholars must use internal evidence from both the language and script to infer its probable time of origin.[17] As one might guess, competent scholars may come to different conclusions in particularly difficult cases.

Although Akkadian is only preserved for us on inscribed tablets and other objects, there is reason to believe that it was largely displaced as a spoken language by Aramaic in the early or mid-first millennium BCE.[18] Thus, Akkadian, as Sumerian before it (sometime during the end of the third millennium BCE), became a dead, recondite language of scribal scholarship.[19] During the last half of the first millennium BCE, Akkadian was increasingly limited in its use to the scholars who worked in the temple communities of urban centers such as Uruk and Babylon.[20]

An Overview of the Textual Record

Scribes used Akkadian in a vast array of genres, ranging from the tediously mundane to the literarily sophisticated.[21] Administrative documents are by far the most numerous cuneiform tablets in museum holdings today. Such documents run the gamut of written records a Mesopotamian institution, business, or individual might need. For example, ration lists, inventories, personnel records,

---

17. Cuneiform paleography is still an underdeveloped area of study within the field. One recent project, Late Babylonian Signs (https://labasi.acdh.oeaw.ac.at/), treats the paleography of cuneiform signs on Babylonian tablets from the late seventh century BCE until the end of the cuneiform tradition.

18. See George 2007a, 61.

19. See Michalowski's important framing of the death of Sumerian (2005).

20. See Clancier 2011.

21. See George 2007a, 32 for a tabular presentation of the various types of texts; Charpin 2010 for a fuller introduction; Radner and Robson 2011 for an extensive treatment of various aspects of cuneiform culture.

accounting documents, and receipts are common text types. Often found with such administrative documents are letters—personal and/or official—as well as legal texts, which might include contracts (loans, marriages, adoptions), judicial rulings, and deeds of sale or inheritance. Occasionally, one finds tablets containing culinary recipes or a handbook describing a craft (e.g., glassmaking and horse training). Royal texts are quite common. Kings commissioned votive and building inscriptions to commemorate their piety and magnanimity. They published annalistic texts to immortalize their military campaigns. They drafted treaties to advance their political agendas. And they promulgated written laws, decrees, and grants of land to exemplify justice and paternal concern for their people. In service to the king or a temple were scribes, scholars, and cultic officials, who created large textual corpora preserving knowledge (revelatory, ritual, and liturgical) related to discerning the divine will and maintaining proper divine-human relations—both of which were central to royal interests. These bodies of knowledge included a vast array of omen collections, prayers, incantations, laments, hymns, rituals, therapeutic procedures, lists of effective plants and stones, and medicinal recipes, among other things. The scholars left behind a sizable body of professional correspondence in which they reported their divinatory findings or made ritual recommendations to the king. Scribes and scholars also produced in the course of their professional activities written lists of culturally important items and observations, ranging from year names to king lists, astronomical phenomena to the price of grain. They preserved mathematical tables and problems in writing. And they developed various written materials related to scribal education (e.g., extensive lists of signs, vocabularies, and synonyms; explanatory commentaries and grammatical treatises; and texts in praise of scribalism). Scholars and priests were also responsible for the creation and preservation of the narrative poems, epics, and reflective poems attested in Akkadian. Alongside all of these institutionally important texts we also find proverbs, folktales, love lyrics, and disputes that may reflect (at some earlier stage, perhaps) the *vox populi*, even if the tablets were found in institutional or professional scribal archaeological contexts. This panoply of Akkadian textual remains is a key component for understanding the vitality and complexity of the Mesopotamian societies that flourished and died during Akkadian's long life span.

The present survey would grow to an unmanageable size if it were to elaborate on all of these genres and text types. Instead, it focuses on a broad selection of texts preserved in Akkadian to give the reader a panoramic view of what one may read in the language. The word "literature," therefore, in the title of this book should be understood in a much broader sense, as is often the case in Assyriological practice, than what we may call literature or *belles lettres* for modern languages.[22] Although narrative poems and traditionally identified literary texts occupy a prominent place in the following pages, satires, proverbs, dialogues, prayers, incantations, and hymns find a place, too. One finds such an inclusive definition of "literature" in Foster's important anthology of Akkadian texts in translation, *Before the Muses* (3rd edition, 2005), which makes an excellent omnibus for much of the material covered herein. In addition to these texts and harking back to an earlier, more expansive definition of "literature" in the field, the survey in this book also includes royal inscriptions, treaties, law collections, omen series, and other scholarly texts.[23] Thus, this book surveys under the label "literature" texts that we might consider having a literary, political, scholarly, and religious character—all anachronistic and artificially separated categories that reflect our own modern conceptual taxonomies. As stated before, the goal of the present book is to acquaint the reader with the critical issues surrounding and the content of a wide selection of texts written in the Akkadian language. A broadly inclusive approach to "literature" achieves this purpose best.

22. See Wasserman 2003b, 185–224 for a very broad definition of Old Babylonian "literary texts," which includes incantations. On the lack of an indigenous concept of *belles lettres* in ancient Mesopotamia, see his comments on p. 183.

23. See, e.g., Bezold 1886; Weber 1907; Jean 1924; Meissner 1927; Dhorme 1937.

CHAPTER I

Prolegomena to the Study of Akkadian Literature

Modern readers typically find Akkadian texts difficult because they are so foreign, not only in their cultural and chronological origins but also in their material production, literary expressions, and social uses. To read these texts with greater understanding the reader needs to acquire a certain level of literary and cultural competence, that is, a knowledge of the historical and cultural contexts of ancient Mesopotamian scribal production as well as the literary and poetic conventions used in Akkadian texts. As a first step toward developing this competence this chapter offers a number of introductory discussions organized under four key rubrics: tablets, scribes, compositions, and audiences. The chapter begins with the physical materials used for writing and moves on to a discussion of the scribes who produced the texts inscribed on this material and the institutional contexts in which they worked. It turns then to a description of the general characteristics of Akkadian compositions with an emphasis on poetic and literary features and concludes with some brief reflections on the various audiences or users of Akkadian texts.

In charting such a course, the present treatment aligns itself with what Niek Veldhuis has called the social-functional approach to ancient Mesopotamian texts, which attempts to understand texts within the institutional contexts that produced and maintained them.[1] The social-functional approach takes seriously both the historical context of the texts, emphasized in what Veldhuis calls the documentarian approach, and their formal features, emphasized in what Veldhuis dubs the poetic approach. Although the present introduction casts its net broader than Veldhuis's treatment (which was written for a discussion of Sumerian literature) to include a greater variety of Akkadian text types, his words about the social-functional approach provide a foundational insight for contextualizing the Akkadian textual record. The texts we investigate, he writes, "tell us about history, not so much the history contained in their narratives, but the history of the people and institutions that wrote and used these compositions.

---

1. See Veldhuis 2004, 39–45.

Where the documentarian approach focuses mainly on contents (history) and the poetic approach on form (style and poetic devices), the social-functional approach looks at form and content from the perspective of the institutional context in which the literary texts were produced and consumed."[2] Acknowledging how this approach connects to texts beyond what may be defined as the literary corpus, Veldhuis states, "no less than administrative tablets, literary texts are tools in the hands of actors who want to achieve a goal by copying, owning, ordering, or disseminating them."[3]

Tablets: From Excavation to Translation

Excavation

Since the 1840s, archaeologists (professional and illicit) have excavated perhaps as many as a million clay tablets inscribed with cuneiform from palaces, temples, and private houses at a great many sites in modern Iraq and Syria as well as, to a lesser extent, in Iran, Turkey, Egypt, and the Levant.[4] Although not all of these tablets bear a text in Akkadian, hundreds of thousands of them do.[5] The most important archaeological sites in Mesopotamia (see map 2) that have yielded a great many Akkadian texts include Nineveh (modern Kuyunjik), Assur (Qalat Shergat), Kalhu (Nimrud), Me-Turan (Tell Haddad), Sippar (Abu Habba/Tell ed-Der), Shaduppum (Tell Harmal), Babylon, Borsippa (Birs Nimrud), Kish (Tell Ingharra/Tell Uhaimir), Nippur (Nuffar), Isin (Ishan Bahriyat), Uruk (Warka), Larsa (Tell Senkereh), and Ur (Tell Muqayyar). Outside of Mesopotamia, Mari (Tell Hariri), Ebla (Tell Mardikh), Emar (Tell Meskene),

---

2. Veldhuis 2004, 43.

3. Veldhuis 2004, 46. The documentarian, poetic, and social-functional approaches that Veldhuis describes have many affinities with traditional historical criticism, new criticism, and new historicism, respectively, in literary theory. See Tyson 2015, 276–77.

4. For material aspects of tablets, including raw materials used in their manufacture, the process and shapes of their manufacture, and the mechanics of their inscription, see Taylor 2011 and the various articles on the clay tablet in *Scienze dell'Antichità* 17 (Taylor 2011). More recently, C. Hess 2015 presents an important argument for taking tablet materiality seriously in our analysis of scribal products. His focus is on the tablets bearing OB epic texts. Other materials besides clay tablets could be inscribed; e.g., stone was often used for monumental and dedicatory inscriptions, as was metal occasionally. Wax-covered writing boards were also used.

5. There is no comprehensive catalog of the tablet holdings in the world's museums. The Cuneiform Digital Library Initiative (http://cdli.ucla.edu/) is undertaking this task. It currently includes records for 335, 072 tablets (as of December 31, 2018). For tabular overviews of the geographical and chronological distribution of cuneiform tablets, see Van De Mieroop 1999, 12; Walker 1987a, 18–19. I do not know of any published estimate of the number of cuneiform tablets inscribed in Akkadian as opposed to those in Sumerian or some other language that used a cuneiform script.

and Ugarit (Ras Shamra) in Syria, Akhetaten (el-Amarna) in Egypt, and Hattusa (Boğazköy), Alalakh (Tell Atchana), and Huzirina (Sultantepe) in Turkey are prominent among sites that have produced Akkadian materials.[6] Of all the sites named, Assurbanipal's library in Nineveh (seventh century BCE), curated at the British Museum, is by far the single most important discovery for the reconstruction of Akkadian literature.[7] In terms of chronology, first-millennium finds far outnumber earlier materials.[8]

As with any ancient artifact, excavated tablets may come out of the ground whole or in a fragmentary state. Their inscribed surfaces vary in quality from almost pristine to severely abraded—in some cases, they are nearly or entirely illegible. This material condition explains why Akkadian compositions often show gaps in their texts, marked with [. . .] and [x] in publications, and why scholars sometimes make restorations. For example, scholars can restore the phrase a-wi-[x] ana É-šu il-[x] to a-wi-[lum] ana É-šu il-[lik], "the ma[n] we[nt] to his house," with as much confidence as you can restore the English phrase "the man we_t to h_s h_use." A restoration is considered conjectural if it is one possibility among several, as would be the case if, for example, the verb in the sentence above were missing: "the man [. . .] to his house." As one can imagine, a large gap of many words or many lines on the tablet, as is often the case, cannot be restored without another tablet that contains the same text (called a duplicate). Many sunbaked tablets are quite fragile when excavated and must be kiln-fired in the field before transporting them. Others are nearly indestructible because they were fired in antiquity accidentally when the ancient building that housed them burned to the ground.

Ideally, tablets are excavated by professional archaeologists who are careful to map their exact find spots. In practice, this has not always been the case. Some tablets, for instance, are from sites that were looted by local residents or profiteers. These tablets have no archaeological context and provenance. Unfortunately, the same is true for some tablets excavated by archaeologists in the nineteenth and early twentieth centuries, when archaeological methods and recording were not up to later standards.[9] Intense scrutiny of museum records

6. For discussion of these sites (and a few others of smaller importance), see, for the Old Babylonian period, Tinney 2011; for the first millennium, Robson 2011; for an overview of sites in the intervening period, Sassmannshausen 2008.

7. See Fincke 2004 and http://www.britishmuseum.org/research/research_projects/all_current_projects/ashurbanipal_library_phase_1.aspx.

8. Some sites are limited to a rather circumscribed time period (e.g., Mari and Hattusa) while others have produced tablets across many time periods (e.g., Uruk, which has produced both some of the earliest and latest tablets found). The reader is advised to check entries in archaeological handbooks (e.g., Meyers 1997) for details about each site.

9. For a brief history of the archaeological exploration of Mesopotamia, see http://cdli.ox.ac.uk/wiki/doku.php?id=a_brief_history_of_archaeology_in_mesopotamia. Rogers 1901, 1:1–253.

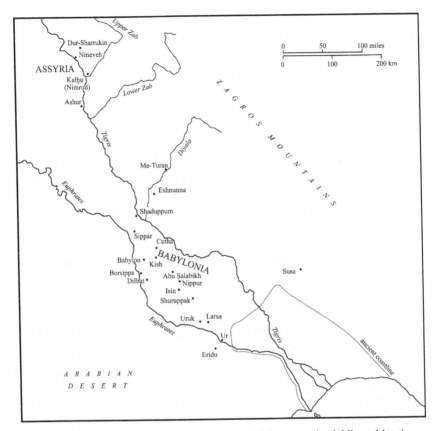

MAP 2. The most important archaeological sites in Mesopotamia yielding tablets in Akkadian.

has ameliorated this problem for some sites (e.g., Assur), but there are many licitly excavated tablets whose precise find spot or even broad provenance (i.e., city of origin) will never be known.[10] Sadly, this includes tablets in Assurbanipal's library, some of which, we know, are not even from Nineveh.[11] Find spots and provenance are often useful data for contextualizing Akkadian texts.

---

recounts the earliest wanderers and explorers in Mesopotamia and continues with a history of excavations up to his time. Likewise Pallis 1956. Larsen 1996 covers the early decades of excavations (1840–1860) in great depth; see also Lloyd 1980, who brings the history into the late twentieth century; Foster forthcoming.

10. For Assur, see Pedersén 1985, 1986.

11. Walker estimates that about 1–2 percent of the tablets in the collection were excavated elsewhere and put together with the Ninevite tablets after delivery to the British Museum (Walker 1987b, 186).

Without these data, scholars must rely solely on internal textual evidence, that is, the evidence in the actual text on the tablet itself (i.e., script, grammar, spelling, and vocabulary).

Curation

Tablets and tablet fragments are housed in various museums around the world, though there are also sizeable private collections (e.g., Martin Schøyen's collection in Oslo, Norway).[12] The most important museum collections, in terms of quantity of tablets, are in the British Museum (London), the Vorderasiatisches Museum (Berlin), the Louvre (Paris), the Arkeoloji Müzeleri (Istanbul), Yale University's Babylonian Collection (New Haven), the Iraq Museum (Baghdad), and University of Pennsylvania's Penn Museum (Philadelphia). There are many other museums and universities with smaller tablet holdings.[13]

Just as some tablets are fired in the field before transporting them, many tablets in museums' holdings need to be fired in a kiln as part of conservation measures. Some may need adhesive inserted into cracks and crevices to stabilize the artifact. And some will need to be cleaned of salts, which leech to the surface due to the heavily salinized clay from which the tablets were made.[14] When fragments or pieces of a tablet are identified as belonging together, conservators glue the pieces together. Assyriologists call this a "join" and indicate it in publications with a plus sign between the museum identification numbers of the pieces joined. A dozen or more such joins of fragments may comprise what was once a single tablet. It is therefore not unusual for a composition to "grow" over time as modern scholars find more fragments that belong to a tablet bearing its text.[15]

Physical Characteristics

Cuneiform tablets present a great variety of shapes and sizes—too many to catalog here exhaustively. Still, there are a few common formats and physical characteristics that describe the material aspects of a great number of tablets. Many tablets contain only a single column of text (fig. 1), inscribed flush left to flush right, top to bottom (like this printed page). Most are written with a "portrait" orientation, that is, the tablet's height is greater than its width, though

---

12. http://www.schoyencollection.com/.

13. An extensive list of museums with collections may be found here: http://cdli.ox.ac.uk/wiki/doku.php?id=cuneiform_tablet_collections.

14. For an older view on tablet curation, see Bateman 1966. For newer techniques of firing, see Thickett, Odlyha, and Ling 2002.

15. A composition may also "grow" as scholars identify more tablets that bear a copy of its text.

FIGURE I. A typical single-column tablet. Notice the ancient
erasure of a half line near the middle right part of the tablet.
Photo © Trustees of the British Museum, London.

one also finds tablets turned to a "landscape" orientation. When the scribe filled the front side of the tablet, called the obverse, he flipped the tablet end over end and commenced writing—again, left to right, top to bottom—on the back of it, the reverse. Typically, the obverse of a tablet is flat and the reverse has a slight convex shape.[16] It is not uncommon to find that a scribe ran out of room on a line and used the side of the tablet to squeeze in a few more signs or wrapped the line around onto the reverse (see fig. 19).[17] Also, one may find the bottom edge of the obverse inscribed, so that the lines of text run continuously from front to back. In the case of a mistake, a scribe could simply rub out the wrong sign and inscribe the correct one over it. Or, if the scribe caught the mistake late in the inscribing process, the scribe could remove many incorrect signs with a deep line impressed into the clay (as in figure 1).

Some tablets are divided into more than one column (see figs. 13 and 14). Two, three, or four to a side is most common, though there are tablets with more.[18] The columns on the obverse are ordered left to right; those on the reverse right to left. Today, scholars number the columns with lower case Roman numerals so that one will find references to, for example, obv. iii or rev. i in text editions and the secondary literature. Obverse iii designates the third column from the left on the front of the tablet; reverse i refers to the first column on the right on the back of the tablet.

Besides the common flat tablets, scribes also formed clay into several other shapes for their writing surface. For example, the famous Cyrus Cylinder is inscribed on a barrel or cylinder shaped chunk of clay. The text is written in long, horizontal lines from end to end of the recumbent cylinder so that its lines wrap around its circumference until its first and last lines meet.[19] A (recumbent) cylinder could also be divided into more than one column (fig. 2), as is a royal inscription of Nabonidus in the British Musuem (BM 91125).

Prisms provide another example. Although similar to cylinders on first glance, they do not have a cylinder's circular profile. Rather, the body of a prism has a distinct number of flat sides so that its profile forms a hexagon, octagon, or such, according to the number of its sides, each of which are treated as are columns on a tablet. The prism remained vertical during the inscription process, and the text the prism bears is written in short lines from left to right on each

16. This is due to the fact that the scribe placed the inscribed obverse face down on a surface while writing the reverse.

17. One may even find a tablet bearing a literary text in which a scribe has inserted a skipped line along the side of the tablet.

18. See C. Hess 2015, 261 for a summary of tablet shape and number of columns for tablets bearing OB epic texts.

19. A photograph of this cylinder, BM 90920, is available at https://cdli.ucla.edu/dl/photo /P386349_d.jpg. See Curtis 2013 for a full treatment of this artifact and the text that it bears.

FIGURE 2. A two-column inscribed cylinder, bearing a Neo-Babylonian royal inscription. Photo © Trustees of the British Museum, London.

side with the lines proceeding from top to bottom of the side before moving on to the next one. A well-preserved, ten-sided example in the British Museum, BM 91086 + (too many joins to list), bears a royal inscription of Assurbanipal, a Neo-Assyrian king (fig. 3).

A regular pyramid-shaped "tablet" provides a final, rare example of an alternative shape. In one example from Babylon, VAT 17489, a scribal student wrote excerpts from various texts (including Enuma Elish and Ludlul bel nemeqi) on all four sides of the pyramid.[20] Because it was found with administrative tablets in a clay jar, it is likely that the pyramid was a kind of keepsake from its owner's school days.[21]

The scribes used lines and cuneiform wedges in various extralinguistic ways to section off the surface of the tablet to be inscribed. For example, sometimes scribes used vertical lines pressed into the clay to mark margins and column parameters on their tablets. They often impressed horizontal lines on the tablet, too. Faint ones were sometimes used for each line of text, from which the scribe would "hang" the signs. This technique insured straight lines of text across the tablet. Scribes also pressed deeper horizontal lines into the clay during the inscription process to indicate divisions within the text. Occasionally, one will find a small wedge in the left margin of a tablet every ten lines; such markers would have made counting the lines of a text—to insure that one had copied the correct number of them—faster.

---

20. See https://cdli.ucla.edu/dl/photo/P347243.jpg for a photograph.
21. See Pedersén 2005, 203–8, esp. 206.

FIGURE 3. A ten-sided prism, inscribed with a Neo-Assyrian royal inscription. Photo © Trustees of the British Museum, London.

Translation

For the last 170 years Assyriologists have worked on cataloging, joining, deciphering, translating, and publishing tablets in museums and collections. The work is extremely labor intensive. In addition to the epigraphic problems of reading multivalent cuneiform signs on what may be a fragmentary tablet with a poorly preserved surface, there are also philological difficulties for the translator, despite the fact that Akkadian is relatively well-studied and now has two complete lexica, *The Assyrian Dictionary of the Oriental Institute of the University of Chicago* (26 vols., 1956–2010) and Wolfram von Soden's *Akkadisches Handwörterbuch* (3 vols., 1972–85).[22] Something as simple as dividing up the cuneiform signs on a line into words can be the source of some debate. There are generally no word dividers or spaces between words as in most modern

---

22. The latter was condensed and translated in Black, George, and Postgate 1999 with updates provided at https://www.soas.ac.uk/cda-archive/.

languages. Rather, cuneiform signs are generally written across the tablet line in a manner that fills the available space, though some poetic texts may show a gap between the two cola (half-lines or versets) that comprise the line.[23]

An example of decipherment and translation may make the process more concrete. Figure 4 shows part of a tablet from ancient Nineveh, held at the British Museum (K.8231), that attests the text of the composition modern scholars call "Counsels of Wisdom" (lines 80–87).

Scholars use a line drawing of a tablet to give an idea of what the decipherer sees on it. Assyriologists call this a copy. Figure 5 shows part of the copy of K.8231 from W. G. Lambert's work, *Babylonian Wisdom Literature* (pl. 28, 1960).

The decipherer transcribes the value of each sign into the Roman script using a system created by scholars and divides the signs into words. The result is called a transliteration. Because the cuneiform script has many homonymous signs, that is, different signs to represent the same sound, transliterations use a combination of accent marks and subscripted numbers to indicate precisely which sign representing that sound is actually on the tablet. These accents and numbers are called indices. For example, in the transliteration below, bé (or be_2) indicates the second BE sign in the standard sign list; lìb (or lib_3) indicates the third LIB sign in the standard sign list; na_4 is the fourth NA in the list, and so on. If there is no accent or index number (e.g., ma), this indicates the first sign for that sound in the standard sign list.[24] Some signs were used in texts to indicate the class to which a word belongs (e.g., a city, a wooden object, or a deity); these were not pronounced when the text was read. Scholars call these signs determinatives and typically indicate them in transliteration by superscripting their value in front of or behind the word to which they are attached (see NA_4 below, which indicates stone objects).[25] Some signs in Akkadian texts are actually Sumerian words that stand for Akkadian words and were only ever read as Akkadian words. Scholars have labeled these logograms; they are indicated in transliteration via capital letters or sometimes small capital letters. For example, KIŠIB in the transliteration below is a logogram representing the Akkadian word for a cylinder seal, *kunukku*. (Cylinder seals were usually made from stone, thus the determinative NA_4 precedes KIŠIB.) This phenomenon of using Sumerian words for Akkadian is similar to our own use of abbreviated Latin as a short hand for an English word. Note how we always read "e.g." as "for example" rather than the Latin "exempli gratia."

---

23. See the example at the end of this section. For the many issues that confront the translator of Akkadian texts, see George 1999, 209–21 and the more general statement in Charpin 2010, 6–16.

24. Although there are many sign lists, the authoritative list for Akkadian is Borger 2010.

25. Determinatives, like logograms to be described momentarily, come from Sumerian.

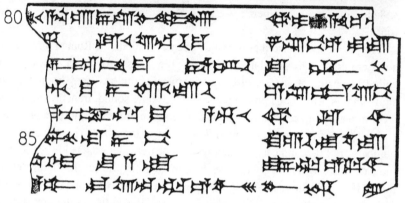

FIGURE 4. (*top*) K.8231. Photo © Trustees of the British Museum, London.
FIGURE 5. (*bottom*) Copy of K.8231. © Eisenbrauns, an imprint of Pennsylvania State University Press.

As mentioned earlier, signs that are missing on a tablet due to damage can often be restored based on what the decipherer believes the tablet originally read or based on another tablet that duplicates the same lines of the composition. Restorations are always placed inside square brackets. If a sign is broken horizontally (i.e., its left or right half is missing), scholars use full square brackets around the broken part of the sign to represent the damage (e.g. [*m*]*a* or *m*[*a*]). Half brackets indicate that a sign is missing its top or bottom part (e.g., ⌈*ma*⌉).

The following presents lines 81–87 of "Counsels of Wisdom" in transliteration:

81. [*ma-r*]*i lu-u lìb-ba-šú-ma*   *šá ru-bé-e at-ta*
82. [*na-a*]*ṣ-ra-am-ma* ^{NA₄}KIŠIB-*šú*   *lu al-lat*
83. [*pe*]-*ti-ma ni-ṣir-ta-šú*   *e-ru-ub ana lìb-bi*
84. [*ul-l*]*a-nu-uk-ka-ma*   *a-ḫu-u ul ib-ši*
85. [*ma-a*]*k-kur la ni-bi*   *qé-reb-šú tu-ut-ta*
86. [*a-n*]*a mim-ma šu-a-tu*   *in-ka e taš-ši*
87. [*a*]-*a ub-la lìb-ba-ka*   *e-pe-eš pu-uz-ru*

Sometimes scholars present the text in what is called "normalized" Akkadian or transcription. This manner of representing Akkadian shows vowel lengths in words and the scholar's grammatical interpretation of the text. Determinatives are not included in this system of representing Akkadian and logograms are converted into their Akkadian equivalent. The transliterated text from "Counsels of Wisdom" may be normalized as follows:

81.	[mār]ī lū libbašu-ma	ša rubê attā
82.	[naṣ]ram-ma kunukkašu	lū allāt
83.	[pe]tī-ma niṣirtašu	erub ana libbi
84.	[ull]ānukkā-ma	aḫû ul ibši
85.	[ma]kkūršu lā nībi	qerebšu tutta
86.	[an]a mimma šuātu	īnka ē tašši
87.	[a]yy-ubla libbaka	epēš puzru

An Aside on Pronunciation: The pronunciation of transliterated and normalized Akkadian is merely a scholarly convention, informed by the pronunciation of related languages.[26] The conventional pronunciation does not represent the ancient language's precise pronunciation, which was not always represented accurately by the cuneiform script and varied over the language's broad area of use and throughout its long history. Most of the consonant letters used to transliterate Akkadian are conventionally pronounced just like they are pronounced in English.

b	bed	m	mile	s	sing
d	dog	n	nine	t	time
g	goat	p	pal	w	will
k	king	q	quick	y[27]	yellow
l	long	r	role	z	zebra

A few of the Roman consonant letters are slightly modified to indicate a sound that existed in Akkadian but not in English or to indicate a sound that is not typically or clearly represented by one letter in English. These are:

ḫ   Ba**ch** (as in German)

ṣ   pi**ts**, **x**ylophone (like the Hebrew letter צ)

---

26. Huehnergard 2011, 1–3. To hear various scholars pronounce some well-known Akkadian compositions, see Martin Worthington's web site at http://www.soas.ac.uk/baplar/recordings/.

27. Some publications use the letter j, under the influence of German, to represent this sound in Akkadian. See, e.g., the *Chicago Assyrian Dictionary*.

ṭ   top (an emphatic t, with no difference in pronunciation from the
         regular t)[28]
š   shin

One special character is used to represent a glottal stop. This consonant is the
sound the throat makes when it is completely closed and then opens briefly to
release a bit of air. The consonant is named *alef*, as in Hebrew and Arabic.

'   the sound at the beginning of both syllables in uh-oh

The four Akkadian vowels are represented in transliteration with the Roman
vowel letters a, e, i, and u. In normalized Akkadian, unaltered Roman vowel
letters represent short vowels: a, e, i, u. The same vowel letters modified with a
macron or circumflex indicate long vowels: ā, ē, ī, ū / â, ê, î, û.[29] These vowels
are conventionally pronounced as follows:

a	top	ā	father
e	get	ē	pain
i	mit	ī	routine (like a Spanish i)
u	put	ū	school

The final goal of decipherment is a translation into a modern language. The
following is my own translation of the lines from "Counsels of Wisdom," transliterated and normalized above. I use parentheses to indicate words that are
supplied for sense and readability. Because an English translation usually cannot indicate the gap between the two halves (cola) of poetic lines and remain
readable, the gaps are not represented.

81. My [so]n, if the prince takes a liking to you,
82. (And) you are entrusted with his [guar]ded seal,
83. [Op]en his treasury; enter therein.
84. There is none [besi]des you (who may).
85. Countless [pos]sessions you will discover within.
86. (But) don't set your eye [on] anything!
87. [Do n]ot be tempted to defraud in secret.

28. Although the ṭ likely had a distinctive pronunciation in ancient times, we do not know what
it was. Thus, it is conventionally pronounced just like t.
29. If the vowel length is due to vowel contraction of two contiguous vowels, then the circumflex is used.

Given the fact that there are so few competent cuneiformists that have regular access to institutional collections, the tedious work of cataloging, joining, deciphering, translating, and publishing tablets has proceeded rather slowly, even if steadily.[30] Many tablets lie in museum trays for decades without attracting much more than a cataloger's brief attention. Moreover, Mesopotamian archaeological sites continue to yield artifacts every year, thereby adding to the backlog of tablets in need of publication. Clearly, there is much work to be done and many surprising finds yet to be made.

Rather daunting material obstacles stand between us and our understanding of ancient Akkadian literature. Yet these very obstacles, alongside the reasonable hope for the discovery of more tablets in the future, make the project a dynamic and exciting intellectual endeavor.

Scribes: Contextualizing Literary Production

Knowing something about the scribes and scholars who produced Akkadian literature, their notions of authorship, and the way they organized some of their texts gives substance to the social contexts of the textual record with which we are concerned.

Scribal Education and Career

Despite several Sumerian compositions that describe the scribal student's training in a school (Sum. edubba'a), scholars believe that scribal education in the Old Babylonian and later periods usually occurred in private houses under the tutelage of a master scribe.[31] In other words, scribalism was taught in much the

---

30. Various digital initiatives promise to diminish the problem of accessibility. For example, the Cuneiform Digital Library Initiative (http://cdli.ucla.edu/), which is cataloging cuneiform tablets from around the world, and the Digital Hammurabi project (http://www.jhu.edu/digitalhammurabi/), which is creating software that will render three-dimensional images (and prints) of tablets.

31. The literature on scribal education and the role of the scribe/scholar in ancient Mesopotamia is vast. The following selection of references should be considered points of entry. Charpin 2010, 17–67; Pearce 1995 offer general overviews; Charpin starts at the beginning of writing ca. 3200 BCE. Also, see Robson 2011; Lenzi 2015b for scribal scholars in the first millennium; Tinney 2011; Delnero 2015 for the OB period. See Dandamayev 1983, 235–42 (English summary of Russian monograph) for a survey of scribes in first millennium Babylonia. For scribes in first millennium temple administrative contexts specifically, see Kümmel 1979 (Uruk's Eanna temple) and Bongenaar 1997 (Sippar's Ebabbar temple). For the Neo-Assyrian court scholars and their royal correspondence, see Parpola 1993; Luukko and Van Buylaere 2002, 137–47. Tanret 2004 tries to reconstruct the work and social position of scribes in OB Sippar-Amnānum from archival documents, which offer information about the best-attested scribe in the OB period, one Shumum-litsi. Van Koppen 2011 investigates Ipiq-Aya, the scribe who produced an important copy of OB Atram-hasis. Visicato 2000

same way that other professions were, namely, through a kind of apprenticeship. As with other professions, the scribal craft was often passed down from father to son. (Professional scribes were usually male.)[32]

The curriculum varied by geography and period, but all periods show the general importance of sign lists, lexical (i.e., word) lists, mathematics, model texts (e.g., letters and contracts), and various compositions (e.g., proverbs, hymns, royal inscriptions, and literary texts). Scribes began their education with very simple exercises that taught them to use a specially cut reed as a stylus to impress into clay the three basic building blocks of the cuneiform script: vertical (⌐), horizontal (⊢), and *Winkelhaken* (◁) wedges. They would then learn basic syllabic signs, comprising various combinations of these wedges. The excerpt in figure 6, which shows the opening lines of an OB syllabary called TU-TA-TI, illustrates the ancient pedagogy quite well. Each line contains three signs, whose basic pronunciations share the same initial consonant but a different vowel—u, a, and i in sequence. Each line begins with a single vertical wedge, transliterated with I below, to indicate the start of a new line. A transliteration of the copy in figure 6 reads:

I TU TA TI
[I] NU! NA NI
I BU BA BI
I LU LA LI!
I ZU ZA ZI

considers scribes in the third millennium. Westenholz 1974/1977 surveys Old Akkadian school texts. Our understanding of scribal education has undergone significant change in the last thirty years due to special attention to the content of individual student tablets and tablet typology. The most important work in this regard for first millennium Babylonia is Gesche 2000 with Veldhuis's review (2003b). Seminal contributions treating the OB period include Veldhuis 1997; Tinney 1999; Robson 2001. Delnero 2010 provides an overview of recent OB scholarship and advances the discussion. See also Veldhuis 2004, 58–66 for a useful, succinct contextualization of OB scribal education. Veldhuis is currently preparing an overview of OB scribal education for *Handbook of Ancient Mesopotamia* (forthcoming). Veldhuis 2000 treats what little we know about the Kassite (mid-second millennium) period. Cohen 2009, 46–64; Cohen and Kedar 2011, 229–38 treat education at Emar in Syria in the late second millennium. Van Soldt 1995 discusses Ugarit; van Soldt 2011 takes in a broader view of the western periphery in the same time period, for which also see Veldhuis 2012. For the Sumerian compositions about scribal training, see Rubio 2009, 58 for a list with references. Some of these compositions were eventually provided with an Akkadian translation and found in first millennium copies (see, e.g., Sjöberg 1972). George 2005b argues that the descriptions of schools in these OB texts actually reflect academies organized and sustained during the Ur III period (2112–2004 BCE), which collapsed with that regime. Be that as it may, scholars agree that these literary texts do not accurately reflect the way scribes learned in the OB or later periods and therefore should no longer be used for historical reconstructions of scribal training in those periods (as they were, e.g., in Sjöberg 1975, and more recently, Volk 2000). See, e.g., Charpin 1986, 420–34; Robson 2001; Tanret 2002 for studies of the tablets from scribal training houses.

32. For female scribes, see Lion 2011, 2008.

ı ḪU ḪA ḪI
ı RU RA RI
ı KU KA KI
ı MU MA MI

The exclamation marks in the transliteration and copy indicate student mistakes. The student wrote a malformed NA in line 2 instead of NU and a TU in line 4 instead of LI, which has a similar shape.[33]

As students continued their education, they would copy advanced sign lists containing hundreds of signs to master the cuneiform script and various lexical lists to learn thousands of vocabulary words. They would also copy excerpts of selected compositions to acquire a knowledge of the language's grammar. The difficulty of these lists and texts increased as students advanced through the curriculum. As many students would spend their scribal careers in service to the major institutions (i.e., the palace and temples), the compositions that were used in their education also inculcated royal ideology (see fig. 14) as well as a knowledge of the gods and the created order.[34] Students would probably need to learn other texts on the job as their specialization required. Yet the depth of the student's learning—in Sumerian grammar and obscure vocabulary, for example—far exceeded the practical requirements of all but the most scholarly of scribal jobs, suggesting scribal education was as much about enculturation, identity formation, and institutional membership as about gaining literacy.[35] How long it took a person to complete scribal training remains unclear.

For the present purpose, it is important to note that the curricula modern scholars have reconstructed for the OB period, especially dependent on sources from the south, centered on the teaching of Sumerian. Sumerian was a cultural language that students learned as a matter of tradition and professional credentialization. Various forms of documentation, however, suggest Akkadian was increasingly taking over as the language of administration in the OB period, especially in the latter half of it.[36] Moreover, based on occasional Akkadian glosses in Sumerian texts and some Akkadian-Sumerian bilingual lexical

---

33. The tablet is IM 51147, housed in the National Museum of Iraq in Baghdad. See https://cdli.ucla.edu/P223453.

34. They might also work privately or in some combination of institutional work and private work.

35. Gesche 2000; Veldhuis 2004, 65–66; Veldhuis 2011, 82–86. Delnero's recent study (2016) suggests that the differences between the scribal curricula at Nippur vs. Ur "was intended to confer different local identities" to scribes (47). This suggests that the generalizations about scribal enculturation and identity must be filled out with an eye for local, particular emphases and absences.

36. It was also the language of administration during the Old Akkadian period. But this practice was discontinued in the Ur III period (2112–2004 BCE).

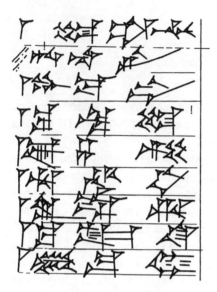

FIGURE 6. This excerpt presents the opening lines of an OB syllabary called TU-TA-TI. My copy follows van Dijk 1976, no. 85.

texts, scribal students and their teachers likely *spoke* Akkadian.[37] Because OB Akkadian liturgical, literary, divinatory, and royal commemorative texts exist, we presume that trained scribes composed and copied them for royal, religious, or personal/scholarly use.[38] To what extent they were part of scribal training, however, is an issue that requires more investigation, ideally on a site-by-site basis.[39] In any case, Sumerian was the main language in scribal training in the OB period. Akkadian texts were not commonly copied; thus, the number of duplicates for OB Akkadian compositions is quite low compared to Sumerian compositions.[40]

In the first millennium the linguistic situation is the exact opposite. All but a small handful of the Sumerian texts used in OB scribal education were forgotten. Moreover, though first millennium scribes still learned Sumerian and there exists a good number of Sumerian-Akkadian bilingual texts, most of the compositions they learned were written in Akkadian, several of which, as the survey shows, present a revised form of the text attested already in the OB

37. For a thorough survey of lexical lists, their long tradition, and their function for scribes in ancient Mesopotamia, see Veldhuis 2014.

38. In a context dealing with incantations, Wasserman writes, "who then were the *literati* that did this if not scribes trained in the Edubba?" (2003b, 181).

39. Delnero 2016, 37 estimates that Akkadian texts comprise only 3 percent of the student tablets at Nippur and 15 percent at Ur during the OB period, which suggests local diversity of practices must be taken into account. Along the same vein: there is some evidence of Akkadian texts being copied by students in the north (see, e.g., van Koppen 2011, 160; and note Charpin 2010, 44).

40. See Wasserman 2003b, 180–81.

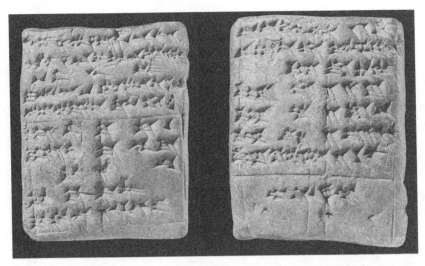

FIGURE 7. A student's tablet containing an excerpt from an incantation in the upper half of the obverse (left). The remainder contains an excerpt from a lexical list. At the end of the reverse is the date the tablet was inscribed. Photo © Trustees of the British Museum, London.

period.[41] In the first millennium, as Petra Gesche (2000) shows, there existed a second stage of scribal training to which some students advanced. This second stage focused on learning Akkadian incantations and various texts used in the professional duties of the exorcists/conjurers (fig. 7). After completion of this level the student would then begin further specialized training as an apprentice to a scholar.[42]

These differing curricula result in an imbalance among the sources for Akkadian literature. Later sources are more numerous than earlier ones; and scholarly texts such as omen collections in fact outnumber other kinds of texts, which usually receive much more extensive treatment in modern surveys such as the present one due to contemporary interests.

As for employment, the palace, temples, and private individuals employed literate professionals in various capacities throughout Mesopotamian history. For example, a scribe might become part of the royal bureaucracy or temple administration; he might specialize in ritual, medical, and/or liturgical texts and serve the temple and/or king in a scholarly capacity as an exorcist, diviner,

41. For a catalog of Sumerian-Akkadian bilingual texts, see the ORACC project "Bilinguals in Late Mesopotamian Scholarship," directed by Steve Tinney and edited by Jeremiah Peterson (http://oracc.museum.upenn.edu/blms/corpus).

42. Scholarly training is described succinctly in Lenzi 2015b, 157–60, based on Gesche's monographic treatment.

ritual lamenter, physician, or celestial diviner; or, he might hire out his services to individuals, performing some ritual or divinatory query or recording various personal and business transactions.[43] Of course, scribes could work in more than one of these spheres. In the first millennium we have a veritable treasure trove of information about the content of a number of scribal scholarly families' libraries (due to the fact that their private residences were excavated), shedding light on their individual professional interests and obligations.[44] In the Neo-Assyrian period we have hundreds of tablets containing the professional correspondence of royal scholars and the kings Esarhaddon and Assurbanipal, whom they served, as well as other documents that give us a glimpse into their everyday life.[45] As is typical in Assyriology, we are inundated with details of uneven chronological and geographic distribution. Bringing these puzzle pieces together to form a more complete picture of the social position and professional activities of scribes and scholars is an on-going process.[46]

Notions of Authorship

Although professional scribes were not the only literate people in ancient Mesopotamia, they were the most qualified to write the literary, historical, and scholarly compositions that have come down to us.[47] Unfortunately, we often can say little more than this about the authors of these compositions because scribes and scholars generally did not take credit for composing a text. Moreover, the traditions that attribute authorship (or editorship) to some works are late and of uncertain reliability.

Authorship in contemporary Western societies refers to a creative individual human who is responsible for the original composition of a text and takes credit for this composition by attaching his or her name to it in some manner. This

43. We know hundreds of scribes by name, since they often appear among the named witnesses in various contracts and legal tablets.

44. See Robson 2011 for a survey.

45. See, e.g., Parpola 1987; Wiggermann 2008; Jean 2006, 172–94.

46. Although literate professionals were often in the employ of the central institutions of Mesopotamian society, namely, the palaces and temples, their textual patrimony may not be entirely devoid of critical discourse aimed at the king. See Finn 2017 for such an argument, based on evidence culled from first millennium sources, both literary and documentary.

47. The content in this section overlaps with material in my previous discussion of authorship in Lenzi 2015b. A basic level of literacy could and was achieved by nonprofessional scribes, both men and women. See Veldhuis 2011 for a discussion of different levels of literacy: functional, technical, and scholarly (with references to the essential secondary literature). The latter two were the reserve of professional scribes. Lion 2011 discusses female literacy; Svärd 2013 treats female agency with regard to authorship. See also Larsen (1976, 305), who believes many of the Old Assyrian merchants could write basic documents, and Parpola 1997, who discusses basic literacy in the Neo-Assyrian period. For Assurbanipal's claim to literacy, see Livingstone 2007.

notion is the product of a long cultural development in the West and is quite foreign to the ancient Near East.[48] Leaving aside mundane letters or reports that include the sender's name and prayers that identify the supplicant by name (see below), claims of authorship in the modern sense did not exist in ancient Mesopotamia, though some works were later attributed to specific gods and scholars.[49] In fact, although internal evidence suggests that some texts were the creative product of an individual (e.g., Erra and Ishum and Ludlul bel nemeqi), many works in the scholarly, lexical, and even literary corpora (e.g., the Standard Babylonian Epic of Gilgamesh) were the culmination of a long textual evolution.[50] If there is evidence that an individual was responsible for a text's latest form, it is usually more appropriate to refer to this person as an editor rather than author.[51] Even in these cases, it is important to keep in mind that such learned scribes were contributors to and custodians (or curators) of bodies of work that were used by other literate professionals (mostly) in institutional service. These men, as van der Toorn writes, "did not write as individuals but functioned as constituent parts of a social organism."[52]

There are some exceptional cases in which the actual name of the text's composer is associated with or attached to the text; all three occur in post-OB compositions that utilize what scholars call an acrostic.[53] In an acrostic text, the first sign of each inscribed line, when read vertically (i.e., the first sign of each line on the left edge of the tablet, read from the top to the bottom), spells out a name or sentence. Despite the acrostics, these cases still lack a strong claim to authorship in the modern sense. Two of the three acrostics occur in two personal prayers written on the same tablet, which includes self-referential instructions at the end of the text for the reader to find the acrostic.[54] The third acrostic text is the Babylonian Theodicy.[55] In the two prayers, the acrostic sentences identify

---

48. See van der Toorn 2007, 27–49 for reflections on authorship in the ancient Near East vis-à-vis the West. For the complicated historical genealogy of "author" in the West, see Pease 1995.

49. For a prayer that names the supplicant, see, e.g., Lambert 1967. For discussion of authorship, see Foster 1991; 2005, 19–20; van der Toorn 2007, 45–49; Charpin 2010, 179–81. For attribution of authorship to gods and scholars, see the catalog edited in Lambert 1962; Helle 2018 provides a nuanced discussion of authorship, canonization, and cultural identity in the Hellenistic and later periods, i.e., during the waning centuries of Akkadian literature.

50. See Foster 1991 for Erra and Ishum; Lenzi 2012 for Ludlul bel nemeqi. These texts are discussed more fully on pages 104 and 175, respectively, below. For more on Epic of Gilgamesh, see page 109.

51. Lambert 1957, 1.

52. Van der Toorn 2007, 47.

53. Wasserman 2015 argues that an officer named Ashmad, mentioned in the OB Zimri-Lim Epic (see page 140), is in fact the author of the poem. Although a plausible idea, this attribution of authorship is a contemporary inference; there is no *explicit* indication of authorship in the text.

54. Oshima 2011, 311–15. The statement is actually found in the tablet's colophon, a scribal note sometimes appended at the end of a tablet. For more about colophons, see page 35, below.

55. For more on this text, see page 173.

the prayers' composer as the supplicant, a man named Nabu-ushebshi. Identifying the supplicant in this way is known in other prayers in which the composer is not the supplicant (e.g., in a prayer written for king Assurbanipal); thus, naming Nabu-ushebshi in the acrostics *may not* be a claim to authorship.[56] In the Babylonian Theodicy the content of the sentence formed by the acrostic announces in first-person voice the scribe's adoration for both god and king; that is, it seems intended to affirm the scribe's loyalty to the institutions he serves rather than to make a strong claim to authorship. Thus, despite naming the scribe, none of these texts shows authorship in the modern sense.

But there are other exceptional cases that do seem rather close to the modern notion of authorship. One authorial claim occurs in the so-called Shitti-Marduk *kudurru* (a royal land grant) in which a diviner named Enlil-tabni-bullit mentions himself as "the writer of the stela" (*šāṭir narî*) just before the final curse section of the text.[57] The presence of this scribal attribution, however, may be more related to the legal nature of the stela (i.e., it granted land and certain exemptions to a village and its leadership) than a concern for literary recognition. But the scribe does identify himself as the writer of the text. The other, and most significant authorial claim in Akkadian literature, comes at the end of a mythological text called Erra and Ishum, where a scribe named Kabti-ilani-Marduk asserts that he is the composer of the poem (*kāṣir kammīšu*, lit. "the composer of its text") but that he also learned the poem in a nocturnal revelation.[58] He professes to have written only what he had received—nothing more, nothing less. The irony, of course, is that this strongest claim of authorship is also a disclaimer of human responsibility since the scribe asserts divine revelation as the ultimate source of his text. Claiming divine inspiration in this manner is not unusual in Mesopotamia. Scholars attributed a divine origin to the textual corpora of the diviners, exorcists, and other scholarly crafts.[59] An important catalog of scholarly and literary texts does the same for a number of works as did many individual incantations.[60] Authorship in the modern sense, it seems,

---

56. For the prayer written for Assurbanipal, see Livingstone 1989, 6–10. A Late Babylonian copy of a Neo-Babylonian prayer may offer an exception in that the prayer's conclusion seems to identify the supplicant as the author explicitly (Finkel 1999). Despite the editor's acceptance of this claim, the literary tradition commends cautious skepticism.

57. See Paulus 2014, 506 (line 25); Foster 2009, 203; 2007, 23. On *kudurru*s generally, see Paulus 2014 and Slanski 2003. This *kudurru* is discussed briefly on page 147, below.

58. For a translation of the passage, see Foster 2005, 910. For more on Erra and Ishum, see page 104, below.

59. Lenzi 2008.

60. Lambert 1962 (with an additional fragment identified by Lambert and published in Jiménez 2017, 113 with 112 n. 307); van der Toorn 2007, 207–9; Lenzi 2008, 119–20. For incantations, see Lenzi 2010.

was as uncommon in ancient Mesopotamia as divine attribution of authorship in the ancient sense is today.

Before leaving the topic of authorship, it seems appropriate to treat the issue of putative authorship in some royal monumental and literary texts. The use of the first-person voice is standard in royal inscriptions and also occurs in law collections (e.g., the laws of Hammurabi).[61] Yet we know that scribes were the ghostwriters of these texts since few kings—whom we might call "honorary authors"—would have been sufficiently literate to produce such original compositions, though there is evidence that they sometimes provided input in the compositional process.[62] The application of writing in the first person to fictional literary texts resulted in pseudepigraphy. That is, the actual writer of the text, the author in the modern sense of the word, masks their own identity by writing their text as though some other person is actually speaking it (i.e., the "I" in the text). Pseudepigraphy attempts to invoke the cultural authority of the putative author (i.e., the first-person speaker of the text) to bolster the narrative's claims and prestige. Most of these texts use a royal speaker, as in the Cuthean Legend of Naram-Sin, and are therefore called *narû*, "stela," literature, in recognition of their similarities to genuine royal inscriptions.[63] Others invoke a culturally important dignitary, as does Ludlul bel nemeqi. In any case, whoever the first-person speaker is in a text, one should not automatically assume they are also the actual author of the text.

Editorial Organization of Texts and Textual Standardization

Scribes curated texts by organizing and editing older materials into a new form. The result could be the creation of a new edition of a poem or a new arrangement of scholarly or religious texts into what scholars call a series, that is, an organized corpus of similar texts copied onto a set number of clay tablets in a specific order.[64] The care that first-millennium scribes claim to have taken in copying their texts provides evidence that these edited materials became authoritative for subsequent generations, as does the production of commentaries.[65] The

---

61. For royal inscriptions, see page 133, below. The laws of Hammurabi are discussed starting on page 150.

62. For the phrase "honorary authors," see van der Toorn 2007, 34. For literacy of kings, see Charpin 2010, 222; Luukko 2007, 228 with references. For royal input, see Frahm 2011, 521–22.

63. On these texts, see page 125 and 145, below.

64. This section also overlaps with material from my previous discussion of editing and standardization in Lenzi 2015b. See also page 42, below on the use of earlier Akkadian materials in various compositions.

65. For the scribal claims, see, e.g., the common colophonic refrain *šaṭir-ma bari* (*kīma labīrīšu*), "written and checked (according to its original)" on some tablets. Examples are cited in

post-OB editing and serialization of scholarly and literary (as well as lexical) texts resulted in a kind of textual "standardization." This process, it seems, took place during the last third of the second millennium, though it did not exclude later editorial refinement. The move toward standardization is quite distinct from what one sees in OB texts and reflects a different understanding of the purpose of writing and approach to textuality in the post-OB context.[66] As Veldhuis has stated—in an admittedly somewhat exaggerated manner, "Old Babylonian texts are the products of authoritative *scholars*, while first millennium *texts* are *themselves* the authoritative sources and bearers of knowledge."[67]

Francesca Rochberg-Halton offers a useful definition of textual standardization for first millennium texts. The term, she argues, should not be understood as referring to a universally established, unchanging text. Rather, standardization should be conceived "in the sense that old material was conscientiously maintained in its traditional form and new material was no longer being incorporated."[68] Standardization, she states, extends to "formal aspects of the text, that is, the number and arrangement of tablets [in a series], while a degree of flexibility remained permissible in the content, in terms of exactly what a particular tablet was to include and in what order."[69] Thus, the term standardization should be understood somewhat loosely when applied to Akkadian texts.[70]

Hunger 1968, 175–76 (s.v. *šaṭāru*). For commentary and explanatory texts, see Frahm 2011; Livingstone 1986, respectively.

66. Veldhuis 1999; Michalowski 1992, 236–37.

67. Veldhuis 1999, 171, emphasis original.

68. Rochberg-Halton 1984, 127.

69. Rochberg-Halton 1984, 128.

70. There has been some debate about Assyriology's use of the word "canonization," which often evokes notions of biblical literature, to describe standardization. The debate at least partly stems from semantics but also from presumptions about the comparanda, especially on the Bible side (see Hurowitz 1999 for a useful survey). If by "canonization" one intends to draw a parallel with the presumed results of the biblical canonization process, i.e., when the books and their wording were rigidly fixed into a corpus (singular) in the early centuries of the Common Era, then the use of the term for first millennium Mesopotamian texts is inappropriate (thus, Rochberg-Halton 1984). Others have noted that the standardized texts of first millennium Mesopotamia compare quite well to the texts that would become the Hebrew Bible (Old Testament) during the last centuries before the Common Era, when the various biblical texts (plural) seem to have had a high level of communal authority but were available in different recensions, showing fluidity in both their wording and internal order (Lenzi 2008, 147–48 n. 57). If this is one's idea of a canonical text in biblical literature (apparently it is for Frahm 2011, 318 n. 1512), then the term may be appropriate to describe first millennium Mesopotamian texts. But it should be noted that biblical scholars will talk about this period of the Bible's history in terms of "canon formation," emphasizing the process leading to rather than the result of canonization. Given these problems, it seems to me that Assyriologists need to invest more energy in clarifying the meaning of the comparative terms. One fruitful avenue recently taken by Rochberg (2016) is to abandon textual attributes in the search for a definition of canonicity and emphasize instead the continued use of certain texts and the power over or force they exerted upon the scribal community. In this vein, see Helle 2018, who argues that the late "Uruk List of Kings and Sages," which lists kings and their sages/scholars, is "a canonical selection of literary works, the

For example, scribes gathered various celestial and meteorological omens (i.e., if X happens, then Y) and arranged them thematically into a series of seventy tablets.[71] They called the series Enuma Anu Enlil. The scribes organized this very long series by topic, so that, for example, lunar eclipse omens could be found in Enuma Anu Enlil tablets 15–22 while omens relating to thunder occur in tablets 44–46.[72] The scribes often ordered the tablets in the series by number in a brief note (a colophon) added at the very end of a tablet. They also indicated the order of the series, as was usual in multitablet series and compositions, by using what modern scholars call catchlines. When the scribes reached the end of one of the tablets in a multitablet series, they would typically draw a line across the tablet to mark the end of the text and then write the first line of the next tablet in the series. This catchline would help the user or reader of the tablet to find the next one in the series. (See figs. 1 and 8 for images of tablets with these organizational features.)

Omens within the various series and sections were also elaborated in a kind of scholasticism that demonstrates systematization.[73] That is, certain "slots" in the wording of an omen—for example, the color of the object of investigation, the day of its occurrence, the number of such objects, the direction of its sighting—were changed in successive omens in order to expand the phenomena covered in a systematic manner. For example, lunar eclipse omens could be listed by day and month of occurrence; within this variable parameter, the omens could be further organized by direction of the wind blowing or the apparent color of the eclipse (among other features).[74]

Despite all of this organization, the evidence indicates that the precise wording (and spelling) of these texts was never rigidly established in the standardization process, as was the case, for example, with biblical canonization in the first centuries of the Common Era.[75] The copyists' statements about faithfully following the wording of their original tablet (e.g., *kīma labīrīšu šaṭir-ma bari,*

implicit promise being that these authors were representative of their tradition—that knowing them and their works was to know Babylonian culture, its values, and its fears" (228).

71. The number of tablets in the series and the series' serialization/standardization is much more complicated than can be indicated here. See Koch 2015, 165–67.

72. For tablets 15–22, see Rochberg-Halton 1988. For tablets 44–46, see Gehlken 2012.

73. See Guinan 1989, 228 for a representative schematic of a section from Shumma alu, a terrestrial omen series; Rochberg 2009, 11–12 for another in Enuma Anu Enlil, an omen series dealing with celestial and meterological signs; De Zorzi 2011 for Shumma izbu, an omen series treating malformed births. For the meaning of left vs. right in omina, see Delnero 2015, 20–21.

74. See Rochberg-Halton 1988, 36–63 for a much more elaborate presentation of the many variables and schemata in the lunar eclipse omens.

75. Note, e.g., the variants in the manuscripts of the SB version of Epic of Gilgamesh collected by George 2003, 1:419–31. He focuses on variants in tablets I, VI, and XI, more than 800 lines of the composition. He characterizes these variants, despite their apparent high number, as "relatively few" and "comparatively minor" (429).

"written according to its original and collated") therefore show some tension between the texts' broader editorial histories, on the one hand, and their individual transmission by copyists, on the other.[76]

Evidence shows that not all texts underwent a standardization process. Further, despite standardization, different recensions (that is, versions or editions) of the same work could exist at the same time in different cities—and sometimes even within the same tablet collection.[77] Moreover, the creation of new texts did not cease. Despite these caveats, the predominant approach to traditional texts in the post-OB periods among scribes emphasized collection, preservation, systematization, and interpretation over new textual production. This approach is imperfectly captured by the term standardization.[78]

Assyriologists believe the late second millennium BCE was the period in which the great literary and learned texts were organized and standardized under the careful editorial eye of scribal scholars, some of whom would be remembered hundreds of years later.[79] But documentation for this claim is mostly indirect, based on inferences from later material.[80] Moreover, this standardization did not disallow later editorial activity in the great library at Nineveh or elsewhere.[81]

As for why the scribes undertook their editorial tasks, one part of the answer comes from the political uses of Akkadian texts in the first millennium. Namely, the massive omen series along with ritual and medical texts were ultimately practical in nature: they were believed to be important for the proper maintenance of kingship, that is, to keep the king in good standing with the gods.[82] Many mythological and epic texts likewise reflect cosmic and theological

76. See a similar comment about internal vs. external textual histories by Veldhuis 2010, 81.

77. See Robson 2011, 572 for a brief discussion of the SB Epic of Gilgamesh and for the celestial divination series Enuma Anu Enlil. On the latter, see also Beaulieu 2010, 11–12.

78. "Standardization" as an editorial process should not be confused with Standard Babylonian, a literary dialect of Akkadian, though many standardized texts were written in SB Akkadian.

79. See, e.g., Lambert 1960, 13–14; Civil 1975, 128; Rochberg-Halton 1987, 327; Frahm 2011, 317–22. For these scribal scholars in later tradition, see Lambert 1962; Beaulieu 2007b, 12–15.

80. There are several lines of evidence, including the continuity of scribal families and ancestry evincing Kassite names in the first millennium (Lambert 1957; 1960, 13–15; the Kassites were a MB dynasty that ruled Babylonia from the mid-fourteenth to the mid-twelfth centuries BCE); a mid-first millennium catalog of texts and putative authors that preserves several of these same names (Lambert 1962; with Jiménez 2017, 113); a few statements in letters (e.g., Parpola 1993, no. 100, rev. 6–7; Hunger 1992, no. 158, rev. 4–5) and colophons that invoke late second millennium scholars and kings in the context of describing editorial work (Frahm 2011, 317–22); and the relatively close genealogical relationship perceived between Middle Babylonian/Assyrian manuscripts of various learned series and those from the first millennium (e.g., Civil 1975, 128; more generally Rochberg-Halton 1984). For a general survey and new evidence, see Heeßel 2011.

81. As proposed by Jeyes 2000 for the extispicy series Barutu.

82. See Pongratz-Leisten 1999a.

themes of importance to proper cultic and/or royal activity.[83] These political uses, however, need not exclude a motivation among learned scribes that was rooted in the desire to bring order to and preserve (especially in times of political and economic turmoil) the Akkadian textual patrimony.[84] The impulse to preserve is certainly supported by textual finds dating to periods after the loss of native kingship—that is, from the Persian period (mid-sixth century BCE) on—when many of the Akkadian texts continued to be used ritually/cultically and also to enculturate young scribes.

Compositions: General Issues

Understanding and appreciating texts written by and for people from a culture other than one's own requires a knowledge of the literary and cultural conventions used in those texts to convey ideas and nuances of meaning. One needs to develop a literary competence attuned to the cultural setting from which those texts derive. One of the best ways to develop literary competence is by increasing one's familiarity with the texts' language and their culture. However, this presents an especially difficult challenge in the case of ancient Mesopotamia, a culture long dead, since the only way to become familiar with Mesopotamian language and culture, aside from archaeological artifacts, is by reading the very texts one wishes to understand. Through the slow process of reading and rereading texts in light of the growing collective understanding of ancient Mesopotamia accrued over the last 170 years, scholars are in a position to offer some generalizations about Akkadian literature. But these generalizations, for the most part, should be understood as progress reports rather than indisputable facts, for the process is on-going, the results tentative, and our ignorance still greater than we would wish.

Dating

Just as we must distinguish between the time period from which a tablet derives and the dialect used on the tablet, especially with regard to tablets inscribed in a literary dialect (see page 4, above), so must we also distinguish between the date of a tablet's origin (i.e., when it was made and inscribed) and the date a composition on a tablet was originally composed (i.e., when it was authored). With tablets not written in one of the literary dialects, for example, one-off letters, treaties, and contracts, there is typically good reason to conflate these

83. As noted by Michalowski 1992, 237.
84. So Frahm 2011, 322; Nils Heeßel, pers. comm.

two points of origins.[85] That is, the tablet was made to inscribe a contemporary text that it now bears; thus the tablet and composition were created in the
same time period—indeed, on the same day. This is not at all the case with
tablets bearing a text written in a literary dialect. It is essentially impossible,
for example, to know the actual time of composition for many texts written in
the Standard Babylonian literary dialect and preserved on a tablet from a Neo-
Assyrian archaeological context such as Assurbanipal's library. The form of the
script on the tablet (the ductus) will represent the one current at the time of the
copying process (thus, Neo-Assyrian), but the text may well have been composed centuries earlier. As N. J. C. Kouwenberg has shown, linguistic clues are
inadequate to specify the date's composition and aligning the events mentioned
in the content of the composition with known historical events is a precarious
and speculative enterprise.[86] Thus, we often do not know the date of Akkadian
compositions, so scholars must be content to speak of Old Babylonian literary,
religious, and scholarly texts, for example, or Standard Babylonian (i.e., post-
OB) ones.[87]

Titles, Rubrics, and Colophons

Ancient scribes typically used the incipit of an Akkadian composition (i.e., its
first line or first few words) for its title. The SB Epic of Gilgamesh, for example,
was referred to as *Ša naqba īmuru*, "He who saw the deep," in ancient catalogs
since this was the epic's first line, while the OB Epic of Gilgamesh was designated *Šūtur eli šarrī*, "Surpassing (all other) kings," which was the first line of
the OB version of the epic.[88] To the dismay of the uninitiated, contemporary
scholars have not adopted this convention consistently. For example, many
scholars will use *Ludlul bel nemeqi*, "I will praise the lord of wisdom," to refer
to the poem about a man who suffers due to Marduk's anger, but very few use
one of the above cited incipits for Gilgamesh to refer to the different versions of
the epic. There is also inconsistency in the use of this convention for the same
composition. For example, a few scholars may use *Bin šar dadmē* to refer to the
Anzu Epic while most others use a modern title such as the Epic of Anzu or the
Anzu Epic (see page 87). If this were not confusing enough, some compositions,
unfortunately, do not have a standard title at all. Scholars may assign their own

---

85. One-off letters are to be distinguished from letters that enter the scribal curriculum and are
copied for generations by students, sometimes coming down to us in multiple copies.

86. Kouwenberg 2012. The exception is royal inscriptions. They are often dated.

87. If tablets bearing a literary text are found in a mid- or late second millennium archaeological
context, one may also speak of a Middle Babylonian or Middle Assyrian version of a composition.

88. The SB version could also be cited as *iškar Gilgāmeš*, "series of Gilgamesh." For an
example of a catalog citing compositions by incipit, see Lambert 1962.

title to it or use one attached to it by a recent translator.[89] In some cases, the publication information of the tablet that bears the composition or the information for the copy most closely associated with the text has become its common title (e.g., *Ugaritica* 5, no. 162, for which see page 178).

Brief remarks that provide information about a composition may occur on a tablet at the end of the composition. For example, after the text of a prayer (and before its attendant ritual) there may be a note, set off from what precedes and follows by deep horizontal rule lines in the clay, that reads "it is the wording of a lifted-hand prayer to Shamash." Scholars call these short notes "rubrics" since they often describe the type of text, its function, or the series to which it belongs. Since rubrics occur after a text's completion and not at a *tablet's* completion, a tablet may contain as many rubrics as it does, for example, prayers (fig. 8).

As mentioned earlier in the discussion about editing, compositions that spanned multiple tablets used the initial line of each tablet as a means of indicating the order in which tablets should be read. The initial line of tablet two in a series, for example, was written at the very end of tablet one—often set off from the previous text by a horizontal rule line in the clay of the tablet. This indicated to the user that the tablet starting with that line of text should be read next in the series. At the end of tablet two, the first line of tablet three would be written. And so on. Scholars call these references to the next tablet catchlines (fig. 8). Sometimes these lines were collected in catalogs to summarize or to reorganize the order of a long series.[90]

The last item included on some tablets was the colophon, a brief note appended at the end of a tablet's inscription (fig. 8). It was typically set apart from the tablet's main text with a rule line or a couple of blank lines. Another way to set the colophon apart from the main text on the tablet was to inscribe the colophon's text with more space between its lines. Though their content and length vary considerably, colophons can offer a wide variety of information, including the contents of the text designated by incipit, the number of lines on the tablet, the tablet's place of origin, the copyist's name and kinship, the care with which the tablet was copied, for whom the tablet was copied (i.e., its owner), the date of its copying, and/or the reason for the tablet's production.[91] As one might imagine, such colophons provide invaluable historical and social information to modern scholars about scribal families and even individual scribes.[92]

---

89. Note, e.g., George's whimsical title for a love poem, "Oh Girl, Whooppee!" (2009, no. 8).
90. See, e.g., Finkel 1988. For recent studies on scholarly text catalogs, see Steinert 2018.
91. Hunger 1968, 1–15.
92. For a striking example of how colophonic evidence can be utilized in tandem with information from contracts and other mundane documents to illuminate a scribe and his family that lived more than 3700 years ago, see von Koppen 2011.

FIGURE 8. A tablet illustrating a number of scribal devices for structuring content. Photo © Trustees of the British Museum, London.

The Neo-Assyrian tablet in fig. 8 illustrates several of these scribal techniques for structuring content. This long tablet includes, from top to bottom, the text of a prayer, its one-line rubric, a three-line ritual, the text of another prayer, its one-line rubric, a one-line ritual, and then the catchline to the next tablet in the series. A horizontal line separates each of these sections. After a blank line, the tablet concludes with a long colophon. The Late Babylonian tablet in fig. 1 is another good illustration of these scribal techniques. The tablet contains a long *shuila*-prayer (see page 166) to the goddess Ishtar. A one-line rubric appears near the bottom of the tablet, set apart by rule lines, followed by four lines of ritual instructions, also set off by rule lines. A catchline and two lines of a colophon complete the tablet.

Genre

We do not have a handbook from ancient Mesopotamia that outlines Akkadian poetics. Nor do we have any treatise that reflects on the nature of genre or catalogs the various text types used in ancient Mesopotamia. This is not surprising given the fact that intellectual activity in ancient Mesopotamia did not focus on the expression of abstract principles or categories, whether in law, science, literature, religion, politics, art, or other spheres of learned inquiry. The absence of a treatise on or catalog of genres, however, does not mean that the Mesopotamians lacked such principles or categories, of course. As Herman Vanstiphout writes, "the unalterable fact that the Mesopotamians never explicitly formulated a framework for their generic system, let alone handed it down, does not mean that it did not exist."[93] We find intimations of their notions of genre (i.e., indigenous concepts of genre) in the use of specific terms to refer to certain kinds of texts; in the listing of thematically similar texts together in catalogs and *Sammeltafeln* ("collection tablets," which gather short compositions onto one large tablet); in the application of rubrics, superscripts, and subscripts to various kinds of discourse; and in the use of known text types for parody.[94] Yet there is much that we do not know

93. Vanstiphout 1999a, 81. See likewise Vanstiphout 1999b, 703. Vanstiphout, perhaps more than anyone, has been a leading proponent of generic research in Sumerian and Akkadian literatures. See Vanstiphout 1986, 1988, 1999a, and 1999b. The results of a 1995 workshop organized by Vanstiphout (and Vogelzang) on Mesopotamian genres, *Genre in Mesopotamian Literature*, never left the press. Other recent general statements on the importance of research into Akkadian literary genres include Longman 1991, 2–21; Wasserman 2003b, 176–78; George 2005a; Neujahr 2012, 75–83, the latter of whom rightly points out the many obstacles and disadvantages an interpreter of ancient texts must overcome with regard to genre analysis that contemporary literary critics simply do not face.

94. For the use of specific terms, see, e.g., Pongratz-Leisten 1999b; 2001, 19–27 on *narû*, "stela"; Beaulieu 1993a on *musarû* in NB and LB times; Parpola and Watanabe 1988, xv on *adê*, "treaty-oath"; Oshima 2011, 33–37 on *šēru* and *zamāru*, "song," both of which were used to designate hymns but the latter is also used for texts we often call epics (e.g., Enuma Elish; see page 83). For catalog

and much work to be done, which means this survey cannot present a selection of texts purely and consistently according to Mesopotamian generic categories.[95]

Modern scholars therefore have had to develop an alternative approach to genre, one in which they have grouped specific texts together due to similarities in form, content, and/or function but also due in part to a similarity with some modern categories deemed useful to literary or historical inquiry.[96] These categorizations have sometimes been created in a kind of intuitive, uncritical manner resulting in categories that prove misleading.[97] However, when constructed thoughtfully, such modern categories can prove quite helpful for specific contemporary purposes (e.g., introducing Akkadian literature). One of the inevitable results of using modern categories to classify ancient texts is that the same text, for example, the Epic of Gilgamesh, may be categorized differently by different scholars, which can easily be a source of confusion.[98] In any case, using a nonindigenous system of classifying texts is the only workable choice at this point in the development of the field.

Orality, Oral Tradition, and Oral Literature

Any discussion of orality in an ancient literature that lacks a continuous tradition to the present is dependent, ironically, on written texts. Despite this handicap, we can be fairly confident that everyday speech patterns and various oral expressions found their way into the body of written Akkadian available to us. One need only consider the way many Akkadian letters begin, "speak to PN (= personal name), thus (says) PN" (*ana* PN *qibī-ma umma* PN-*ma*). Letters also

---

listings, see, e.g., the catalog of love lyric incipits presented by George 2009, no. 12; now also edited in Wasserman 2016, no. 18. A *Sammeltafel* bears several similar texts on one physical tablet, even though those texts may have had different origins and circulated separately at some point in time. E.g., several of the Neo-Assyrian prophecies were rewritten together onto one large tablet. See Parpola 1993, nos. 1–3. On rubrics, superscripts, and subscripts, note, e.g., Sumerian ÉN before the wording of Akkadian incantations or DÙ.DÙ.BI before ritual instructions that follow the wording. It should be noted, however, that these scribal conventions are often indicative more of the use or function of the text than their form. And even when they are present, they may be vague or inconsistent (on which point, see Pongratz-Leisten 1999a, 217–19 for a discussion of the indigenous terminology for the "Gottesbriefe," for which see page 137, "Letters to the Gods," below). For parody, see, e.g., Vanstiphout 1988; Veldhuis 2003a, 23–27; Jiménez 2017, 79–99.

95. In making this statement, I am following the majority of other scholars who have surveyed Akkadian literature. See Pongratz-Leisten 2001.

96. See, e.g., Neujahr 2012, 83–112 for the debate over the generic identification of the so-called "literary prophecies" (what Neujahr prefers to call "*ex eventu* texts," for which see "Literary Prophecies/Ex Eventu Texts" on page 143, below). As examples of useful modern categories, see Grayson 1980 on royal inscriptions; Lenzi 2011, 2–23 on prayers; Noegel 2005 on epics; Wasserman 2016, 19–20 on love lyrics.

97. E.g., "literary prophecies" (see Neujahr 2012, 101–2).

98. Thus, Vanstiphout's lament (1999a, 80–81).

frequently quote what others have said to them or invoke for rhetorical purposes traditional proverbs, some of which do not appear in any written form beyond the one text in which they occur.[99] Yet letters present a simpler situation than do narrative poems or royal inscriptions. Identifying genuinely oral expressions in these written texts (see the discussion of oral literature below) in a methodologically sound manner is quite challenging. Indisputable examples are rather rare, making us, as Nathan Wasserman so aptly notes, "almost entirely deaf today to this type of oral expression."[100]

As for oral traditions: We know something about the *existence* of oral traditions from the written texts that have come down to us, but our knowledge of the actual content of these traditions varies rather widely. First millennium scholars, for example, sometimes invoked the phrase "according to the scholars" (lit. "of the mouth of the scholars," *ša pî ummâni*) in their efforts to explain a phenomenon to the king (in a letter or report). Yaakov Elman believed the phrase pointed to the existence of an authoritative oral tradition among scholars that was on par with but distinct from their written corpora.[101] Recent scholarship, however, suggests the phrase refers to the ancient scholars' oral teachings, some of which may have been written down in commentary texts.[102] If so, then we have a sizeable body of evidence for these pedagogical oral traditions in writing. There is also good reason (beyond common sense) to believe that many of the professional crafts, including scribal and scholarly ones (such as divination, exorcism, and medicine), had an oral component.[103] Some scholars believe ritual instructions, for example, were supplemented with orally transmitted instructions because these texts do not contain enough information to execute all of the prescribed ritual activities precisely.[104] If so, we only have a general sense of the content of these ritual oral traditions.

Finding oral expressions in letters or glimpses of an oral tradition in various crafts is one thing. Oral literature, that is, as Bendt Alster defines it, "literature

99. See Hallo 1990 for many examples (with references), including many in epistolary contexts that span the chronological spectrum (208–9); Cohen 2013, 213–31.

100. Wasserman 2003b, 173, where he offers a few other examples of oral expressions in written texts. Lambert's statement (1968, 123) in a discussion of "literary" (i.e., narrative poetic) texts, "when writing was invented and texts were written down the oral aspects of it continued exactly as before," overstates the case. See the discussion on oral literature, below.

101. Elman 1975.

102. So, e.g., Veldhuis 2010, 82 n. 18 (citing Koch-Westenholz 1999, 151); Frahm 2011, 44–45; Gabbay 2012, 278–80.

103. See Lenzi 2015b.

104. E.g., instructions may tell the ritual expert to set up a censer but without providing further details. See, e.g., Linssen 2004, 4, who notes the laconic nature of ritual instructions in Hellenistic ritual texts; Maul 1994, 119, who asserts the idea that many ritual activities were so self-evident to the ritual expert that they could be left out. Both cases assume a kind of oral tradition that informs the ritual expert.

created, transmitted, and recited without the help of writing," is quite another matter.[105] Of course, few would deny that the ancient Mesopotamians must have told stories and shared vignettes orally and that these existed both before writing and, after its invention, alongside it; but these are and always will remain presumptions, for, as Jerry Cooper writes, "actual Mesopotamian oral literature is what by definition we can never have."[106] This has not kept scholars, however, from claiming to find an oral background in the written texts, literary or otherwise.[107] For example, Wasserman, addressing the oral background of OB texts, writes, "not only incantations, but also other literary *nuclei* stemming from the popular, unbookish strata of society were penetrating the circles of the Edubba [that is, the scribal training house]. Once brought in, these literary embryos were modified to fit the matrices of the literary conventions of the period.... The literary product which emerged from this process [which we now have in the form of inscribed tablets] no longer belonged to the sphere of oral literature."[108] This is not at all an implausible scenario. But what evidence could we muster in the written texts to prove it?

The methodological problems surrounding the attempt to find an oral literature behind the written texts were laid bare in the results of a conference organized by Marianna Vogelzang and Herman Vanstiphout in Groningen in June 1990 on the theme of the oral or aural character of Mesopotamian epic.[109] One of the purposes of the conference was to explore the usefulness of the Parry-Lord paradigm for understanding the oral origins of Sumerian and Akkadian epic texts. The Parry-Lord or Oral-Formulaic Theory is, as John Foley summarizes it, "an approach to oral and oral-derived texts that seeks to explain the performance and transmission of folkloristic and literary material through a series of structural units: formula, theme, and story pattern. The formula is a

105. Alster 1992, 23.

106. Quotation from Cooper 1992, 105. See Cooper 1992, 104–5 for a colorful way of putting this presumption in a prewriting context. For the presumption of an oral literary tradition alongside the written products of scribes, see Cooper 1992, 109; Elman 1975, 22; both of whom cite Oppenheim and Reiner 1977, 22 (whose statement is somewhat convoluted); likewise, e.g., J. Westenholz 1992, 127; Vogelzang 1992, 265–66. Many others could be cited. Some scholars might presume that stories about certain heroes, e.g., Enmerkar (in Sumerian literature) and Atram-hasis, were floating around (see Vanstiphout 1992d, 260; van Koppen 2011, 144). But these versions are not necessarily to be equated with the written ones available to us.

107. See Cooper 1992, 103, 112 for examples of scholars who believe that our written sources are close to or derived from presumed oral predecessors. One could also add, significantly, George 2003, 1:21, who seems to favor the possibility that the Akkadian Epic of Gilgamesh was influenced by oral tradition. In contrast, Lambert (2013, 444) refuses to speculate about the oral background of Enuma Elish.

108. Wasserman 2003b, 182.

109. Vogelzang and Vanstiphout 1992. This is the same volume from which the quotations from Alster and Cooper just above are taken.

substitutable phrase that provides the performer with a malleable, ready-made idiom that simplifies the task of oral composition in performance; the theme and story pattern amount to formulas at the higher levels of the typical scene and tale type, respectively."[110] Although Milman Parry forged his ideas in the intellectual context of understanding the creation and transmission of the Homeric epics, he and his student Albert Lord extended their analysis to the living oral epic traditions in the Balkans, specifically Albania and the former Yugoslavia. Lord provided an important innovation in the theory with the development of what he called "formulaic density." According to this idea, one could determine the oral origins of a composition by calculating the percentage of formulas present in it.[111] Although most of the Assyriologists at the Groningen conference found the Parry-Lord Oral-Formulaic Theory to be lacking significant merit when applied to the Mesopotamian materials, some participants were more willing than others to consider oral influence on and origins of the written texts.[112] Piotr Michalowski's cautionary statement is worth citing at length. He writes, Mesopotamian literature is "a highly coded, written tradition that may have sometimes been transmitted orally but that was in many ways a separate mode of communication, different from the vernacular literatures that must have existed. To be sure, one may posit some mutual influence between the written and the oral literatures but one cannot hope to recover any documentation for the range of interaction between the two traditions."[113] Overall, there was a general sense that, as one participant summarized the findings, "aurality, rather than orality is what can be investigated" in Mesopotamian texts.[114]

Literary Sources, Borrowing, and Textual Variation

Given the bilingualism of ancient Mesopotamia and the influence of Akkadian and Sumerian on one another, it should come as no surprise that material found in Akkadian literary texts is sometimes related to or perhaps in some way derived

110. Foley 2012, 976.

111. Foley 2012, 977.

112. For those finding it lacking, see Alster 1992, 27; Black 1992, 91; Cooper 1992, 111–12; J. Westenholz 1992, 123–25, 137–38; Izre'el 1992, 156; Michalowski 1992, 232, 244; Vanstiphout 1992d, 247–48; Vogelzang 1992, 267. See similarly already Komoróczy 1975, 63. For the varied opinions on oral influence on or origin of written texts, compare, e.g., the contributions from Alster and Black to those by Cooper and Michalowski. Note also J. Westenholz's acceptance of the role of oral transmission between written versions of a text (1992, 153–54) and Vogelzang's exploration of what she calls the "impression of orality" in the short (written) versions of Nergal and Ereshkigal and Adapa from el-Amarna (1992, 271). Despite her interest in the oral sense of the texts, she has no intention to prove an oral origin or composition for these works (see esp. 267, 269–71, and 274).

113. Michalowski 1992, 245.

114. Izre'el 1992, 155.

from earlier Sumerian literature (from Ur III or Old Babylonian times).[115] To cite the clearest examples for which we have both Akkadian and Sumerian texts: Several scenes in the Epic of Gilgamesh also occur in earlier Sumerian versions (Bilgames and Huwawa, Bilgames and the Bull of Heaven, Bilgames and the Netherworld, and The Death of Bilgames), and the SB Descent of Ishtar represents a shorter version of the Sumerian myth Descent of Inanna.[116] How these Akkadian texts relate to the earlier Sumerian ones precisely (e.g., via oral tradition, a common source, through direct translation of an intermediary version, or free adaptation) is an open matter. We also have cases in which Akkadian texts were clearly influenced by well-known Sumerian genres but the Akkadian text does not have an exact Sumerian equivalent with which to compare it. Stefan Maul, for example, notes the influence of the Sumerian *ershahunga*-prayer genre on an Akkadian *shuila*-prayer to Marduk, though no similar Sumerian prayer to Marduk exists (yet) to which one could point as its source.[117] It seems rather clear that Sumerian compositions influenced Akkadian ones. Defining this influence precisely, however, and delineating its mechanisms and channels of transmission are much more difficult historical endeavors. Investigations must proceed on a case-by-case basis in full recognition that we may not have in our preserved texts all of the evidence necessary to answer our many questions in such matters.[118]

Akkadian texts also drew upon earlier *Akkadian* texts as source material. As there was no sense of copyright or plagiarism among ancient Mesopotamian scribes, they freely edited and modified earlier versions of compositions to create new ones. For example, the SB versions of Gilgamesh, Atram-hasis, Etana, Anzu, Adapa, and Nergal and Ereshkigal (among others), known from first millennium sources, have OB and/or MB versions, too, which substantially differ from the later SB ones. The scribes also incorporated material or passages (sometimes verbatim) from one text into an entirely different composition.[119] Some scholars have even suggested that scribes created deliberate structural

115. A dated but useful overview is Komoróczy 1975, 45–49. For the general influence of Sumerian on Akkadian in "epic" poetry, see Hecker 1974, 187–96.

116. For Gilgamesh and Bilgames, see George 1999, 141–208 for translations of the Sumerian poems; George 2003, 1:17–22 for a discussion of the relationship between the Sumerian and the Akkadian (with references to earlier literature). His conclusion: "The author [of the OB Akkadian epic] may have known the Sumerian poems but I doubt that he actually used them as primary sources. It is easier to allow that these poems informed his work in a secondary way, as general background, but equally possible that the similarities between the Sumerian and Babylonian material is the result of their dependence on old legends, motifs and other traditional material held in common" (21). For the relationship between the Descents of Inanna and Ishtar, see Falkenstein 1968.

117. Maul 1988, 16.

118. See Chen 2013 for an attempt to determine the influence of the Sumerian flood tradition on the Akkadian Atram-hasis; see Lenzi 2015c for my review.

119. See Chen 2013, 13.

and thematic developments between several compositions.[120] Very conspicuous cases of borrowing from one composition to create something new in another are the insertion of the flood story from some version of Atram-hasis into Tablet II of the SB Epic of Gilgamesh and the incorporation of the names of Marduk in Tablets VI and VII of Enuma Elish from some earlier list(s) of divine names.[121] Likewise, common passages in Descent of Ishtar and Nergal and Ereshkigal, on the one hand, and Descent of Ishtar and the SB Epic of Gilgamesh, on the other, point to either borrowing one from the other or a shared source.[122] Related to this large-scale borrowing, scribes sometimes changed a source text only slightly in order to adapt it to a new purpose. For example, an Assyrian scribe made a rather superficial attempt to create an Assyrian recension of Enuma Elish by replacing the name of Marduk, the high god of Babylon's pantheon, with that of the patron god of Assyria, Assur.[123] Narrative poems are not alone in these various forms of textual pilfery. Prayers, incantations, hymns, and ritual series could likewise borrow and/or adapt materials to suit a new ritual context, to address a different deity, or to accommodate a different supplicant.[124] Finally, scribes sometimes updated royal annals after successive campaigns; thus, early campaigns could be revised in light of later political and military developments—often with significant changes.[125]

In light of all of this, the reader of Akkadian texts should *expect* textual variation in the actual wording of compositions; it is a very common feature of texts preserved in multiple copies. Moreover, the scribal propensity to borrow and adapt texts for new purposes and the scribal necessity to copy compositions one manuscript at a time by hand over centuries in different cities rightly informs and tempers our definition of standardization of literary and scholarly compositions (see page 28, above).

---

120. Machinist 2005 sees a conscious and deliberate thematic development from Anzu to Enuma Elish to Erra. See also Frahm 2011, 345–49. The idea is significantly developed, drawing intertextual connections to a number of other works, in Wisnom 2014.

121. For Gilgamesh, see George 2003, 1:18. For Enuma Elish, see Lambert 2013, 147–60.

122. See, conveniently, Foster 2005, 24; Lapinkivi 2010, xi for references. Note also that all three compositions share lines in two different passages.

123. See Lambert 2013, 4–6; 1997.

124. For adaptations to a new ritual context, see, e.g., the discussion of "boilerplate" composition of incantations in Abusch 2002, 200 n. 11. For changing the deity's name, see, e.g., Mayer 1976, 450, where textual variants in seven MSS of a prayer show how a prayer could be directed to different goddesses, in this case, Gula (four MSS) or Belet-ili (three MSS), simply by switching the divine name. For changing the supplicant, see, e.g., the shuila-prayer directed to the moon god in Butler 1998, 379–98 (previously, Mayer 1976, 490–94), where two different royal supplicants are named in different MSS of the prayer (and at different places in the prayer). The prayer is an excellent example of ritual adaptation and fluidity in contents, too. The prayer was used in at least two different kinds of rituals. And the nine MSS show significant differences among themselves. See Lenzi 2011, 386; 2016.

125. See Van De Mieroop 1999, 40–56 for an overview with examples.

Poetics

Verse and Prose

Scribes writing in Akkadian could choose to communicate in verse or prose. While a great many of the texts discussed in this book were written in verse, a significant number, especially among royal inscriptions, were composed in prose. Deciding whether a text is written in verse or prose is a fundamental issue when deciphering a text, which raises the all-important question: What are the most distinctive identifying features of verse and prose in Akkadian? Excerpts from two religious texts will provide the material with which to consider this question.

A hymn to Shamash, sun god and god of justice, reads: "Illuminator of all, the whole of heaven / who makes light the darkness for humankind above and below / Shamash, illuminator of all, the whole of heaven / Who makes light the darkness for humankind above and below / Your radiance spreads out like a net over the world / You brighten the gloom of the distant mountains."[126] (The forward slash in this citation indicates line breaks on the tablet.) An OB letter-prayer (fig. 9) to a little-known deity named Ninmug states: "Ishum will listen to what you say, intercede for me with Ishum for this sin that I have committed. When you have interceded for me, I, radiant with happiness, will bring Ishum an offering, and I will bring you a sheep. When I sing praises before Ishum, I will sing your praises as well."[127]

Even from the English translation one can see that the former quotation is marked by rich imagery, redundancy/repetition, and, in the last two phrases, semantic parallelism (that is, both phrases describe the same idea with different wording: Shamash shines over the lands; see page 53, below, for more on parallelism). A glance at the Akkadian will reveal several telltale signs of verse. First, all of the lines in the hymn to Shamash have a similar length (here, four to five Akkadian words; note that prepositions, relative pronouns, and conjunctions do not count as independent words). Second, semantic units break with the lines on the tablet (separated by slashes in the translation); in other words, each line presents a self-contained idea. And third, the syntax or word order in the phrases (where obvious repetition is lacking) is varied. This point is quite obvious in a word-for-word translation of the last two lines of the citation: "they spread out like a net over the world your sunbeams / of the mountains

---

126. Foster 2005, 627–28. I have removed brackets in his translation now that the text is essentially fully restored.

127. Foster 2005, 219.

FIGURE 9. An OB letter in prose sent to a deity as a prayer. The tablet measures only 3.8 × 6.1 cm (1.5 × 2.4 in.). Photo © Trustees of the British Museum, London.

distant their gloom you brighten."[128] Finally, reading the Akkadian text aloud reveals both consonance and assonance. (Bold print marks the accented syllables.)[129]

mušnammir gimir[130] *kala šamāmī*
mušaḫli ekletu ana nišī eliš u šapliš
Šamaš mušnammir gimir kala šamāmī
mušaḫli ekletu ana nišī eliš u šapliš
saḫpū kīma šuškalli erṣetu šarūrūka
ša ḫuršāni bērûti eṭûttšunu tušpardi

These are all clues that the text is written in verse.

128. See Lambert 1960, 126 for the Akkadian text with the excerpt of the school tablet BM 36296, transliterated and translated in Oshima 2011, 190, which restores the lacunae of the opening lines in Lambert's edition. I have not indicated minor restorations.

129. See Huehnergard 2011, 3–4 for the rules of accentuation followed here.

130. I am assuming a mistake in the text here and in the third line of the quatrain: *gimillu*, "favor," should be *gimir*, "totality" (perhaps the MIR sign in the NB script was read as the signs MIL and LU). See similarly Oshima 2011, 190 n. 71.

The letter-prayer's text, in contrast, is straightforward in terms of its content. It conveys information, makes a request, and promises to respond in kind for a favorable reply. The text also follows typical Akkadian syntax. Most conspicuous in this respect is the placement of each verb in the text at the end of the clause in which it occurs. Moreover, clauses and phrases do not always break at the end of a line, as did the hymnic text. Again, a literal translation following the Akkadian word order brings this out more clearly (with slashes separating lines of text on the tablet):[131] "Your speaking Ishum hears. / For this sin / that I have committed, my hands / with Ishum take.[132] / When my hands you have taken, / with a shining face / to Ishum an offering / I will bring. / And to you / a sheep I will bring. / When praises / before Ishum / I praise, / then [Akk. *u*] your praises / I will praise." Finally, although the letter-prayer does not lack parallel constructions (note the last sentence), it is not graced with any imagery beyond the self-description of the subject (*ina pānīn namrūtim*, literally, "with a shining face"). These are all clues that the text is composed in prose.

This differentiation between poetry and prose is not simply a modern construct foisted on our ancient texts. As pointed out above, scribes generally inscribed one poetic line on one line of a tablet. Prose was generally inscribed without regard for line breaks on the tablet. This is a very clear signal that the scribes shared our conceptual distinction between poetry and prose. And this is an important clue to the proper reading of a text.

In light of the above, it may be tempting to view verse and prose in opposition to one another. As Timothy Steele writes in the entry "Verse and Prose" of the fourth edition of *The Princeton Encyclopedia of Poetry and Poetics*: "Verse involves measure—it organizes speech into units of a specific length and rhythmical character—whereas prose flows more freely at the discretion of the writer or speaker employing it."[133] But this stark opposition is not without problems. As Steele explains, "in one respect, we exhaust the subject by noting the difference between verse with its rhythmical organization and prose with its rhythmical freedom; yet in other respects, many factors complicate the relationship of the two media and blur the boundary between them. Throughout lit.[erary] hist.[ory], verse writers and prose writers share stylistic concerns and rhetorical strategies, and their methods of composition overlap in fascinating ways."[134] This generalization is no less true for Akkadian. For example, the Assyrian royal inscriptions are generally written in prose (thus, the verb is

131. See van Soldt 1994, no. 164 for the Akkadian text.
132. "Taking the hands" here is an idiom for intercession. Presentation scenes on cylinder seals, wherein a *lamassu*, holding a person's hand, leads the person into the presence of a seated deity, illustrates the idiom well. See Collon 1990, 46 and the image in fig. 18 for examples; Frechette 2012, 56 n. 182 provides recent bibliography.
133. T. Steele 2012, 1507.
134. T. Steele 2012, 1507–8.

often sentence final, and sentences do not correspond to line breaks), but many of these texts show substantial sophistication in their literary artifice, including penultimate placement of the verb in the sentence and a penchant for rare words, literary allusions, and rich metaphors and similes.[135] Atypical "poetic" syntax also occurs, for example, in the everyday language of OB letters.[136] Parallelism, although dominating verse, shows up in prose, too.[137] Thus, "verse" and "prose" are useful categories from the ancient as well as the modern literary perspective, but viewing them in rigid opposition to one another will improperly diminish appreciation of the literary sophistication of Akkadian prose.[138]

Verse Structure and Poetic Meter

As stated above, Akkadian texts were frequently composed in verse.[139] Given the diversity of genres and content as well as the longevity of the language's use, it will not be surprising to learn that for nearly every general observation one offers about Akkadian verse structure, one can also mention qualifications, exceptions, and variations. For example, line breaks on a tablet *usually* correspond to a single poetic verse.[140] We must qualify this statement with "usually" because there are exceptions, including occasional cases of enjambment, that is, "[t]he continuation of a syntactic unit from one line to the next without a major juncture or pause."[141] Note in the following excerpt from a Standard

135. As a random example of royal inscriptions, see lines 9–12 of a stela from Adad-Narari III, discovered in Tell al-Rimah (Grayson 1996, 211). Reiner refers to royal annals and votive inscriptions as "sustained elevated prose" (1985, 17). For a highly artificed royal inscription in prose, see Sargon's Eighth Campaign (Foster 2005, 790–813). For penultimate verb placement, see George 2007, 41; 2013b, 43. For rare words and literary allusions, see, e.g., Weissert 1997. For rich metaphors and similes, see Marcus 1977; Zaccagnini 1978; Ponchia 1987; Rivaroli and Verderame 2005; Nadali 2009; Van De Mieroop 2015, who also points out literary allusions.

136. For example, J. Westenholz cites many examples of the inverted genitive (exemplified by "of the mountains . . . their gloom," cited above) in OB letters (1997b, 193–95).

137. See, e.g., the diplomatic letter edited in George 2009, 113–20, where George also reflects on and rejects the artificial dichotomy between verse and prose, and the three el-Amarna letters treated by R. Hess 1993.

138. Hecker sees the transition between verse and artful prose as fluid (1974, 114). George (2009, 119) approvingly cites Michalowski's idea (1996, 146) to do away with the distinction altogether.

139. For an interesting project that collects various scholars' ideas of how Akkadian texts might have sounded, including several poetic texts, see Martin Worthington's web site at http://www.soas .ac.uk/baplar/recordings/. Scholarship on Akkadian verse from the last several decades includes Hecker 1974, 101–60; Polentz 1989; Buccellati 1990; the many studies in Vogelzang and Vanstiphout 1992, 1996; Black 1990; J. Westenholz 1997a, 24–29; 1997b; Izre'el 2001; Wasserman 2003b; Streck 2007b; Lambert 2013, 17–34; Helle 2014; Wisnom 2015; C. Hess 2015. Reiner and Farber 2012 present a brief overview.

140. Thus, for Lambert the line is the "one basic and unmistakable element of Akkadian poetry" (Lambert 2013, 17; contrast Hecker 1974, 142, who gives preference to the couplet, and Wisnom 2015, 500, who looks to the half-line as fundamental).

141. Brogan, Scott, and Monte 2012, 435.

Babylonian hymn to Shamash that the first poetic line can only be fully understood with its continuation in the second: "To unknown distant regions and for
uncounted leagues / You press on, Shamash, going by day and returning by
night."[142] Another exception to the congruence of tablet lines with poetic verses
is that some manuscripts of poetic works, especially from the OB period, distribute the constituents of a single verse over two, rarely three, lines of the tablet.[143]
Finally, a third exception is that one occasionally finds two poetic lines written
on one line of the tablet, often divided with a cuneiform "colon" (𒑱).[144] Another
generalization worthy of mention: Rhyme is not a typical feature of Akkadian
verse; but again there are exceptions. Indeed, there are enough of these exceptions for Wasserman to devote a whole chapter of his monograph *Style and
Form in Old-Babylonian Literary Texts* to rhyming couplets in OB verse.[145]
In yet another oft-repeated generalization, one might note that Akkadian verse
usually ends with a trochee (i.e., a series of two syllables in which the first one
is accented; e.g., **šar′-**ru) or amphibrach (i.e., a series of three syllables in which
the middle one is accented; a-**wi′-**lum).[146] But once again there are exceptions.[147]
In fact, attempting to turn the trochee/amphibrach observation into a law results
in a Procrustean theory that distorts normal stress in words and vowel length
at the end of lines and thereby potentially overlooks expressively significant
variations.[148] Thus, it is best to consider this feature of Akkadian verse a very
common tendency rather than a law.

142. The translation follows Lambert 1960, 129, lines 43–44. The example is cited by Groneberg
1987, 184–85; see also Hecker 1974, 142–43.

143. See, e.g., George 2003, 1:162 for OB examples, and 1:351 for later (mostly Western but
also including Assyrian) examples of manuscripts of Gilgamesh. In some of the later manuscripts,
poetic lines may even break in the middle of lines on the tablet. The poetic lines in the el-Amarna
MSS of Adapa and Nergal and Ereshkigal also do not always coincide with the lines on the tablet
(see Izre'el 1992, 180; 2001, 72). For an overview of several OB compositions that distribute poetic
lines over more than one line on the tablet, see the texts presented in von Soden 1981; 1984, 213–15.
For a kind of inventory of such in OB epic, see C. Hess 2015, 262–67.

144. See, e.g., AO 4462, the only manuscript of the OB Man and His God (Lambert 1987). This
composition is discussed on page 172, below.

145. Wasserman 2003b, 157–73, who also notes the fact that Akkadian verse seems to avoid
the creation of rhyme in some cases (158–59, citing Kinnier Wilson's work on this issue in n. 9).
See also Hecker 1974, 143–45 for various patterns of rhyme that arise due to repetition of the same
words across couplets.

146. See, e.g, Landsberger 1926, 371 (English translation, 1976); von Soden 1981, 170–72; Izre'el
and Cohen 2004, 30; Lambert 2013, 18–20; Helle 2014, whose work is especially interesting for pointing out what is typical while recognizing variation. George 1999, 219–20; Jiménez 2017, 76–77 offer
illustrative passages with accents marked.

147. See Hecker 1974, 101–8 for discussion and exceptions. See also Lambert's comments about
exceptions (2013, 18–20).

148. For the former, see, e.g., Edzard 1993–95, 149; West 1997a, 182; Wisnom 2015, 489. For the
latter, see Helle 2014, esp. 68.

Just as flexibility and openness to variation must characterize any approach to Akkadian verse structure, likewise with meter. Wasserman captures the issues well: "An analysis of the Old Babylonian literary corpus shows that if a basic rule concerning its general prosodic characteristics can be drawn, it is the penchant for variation, whether in quantity, quality or frequency of syllables; alteration in sequence of pitches, stresses, accents or pauses; or variability in the position of alliterating elements, balancing segments (i.e., words), or even suprasegments (i.e., notions or ideas). Simply stated, Akkadian literary texts were not normally constructed following a single obligatory metric or prosodic form."[149] After his brief review of various proposals for discerning an Akkadian meter, Wasserman concludes that there is no metrical system in Akkadian poetry like that in Classical texts, that is, with a "regular and predetermined number of syllables." Rather, Akkadian verse "interweaves syntactic structure with basic semantic units, mostly within the boundaries of a single line or a couplet."[150]

It may therefore be better to speak of an Akkadian poetic rhythm rather than meter, formed by weaving together, in Wasserman's words, "syntactic structure with basic semantic units" (though rhythm includes other features, too, as noted below).[151] Shlomo Izre'el calls these units "metremes," which are most simply defined as "syntactic units ... carrying a single (main) stress each."[152] (Some scholars will describe this stress as the unit's "beat.")[153] Izre'el's fuller explanation of a metreme, offered in the context of his discussion of the Babylonian Theodicy, reveals, however, that these units are not so easily defined.[154] He writes, "[a] metreme is usually identical with a word, a genitive construct [two words syntactically bound to one another, e.g., *bēl bīti*, "the house's owner"] or a word with proclitics (i.e., prepositions, negations, the relative particle or the conjunction)," for example, *ana bēl bīti*, "to the house's owner."[155] In each of these cases, only one syllable would typically carry the main stress. "However," he continues, "this is not always the case, and thus we may find

149. Wasserman 2003b, 157–58. Although the statement occurs in a monograph on OB literary texts, it applies to later Akkadian texts, as his last sentences suggests, just as well. See likewise Foster 2009, 138; compared with 2005, 16.

150. Wasserman 2003b, 162. Wasserman 2003b, 159 n. 14 updates West's bibliography of earlier work on Akkadian meter (1997a, 175 n. 1). Add van Rensburg 1990; Tropper 2012; Helle 2014; Wisnom 2015, who suggests "that perhaps the reason no system of stress patterns has been found is that we have been too strict in our criteria for what such a system should constitute" (485). She goes on to suggest a flexible system of meter, elucidated by a comparative look at Old English verse.

151. Wasserman 2003b, 162.

152. Izre'el and Cohen 2004, 30.

153. See, e.g., George 1999, 219; 2003, 162–63.

154. The Babylonian Theodicy is a favorite text to discuss in works on Akkadian meter for reasons that will appear below. See, also, e.g., West 1997a; more briefly, von Soden 1981, 161.

155. Izre'el 1992, 186.

metremes comprising of larger units ... and smaller units."[156] The larger units may be an entire line and the smaller units may be the result of the separation of, for example, a genitive construct, whose components are typically inseparable, into its two constituent parts.[157] The number of metremes in a given line of verse can differ. Lines with three units are common; lines with four dominate many poems (e.g., Epic of Gilgamesh, Enuma Elish, and Ludlul bel nemeqi, among others). Yet lines of verse with fewer (two) and more units (as many as six) may also occur.[158] Moreover, scholars will not always agree on how to divide a line into metremes. Thus, there seems to have been flexibility and variation in how the Akkadian poets used these building blocks to compose Akkadian verse; and our understanding of these units is imperfect.[159]

The arrangement of verses in some manuscripts of poetic compositions supports the idea that lines are in fact formed by way of these smaller building blocks.[160] Such manuscripts sometimes show a gap on the tablet about half way through each line (in which tablet and verse lines correspond), as the tablet containing Counsels of Wisdom 81–87 illustrates in figures 4 and 5.[161] This caesura suggests that verses were conceived as comprising two half-lines (sometimes called versets or cola).[162] Other manuscripts suggest that these half lines could be understood as containing yet smaller constituent parts. A manuscript of Enuma Elish VI from Tell Hadad (ancient Me-Turan) shows a gap on the tablet at the halfway point in each line and then another gap at about three-quarters of the way through the line. The second gap corresponds largely with the division between two metremes that constitute the second half of the verse.[163] Three

---

156. Izre'el 1992, 186. See similarly George 1999, 219, both cited by Wasserman 2003a, 161. For Izre'el's more recent statement on meter in his reading of Adapa, see 2001, 81–90.

157. For the separation of genitive constructs, see the brief discussion of the Babylonian Theodicy below.

158. See Hecker 1974, 109–19.

159. Likewise, Hecker 1974, 114.

160. See generally Foster 2005, 13.

161. Further, see, e.g., the copy of VS 10 214 (from Assur in Zimmern 1913; as noted by Groneberg 1996, 66 n. 54), which contains the OB Agushaya Hymn; the copy of MS i (SU 1951 32 = STT 33 from Sultantepe) of Ludlul bel nemeqi II in Lambert 1960, pls. 8–11; the copy of VAT 10610 (from Assur) of a bilingual hymn to Ninurta, probably dating back to Middle Assyrian times, in Lambert 1960, pl. 31; and the copy of MS a of Enuma Elish I (1924 790+1813+2081 from Kish) in Lambert 2013, pl. 3.

162. Thus, lines (on the tablet) of some OB texts should be construed in fact as half lines of verse.

163. As noted by West 1997a, 177; see Al-Rawi and Black 1994, 136–39 for a copy of the tablet. In an odd variation: a witness to Ludlul bel nemeqi I shows a gap in the middle of the physical tablet but three-quarters of the text in each poetic line has been written before the gap and only one quarter of the wording after the gap; see Lambert 1960, pls. 1–2 for the copy (his MS m = SU 1951 10 = STT 32 from Sultantepe).

manuscripts of the Babylonian Theodicy go the next step by marking quarter lines of each verse.[164] However, these quarter lines are not distinguished by gaps on the tablet; rather, three vertical lines are inscribed on the tablet, and each quarter of the line, each metreme, presumably, is written in the resulting columns. Interestingly, there are ten lines in which the two members of a genitive construct are separated into adjacent columns, thus—assuming the copyist's divisions represent a common Mesopotamian poetic sense—problematizing how we might divide unmarked poetic lines into constituent metremes.[165] Again, it would seem that even the identification of metremes was variable and flexible.

As the previous section on prose and verse suggested, the syntax within verses and cola may vary significantly from prose. For example, verbs need not occur in final position, adjectives may precede the noun they modify, and elements typically kept together (e.g., nouns in apposition, adjectives and nouns, or a noun and its qualifying prepositional phrase) may be separated by another word in the phrase.[166] Word selection and their arrangement within the cola and verse might have been motivated by consonance, assonance, rhyme, word play, or the desire to create a trochee/amphibrach at the end of the verse.[167] The needs of parallelism within the verse or with another verse with which it forms a couplet might have influenced syntactical arrangement. The same could be said for chiasmus, "the repetition of a pair of sounds, words, phrases, or ideas in the reverse order, producing an *abba* structure."[168] The possibilities are too

---

164. Copies of two of these tablets, BM 34773 and BM 35405, are available in Lambert 1960, pls. 19, 24 and 20, respectively. See Oshima 2014a, pl. XV for a third (BM 47745). Also, his plates LIII–LVI provide photographs of BM 34773 and BM 35405.

165. West 1997a, 177. Perhaps the most illustrative example is line 254: *lē'u | palkû | šu'ê | tašimti*, "O capable one | wise one | master of | sagacity." On the other side of the problem, West notes that there are some cases of a particularly long word in one cola of a verse that seems to balance another cola in the verse or couplet with two beats, thus suggesting that the long word has two beats; but there are other cases of similarly long words that must be construed as having only one beat (1997a, 176). This entire analysis, however, may be overgeneralizing, deriving more about Mesopotamian poetics than these manuscripts of the Babylonian Theodicy can bear. We may only be witnessing one poetic tradition. Moreover, this tradition could be a secondary development foisted upon the text, as there is no way to determine if the copyists who produced these ruled tablets were reading the text as the author intended. See likewise Foster's reaction to Izre'el's suggestion (1992, 181–91; see now Izre'el 2001, 81–90) about the metremic significance of the "red dots" in the el-Amarna versions of Adapa and Nergal and Ereshkigal (Foster 1994, 590).

166. See George 2003, 1:434–35 for examples of these syntactic arrangements in Gilgamesh; also, more briefly, Groneberg 1987, 175–79, who also notes the unusual position of interrogatives (176).

167. For word play, see, e.g., Hecker 1974, 138–41; Groneberg 1987, 184; 1996, who cites several other studies on p. 67; J. Westenholz 1997a, 29. For more on word play (i.e., paronomasia), see page 63, below. For the desire to create a trochee/amphibrach, see the examples in George 2003, 1:434.

168. Brogan, Halsall, and Hunter 2012, 225.

extensive to document here.[169] As Sophus Helle has emphasized, all of these features of Akkadian poetry factor into poetic rhythm, which is "flexible and interwoven with the semantics of expression," "an interplay between meaning and sound, where different aspects of speech (stress, meaning, word order, consonance, assonance, pauses, etc.) converge."[170]

Looking at Akkadian verse diachronically, one sees a tendency for shorter lines of verse in the OB period and longer lines in the later period.[171] Compare, for example, these lines of the flood story in the OB version of Atram-hasis (III 36–37):

> *anāku ina puḫri ša ilānī*
> *kī aqbi ittīšunu gamertam*

"In the assembly of the gods,
How did I, with them, command total destruction?"[172]

with these similar lines in the SB Epic of Gilgamesh (XI 121–122):

> *kī aqbi ina puḫri ilānī lemuttu*
> *ana ḫulluq nišīya qabla aqbī-ma*

"How was it I spoke evil in the assembly of the gods,
(and) declared a war to destroy my people?"[173]

The couplet in the first excerpt has three metremes per line; the one in the second has four. Lines of verse reach their greatest length in compositions such as Erra and Ishum and the royal Epic of Tukulti-Ninurta I.[174] Note, for example, Erra I 39–44:

169. See Hecker 1974, 120–45, who has treated this aspect of verse and couplets extensively within his corpus.

170. Helle 2014, 68–69, note his case study of Enuma Elish I 1–9 on pp. 69–71 (and now compare Wisnom 2015, 499–500).

171. See, e.g., West 1997a, 178–80; Wasserman 2003a, 160; Wisnom 2015, 486. The observation remains true even if one assumes that a poetic line in some OB texts often occupied more than one line on the tablet. But here too one can cite exceptions. E.g., note the relatively long lines of the OB Man and His God (Lambert 1987), which are still rather long even after recognizing two lines of poetry often are written on one line on the tablet.

172. See Lambert and Millard 1969, 94–95.

173. See George 2003, 1:711. A near verbatim parallel exists, e.g., in Gilgamesh XI 112–113 and Atram-hasis III 12–14. However, the former adds one word to specify the subject of the verb in the second line.

174. West 1997a, 180; Hecker 1974, 135, who refers to these compositions as "Kunstprosa." For Epic of Tukulti-Ninurta I, see page 141, below.

ultu šīmat Sibitti napḫaršunu išīmu Anum
iddiššunūtī-ma ana Erra qarrād ilānī lillikū idaka
kī ša nišī dadmē ḫubūršina elīka imtarṣu
ublam-ma libbaka ana šakān kamāri
ṣalmat qaqqadi ana šumutti šumqutu būl Šakkan
lū kakkūka ezzūti šunū-ma lillikū idaka[175]

After Anu had ordained destinies for all of the Seven,
He gave those very ones to Erra, warriors of the gods, (saying),
   "Let them go beside you.
"When the clamor of human habitations becomes noisome to you,
"And you resolve to wreak destruction,
"To massacre the people of this land and fell the livestock,
"Let these be your fierce weaponry, let them go beside you."[176]

Poetic Units Above the Verse and Parallelism

Akkadian lines of verse may stand alone (e.g. Ludlul II 33), but it is much more common for verses to occur in larger units. Sometimes these units are marked on the tablet with rule lines; but this is quite inconsistent across witnesses to compositions, and sometimes these rule lines have nothing to do with the poetic delineation of the verses.[177] The few comments in this section offer some broad generalizations about poetic units above the verse, but they cannot fully convey the difficulties in identifying larger poetic units, about which competent scholars often disagree.

The most common arrangement in Akkadian poetry is to bind two lines of verse together to form a couplet.[178] This arrangement allowed for the development of extensive forms of parallelism between verses. Parallelism, as Foster has succinctly stated, is the "repeated formulation of the same message such that subsequent encodings of it restate, expand, complete, contrast, render more specific, complement, or carry further the first message."[179] Parallelism can operate

---

175. See Cagni 1969, 62 for the text.
176. The translation follows Foster 2005, 883.
177. See Groneberg 1996, 65–66 for a brief discussion with examples.
178. Some scholars prefer the term distich. See Hecker 1974, 142–45 for a brief treatment of couplets. Hecker actually calls the couplet the basic unit of Akkadian poetry because the presence of a couplet is sometimes the only way to identify a text as poetry rather than prose (142).
179. Foster 2005, 14, with examples on 14–15; see also Foster 2009, 138–40; Groneberg 1987, 181–90 for more examples. Streck 2007b uses a narrower definition of parallelism; he provides several examples in OB hymns. Related to parallelism is repetition, which, as Vogelzang states, "in its broadest sense . . . is part of all poetry" (1996, 168). Her analysis highlights repetition at different levels and in different aspects of Akkadian verse (repetition of sounds, grammatical forms, syntax,

on numerous levels, including the semantic, grammatical, phonological, and lexical.[180] Some lines from OB Gilgamesh (Pennsylvania tablet) I 90–93 provide a good example of how two verses can form a couplet and work together in parallel. Note, by the way, how each verse occupies two lines on the tablet:

> [90] <u>ul īde</u> Enkidu [91] <u>aklam ana akālim</u>
> [92] <u>šikaram ana šatêm</u> [93] <u>lā lummud</u>

> Enkidu <u>did not know how</u> to eat bread,
> <u>How</u> to drink ale <u>he had never been shown</u>.[181]

As the underlining shows in the Akkadian, the outer grammatical elements in the two verses form a syntactic chiasm in the couplet that binds the verses together. That is, the syntax of the outer elements of the two verses mirror one another: <u>negated verb</u> (A), subject, <u>predicate</u> (B); <u>predicate</u> (B), [elided subject], <u>negated verb</u> (A). Only the stated subject in the middle of the first verse, Enkidu, is without grammatical parallel in the second verse. As it would be redundant to include it, it is elided. Lexically speaking, the two main verbs are synonymous whereas the other elements in the couplet are logical opposites: eat/drink (encapsulating all forms of acquiring nourishment) and bread/beer (representing the two staples of the Mesopotamian diet and metonymically standing in for all solids and liquids).[182] Semantically, all of these elements work together in the couplet to communicate a broader image than would be possible in either individual verse. The couplet communicates Enkidu's beastly, uncivilized comportment; he does not know what to do with human nourishment.

Couplets may also contain two verses that contrast, wherein the larger message is advanced. Many examples occur in the hymnic prologue to the Standard Babylonian poem Ludlul bel nemeqi. For example, I 17–18 reads:

> akṣat ana surri ennittašu kabitti
> ikkarriṭ-ma zamar itâr ālittuš

---

and words of the same semantic domain). Although parallelism occurs between verses, it also occurs at other levels (e.g., between cola within the verse or between couplets in quatrains). See below. The student of Akkadian verse can learn much from scholarship on parallelism in Biblical Hebrew poetry; see especially the Roman Jakobsen-influenced treatment in Berlin 1985.

180. See Annus and Lenzi 2010, xxx–xxxiv (which is indebted to Berlin 1985) for my treatment of these four areas with reference to couplets from Ludlul.

181. The example is cited by Hecker 1974, 142. The text, line numbers, and translation follow George 2003, 1:176–77.

182. For akālu and šikāru as merismatic pairs, see Wasserman 2003b, 94–95.

His grievous punishment is immediately overbearing,
He shows pity and instantly becomes motherly.[183]

Interestingly, the semantic contrast between verses here is complemented by the phonological correspondences (alliteration and assonance): the /k/ and dentals in *akṣat* and *ikkarriṭ*, the sibilants and /r/ in *surri* and *zamar*, and the /t/, /š/, /a/, and /i/ sounds in *ennittašu kabitti* and *itâr ālittuš*.[184]

Verses can be arranged into units larger than the couplet, though scholars often do not agree about the delineation of these larger units. Tercets (three verses) are sometimes found bound together, as at the start of tablet V of the SB Epic of Gilgamesh.

> *izzizū-ma inappattū qišta*
> *ša erēni ittanaplasū mēlâšu*
> *ša qišti ittanaplasū nērebšu*

> They stood marveling at the forest,
> Observing the height of the cedars,
> Observing the way into the forest.[185]

But quatrains, that is, four lines of verse, are the most common unit after the simple couplet. Andrew George, for example, arranges the OB Epic of Gilgamesh in quatrains; Philippe Talon does the same for Enuma Elish.[186] Quatrains exhibit a number of patterns.[187] The following is but a small sample.

Quatrains sometimes consist of two nearly identical couplets, as the opening lines of the hymn to Shamash, cited earlier, show.

> *mušnammir gimir kal*[*a*] *šamāmi*
> *mušaḫli ekletum ana niš*[*ū*] *eliš u šapliš*
> *Šamaš mušnammir gimir ka*[*la*] *šamāmi*
> *mušaḫli ekletum ana niš*[*ū el*]*iš u šapliš*[188]

---

183. The text and translation follow Annus and Lenzi 2010, 15, 31. See also Oshima 2014a, 78–79.

184. This paragraph follows my previous treatment of this line in Annus and Lenzi 2010, xxxii closely.

185. George 2003, 1:602–3.

186. George 2003, 1:162–65; Talon 2005 (with only two exceptions noted on p. x). Lambert 2013, 28–30 argues against Talon's understanding.

187. On patterns within quatrains, see further Hecker 1974, 146–51.

188. For the text, see Lambert 1960, 126; the fragment that fills the gaps in Lambert's edition is in Oshima 2011, 190. As Oshima notes (n. 71), *gimillu* in lines 1 and 3 is probably a scribal mistake for *gimir* (see note 130, above).

Illuminator of all, the whole of heaven,
Who makes light the darkness for humankind above and below,
Shamash, illuminator of all, the whole of heaven,
Who makes light the darkness for humankind above and below.[189]

Obviously, the two couplets are repeated nearly verbatim, except the third verse specifies the deity's name at its head. This reflects an old Sumerian hymnic pattern that finds its way into various Akkadian hymns and hymnic passages (as at the beginning of Ludlul bel nemeqi and various prayers).[190]

Sometimes the couplets forming the quatrain exhibit slight alterations of wording in order to restate the message of the stanza through parallelism, just as would two verses in a couplet. For example, Ludlul bel nemeqi I 29–32:

bēlu mimma libbi ilānī ibarri
manāma i[na] ilān[ī] alaktašu ul īde
Marduk [mi]mma libbi ilānī ibarri
ilu ayyumma ul ilammad ṭēnšu

The lord, he sees everything in the heart of the gods,
But no one among the gods knows his way.
Marduk, he sees everything in the heart of the gods,
But no god can learn his counsel.[191]

Quatrains may also consist of two semantically contrasting couplets to communicate a unified idea. Note, for example, the grammatical parallelism between the following two couplets that also portray in their semantic contrast the cosmographic divide between the celestial and chthonic deities. The lines are from the beginning of the myth Nergal and Ereshkigal (lines 36–39).

umma att[ī-m]a ul ša elî
ina šattī[k]ī-ma ul tellī ana maḫrīni
u nīnū-ma ul ša arādi
ina ar[ḫ]īni-ma ul nurrad ana maḫrī[k]i[192]

You are not able to come up,
Not (once) in a year can you come up before us.

---

189. The translation follows Foster 2005, 627–28. I identify these lines as a quatrain despite rule lines between couplets on the tablets bearing the text (see Lambert 1960, pls. 33–36).

190. See, e.g., Mayer 1976, 40–41.

191. See Oshima 2014a, 80–81 for the text and Annus and Lenzi 2010, 31–32 for the translation. Note how this quatrain plays with the hymnic pattern noted previously.

192. For the text see Ponchia and Luukko 2013, 13 with their comment on p. 34.

We cannot go down,
Nor (once) in a month can we descend before you.[193]

Quatrains sometimes comprise two couplets in which each verse within a couplet extends the idea of the previous, and the second couplet builds on the first in some way. Note, for example, the opening lines of an OB hymn to Nanay:

iltam šamaš nišīša
Nanāya suppiā šubbā[194] nazzāssa
šātu kīma arḫim annaṭālim[195]
igisuṣillaša šarūri za'nū[196]

To the goddess, sun of her people,
To Nanay pray, and praise her rank:
For she is like the moon to look on,
Her wondrous features full of brilliance.[197]

The first couplet is a call to praise and the second provides reasons to do so. Contrasting word pairs introduced in the first verse of each couplet, the sun and the moon, work together to convey the idea of divine effulgence and cosmic position (see *nazzāssa*, "her rank" in the second verse). Within the couplets, the second verse identifies by name the goddess mentioned in the first and then advances the thought of the first verse by providing two verbs (imperatives), which call on her people to praise her (and her rank). The third verse compares the goddess to the moon, providing a reason to praise the goddess, and the fourth advances this idea by specifying a feature of the goddess and then elaborating the significance of the lunar simile.

Stanzas of more than four verses occasionally occur. For example, Ludlul II 12–22 seem to form a single poetic unit as do the lines describing Ishtar's ascent from the netherworld in Descent of Ishtar 119–125.[198] Although most of the tablets witnessing to the text of the Babylonian Theodicy mark eleven line units

---

193. The translation follows Foster 2005, 512.
194. See Streck and Wasserman 2012, 191 for this problematic word.
195. A sandhi writing for *ana naṭālim*.
196. See Streck and Wasserman 2012,187 for the text.
197. The translation follows Foster 2005, 89, except I have removed the word "new" before the word "moon," as its presence negates the purpose of the simile. *Arḫum* can simply mean "moon." Interestingly, this hymn consists of fourteen quatrains, which are each separated on the tablet by a rule line. See likewise the OB hymn to Ishtar, translated by Foster 2005, 85–88; the reverse of the tablet is pictured in fig. 19.
198. See Foster 2005, 398–99 and 503–4, respectively. See also Groneberg 1996, 74, where she treats Ludlul I 57–65 as one poetic unit.

with a rule line, these blocks of text comprise a mix of couplets and single line verses.[199]

Other Literary Characteristics

Repetition

Akkadian literary sensibilities show no discomfort with repetition.[200] Phrases, short passages, and long episodes are often repeated, sometimes multiple times.[201] The conventional formulas for the introduction of speech in narrative poetry perhaps best exemplify repetition at the phrase level.[202] A couple of the more common renditions appear very frequently and sometimes in close succession. For example, in the SB Epic of Gilgamesh the phrases "he answered [lit. made his mouth] and spoke,[203] saying to PN" (*pâšu īpuš-ma iqabbi izakkara ana* PN) and "PN₁ spoke to him/her, to PN₂," (PN₁ *ana šâšu/i-ma izakkar ana* PN₂) both occur nearly forty times in the epic. In one passage, the former phrase occurs three times in seven lines (IV 211–217); in another, the latter phrase appears three times in eight lines (XI 212–219).[204] Obviously, these phrases mark transitions between speakers and help the reader/listener follow the flow of the plot. Yet they are to be considered an element of style, since identifying the speaker in this way was not always thought necessary.[205] As others have pointed out, these introductory formulas may be left out in passages that are emotionally tense or aim to step up the narrative pace.[206]

---

199. The lines in each unit also begin with the same sign. See Lambert 1960, pls. 19–25.

200. For a substantial treatment of hendiadys, *tamyīz, damqam-īnim*, merismus (including an extended discussion of word pairs), simile (treated below under imagery), and rhyme in Old Babylonian literary texts, see Wasserman 2003b. For repetition, see Foster 2005, 15–16; Vogelzang 1996; Hecker 1974, 56–65, 154–60.

201. E.g., the same two-line refrain occurs nine times in the SB Epic of Gilgamesh IX, between lines 139–166 (George 2003, 1:672–73).

202. See Sonnek 1940 for the various formulas with updates in Hecker 1974, 174–77. Vogelzang 1990 does not study the conventional formulas for direct speech as much as their literary contexts. Edzard 1990 argues for several examples of soliloquy and monologue in Akkadian literature, which exhibit distinctive but not standardized introductory formulas. For the role of repetition at a level lower than the line or phrase, see Vogelzang 1996, who states that "in its broadest sense repetition is part of all poetry" (168), including the repetition of sounds (i.e., alliteration and assonance).

203. Alternatively, "he made ready to speak" (Foster 2005, 31).

204. See George 2003, 1:598–99 and 716–17, respectively. To give another example: similar conventional formulas introducing direct speech occur over twenty times in Etana tablets II and III, which together comprise a little more than three hundred lines.

205. Jiménez 2017, 92–93 notes that these introductory phrases occur predominantly in epic poetry and the disputations (though see his n. 246 for exceptions), which seem to be appropriating the high literary style for a parodying effect.

206. See, e.g., Reiner 1986, 3; Vogelzang 1992, 275; Foster 2005, 31.

Repetition serves a variety of narrative purposes. Repetition may signal narrative structure. Note, for example, the (near) repetition of lines 64–68 of The Poor Man of Nippur in lines 109–113 and 135–139.[207] In each case, the protagonist calls out behind him as he exits the city gate that he will exact or has exacted his three-fold revenge upon the mayor of Nippur. The repeated lines signal the closing of each scene. At the other end, a repeated phrase such as *ina* N *gerrīya*, "on my Nth campaign" and *ina* N *palêya*, "in my Nth regnal year" signals the beginning of successive military campaigns or the activities of successive regnal years in Assyrian inscriptions. The repetition of SB Epic of Gilgamesh I 18–23 at the end of Tablet XI (lines 323–328) offers another clear example of structure. In this case, the repetition creates a ring structure around the entire epic, bringing the audience back to the walls of Uruk, where Gilgamesh's story began.[208] Repetition of lines or passages (with slight changes between each iteration) sometimes represents movement between scenes in the plot. For example, Ishtar's entering and exiting of the netherworld through seven gates, where she strips off (during entry) or puts on (during exit) an item of clothing or adornment, is presented in highly repetitive but slightly varied lines (42–62; 119–125) as is Gilgamesh and Enkidu's journey to the cedar forest and nightly encampment, at each of which Gilgamesh has a different, foreboding dream (IV 1–183).[209] At the end of the repetitive section, the protagonist arrives at the next scene of the narrative (see also Gilgamesh IX 139–170). Repetition of lines (again with slight variations) also shows progress within a scene or fulfillment of previous expectations in a later scene. This progress may move from a proposed action to its realization, as in The Poor Man of Nippur 12–15:[210]

"I'll strip off my garment, for which there is none to change,
I'll buy a ram in the market of my city, Nippur."
He stripped off his garments, for which there was none to change,
He bought a three-year old nanny goat in the market of his city
     Nippur.[211]

Or, the progress may move from a command to its fulfillment, as in SB Nergal and Ereshkigal 125–134, where Ea commands Nergal to resist accepting the

---

207. See Foster 2005, 932–34 for a translation. Cooper (1975, 165–66) noted the structural significance. The text is discussed on page 189, below.

208. Vogelzang calls this an "envelope figure" (1996, 174).

209. For Descent of Ishtar, see Lapinkivi 2010, 26, 27–28, 30, 32; see also Hecker 1974, 45–46. For Epic of Gilgamesh, see George 2003, 1:588–97, with explanation on 463; see also Hecker 1974, 57–59.

210. See Cooper 1975, 167.

211. The translation is Foster's (2005, 931).

hospitalities offered him in the netherworld, and later in lines 209–218, where Nergal complies.[212] Repetition may also be used to slow down narrative progress, as seems to be the case with the long, unvarying speech presented twice in Enuma Elish III, once by the sender of a message to the messenger and again by the messenger to the final recipient (a command/fulfillment repetition).[213] Finally, repetition of lines may also be used to heighten intensity, as is probably the case with Ea's repetitive recommendations for thinning human population after the flood in SB Gilgamesh XI 188–195.[214]

In a slightly different example of textual repetition we leave literary sensibilities to consider architectural aesthetics. Inscribing stone objects (such as wall reliefs, colossi, door sockets, thresholds, steps, etc.) in temples and palaces was a common architectural practice from the third millennium on. Such must have been an especially favored decorative style among Assyrian palatial interior designers. The same text, the so-called Standard Inscription of Assurnasirpal II, which lauds the king, his conquests, and his building activities, were inscribed onto more than four hundred stone slabs lining the North West Palace walls at Kalhu![215] (See the relief pictured in fig. 10.)

Imagery, Simile, and Metaphor

On the one hand, the significance of many images, similes, and metaphors in Akkadian literature is often rather clear to modern readers because they are rooted in environmental, physiological, and cultural experiences that have some parallel or analogy in our own modern lives.[216] Modern readers can easily understand when a suffering person likens his stopped up ears to those

---

212. See Ponchia and Luukko 2013, 15–18, 25–28 for the text. Interestingly, SB Descent of Ishtar omits the expected fulfillment (via repetition) of Ea's instructions to Atsushunamir, his messenger, as given in lines 93–99. Instead, line 100 immediately indicates Ereshkigal's reaction to Atsushunamir's words, even though we do not read about her hearing them. See Lapinkivi 2010, 11–12, 31 for the text. Foster (2005, 502 n. 5) and Reiner (1985, 44) entertain the idea that this is a scribal error (via parablepsis).

213. See Lambert 2013, 76–83. The fact that this speech repeats earlier material from tablets I and II heightens its torpid monotony.

214. George 2003, 1:714–17. See, also, the use of *tuštamīt*, "you have put to death," at the end of each line in Erra and Ishum V 104–111, cited by Vogelzang 1996, 172–73.

215. See Grayson 1991, 268–76 for the text and its witnesses. For the architectural context of the inscriptions, see Russell 1999, 30–41.

216. Two essential studies are Streck 1999, who examines similes and metaphor in Akkadian epic texts (the corpus is listed on p. 54), and Wasserman 2003b, 98–156, who treats similes in Old Babylonian literary texts (the corpus is cataloged on pp. 185–224). Streck reviews the most relevant studies prior to 1999. Wasserman uses the same semantic domains as Streck for his analysis, making comparison of the two corpora easier. See also Foster 2010 for similes in Gilgamesh with reflections on similes in Akkadian literature more broadly considered. For similes and metaphors in Assyrian royal inscriptions, see note 135.

FIGURE 10. A Neo-Assyrian palace wall relief containing Assurnasirpal II's Standard Inscription. Photo © Trustees of the British Museum, London.

of a deaf man, when a king trapped within his city under siege is likened to a caged bird, or when something is described as bright as the rays of the sun.[217] These similes are clear. Since, however, contemporary readers are far removed from ancient Mesopotamia in terms of time, (usually) place, and way of life, we often lack the background knowledge of Mesopotamian flora, fauna, material existence, and other aspects of cultural life necessary for appreciating some of the imagery, similes, and metaphors found in Akkadian texts. Few readers will have the specialized knowledge of bovine behavior to understand the simile in Ludlul bel nemeqi I 20, "like a cow with a calf, he [i.e., Marduk] keeps looking behind him." It intends to convey Marduk's constant attention to his protégé. And few moderns will readily discern the meaning of Ereshkigal's face growing pale like a cut tamarisk and her lips darkening like the edge of a *kuninnu*-bowl when she hears of her sister's arrival at the gates of the netherworld in Descent of Ishtar, lines 29–30. Both similes use colors, green-yellow and blue-black, respectively, that are associated with an emotional reaction of shock, fear, and/or anger.[218] Even when we moderns may have experience with or knowledge of some item used in an ancient image, simile, or metaphor (e.g., clay), we may very likely still miss its full significance (the use of clay in, e.g., the various Mesopotamian anthropogonies, i.e., mythical accounts of human creation) because our experience with the item does not correspond to that of the Mesopotamians (who knew clay primarily as a *building* material and its role in the birthing process in the form of birthing-bricks).[219] Despite all of the knowledge we possess about ancient Mesopotamia via archaeological and textual records, some images, similes, and metaphors remain opaque.[220] This may be due to our inability to identify precisely a term used in the figure or to determine the point of comparison. For example, what does it mean when a supplicant prays to Nabu, "[Before] humankind I am like a whirlwind!"[221] Or, what cluster of ideas does the poet's metaphors intend to evoke when he states a goddess's thighs are a gazelle, her ankles are an apple, and her heels obsidian?[222] Perhaps future research will provide some insight on these and other difficult cases.

217. See Nadali 2009 for the caged bird simile in Neo-Assyrian royal inscriptions, which he argues depicts an Assyrian military strategy.

218. See Streck 1999, 71–72 for a discussion.

219. For a treatment of ceramic imagery in ancient Near Eastern literature (including Sumerian, Akkadian, Egyptian, and biblical texts), see Polinger Foster 1991.

220. An excellent resource for looking into specific cultural features is the multi-volume *Reallexikon der Assyriologie und Vorderasiatischen Archäologie* (Berlin: de Gruyter, 1928–2018).

221. See Foster 2005, 697 for the line and n. 1 for his ideas about the meaning of the simile. See also Lenzi 2011, 331 for several suggestions.

222. Livingstone 1989, 36, lines 5–7.

Paronomasia

Mesopotamian scribes relished the use of paronomasia, that is, "wordplay based on like-sounding words," in texts of all kinds.[223] Although paronomasia may have contributed to literary artifice and demonstrated scribal virtuosity, it was also, as Foster notes, "a primary message-bearing device . . . for serious and significant communication."[224] For example, in Ludlul bel nemeqi I 49, in the context of the sufferer reporting on the results of his divine abandonment, he asserts, "portents of terror [*piritti*] were established for me." Since omen results were sometimes considered secret (*pirištu*), this line may be making an implicit contrast between an unfavorable descriptor of omens (*pirittu*, "terror") with a more appropriate one (*pirištu*, "secret," i.e., revelation).[225] A more complicated example occurs in the SB Epic of Gilgamesh XI 42–47 when Ea tells Uta-napishti, the flood hero, to say the following to his contemporaries when he needs to explain to them why he is building an ark: "[I shall] go down to the Apsu, to live with Ea, my master; he will rain down on you plenty! [*nuḫšu*]. . . . In the morning he [Ea] will rain down on you bread-cakes [*kukku*], in the evening, a torrent of wheat.'"[226] These rather benign sounding words are rife with sinister double meanings. As noted by George, *nuḫšu* sounds like *nuḫḫusu*, "sobbing" and *kukku* "is chosen for its similarity to *kakku*, 'weapon; warfare', which represents the coming 'battle' and also means 'ominous sign', as in extispicy. Possibly there is also an allusion to the imminent demise of mankind, for . . . *kukkû*, 'the Dark', is a name of the Netherworld."[227] Thus, Uta-napishti cryptically conveys a horrific message to the poor souls not boarding his boat. Examples could easily be multiplied in narrative poetry, religious texts, and other genres.[228]

Paronomasia was especially ubiquitous in omen literature, which uses the figure to connect an omen's typical constituent parts, the protasis (if-statement) and the apodosis (then-statement). A simple example illustrates the point: "If a man dreams that he is eating a raven [*arbu*]; he will have income [*irbu*]."[229]

---

223. A monographic treatment on word play in ancient Near Eastern texts is currently in preparation by Scott Noegel, who has contributed significantly to this topic. With regard to Akkadian texts, see esp. Noegel 1996, 1997, 2000 (selected chapters), 2007 (esp. 1–88), 2010, 2011, and 2016. Quotation from Cook 2012, 1003.

224. Foster 2005, 16.

225. See Annus and Lenzi 2010, xxxiv.

226. George 2003, 1:704–7.

227. George 2003, 1:511. George 2003, 1:510–12 provides a fuller explanation, including several other possible word plays in this passage.

228. Note, e.g., the role of paronomasia in the prologue and epilogue of the laws of Hammurabi as identified by Hurowitz 1994, 9, 21, 27–28, 39, 42, 76, 81.

229. Cited in Noegel 2007, 20, in a context that discusses puns in omina (11–24).

The phonological similarity of the two words *arbu* and *irbu* was considered intrinsic—not merely coincidental—to the nature of reality. The scribes used such cases of homonymy or near homonymy, along with many other hermeneutical techniques in both language and cuneiform script, to forge meaningful connections between real world objects.[230]

Although rooted in omen literature and most creatively deployed in explanatory and commentary texts of the first millennium, similar hermeneutical creativity appears to a lesser degree in compositions probably composed in the late second millennium.[231] Two notable examples include the exposition of Marduk's fifty names in Enuma Elish VI–VII and in the lines describing the sufferer's passing through the twelve gates of the temple precincts in Ludlul bel nemeqi V.[232] Enuma Elish VII 35 provides a straight-forward illustration of how a scribe could use this literary and interpretive device in a composition. In VII 35 Marduk receives his eighteenth name, Shazu, which means "midwife" in Sumerian. The poem ignores this meaning, however, and rather explains "Shazu" with the Sumerian meaning of each of the name's constituent syllables considered separately, arriving at the idea that Marduk is "the heart" (Sum. šà) "knower" (Sum. zu) among the gods. The following passage then elaborates on the theme of Marduk's omniscience and execution of justice (VII 35–40).[233] The implication is that these divine attributes attached to Marduk are intrinsically contained in the name Shazu itself.

Intertextuality and Literary Allusion

For the purposes of this discussion, the most important distinction between "intertextuality" and "literary allusion" is intention.[234] "Literary allusion" denotes an intentional strategy of an author. It is the label that describes an author's deliberate attempt to point to or draw upon another text within their literary sphere, signaled to readers via some linguistic marker (i.e., words, phrases, themes, typical forms, etc.), so as to achieve some rhetorically desired effect within the text the author is composing.[235] This text, it should be noted, is the

---

230. See briefly Frahm 2011, 20–23; Noegel 2010.
231. For explanatory texts, see Livingstone 1986; for commentaries, Frahm 2011.
232. See Danzig 2013; Lenzi 2015d, respectively.
233. See Lambert 2013, 484–85; Danzig 2013, 74–76.
234. B. Sommer 1998, 6–20, upon which the present discussion draws, offers an informed presentation of the differences between intertexuality and allusion. Despite the fact that Sommer uses the latter to explore the biblical Second Isaiah, his treatment is methodologically illustrative for those interested in allusion in Akkadian texts.
235. See B. Sommer 1998, 11–12 for a brief review of what may constitute such a marker. For obvious reasons, identifying an allusion works within the realm of hypothesis, as noted by, e.g., Finet 1986, 14. Plausibility rather than certainty is usually the best one can achieve.

only available evidence we have from which to infer an author's intention to allude to another.[236] Obviously, the text upon which one thinks an author draws must be chronologically prior to the main text being composed. Yet the uncertain dating of many texts often presents a significant obstacle to establishing the plausibility of an allusion. In any case, the study of allusions investigates texts from a diachronic perspective. "Intertexuality," in contrast, is more reader-centered and concerns itself with connections much more broadly defined and unanchored chronologically. Authorial intention plays little or no role. As Sommer explains it,

> "Intertexuality" ... encompasses manifold connections between a text being studied and other texts, or between a text being studied and commonplace phrases or figures from the linguistic or cultural systems in which the text exists. ... These connections do not arise exclusively from an intentional and signaled use of an earlier text, such as citation. ... The connections may result from the way that expressions in a given text reflect linguistic, esthetic, cultural, or ideological contexts of the text at hand; other texts may share those contexts, and hence links among many texts may be noticed, whether the authors of the texts knew each other or not.[237]

Intertextuality, as defined here, is the broader, more diffuse concept and has received very little explicit attention in Assyriological secondary literature, even though it is common in practice (since contextualizing and interpreting an ancient text is often an implicit form of intertextual analysis).[238] Allusion, on the other hand, has attracted a sizeable amount of Assyriological interest.[239]

---

236. On the thorny issue of authorial intention in intertextuality/allusion (and texts in general), see Wisnom 2014, 4–7, who takes a text-centered perspective. In summarizing the position of M. Heath, she writes, "asking about intentions is not to ask about unknowable psychological states, but rather to enquire into the text as the product of purposive behaviour" (6). Moreover, she correctly notes that "as Assyriologists we are in no danger of falling into the traps of the extremes of the intentional fallacy ..., because we know nothing about our authors' lives, in most cases not even their names. However, certain assumptions have been made about them based on what we find in texts, and this seems to me to be entirely legitimate" (6).

237. Sommer 1998, 7.

238. Intertextuality is often used for what I have defined as allusion. My study of the phrase *šiptu ul yattun* (Lenzi 2010) may qualify as an intertextual study, though I did not frame it explicitly in those terms. See also my suggestion for what scribal students could have reasonably understood (due to a text in their scribal curriculum) when they read the word *ummânū* in the flood story in the SB Epic of Gilgamesh. My interpretation is based on the intertextual suggestion that the ancient reader (in this case, scribal students) would have read the word in question through its use in the first entry of a lexical list that many first millennium scribal students would have copied. See Lenzi 2014.

239. For two general statements with much literature cited, see Foster 2005, 22–26; 2007, 113–14. Seri 2014 also provides a general statement with several examples before turning attention to Enuma

Two major factors frame the issue of allusion in Akkadian texts: the limited size of the Akkadian corpus and the nature of scribal education. As for the first, throughout Mesopotamian history the number of Akkadian literary and scholarly texts in circulation at any given time was relatively small. Even in the first millennium, when the corpora of the scholars had grown to their largest extent, these materials were not so vast that they were beyond the capability of individuals to control with competence.[240] Indeed, we know that some individuals distinguished themselves by way of their *mastery* of the Akkadian textual tradition current in their time.[241] The second factor lies in the nature of scribal education. Alongside the practical goal of preparing scribes for a career, an important element in scribal education was to pass on (mainly through rote memorization) a common literary heritage to its pupils through the curriculum that was formative to their cultural identity and institutional membership.[242] By the first millennium, the curriculum was heavily weighted toward Akkadian literary and scholarly texts.[243] Given these two factors, it should be no surprise to find scribes, especially in the first millennium, deliberately alluding to well-known Akkadian texts when writing another.

Published examples of allusions in Akkadian texts are numerous and occur in a variety of genres. Take, for example, royal inscriptions and related texts. There is an allusion to Enuma Elish in Sennacherib's report of the Battle at Halule; Nabonidus's Harran Inscriptions allude to Ludlul bel nemeqi; and the Vassal Treaty of Esarhaddon may allude to Erra and Ishum.[244] New literary compositions may also allude to earlier texts for some rhetorical purpose. For example, the author of Enuma Elish appropriates elements of Ninurta's mythology as depicted in Anzu in an effort to exalt Marduk.[245] The authors of the Akkadian

---

Elish. Wisnom 2014, 3–17 offers a broad methodological introduction to the issues, drawing especially from Classical scholarship. Jiménez 2017, 79–82 summarizes recent perspectives, classifying them between a minimalist and a maximalist view. For reflections on allusions between the Old Testament/Hebrew Bible and other ancient Near Eastern texts, including Akkadian ones, see Hays 2008.

240. Reiner 1978, 155, citing Oppenheim and Reiner 1977, 13–18, estimates about 1500 distinct literary and scholarly texts in the famous Neo-Assyrian library of Assurbanipal.

241. The great Neo-Assyrian scholar Nabu-zukup-kenu is a prime example, for whom see Baker and Pearce 2001. See also the Neo-Assyrian letter SAA 10 160 (Parpola 1993, 121–24), in which a certain Marduk-shapik-zeri lists his wide-ranging scholarly knowledge and also lists twenty young scribes at his disposal, several of whom had training in more than one scholarly specialization.

242. See Gesche 2000; Veldhuis 2004, 65–66; Delnero 2016, 19–28.

243. See Gesche 2000.

244. For Enuma Elish, see Weissert 1997. See also Van De Mieroop 2015, who analyzes metaphors and literary allusions in the same episode as well as several other battle passages in NA Sargonid royal inscriptions. For Ludlul bel nemeqi, see Lambert 1960, 284. For Erra and Ishum, see Watanabe 1984. For further reflections on the role of intertextuality/allusion in royal inscriptions, see the remarks of Frahm 1997, 297–80; Da Riva 2013, 20–29.

245. Lambert 1986. For a recent treatment of textual borrowings in Enuma Elish, see Seri 2014; Wisnom 2014, 90–207.

disputations allude to epic and narrative poetry with a high literary register of Akkadian to signal their works as humorous parody.[246] Some Neo-Assyrian prophetic oracles allude to well-known literary texts, including Gilgamesh, Atramhasis, and Adapa.[247] Even letters to a king can allude to important literary works, thereby showcasing the author's scholarly credentials even while couching his appeals in affective language.[248] Allusions are not limited to a few words or phrases. Veldhuis identifies whole genres being alluded to for the purpose of parody in the satirical Aluzinnu-text.[249] Likewise, I have argued recently that Ludlul bel nemeqi adopts and adapts the language and form of the incantation-prayer in order to present this hymn-like poem of thanksgiving in the language of supplication so those still in need (supplicants) could use the text as a kind of proleptic thanksgiving.[250]

Given what we know about scribes, their education, and their propensity to borrow from and allude to other texts, the exploration of literary allusions in Akkadian texts is an area rich with potential.

Audiences: Who Read These Texts?

Despite a changing view that functional literacy may have been more common than previously thought, there was nothing like a reading public in ancient Mesopotamia.[251] Who then were the audiences for the texts that have come down to us? What seems to be a simple question is in fact quite difficult to answer satisfactorily, which may explain why the issue of audience is often passed over in introductions to Akkadian literature.[252]

---

246. Jiménez 2017, 79–99.

247. Halton 2009. For a proverbial saying that appears a few times in OB letters reporting prophetic oracles, see Sasson 1995.

248. See the Neo-Assyrian letter SAA 10 294 (Parpola 1993, 231–34), in which both Parpola (1987) and Hurowitz (2002–2005) have identified various allusions to literary texts. Finet (1974, 1986) has suggested several "réminiscences" (1986, 15) in some OB letters from Mari to OB Atramhasis, Gilgamesh, and other works (including several proverbs).

249. Veldhuis 2003a, 23–27. The text is also known as "The Jester" in Foster 2005, 939–41.

250. Lenzi 2015a. Similarly, historical-literary texts adopt some stylistic aspects of omens, see Grayson 1976, 15–16. More provocatively, Wisnom has argued that Erra and Ishum draws on the structure of the Sumerian Lamentation over the Destruction of Sumer and Ur (2014, 262–86).

251. For functional literacy, see Veldhuis 2011. On the lack of a reading public, see, e.g., Foster 2005, 45.

252. See the brief remarks in Röllig 1987, 49; McCall 1990, 36–37. It should be stated, however, that the audience of particular kinds of texts, as noted below, has generated interest in the secondary literature. Note, e.g., the essays in Vogelzang and Vanstiphout 1992, which often raise the issue of audience while considering the oral backgrounds to Mesopotamian epic literature.

What Is an Audience?

How does one define an audience? As we are dealing with a body of written literature—texts on tablets—rather than oral tradition (which is as irretrievable as it was likely to have existed), it seems appropriate for the present purpose to circumscribe our notion of audience to people who read or heard the texts inscribed on clay tablets and other material supports. We therefore are dealing with a mediated audience, who received the text at some distance from its creation. Within this restricted view, we may then ask: Who was *supposed* to have read/heard the texts these tablets bear (a primary or target audience)?[253] And who else might *also* have read/heard them (a secondary or indirect audience)? As the following discussion demonstrates, the answers to these questions—to the extent that evidence may even suggest answers—depend on the kind of text under consideration. Since we cannot investigate the audience of every single text in detail, the following comments consider the possible (primary and secondary) audiences for several broad categories of texts (scholarly, religious, narrative poetic, and royal) and the issues involved in discerning these audiences. The discussion must operate at a rather general level, though there is no doubt that practices throughout Mesopotamian history would have varied from one place to another within these broad categories of texts.[254]

Scholarly Texts

The audience for learned texts, that is, omen collections, ritual instructions, lists of *materia medica* (e.g., stones, plants, etc.), various lexical and sign lists, catalogs of incipits, and so on, is rather easy to identify.[255] There is little room to doubt that these texts were written primarily by scholars for scholars and secondarily for their advanced scribal students. Still, *how* these texts were used in their professional practice, for example, during an examination of animal entrails for omens, is a difficult question that Assyriologists are only beginning to address.[256] We may be misguided by our own scholarly practices if we assume diviners, for example, always used their massive series of texts as we use reference books (instead of relying on their memory or common practice). It does seem, however, that scholars sometimes read texts directly from a tablet during, for example, a ritual, as suggested by this line attested in colophons: *ana ṣabāt*

253. The primary audience may be identical to, a portion of, or entirely different from the implied audience of a text, which is the audience the text constructs for some rhetorical purpose.

254. For an attempt to understand the audience of a particular text (Ludlul bel nemeqi), see Lenzi 2012.

255. See pages 155, 160, below, for a description of some of these texts.

256. See, e.g., Robson 2008, 2011.

epēši ḫanṭiš nasḫa, "quickly copied for a ritual performance."[257] But surely memory would have played a role in a scholar's day-to-day work, too. As if to give us a peak into a scribe's anxiety about his unreliable memory, one colophon states *ana taḫsisti zamar nasḫa*, "quickly copied as an aide to memory."[258] Whatever their precise manner of use, scholarly texts were intended for scholars and their apprentices.

Religious Texts

Establishing the audience of hymns, prayers, laments, incantations, and incantation-prayers is rather easy, too.[259] The primary, putative audience is the divine being(s) to whom such compositions are directed. Yet this recognition does not exhaust the potential extent of the audience. As scholars of religion have suggested, texts addressed to divine beings (e.g., prayers) are often utilized to exhort, comfort, and/or teach the humans who read, speak, and/or hear them. In this way, the values and ideals latent in such texts are communicated to the human reader/speaker as well as anyone within earshot of the texts' vocal execution. In other words, religious texts, even ones used by individuals, can be communally oriented and thus have a secondary audience or indirect recipients besides the divine beings to whom they are explicitly and primarily directed.[260] Looking at ancient Mesopotamia, this broader view of the audience of religious texts seems quite reasonable, even if the community was limited to the student scribes copying the religious texts (and thereby being indoctrinated into the institutional theological system of the elites), the actual participants in a ritual, the temple staff nearby, or people gathered at a public event of some kind in which religious texts were used.[261]

But there is a problem that crops up at this point and, in fact, dogs the entire issue of determining the audience of most Akkadian texts beyond the gods and the scribes and scholars who possessed or were developing a very high level of literacy. Namely, the language of the texts being read or heard was not always, indeed, usually was not identical to the vernacular of the people in the street.[262] We cannot be sure that a semipublic recitation of a prayer or incantation in the

---

257. Hunger 1968, nos. 197 and 198.
258. Hunger 1968, no. 336.
259. See page 161, below, for a description of some of these texts.
260. Gill 1987, 490.
261. For the participants, see Lenzi 2011, 2–23 for a general discussion; 2010, 153–54 for a more limited view of the potential impact an incantation could have had upon the ritual officiant speaking it.
262. Michalowski has emphasized this general point in several publications. See, e.g., 1990, 60; 1992, 245 (see also Cooper 1992, 118); 1994, 59. For the changing linguistic landscape and the receding influence of Akkadian in first millennium Mesopotamia, see Beaulieu 2006b. For a survey

Standard Babylonian literary dialect, for example, communicated to those not officiating the recitation much at all beyond what the sight of such an activity itself communicated because the language may not have been easily intelligible to a speaker of Neo-Assyrian, for example, or Late Babylonian.[263] This same problem arises with regard to both narrative poems and royal inscriptions.

Poetic Texts

Many of the narrative poems in Akkadian have indications that might be interpreted as requiring or commending an oral recitation or reading of the text (from the tablet).[264] For example, several narrative poems describe themselves as songs (*zamāru*), which we might presume therefore would need to be sung.[265] Further, several poems begin with lines that might be read as though a bard is gathering an audience, thus suggesting the (written) text was intended for oral recitation.[266] Moreover, a few texts actually describe or commend the recitation of the poem, as, for example, the OB version of Atram-hasis, which concludes with these lines:

> This [my] song (is) for your praise.
> May the Igigi-gods hear,
> let them extol your great deeds to each other.
> I have sung of the flood to all the peoples: Listen![267] (III viii 14–18)

---

of the history of Akkadian that also notes the linguistic gap between the vernacular and the language of chancery or literature at various stages of the language's history, see George 2007a.

263. Kouwenberg 2012, 434 n. 3 remarks that Babylonian and Assyrian would very likely have been mutually intelligible; however, he qualifies this somewhat for later periods (with due regard for conservative orthography, 436). Moreover, comparing Standard Babylonian to, e.g., Neo-Assyrian has diachronic and socio-linguistic elements to it since Standard Babylonian represents a mid-second millennium literary dialect whereas Neo-Assyrian is a mid-first millennium vernacular. Thus, the level of mutual intelligibility is unclear.

264. The most recent and detailed argument for this point is West 1997b, 593–602. See also his briefer treatment in West 1997a, 180–81. Narrative poems are treated in the second half of the book under sections that discuss myths and epics (pp. 78–123), legends of Akkadian kings, (pp. 123–132), and meditations on human suffering and the divine (pp. 172–178).

265. E.g., Atram-hasis (see III viii 16; Lambert and Millard 1969, 104–5), Enuma Elish (VII 161; see Lambert 2013, 132–33), and Erra and Ishum (V 49; Cagni 1969, 126–29).

266. See Wilcke's essay on how Akkadian epics begin (1977), who, it should be noted, does not believe any of these compositions were actually written down or dictated to a scribe by such a bard (215–16).

267. Foster 2005, 253; for the text, see Lambert and Millard 1969, 104–5. Note also Enuma Elish VII 157–64 (Lambert 2013, 132–33; Oshima 2011, 36–37), Erra and Ishum V 48–61 (Cagni 1969, 126–29; Foster 2005, 910–11), and the didactic intent mentioned throughout Ludlul bel nemeqi (see esp. I 39 and IV §C, line 6‴ [in Oshima 2014a, 96, 104], noted by Annus and Lenzi 2010, xix). If George's reading of the final line of the OB mythological text that he calls The Song of Bazi is

To utilize this internal evidence to prove oral recitation, of course, requires one to assume that it is to be taken literally—or at face value, which is something that must be established rather than presumed. To this end, one might point, as does M. L. West, to a tablet archive belonging to a family of chief singers (*nargallū*), which contained copies or portions of several narrative poems, including the SB Epic of Gilgamesh, Descent of Ishtar, Enuma Elish, Anzu, and Etana, among other texts.[268] Were these texts among those that they sang? Possibly. Despite this rather incomplete evidence, one might still be inclined to believe these narrative poems were recited to an audience.[269] Even if one accepts this conclusion as both reasonable and plausible, there is a problem: we know next to nothing about how or where such recitations actually happened.[270] Moreover, would these compositions in the OB and SB literary dialects be understood by people outside learned circles? The humbling fact of the matter is that we know next to nothing about the intended or primary audience of such texts. Scenarios may be suggested, as, for example, Frans von Koppen does for OB Atram-hasis: "An original context for the performance of Atram-hasis is not known either, but we are presumably not too far off when we situate this at a royal court or other elite setting, where much of the early Mesopotamian literature began as entertainment for the privileged."[271] As plausible as this seems, it is only a surmise. We have no evidence for royal performances of narrative poems. Even when we consider the fact that the recitation of Enuma Elish is prescribed in a first millennium New Year's ritual, we *still* do not know the (secondary human) audience of the text beyond the god Marduk himself (the primary audience) since the poem would have been recited in Marduk's cella rather than in the temple courtyard or in some other more public setting.[272]

The only audience, therefore, that we can know actually read (or heard) the narrative poems discussed in this book were the scribes and their students who copied them.[273] As these students copied these highly theological texts, they would have (ideally) been indoctrinated into the values and worldview such

---

accepted (see George 2009, no. 1), then we may have a text that prescribes its own singing in its subscription.

268. West 1997b, 600, citing Pedersén 1986, 34–41. Note, however, the cautionary remarks about the literacy of singers in J. Westenholz 1992, 152–53 (also cited by West).

269. See, e.g., Vogelzang, who believes the debate poems "must have been mainly intended for public performance" (Vogelzang 1991, 54). See page 184 for the debate poems.

270. See, e.g., Wasserman 2003b, 160; George 2003, 1:35; Cooper 1992, 117, 121; J. Westenholz 1992, 153; Vogelzang 1992. Even West 1997b, 602 must admit our ignorance on these points.

271. Von Koppen 2011, 144. See George 2003, 1:21 for a similar idea about the oral recitation of the OB Epic of Gilgamesh.

272. See the discussion in Oshima 2011, 36.

273. George concludes the same about the presence of narrative poems in the singers' library at Assur (2003, 35). See similarly George 2005a, 41.

texts communicated.[274] This is the only audience that can be securely reconstructed, even if we suspect there were others.

Royal Inscriptions

Royal inscriptions generally address two groups and therefore have two primary audiences: the gods, whom the king sought to please with the reports of his actions, and/or future kings, who—as many texts anticipate—may someday find the inscriptions and are therefore admonished to give them proper respect.[275] If we accept this prima facie reading of the texts, then we might believe that royal inscriptions ignored contemporary people altogether, aside from the scholar-scribes who wrote them and a handful of important administrators who may have taken part in composing them or had direct experience of them in some way.[276] One might suppose, of course, that royal inscriptions could indirectly or secondarily find an audience with any literate person who might care to read the inscription in situ (e.g., display inscriptions in palace corridors [fig. 10], votive inscriptions on statues or objects, or building inscriptions on a temple, city wall, or nearby canal).[277] In this way, a few more people (both contemporary and later) could have learned the contents of some texts in detail, but this was clearly not possible for all royal inscriptions, as some of them were inscribed or set to rest in inaccessible places (e.g., on cliffs and on clay cylinders or tablets of precious metal interred in building foundations).[278]

274. See Gesche 2000, 210–12 for a summary of scribal education in the first millennium and the role of various narrative poems therein.

275. Royal inscriptions are described below on pages 133–138. For future kings as audience, see, e.g., Oppenheim and Reiner 1977, 147–49; Charpin 2010, 215; Liverani 1995, 2354. For later kings' archaeological endeavors, looking for and finding earlier royal inscriptions and projects (e.g., temples), see Winter 2000. For a discussion and collection of references in inscriptions to predecessors, see Radner 2005, 203–34.

276. Of course, it would have been crucial to any king to keep this inner group informed and convinced of his legitimacy and effectiveness, as Liverani points out (1995, 2354; 1979, 302; see also Porter 1993, 109–10; 1995, 57, 69). For the role of scholars and administrators in the writing of royal inscriptions, see, e.g., Luukko 2007, 228, with references.

277. See, e.g., Grayson 1980, 164 for the general point and 157, 162 for dedicatory inscriptions. Russell identifies twelve groups of people who could have had access to palace reliefs and their inscriptions (Russell 1991, 223–40), though he does not equate these people simplistically with the intended audience of the reliefs. The intended audience, as he understands it, was probably limited to "the king and his court and, at a more abstract level, future kings and perhaps the gods" (251), though he also mentions the likelihood that diplomats and foreign visitors were included in the reliefs' audience (252). Porter argues that copies of some Neo-Assyrian royal inscriptions were deposited in temple libraries and therefore were accessible to literate priests and temple officials (1993, 110–12; 1995, 63–65). Indeed, we would not have even known of some royal inscriptions had scribes not copied them from their original material supports. The classic example is Old Akkadian royal inscriptions copied from votive statues in temple courtyards (see Buccellati 1993 in particular; Radner 2005, 244–50 for this and other examples).

278. But see below on the problem of language and script.

Several scholars have recently argued that the general message, rhetorical construction, and potential propagandistic value of royal inscriptions suggest the texts possessed a broader primary audience than the gods, future kings, and incidental literate passers-by. They find this audience among the texts' contemporaries, namely, some fraction of the gathered public, who could have heard the texts read aloud or in some way orally presented in speeches during a ceremony of some kind.[279] Although plausible on the face of it, this suggestion requires the resolution of several difficult matters.[280]

Perhaps of primary importance is intelligibility. Would the audience have understood the language of these inscriptions, which were often written in a high, literary register of Akkadian quite different from the vernaculars? Moreover, some royal inscriptions were written in an entirely different language than that spoken on the streets, for example, Sumerian when people spoke Akkadian or Akkadian when people spoke Amorite or Aramaic. How well would these texts have communicated to people?

Barbara Porter considers this problem in regard to Neo-Assyrian royal inscriptions (when Aramaic was the everyday language of most people) and suggests that elites and other major political stakeholders were the ones primarily addressed when the texts were read aloud or presented publicly, though others may have understood some of it, too.[281] These elites, she suggests, were likely to have known some Akkadian or could have had scribes available to interpret or translate the texts for them.[282] Still, the issue of language persists in

279. See Porter 1993, 104–17 for the most developed argument. Her argument for oral presentation of at least some inscriptions arises from her astute observations on the carefully shaped rhetoric of some of Esarhaddon's building inscriptions, some of which were intended for an Assyrian and others for a Babylonian audience. See also Schaudig 2001, 66–67 with literature for and against this view in n. 219; Da Riva 2008, 26; Liverani 1979, 302. Fales 1999–2001, 127, 130 is more cautious, it seems; or at least, less explicit. Oppenheim made a more circumscribed argument for a public reading of Sargon's Eighth Campaign (1960, esp. 143–47). Porter 1995 offers a study of the reception and the differing audience of three different kinds of inscriptions laid to rest in three different locales (a monument outside the imperial heartland, a foundation deposit in Assyria, and a [Sumerian] brick inscription in Babylon). Notably, all of these scholars are treating first millennium Assyrian or Babylonian inscriptions. For the suggestion of a ceremony, see Porter 1993, 112–15; see also Liverani 1979, 302–3; Porter 1995, 61. Since a *copy* of the text could be read, this hypothesis also covers inscriptions that were inscribed in inaccessible places or eventually interred in buildings' foundations.

280. See likewise Russell 1991, 254–55 for the difficulties of a visitor understanding the inscriptions on palace reliefs.

281. The texts, she writes, "would also have been comprehensible to the [Aramaic-speaking] populace as a whole, rather in the way that the archaic English of the King James Bible is still relatively comprehensible to modern audiences because they are accustomed to hearing it on ceremonial occasions" (Porter 1993, 116). It is difficult to assess this idea because the level of intelligibility between Standard Babylonian, the language of the inscriptions, and Aramaic has not been properly studied.

282. Porter 1993, 116. Michalowski also imagines that such a view would require the intervention of a translator (1992, 245; see also Russell 1991, 233 for the use of an interpreter with palace reliefs).

raising problems. The Neo-Assyrian royal inscriptions were written in Standard Babylonian rather than the Neo-Assyrian dialect of Akkadian, which was the language of administration and royal correspondence. It is difficult to know how well elites without extensive scribal training (in Standard Babylonian literary texts) would have understood the literary dialect of the inscriptions since the level of intelligibility between Standard Babylonian and Neo-Assyrian Akkadian has not been properly studied.[283] More to the point: if the texts were going to be read aloud or presented orally to the citizenry, why weren't they simply composed in Neo-Assyrian, the official administrative language that many elites would have understood? Is it not significant that king Esarhaddon, who imposed a treaty on his own people, had the text of his treaty composed in the Neo-Assyrian dialect rather than literary Standard Babylonian?[284]

Another issue is the fact that there is no evidence that the royal inscriptions were read aloud let alone translated/interpreted at the time of reading (or at some later time). Porter discusses several references to texts being read aloud in the ancient Near East and mentions the fact that kings sometimes delivered royal proclamations to the people orally. She also notes a few literary texts that suggest within their lines an oral recitation (treated below), though she recognizes that "the extent to which such literary conventions reflect actual practice is not clear."[285] No doubt there were various oral proclamations from the king; but apart from more evidence, we cannot be sure that the textual records we possess were in fact the wording of any of them.

Although not directly relevant for the issue of Neo-Assyrian royal inscriptions being read aloud, the OB laws of Hammurabi contain a passage that some might construe as evidence to support the notion that some royal inscriptions were expected to elicit public interaction with its text. There is an exhortation in the laws' epilogue for people to consult the stela in matters of justice. It reads: "Let any wronged man who has a lawsuit come before the statue of me, the king of justice, and let him have my inscribed stela read aloud to him,[286] thus may he hear my precious pronouncements and let my stela reveal the lawsuit for him."[287] The several stelae bearing this text, we know, were erected in various cities as public monuments and were therefore accessible (see fig. 16).[288] However, there is a logical problem here. In order to accept this text as evidence for the expectation of public interaction with the text of royal inscriptions (if only

283. Porter is less sanguine about the number of people who would have been able to understand the royal inscriptions in her later article on the subject (1995, 57, 65, 69).

284. For the treaty, see Parpola 1993, 7–8 (texts no. 6–7). The treaty may have been about rightful succession, see Parpola 1983, 3–5.

285. Porter 1993, 115.

286. Or, perhaps simply, "let him read my inscribed stela."

287. Roth 1997, 134 (xlviii 3–16).

288. See, e.g., Roth 1997, 73.

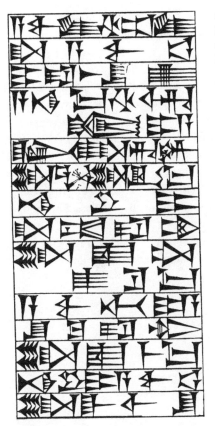

FIGURE 11. An excerpt from the laws of Hammurabi in an archaic lapidary form of cuneiform. From Harper 1904, pl. LXXIV.

by request!), one must first assume the text was in fact read aloud to the public. How else would a wronged person know about the legal provision?[289] Though there is evidence that the OB kings promulgated decrees to their people, there is no evidence of them reading laws aloud to the public.[290] Moreover, given the facts that the stelae bearing the laws were inscribed in an archaic lapidary cuneiform script (see fig. 11, which was different from the cursive script used by regular, work-a-day scribes in the OB period) and erected toward the end of Hammurabi's reign, this passage is probably better understood as royal rhetoric, a flourish to aggrandize Hammurabi's commitment to the ideal of justice.[291]

289. If the alternate rendering of the key phrase is preferred (see note 286), there is still the problem of the archaic script, noted just below.

290. See Finkelstein 1961, 103, who notes, unlike the edicts of remission (*mīšarum*), also mentioned by Porter (1993, 114), the absence of any kind of event surrounding the erection of the stelae.

291. Likewise, e.g., Van De Mieroop 2016, 177; differently, Slanski 2012. The passage is also an early example of Akkadian literature's penchant for self-referentiality. See the prologue of the SB Epic of Gilgamesh and the endings of both Erra and Ishum and Enuma Elish for other examples.

Thus, even this rather explicit reference to public outreach in a royal inscription commends caution in identifying the presumed (and in this case, explicitly stated) audience of a text.

Where does this leave us for determining the audiences of Akkadian royal inscriptions beyond the gods, future rulers, and a few literate passers-by? The matter must remain open. But perhaps we ought to consider it from another angle. Might the royal inscriptions have communicated to the vast majority of normal people in the street or foreign visiting diplomats in only an indirect, silent manner? What if these people viewed the monuments and texts more as icons of royal power than as texts to be heard or read?[292] Along these lines, Mario Liverani, speaking of the Assyrian citizenry's reception of royal inscriptions, notes, "although they have no access to writing, nonetheless they gain[ed] some access to the content of the message through the channels of oral transmission, ceremonial staging, and iconic representation."[293] This is reasonable and plausible but rather vague (and ultimately unprovable). Still, this may be the best we can do without further evidence.

292. So, e.g., Fales 1999–2001, 127, who notes that the medium was "at least in certain cases" the message. Note also Slanski's argument for the communicative role of the iconography at the top of the laws of Hammurabi (2012).

293. Liverani 1995, 2354–55. Porter also recognizes informal opportunities for illiterate people, e.g., at the royal court, to learn about the contents of royal inscriptions (1993, 109 and n. 36).

CHAPTER 2

Survey of Selected Text Groups

The survey of selected texts in this book, as mentioned in the brief discussion of genre, cannot proceed using an indigenous Mesopotamian classificatory system because the Mesopotamian scribes never developed one explicitly. Instead, as with all other surveys, the categories used here are modern creations, formed on the basis of perceived similarities of content and/or form and sometimes also with the help of scribal clues that hint at indigenous methods of organization. The following sections therefore are intended to be convenient groupings, a heuristic to organize data.[1]

The reader working through a selection such as the one that follows should not mistake what is represented here as the entire corpus of Akkadian textual materials. Considerations of space in a book that presents itself as a relatively short introduction have required that some texts and even some kinds of texts be omitted. Several print anthologies and online projects provide valuable resources to expand one's view of Akkadian textual materials. These offer contemporary translations of a wide variety of Akkadian texts. Print resources include *Before the Muses*, 3rd edition (Foster 2005)—the most comprehensive anthology of exclusively Akkadian texts; *The Context of Scripture*, 4 vols. (Hallo and Younger 2003–2016); and *Texte aus der Umwelt des alten Testaments*, with eight volumes in the new series so far (2004–) and three in the old (1982–1997, with a supplement in 2001). The latter two works include translations of texts in other ancient Near Eastern languages alongside ones in Akkadian. The older anthology *Ancient Near Eastern Texts Relating to the Old Testament*, 3rd edition with supplement (Pritchard 1969) is now quite outdated.[2] Halton and Svärd have produced a thematic anthology of texts, dedicated to the writings of women from ancient Mesopotamia in both Sumerian and Akkadian (2018). Among online resources, two projects stand out: "Sources of Early Akkadian

---

1. In this pragmatic approach, I follow Foster 2007, 3, who offers a brief overview of alternatives, and Röllig 1987.

2. For a historical survey of ancient Near Eastern anthologies, see Younger 2006.

Literature" (SEAL), under the direction of Michael P. Streck and Nathan Wasserman (http://www.seal.uni-leipzig.de/), which provides editions and translations of many Akkadian texts from the third and second millennia (2400–1100 BCE); and "The Open Richly Annotated Cuneiform Corpus" (ORACC), steered by Eleanor Robson, Steve Tinney, and Niek Veldhuis (http://oracc.museum.upenn .edu/index.html), which is a kind of portal to a wide variety of online text-based cuneiform-related projects (Sumerian and Akkadian).[3] These resources provide the student of Akkadian literature with a lifetime of study material.

Two more qualifications should be mentioned here. First, what follows in this section of the book is a survey and description of texts. Although it is not devoid of interpretive decisions and at times mentions some key interpretive debates (indeed, interpretation begins with decipherment and translation), the presentation of the material does not attempt full literary-critical interpretations of the works surveyed, which would require a much larger book. This second part of the book intends to give readers some idea of what there is available to read in Akkadian literature and to provide some sense of the contents of these works. The footnotes point readers to further information, including text editions, historical studies, interpretive essays, and other relevant materials. Second, the sections comprising this part of the book are mostly self-contained. Although one may plow straight through what reads like an extensively annotated catalog of compositions—consider this fair warning, a reader may also jump to a particular section of interest without too much concern that some essential point to understanding the material there has been lost.

Mythological and Heroic Epics

The many textual sources that have come down to us reveal thousands of divinities and other suprahuman entities.[4] We know next to nothing about the vast

---

3. The editors of SEAL also intend to produce a series of volumes in print. Wasserman 2016 is the first, which presents Akkadian "love literature" of the third and second millennia, a category broadly defined as texts relating to the theme of love and/or sex. After a very useful introduction to the corpus and various themes, semantic fields, and metaphors surrounding love and attraction (15–62), Wasserman edits "twenty non-homogenous texts: monologues, dialogues, hymnal compositions, as well as descriptive texts" (16). Some attest human lovers (a man and a woman); others involve love/sex between deities. About a quarter of these texts were likely used only in the private sphere; the others were probably used in a cultic setting (21). In parts two and three of the work, Wasserman edits three catalogs of incipits and fifteen love and/or sex-related incantations, respectively. (He notes a further unpublished tablet on p. 18, to appear elsewhere.) For the first millennium texts often included within this broadly defined category, see Wasserman 2016, 15; Foster 2007, 40–42; 2009, 210–12. "Love literature" is not treated further in the present survey. For the broader theme of sex and eroticism in Mesopotamian literature (Sumerian and Akkadian), see Leick 1994.

4. For an excellent, succinct survey of Mesopotamian myths, both Sumerian and Akkadian, see Heimpel 1993–1995. Edzard 1965 offers a brief introduction to the topic and concise entries,

majority of these beings beyond their names and, in some cases, perhaps one or two isolated facts. Of the thousands of divine names that scholars, both ancient and modern, have collected in various lists and catalogs, the deities that rank among the most important number only a few dozen.[5] Among these, a still smaller number dominate, as one will see, the various Akkadian mythological texts. The gods were organized into a hierarchical pantheon, each with their own families, servants, and households (i.e., temples), where a staff of priests and servants cared for them.[6] Although a deity may be identified with some element in the cosmos (e.g., the sun, the wind, brick-making, or writing) and could be described as residing in the heavens, they were also given concrete form in an anthropomorphic image that lived in a temple, which occupied a prominent place in the urban landscape.[7]

The texts considered in this section are centered on these gods and set in many cases during a primordial time—an age before the world as it is now. Alongside them are the stories of a few outstanding heroes, Atram-hasis, Etana, Adapa, and Gilgamesh, who were either partly divine themselves (as was Gilgamesh) or who had extraordinary interaction with the gods. We have no reliable historical records about the actual lives of these men. Mainly on the basis of their general similarities with those of Western literary history, these texts of gods and heroes comprise a rather circumscribed group of narrative poems that modern scholars have identified as myths and epics.[8] However, the use of the

---

arranged alphabetically, of most of the key deities and their stories. Likewise, Leick 1991 and Black and Green 1992, the latter of which is limited to gods, demons, and other suprahuman entities that appear in mythological texts. Bottéro and Kramer 1989 provides an extensive treatment of the myths, including introductory essays and French translations of the most important texts in both Sumerian and Akkadian. Reiner 1978, 159–75; Foster 2007, 49–73; 2009, 164–85 give substantial but shorter presentations of the Akkadian materials. Relatively new mythological texts are not represented in the handbooks. See, e.g., the OB mythological text in George 2009, no. 1, which he calls The Song of Bazi, and the text edited by Oshima 2010. For a brief methodological orientation to interpreting ancient Near Eastern mythological texts, see Walls 2001, 1–8. For a concise introduction to various ancient Near Eastern epic texts, see Noegel 2005, with numerous references to the literature, to which add Pongratz-Leisten 1999b and 2001. Guichard 2014, 71–75; C. Hess 2015, 254–57 provide recent discussions of the use of the term "epic" for Mesopotamian texts. Haubold 2013, 18–72 offers an insightful comparative reading of Greek (Homer and Hesiod) and Akkadian (Enuma Elish and Gilgamesh) epic materials. And Helle (forthcoming) offers the provocative suggestion that many Akkadian epics—six of the nine he examines—as well as several nonepic texts (e.g., The Poor Man of Nippur, among others) utilize a two-act literary structure wherein the second act expands and in some way mirrors the first.

5. For two important ancient god lists from the first millennium, see Litke 1998. A modern catalog, though now quite dated, is Tallqvist 1938.

6. The classic essay is Oppenheim's "The Care and Feeding of the Gods" (with Reiner 1977, 183–98).

7. See Bottéro 2001, 44–77 for one panoramic presentation of Mesopotamian deities. Hrůša 2015 provides a general description of things we deem religious in ancient Mesopotamia.

8. So, e.g., Reiner 1991, 293–94.

terms "myth" and "epic" is problematic since, as Vanstiphout has noted, "we do not as yet possess any analytical insight, and still less an analytical tool, for either lumping together or precisely distinguishing" these poems from other narrative poems from Mesopotamia. "And certainly not enough relevant study has been done on these texts for allowing us to group them with e.g. the epics of the Classical Age, or of the Western European Middle Ages."[9] Further, despite the development of a sort of modern scholarly tradition around which texts should be included in this category, there is no agreement about how one should separate myths from epics. As Foster writes, "[t]he modern distinction . . . is blurred in Assyriology, as different scholars refer to the same text as one or the other."[10] Thus, this category, like many of the subsequent ones, must be understood as something of an organizational convenience to the reader rather than an analytical statement of the nature of the Akkadian poetic tradition.[11]

Atram-hasis

Atram-hasis is the longest and most celebrated Akkadian mythological narrative poem that has survived from the OB period.[12] Alongside the OB version, the

9. Vanstiphout 1988, 207–8. See Pongratz-Leisten 1999b and 2001 for reflections on Mesopotamian epics within the broader epic tradition.

10. Foster 2007, 49.

11. Despite the fact that all of the texts treated here are written in a poetic register of Akkadian, some are stylistically more sophisticated than others. Such differences exist not only between different poems but also between chronologically distinct versions of the same composition. For example, the OB Epic of Gilgamesh uses high literary style rather sparsely, according to George 2003, 1:162. Acquiring an eye to discern such literary subtleties, needless to say, will involve learning to read Akkadian very well. For a brief but informative essay on evolution and change in Akkadian literature, see Foster 2007, 99–111.

12. Atram-hasis is the name of the human protagonist in the story. The ancient incipit is *Inūma ilū awīlum*, "When the gods were man," but contemporary scholars never refer to the poem in this way. Lambert and Millard 1969 is the most recent edition. Von Soden 1978 reedits OB tablet I. Additional witnesses have come to light since Lambert and Millard's edition, including Lambert 1980a, 71–76 (several late fragments and joins, mostly from Nineveh); 1991 (one OB and two NA fragments); Groneberg 1991 (an OB tablet of unknown origin, housed in Paris); George and Al-Rawi 1996 (four NB witnesses from Sippar); Böck and Rowe 1999–2000 (a LB fragment); Spar and Lambert 2005, no. 42 (a LB tablet); George 2009, no. 3 (an OB excerpt). Moran 1971, 1987; Wilcke 1999 are important expository essays. Shehata 2001 offers an expansive overview of the contents of the poem (4–22) and an indispensable line-by-line bibliographical commentary to the Akkadian text. For a recent English introduction and translation, including extensive notes, references to secondary literature, and translations of the various versions of the poem, see Foster 2005, 227–80. Other translations include Dalley 2000, 1–38; von Soden 1994; Bottéro and Kramer 1989, 526–601. For allusions to Atram-hasis in the Epic of Anzu, Enuma Elish, and Erra and Ishum, see Wisnom 2014. Chen 2013 treats the myth within his broader study of flood and antediluvian traditions. Finkel 2014 discusses the myth in relation to a new sixty-line tablet (see 107–10, 357–68 for his translation and edition) containing a flood account that mentions Atram-Hasis by name. Finkel also argues that the flood hero's boat was shaped like a coracle—it was round (123–55).

poem is also known from two mid-second millennium tablets from Nippur and Ugarit (on the Mediterranean coast) and is found in Babylonian and Assyrian versions from a number of first millennium witnesses.[13] All of these attest to the popularity of the composition among scribes. The focus here will be on the classical OB text, which was written over three tablets, totaling more than 1200 lines. The recovery of the poem is still incomplete.[14]

The story opens with a group of gods doing hard labor, digging the Tigris and Euphrates Rivers at the behest of the great gods. The gods grow angry under the oppressive labor and determine to rebel. They burn their tools and storm the temple of Enlil, the chief god of the pantheon, in the middle of the night, causing great anxiety and dismay in the high god. Enlil calls the other major gods, the sky god Anu from the heavens and Enki (a Sumerian name of the god Ea), god of wisdom and magic, from the subterranean waters, to take counsel. After some deliberation among themselves and discussion with the angry gods, Enki proposes that the high gods create human beings to do the miserable work of the angry gods. With the cooperation of the birth goddess, Enki creates human beings (*awīlū*) from clay mixed with the flesh and blood of the rebellious gods' leader, a deity named Aw-ila—a pregnant etiological wordplay on the nature of human beings.[15]

Twelve hundred years elapse. Humanity has reproduced to the point that their clamor annoys Enlil, causing him to lose sleep, so he decides to send a plague.[16] Enki undermines Enlil's efforts by communicating to a man named Atram-hasis (meaning, "Extra-wise"), the human protagonist of the remainder of the story, about how to avert the plague. Enki tells Atram-hasis to command the people to direct all of their offerings to Namtar, the deity responsible for the plague, until he is shamed into relenting. They do, and he does. The same scenario plays out two more times in tablet II: the people increase, Enlil is annoyed and decides to destroy them with a drought and then a famine, but Enki intervenes in both instances in some way to save humanity. At the end of tablet II, after one of several breaks in the text, we learn that the gods have decided to send a flood to wash the earth clean of humanity, and they have bound Enki with an oath this time so he cannot intervene.[17]

---

13. Foster 2005, 228–29 conveniently provides a synoptic tabulation of the contents of each version.

14. Van Koppen 2011 investigates the social context of the copyist of the most important OB witness on the basis of archival documents belonging to his family.

15. The name of this god is read variously (e.g., We-ila); see Shehata 2001, 68–69 for a review of the options.

16. On the topic of sleep in ancient Near Eastern (and other) mythological texts, see Batto 1987; Oshima 2014b.

17. A very similar flood account is preserved in the SB Epic of Gilgamesh XI. On the flood narratives in ancient Mesopotamia, see Chen 2013.

At the beginning of tablet III we find Enki—the clever god of wisdom—circumventing the oath by speaking to the wall of a reed hut, behind which Atram-hasis happens to be lying; thus, Atram-hasis learns "accidentally on purpose" that he must build a boat to preserve life.[18] After Atram-hasis builds the boat and loads it with his family and various animals, the flood comes with such force that even the gods are afraid. The vivid description is worthy of full citation:

> [Anzu {a fierce mythological bird} rent] the sky with his talons,
> . . . .
> He broke its clamor [like a pot].
> . . . .
> Its destructive power came upon the peoples [like a battle].
> One person did [not] see another,
> They could [not] recognize each other in the catastrophe.
> [The deluge] bellowed like a bull,
> The wind [resound]ed like a screaming eagle.
> The darkness [was dense], the sun was gone,
> [The offspring became] like flies.
> [The gods became afraid of the clamor] of the deluge,
> They took [refuge in heaven],
> They [crou]ched [outside]. (III iii 7–8, 10, 12–22)[19]

As the flood continues to wreak devastation, the gods lament but also grow hungry and thirsty because there are no people to make offerings. After seven days and nights, the flood ends and Atram-hasis offers a sacrifice, around which the malnourished gods flock like flies. Enlil is furious that someone survived the flood, and Enki confesses that he is to blame. Enki then suggests that the gods institute death rather than practice indiscriminate attempts to annihilate humans, thus explaining the natural limitation on human lifespan.[20] Enki also suggests several measures to control the human population: some women should be made barren, others should be made celibate priestesses, and a demon ought to be established that would steal the life of newborn children—all three overt etiologies for the reproductive fate of various kinds of women in society.[21] The text concludes with a paean to a deity, as is quite typical in Sumerian and Akkadian poems, in this case to Enlil for bringing the flood.

18. See Weinfeld 1988, 1997–1998.

19. Foster 2005, 249.

20. Apparently humans could only die from an accident or illness previously. For the idea of instituting death in this passage, see Lambert 1980b, 58.

21. See Kilmer 1972.

As already noted above, scholars have identified a number of etiologies in this interesting myth that explain various aspects of divinity and humanity as well as their relationship—clearly, it's complicated. Interpreting the precise significance of these etiologies, however, is rather difficult, leading to a diversity of interpretive outcomes among readers. For example, the very first line of the poem, a mere three words, elicits debate: *inūma ilū awīlum*. Literally translated, the line reads "when the gods a man." What does this mean? Should we conclude that the working gods at the beginning of the poem were actually human men in earlier times or were they only *like* men (i.e., they labored for the high gods as would men)? There is no verb in the terse phrase; and the line lacks an Akkadian word for "like" (e.g., *kīma*).[22] The translation of these words is itself a highly significant interpretive decision, with implications for the primeval character of some of the deities in the story. Another interpretive crux surrounds the phonological conincidence between the word for humans (*awīlū*) and the name of the god slain in their creation (Aw-ila). This is an obvious attempt to explain the nature of human beings. However, scholars debate the contemporary understanding of this ancient explanation and thus the overall meaning of the passage (I 192–248).[23] Is it significant that the deity slain in the creation of humans was the leader of the rebel gods? What do we make of the fact that this deity is the one who, according to the text, had *ṭēmu*, an Akkadian word variously translated "personality," "inspiration," and "intelligence," among others?[24] Our answers to these questions—our interpretations—have profound implications for understanding the myth's view of human beings. As for the relationship between the gods and humanity, should we interpret the interdependence that develops between the humans who do the work for the gods and the gods who receive sustenance from humans as merely an explanation of the religious system (i.e., the status quo), or is the representation in the poem intended to be critical of the status quo?[25] These are but a few of the interpretive questions that exercise readers of this Old Babylonian mythological masterpiece.

Enuma Elish

Enuma elish, "when on high," is the incipit and thus title of a long narrative poem that chronicles the god Marduk's rise to the head of the Babylonian

---

22. Ziegler 2016 has recently reviewed the literature on this matter.

23. For an important study of this anthropogony and the paronomasia utilized therein, which extends to words in the text not mentioned above, see Abusch 1998.

24. See Lambert and Millard 1969, 58 at I 223. The translations above come from Lambert and Millard 1969, 59; Foster 2005, 236; Abusch 1998, 366, respectively. Shehata 2001, 69 provides other translations with a brief discussion.

25. On the religious and political criticism in the myth, see, e.g., Wilcke 1999, 99–105; Chen 2013, 197–253.

pantheon (displacing Enlil) through the violent defeat of the chaotic female monster Tiamat.[26] In the course of the poem, the text also explains the origin of the gods (theogony), the making of the world (cosmogony), as well as the creation of human beings (anthropogony). The most recent reconstruction of the poem attests 1096 lines across seven tablets. The text may date to the Middle Babylonian period (mid- to late second millennium), though this is uncertain and disputed.[27] The poem is often called *the* Babylonian creation story, despite the facts that Marduk's rise to the head of the pantheon is the main purpose of the text and there are several other Mesopotamian theogonic, cosmogonic, and anthropogonic accounts preserved on cuneiform tablets.[28] Still, Enuma Elish must have been one of the most important texts in first millennium scribal culture if its many copies, its two ancient commentaries, and its ritual use in the Akitu (New Year's) ceremony are any indicator.[29] The fact that the Assyrians tried to adapt the text to exalt their own chief god, Assur, to the head of the pantheon also bespeaks the text's theological cachet.[30]

The author of the poem drew on a diverse body of traditional mythological and scholarly materials, and, as Lambert noted, "has interwoven this material together in an unparalleled fashion."[31] Figuring prominently among such was the mythology of the warrior god Ninurta (see the Epic of Anzu on page 87

26. The newest edition of Enuma Elish is Lambert 2013, who provides extensive discussions of historical and thematic aspects of the text. See also Kämmerer and Metzler 2012, whose bibliography is more up-to-date than Lambert's. For a classic interpretive essay, see Jacobsen 1976, 167–91. Gabriel 2014 offers a recent monograph-length interpretation of the poem. Foster 2005, 436–86 provides a translation with a great many notes and references to the literature that cannot be repeated here. Other translations include Lambert 1994a, 2008; Dalley 2000, 228–77; Bottéro and Kramer 1989, 602–79, the last of whom also provides extensive discussion (653–79). For the reception history of Enuma Elish in the ancient world, see Frahm 2011, 345–68 (earlier 2010). The literature on Marduk is extensive. Essential references may be found in Sommerfeld 1982, 1987–1990; Lambert 2013, 248–77; Oshima 2011, 2014a. Oshima's two works, though not centered on Marduk as a deity, contain a great deal of relevant material.

27. See Lambert 2013, 439–44 for a defense of the view presented above. The *Chaoskampf* motif (the battle against chaotic forces) attested in the poem is much older, as proven by an OB prophecy from Mari that alludes to the storm god Adad's defeat of the Sea (see Durand 1993; Foster 2005, 144 for a translation).

28. See Lambert 2013, 464–65 for the common misconception about the poem being *the* Babylonian creation story. Lambert 2013 provides a critical edition for several other creation accounts that cannot be summarized here. For the Sumerian and Akkadian texts relevant to anthropogony specifically, see the dated treatment in Pettinato 1971; and the broader treatment of Mesopotamian conceptions of human nature in Steinert 2012.

29. See Frahm 2011, 112–17 for a description of the two commentaries and related texts. Lambert 2013 now provides editions of the two commentaries with discussion. Bottéro 1977 remains a valuable study. For the Akitu festival, see Linssen 2004, 81; Pongratz-Leisten 1994, 52 and throughout.

30. See Lambert 1997; 2013, 4–6.

31. Lambert 2013, 457. See Vanstiphout 1992b for broad reflections on this aspect of the poem, which he concludes is not so much an epic but "a theological didactic poem" (52, 56).

below) and traditional god lists.[32] The resulting poem is a sophisticated and learned work of literature that continues to challenge philologists and interpreters with its many subtleties and obscurities.

The poem opens with two primeval deities, the female Tiamat, "Sea," and the male Apsu, "Subterranean Fresh Water," mingling their waters in the most ancient of times, a time before anything had yet been named and thus before anything had been created.[33] From this union arise the primordial gods Lahmu and Lahamu, who produce the primordial gods Anshar and Kishar, from whom come the god Anu, god of heaven. With Anu the epic introduces a major god in the pantheon who was revered widely throughout Mesopotamian history.[34] Anu then begets a son called Nudimmud, which is another name for Ea (Sumerian Enki), the god of water and wisdom. The gods disturb the waters of Tiamat with their noise. Apsu, annoyed at the commotion, counsels to destroy them. But Tiamat will not countenance it. Nevertheless, Apsu hatches a deicidal plan, which Ea discovers and thwarts. Ea kills Apsu and makes his divine abode from the corpse, explaining thereby how Ea came to inhabit the subterranean fresh waters. In Ea's watery realm Marduk, the future god of Babylon, is born to Ea and his wife Damkina.

Marduk, with the four winds granted him by his grandfather Anu, disturbs Tiamat and the other gods dwelling within her. After complaints and cajoling, Tiamat accedes to destroy the gods in Apsu. She creates eleven fierce creatures to do her bidding and sets a minor deity named Qingu, her new lover, in charge, whose authority is symbolized by the fact that he holds the tablet of destinies.[35] It can be no accident that a male deity holds the instruments of power.[36]

Ea hears about Tiamat's plans and seeks counsel from Anshar, repeating everything that Tiamat had said to Qingu in tablet I. Distraught, Anshar blames Ea for provoking the aggression with his murder of Apsu.[37] Anshar dispatches Ea to fight Tiamat with the power of his incantation. Ea sets out to fight but

32. On Ninurta specifically, see Lambert 1986; Lambert 2013 explores the poem's use of previous traditional materials thoroughly. Seri 2012 examines the use of creation traditions in the poem; Seri 2014 sheds light on the intertextuality of the poem. Wisnom's close reading of the poem finds allusions to and structural affinities with the Epic of Anzu, Atram-hasis, and the Sumerian text Lugal-e, which was provided with an Akkadian interlinear translation (2014, 90–207).

33. The opening lines of the poem have generated considerable controversy and literature. For a recent review of the issues and a new translation, see Haubold 2017, 221–28. On the likely West Semitic origin of Tiamat, see Wisnom's recent review of the literature (2014, 24–29).

34. For a brief statement of Anu (Sum. An), see Black and Green 1992, 30.

35. For the monsters of Tiamat's army, see Wiggermann 1992, 145–64. For more on Qingu, see Krebernik 2006–2008. For the significance of the tablet of destinies in Enuma Elish, see Sonik 2012.

36. For a discussion of gender and Tiamat's role in Enuma Elish—from primeval element to murderous mother/wife to chaotic monster, see Sonik 2009.

37. For Ea's reply to Anshar (specifically the difficult lines in II 69–70), see the new translation suggested in Haubold 2017, 228–36.

turns back, disheartened by Tiamat's power. Anshar then sends Anu out against Tiamat, but he likewise turns back, repeating Ea's excuse verbatim. Ea encourages Marduk to step forward for battle. Marduk volunteers and Anshar agrees to let him go. But Marduk stipulates that Anshar must make him the head of the pantheon.

Tablet III barely advances the plot due to the large sections of repeated material. Anshar sends Kakka, his vizier to Lahmu and Lahamu, to assemble the gods. Anshar's message to Kakka repeats Tiamat's words from the end of tablet I and the words from tablet II describing the failures of Ea and Anu and Marduk's volunteering to fight. Kakka, as a good messenger, goes and repeats to Lahmu and Lahamu all of Anshar's words. The gods assemble as Anshar requested for a banquet, where they agree to make Marduk their champion.

As tablet IV opens, the gods are exalting Marduk to the head of the pantheon. They ask him to demonstrate his powerful decree, which Marduk does by commanding the disappearance and reappearance of a constellation. Marduk arms himself for battle and advances. He is dismayed at first but then takes courage. Marduk addresses Tiamat and the two engage in battle, which lasts only about a dozen lines. Marduk's winds rush inside Tiamat, distending her body, and his arrow splits her in half. Marduk captures the rebellious gods and takes the tablet of destinies from Qingu. From the corpse of Tiamat Marduk creates the frame of the cosmos and stations Anu, Enlil, and Ea in their respective shrines/domains (i.e., the heavens, the earth, and the subterranean waters). Marduk's creation continues into tablet V, where he appoints the gods to their constellations and sets up the celestial bodies, especially the moon, that/who regulate the calendar. Tiamat's body becomes the Mesopotamian landscape: her eyes are the sources for the Tigris and Euphrates rivers; her breasts become distant mountains. The gods rejoice at Marduk's victory. He takes on the accoutrements of kingship and the gods submit to his newly earned authority. The end of tablet V is still not fully recovered, but it is clear that Marduk decides to build his shrine in Babylon.

At the beginning of tablet VI Marduk has the idea to create humans to serve the gods. Ea suggests they be made from the blood of Tiamat's ringleader, Qingu, whom the divine assembly hands over for the purpose. After Marduk apportioned all of the gods to their places, they ask what they may do for Marduk. He asks them to build his shrine in Babylon, which they do. Marduk holds a banquet in his new shrine where the gods once again affirm Marduk's supremacy and their loyalty. Starting in VI 137, the gods proclaim Marduk's fifty names. As fifty is the traditional divine number of Enlil, giving Marduk fifty names is a clear indication that Marduk has usurped the older head deity's position. With each name is a brief explanation of its significance, many of which derive from translations or expositions of the Sumerian names using traditional scholarly hermeneutical methods.[38] The myth ends with an exhortation for people to learn the text, now called Marduk's song (*zamāru* in VII 161), and pass it on to future generations.

There is broad consensus among scholars that Enuma Elish was written to exalt Marduk to the head of the pantheon (thereby replacing Enlil), which simultaneously raised the profile of the city that became host to Marduk's shrine, Babylon. Along the way, the myth also explains the origins of the gods, the world, and humanity. Despite this consensus about the text's purpose, scholars do not agree on the religio-political implications of the myth because they differ on its time of composition. Lambert searches a myriad of texts to establish the historical context for Marduk's rise to preeminence in the Babylonian pantheon. He concludes that it took place during the reign of Nebuchadnezzar I (1125–1104 BCE).[39] This date, however, as he rightly points out, can only serve as the earliest point in time for the myth's composition. As he observes, "it is hardly possible to judge from the text of the Epic whether it was composed as part of the movement which instated Marduk above the other gods or whether it was a literary expression of views which had been current for centuries."[40] The latest point in time for the myth's composition must be established on the basis of the oldest tablets (currently known) that bear witness to its text. Lambert dates these to about 900 BCE.[41] Given this rather wide historical window for the origin of the poem, it is difficult to pin down its religio-political purpose. Was it written to justify a new prominence for Marduk and Babylon, for example, in the late second millennium, as Lambert contends?[42] Was the poem an emphatic statement of this prominence at a later time, perhaps at a time of Babylonian decline? Was it written for some other, perhaps celebratory, purpose? One's view on the dating of the poem will inform one's answers to these questions. Without better evidence, however, various datings will continue to compete within the murky realm of historical plausibility.

Epic of Anzu

Drawing on a reservoir of ancient Near Eastern traditions of mythical battles against the forces of chaos (*Chaoskampf*) and Sumerian mythology surrounding

---

38. For an example of how the text explains the various names, see page 64. For a scholarly exposition of the names in the text, see now the master's thesis by Danzig (2013), prepared under the direction of Eckhart Frahm. For their structure and function within the poem, see Seri 2006. For an investigation into how the ancient commentary used scribal hermeneutics to explain the names within the text, see Bottéro 1977.

39. Lambert 2013, 248–77, esp. 273–74 for his conclusions.

40. Lambert 2013, 248.

41. See Lambert 2013, 442. His judgment is an estimate, based on a paleographical evaluation of specific tablets from Assur.

42. Lambert 2013, 443.

Ninurta, the Epic of Anzu recounts the rise of rebellious Anzu, a fierce mythological bird, and his destruction by the warrior god Ninurta.[43] The Akkadian poem is known in an OB and SB version. The OB version, which identifies the warrior god as Ningirsu, is represented by only a couple of quite fragmentary tablets.[44] The SB version is much better attested and shows a longer text. Currently, almost 550 lines divided over three tablets have been recovered.[45] Tablets I and II are well-preserved; the third and final tablet breaks off before its completion. As Vogelzang has demonstrated, the SB version is marked by expansions, repetition, and narrative symmetry.[46] It may date back to as early as 1200 BCE.[47] The following description is based on the SB version. As one will readily see, the poem has close affinities to Enuma Elish (see page 83, above) since the latter drew on Ninurta mythology for its characterization of Marduk.[48]

After a brief hymn to Ninurta describing his many attributes and martial conquests, the poem describes the world before its present condition: the gods had no shrines and the rivers, though formed, were not filled with water. At that time Enlil, depicted here as the chief god of the pantheon, received word about the birth of Anzu on Sharshar Mountain (perhaps Jebel Bishri in present day Syria). Anzu is described in terms that associate him with strong winds and a flood of

---

43. The incipit to this poem is *Bin šar dadmē*, "Son of the king of habitations," though scholars only occasionally use it to refer to the poem (see note 128, below, for a connection to Erra and Ishum). Vogelzang 1988 offers a critical edition of all Akkadian versions, including two witnesses (STT 23 and STT 25) that seem to attest a different text about Ninurta or a quite different tradition. The most recent edition is Annus 2001, which includes some material published since Vogelzang's (notably Saggs 1986). Lauinger 2004 presents a new fragment of tablet III in the SB version. Foster 2005, 555–78 provides an English translation with notes and references. Other translations include Dalley 2000, 203–21; Bottéro and Kramer 1989, 389–418; Hecker 1994. In addition to an edition of the OB and SB versions of the poem, Vogelzang 1988 includes several chapters of broader interest, including a treatment of the differences between the two versions, the poem's overall structure, its use of specific narrative devices (esp. repetition and parallelism; see already Vogelzang 1986 for the former), and its relationship to other texts attesting the Ninurta mythology. Streck 2009, 477–84 provides collations and notes on the OB version, which has now been reedited for the SEAL project (text 1.1.2.1). Feldt 2013 emphasizes the role of Ea's "cunning intelligence" in the story and in the ideology of political sovereignty. Wisnom 2014, 56–89 finds allusions in the Epic of Anzu to the Sumerian narrative poems Lugal-e, An-gin₇, The Return of Lugalbanda, as well as the Akkadian mythical texts Labbu and Atram-hasis. (The fragmentary Labbu myth is not treated in this book; see Lambert 2013, 361–65 for an edition; Foster 2005, 581–82 for a translation.) For *Chaoskampf* and Sumerian mythology, see Annus 2001, xiv–xxi and Vogelzang 1988, 170–76. For Ninurta, see Annus 2002.

44. In fact, this OB version is based on two tablets from Susa that may be MB or NB copies. These later copies seem to preserve an OB text (see Foster 2005, 577; Vogelzang 1988, 111–18).

45. The SB text is reconstructed from fifteen manuscripts at present, a mix of MA (MSS C and E), MB (MS t), NA (A, B, F, H, I, J, K, R, and Lauinger 2004), and NB (MSS d, g, and p) tablets.

46. See Vogelzang 1986; 1988, 190–224.

47. See, e.g., Vogelzang 1988, 8.

48. See note 32, above.

water.[49] As Enlil contemplates what to make of Anzu, Ea, the god of wisdom, suggests the creature stand guard in Enlil's cella. Enlil agrees; but Anzu takes advantage of his proximity to power. He covets the trappings of kingship: Enlil's crown, his divine garment, and the tablet of destinies—a symbol of authority and governance; and he plots to overthrow Enlil's kingship.[50] When Enlil removes his clothes to bathe in his shrine's pure waters (the availability of which seem related to Anzu's domestication), Anzu takes the tablet of destinies, the ultimate source of Enlil's power, and flies off to the mountains.[51] The impact of the tablet's absence is immediate and obviously devastating, as the narrator states:

> He took control of the tablet of destinies,
> He took supremacy, [authority] was overthrown!
> Anzu soared off and [made his way] to his mountain,
> Awful silence spread, deathly sti[llness] reigned. (I 80–83)[52]

The gods, dismayed by this development, take immediate counsel to determine who should pursue the fiend, kill him, recover the tablet, and restore order. As a reward for his valor, the savior would gain a multitude of shrines and thereby a great name (*gašru*, "Strong One"). In a long, repetitive passage, three gods are nominated, Adad, Girra, and Shara, and each refuse to go, citing the identical reason: Anzu's possession of the tablet of destinies. Such is the power of this tablet that whatever Anzu commands actually happens.[53] Ea steps forward and wisely suggests to Anu and the assembled gods that he be allowed to intervene. He tells them to bring in the goddess Belet-ili, whom they flatter in their assembly with praise and honor with a name change (she becomes Belet-kullat-ili, "lady of all the gods"). They then ask her to volunteer her son Ninurta for the mission. She agrees. Tablet I ends with her briefing Ninurta about the situation, and tablet II opens with her instructing Ninurta how to destroy Anzu (part of which repeats earlier instructions to the three previous candidates).

Ninurta then sets out to kill Anzu. The two meet in the battlefield. After a volley of verbal retorts, a fierce battle ensues, in which Anzu turns Ninurta back. Using the power of the tablet of destinies, Anzu commands the components of the arrows Ninurta fires at him to return to their respective places of origin:

---

49. Annus notes, with references, that Kassite cylinder seal iconography confirms this (2001, x).

50. On the tablet of destinies and kingship, see George 1986. For its role in Anzu, see Groneberg 2008.

51. On the availability of pure water, see Annus 2001, x–xi and Vogelzang 1988, 76–77.

52. Foster 2005, 564.

53. See Marduk's similar power in Enuma Elish, page 86, above. For the effective word in the ancient Near East, see Greaves 1996.

The shaft did not approach Anzu but returned!
Anzu cried out against it,
"Shaft that has come, go back to your thicket,
"Frame of the bow to your forests,
"Bowstring to the sheep's sinews, feather to the birds: go back!"
Because he held the tablet of destinies of the gods in his hand,
The bowstring brought forth arrows, but they did not approach his body.
    (II 61–67)[54]

In the remainder of tablet II Ninurta enlists Sharur, his deified weapon and trustworthy adviser, to report the situation to Ea and seek advice.[55] Ninurta's message comprises earlier lines from the narrative taken verbatim, including Anzu's words (and thus the message contains a speech within a speech). Sharur then delivers the message to Ea (which now has a speech within a speech within a speech). Ea, realizing that they must turn the power of the tablet of destinies against Anzu somehow, gives specific instructions for Ninurta to Sharur, who then repeats them to Ninurta. Tablet II ends with Ninurta preparing for a second assault.

Tablet III opens in the throes of battle. Ninurta tires Anzu out so that his wings begin to droop. Ninurta then carries out Ea's plan:

He [Ninurta] took a sword behind his arrows and
cut off his wings, detached(?) right and left.
When he [Anzû] saw his feather(s), it brought out the utterance of his
    mouth.
When he cried, "Feathers to feathers!" the arrow found him.
The arrow passed through his heart.
As for the wings and feathers, he made the arrow pass through them.
The arrow cut through the heart and the lungs. (III 10–16)[56]

Just as Anzu's effective command had made the components of Ninurta's arrow in the first battle return to their place of origin, so Anzu's command here intends to restore his dismembered feathers to their place of origin, that is, on his own body. Ironically, as Ea knew, all the feathers within range of the command would obey Anzu's word, including the ones on Ninurta's arrows. Thus, Anzu's own order ironically and effectively kills him.[57]

---

54. Foster 2005, 570.

55. Sharur is a deified weapon in Lugal-e, a similar story to Anzu about Ninurta in Sumerian. Sharur's equivalent in Enuma Elish is Anshar's vizier, Kakka (Wisnom 2014, 64), a name that means "weapon."

56. The translation is from Studevent-Hickman 2010, 290–91.

57. For a fuller presentation of this interpretation (and a reading of the poem that gives due attention to the power of language within the poem), see Studevent-Hickman 2010, esp. pp. 290–91.

Ninurta recovers the tablet of destinies and news of Anzu's death reaches the gods, whereupon they rejoice and invite Ninurta into their exclusive council. The gods request Ninurta to return the tablet of destinies, which he does, perhaps with some hesitation (the lines are fragmentary).[58] The poem then ends with a long passage of praise for Ninurta, including the pronouncing of his various names (in much the same fashion as Enuma Elish does for Marduk).

Although the narrative poem contains in its opening section an environmental etiology that explains the origins of the Tigris and Euphrates Rivers—a defining characteristic of Mesopotamia (Greek μεσοποταμία, "land between the rivers"), its most important theme is related to political ideology, specifically, the nature of kingship and the justification of the use of force against enemies who threaten stability and the status quo. Given the importance of Ninurta to Assyrian royal ideology, especially from the MA period on, it is no surprise that so many tablets bearing witness to the poem come from Assyria, eleven of fifteen total, and that many of the Assyrian royal inscriptions incorporate the mythology of Ninurta in their descriptions of the Assyrian king, who is represented as fulfilling the divine hero's role.[59]

Adapa

The narrative poem contemporary scholars call Adapa is known primarily from an incomplete fourteenth-century tablet of (now) seventy-one lines found at el-Amarna in Egypt.[60] Five other fragments of the story are known from Assurbanipal's library in Nineveh, which date to some seven hundred years later.[61] A couple of these later fragments (which scholars have labeled A and A₁) provide an introduction to Adapa, the sage and protagonist of the poem, that are absent in the older version. Another fragment (labeled D) provides a different ending to the story and appends an incantation invoking Adapa against the South Wind.[62]

58. Vogelzang 1988, 139 thinks it plausible that Ninurta wants to keep the tablet of destinies for himself. Likewise, Foster 2005, 556. Annus 2001, xiii does not see sufficient evidence for such a view.

59. For the importance of Ninurta, see, e.g., Maul 1999, 209–12; Annus 2002, 39–47; Pongratz-Leisten 2015, esp. ch. 6. For a survey of the Assyrian king as Ninurta see Annus 2002, 94–101; Pongratz-Leisten 2015. The characterization of the king as the "fulfillment" of Ninurta comes from Pongratz-Leisten 2015, 38.

60. The most recent edition of the Akkadian text with extensive philological commentary and discussion of the poem's literary character and mythological significance is Izre'el 2001. Recent translations include Foster 2005, 525–30; Dalley 2000, 182–88; Hecker 2001, 51–55. See also Kilmer's translation in Izre'el 1996, 111–14. For a study of Adapa and its intertexuality with the scholarly texts belonging to the exorcist, see Annus 2016. The el-Amarna witness is probably a student's tablet (Izre'el 2001, 51–54).

61. See Izre'el 2001, 5–6 for the manuscripts. An extensive Sumerian version was found at Tell Haddad (Cavigneaux and Al-Rawi 1993, 92–93; Cavigneaux 2014b). For its possible relationship to the Akkadian materials, see Milstein 2015b.

62. See Izre'el 2001, 5–6, 108–10.

According to the introductory material from fragments A and A₁, Adapa is a wise sage and servant of Ea, god of wisdom, living in the southern city of Eridu, Ea's hometown. "To him he [i.e., Ea] granted wisdom," fragment A states, "eternal life he did not grant him" (A 4').[63] Adapa is so dedicated to his god that he personally prepares the deity's meals, including baking the bread and catching the fish himself. While out fishing one day, the South Wind capsizes Adapa's boat, casting him into the sea.[64] In his anger, according to the beginning of fragment B, he curses the South Wind ("I will fracture your w[in]g," B 5').[65] His curse is effective, and the wind ceases its blowing.[66] After a week, the high god Anu takes notice and queries his adviser about the stillness of the South Wind. When he learns that Adapa is responsible, he calls Adapa up to heaven to give an account of his actions. Ea, knowing that Adapa was summoned, devises a cunning plan: he dishevels Adapa's hair and clothes him in a mourner's garment so that on arrival to heaven Adapa would appear to be in mourning. He then advises Adapa to tell the two gods standing at Anu's gates that he is in mourning for the gods Dumuzi and Gizzida that had disappeared from the earth. As these are the very gods who stand guard at Anu's gate, this deception would make them favorably disposed to Adapa. Ea also tells Adapa not to eat or drink what Anu offers him, which Ea characterizes as food and water of death.

Adapa then ascends to heaven and greets the two deities just as Ea had instructed. Pleased, they lead him into Anu, who demands an account from Adapa for cursing the South Wind. It is at this point that we learn about Adapa's trouble at sea (B 49'–54'), which is absent from the beginning of the story. Although Anu is enraged, Dumuzi and Gizzida put in a good word for Adapa. Anu then asks Adapa a couple of questions that have been something of a crux for understanding the poem: "Why did Ea expose to a human what is bad in heaven and earth? (Why did he) establish a 'fat heart' (in) him?" (B 57'–58').[67] Anu offers Adapa food and drink, which are now called the food and water of life, and some oil and a garment. Adapa, in obedience to Ea, refuses the former items and accepts the latter. Anu laughs and questions Adapa's refusal.[68] Adapa explains that Ea had advised him against eating and drinking what is offered.

---

63. Foster 2005, 526.

64. It seems that Adapa drowns (so Izre'el 2001, 141, Milstein 2015b, 35, 37; 2015a, 197, 204, 208).

65. Foster 2005, 527.

66. See B 3'–6' and, in a fuller description, B 49'–54'.

67. Izre'el 2001, 18–21.

68. Anu's direct speech to Adapa includes the phrase *lā balṭāta â nišī dallāti* ("Won't you live? Alas for the wretched peoples!" [Foster 2005, 529] or "Hence you shall not live! Alas for inferior humanity!" [Izre'el 2001, 21] in B 68'. Its significance is disputed. Is immortality on offer here (so Izre'el 2001, 32) or simply a restoration to health (for a drowned Adapa, so Milstein 2015a, 208)?

Anu then orders him to be returned to the earth.[69] An alternate ending is pre-served in fragment D, in which Anu seems to free Adapa from Ea's service (D 9′–10′) and decides to keep Adapa in heaven with him.[70] A broken incantation that invokes Adapa's unique power concludes the story.

This short mythic tale raises a host of interpretive questions. Did Ea trick Adapa to deprive him of immortality? Was Ea mistaken about the nature of the divinely offered victuals? Scholars offer a very wide variety of interpretations of this myth and its purpose. For example, Piotr Michalowski sees an etiology for the discovery of magic.[71] Sara Milstein sees a myth that mirrors the structure of a magical healing ritual.[72] Benjamin Foster sees a kind of a fortiori argument against human immortality: "if a man so perfect could not obtain immortal-ity, despite his close relationship to a great god, who else could expect to?"[73] Shlomo Izre'el focuses his interpretation on the use of language, wisdom, and differentiating humans from gods.[74] Most compelling is Mario Liverani. Using a structuralist methodology, he finds an etiology for the priesthood, who may enter the god's house and accept a measure of hospitality (symbolized by a liquid and solid applied to the outside of the body: oil and a garment) but may not become a permanent member of the community of residents (symbolized by a liquid and a solid that goes inside the body: water and food from the divine table).[75] There is little reason to think, however, that anyone has written the final word on this brief, enigmatic tale.

Etana

The poem known today as Etana is a unique blend of a fable about an eagle and a snake and a story about a man's quest to acquire an heir, a theme attested elsewhere in the ancient Near East.[76] The poem currently exists in OB, MA, and

69. Or possibly Adapa is sent to the netherworld, since *qaqqaru* can have that meaning, too (so Izre'el 2001, 141–42 [and p. 33 for the philological issues with the precise form, *qaqqarīšu*]; Milstein 2015b, 35 n. 24).

70. For Anu freeing Adapa, see Izre'el 2001, 38–39. For keeping Adapa in heaven, see Izre'el 2001, 42; and the developed idea in Annus 2016, 81–85; Sanders 2017, 58, both of whom connect Adapa in heaven in this myth to the throne of Anu mentioned in the topographical text Tintir (in II 2). For Tintir and other topographical texts, which are not covered in the present book, see George 1992.

71. Michalowski 1980.

72. Milstein 2015a.

73. Foster 2005, 525.

74. Izre'el 2001.

75. Liverani 2004.

76. The Akkadian incipit is *Āla īṣurū*, "they planned out a city," though scholars do not use it. The most recent critical edition is Haul 2000. Earlier critical editions include Saporetti 1990; Kin-nier Wilson 1985. Novotny 2001 offers a teaching edition with a succinct but rich introduction to the poem and scholarship on it. Kinnier Wilson 2007 provides some new material and discussion of affected scenes. Foster 2005, 533–54 is the most recent translation. See also Dalley 2000, 189–202;

SB recensions, but we have evidence in Sumerian and in cylinder seal art that the story was known even earlier.[77] The OB and MA versions of the story are rather fragmentary and incomplete, having come down to us in but a handful of tablets and fragments. The SB version is preserved on many more tablets and fragments, providing a much fuller presentation of the story in about 330 preserved lines, though it too is incomplete. Unfortunately, just how incomplete it is remains unclear, since the number of tablets comprising the poem—and thus its original length—ranges in scholarly opinion between three and as many as six (or eight!). To complicate matters further, the ordering of the material after tablet II is disputed, thus even the plot of the story varies among translators.[78] One of the greatest disappointments about the fragmentary state of the poem is the fact that we still do not have its ending. Did Etana reach heaven and acquire his heir? As several scholars have noted, the Sumerian King List records the name of Etana's heir, which may give some reason to believe he was successful. Yet this evidence is sometimes doubted; and if it is accepted, the details about how his success was achieved remain uncertain.[79] The description presented here follows the SB recension via Foster's most recent and accessible English translation of the poem, which orders the material much like the editions of Novotny (2001) and Haul (2000).[80]

The first tablet is unfortunately rather incomplete. As the story opens, the gods plan and found a city, which needs a leader. The high god Enlil and Ishtar, goddess of sex and war, search high and low and agree to appoint Etana from the city of Kish as king. After a gap, there are a few lines that mention Etana's wife and a dream (on MS K). The remainder of tablet I is lost.

Hecker 2001, 34–51. Novotny 2001, xi includes references to several others. Horowitz 1998, 43–66 discusses the cosmographical implications of Etana's flight to heaven. Streck 2009, 484–86 provides collations and notes on the OB version, which is now reedited for the SEAL project (text 1.1.6.1). For the theme of a quest for an heir, see, e.g., the Ugaritic Kirta Epic and the story of Abraham in the biblical book of Genesis.

77. For a chart of how the different versions' contents line up, see Foster 2005, 534. The Sumerian King List mentions Etana's flight (see ETCSL 2.1.1, lines 64–70). Numerous cylinder seals may depict the story (or some version of it). See Steinkeller 1992, 248–55; Hrouda 1996.

78. For scholarly opinions and references on both the number of tablets and the arrangement of the material after tablet II, see conveniently Novotny 2001, xiii–xviii (and add Kinnier-Wilson 2007, 87–89). Novotny also provides a concordance to the ordering of the materials in his and the three other editions of the poem (53) as well as a concordance for his edition vis-à-vis Dalley's (2010) and Foster's (first edition of his anthology, *Before the Muses*, 1993) English translations. Foster's third edition of *Before the Muses* (2005) now follows Novotny's order. Haul 2000 offers an extensive introduction to the sources and their ordering, the figure of Etana in Mesopotamian tradition, the interpretation of the tale (with a discussion of competing approaches [add the interesting structuralist interpretation offered in Koubková 2016]), and the story's relationship to folktales of similar content.

79. An unpublished tablet reports that Etana did not make it to heaven (pers. comm., Benjamin Foster).

80. Foster 2005, 544–53.

Tablet II introduces an eagle and a snake, who have made their homes in the boughs and roots, respectively, of a large tree near some cultic structure. The two make a pact of mutual respect and friendship; they hunt together and feed their young in harmony. All goes well, it seems, until the eagle's children are grown and the eagle has a change of heart. He conspires to eat the serpent's young and vocalizes his plan to his offspring. The youngest (and wisest, the text notes) protests against his father's evil plan, citing the punishment that Shamash, the sun god and god of justice, whose rays see everything under the heavens, would impose.[81] But the eagle eats the serpent's young anyway. The bereaved serpent cries out for justice to Shamash, who conveys his own plan for the serpent to have his revenge. Shamash has killed an ox in which the serpent will hide. When the eagle comes to feed, the serpent will strike at his wings and feathers so as to ground him and then throw him into a pit to die. The serpent does as he is told. When the eagle espies the ox, he tells his young, wise son that they should go down to feed. The son warns the father that it's a trap; the serpent could be lying in wait. The eagle does as he wishes, despite the warning, and finds himself stranded in a deep pit, left for dead.[82] The eagle cries out to Shamash for help. Although Shamash tells the eagle he deserves what he has received, he also announces that he will send a man to rescue him. That man is Etana, who has been praying to Shamash for salvation, too; he is praying for Shamash to grant him the plant of life so he can finally produce an heir. Shamash tells him about the eagle, who will reveal the plant to him.

As tablet III begins, the eagle and Etana are granted the ability to communicate to one another. Etana explains how he needs the plant of life, which is located somewhere only birds can fly. The eagle agrees to hunt for it, but he cannot find it on earth.[83] The eagle then suggests they fly together to heaven to get help (or the plant?) from the goddess Ishtar. With Etana on his back, the eagle ascends into the heavens. With each league they ascend, the eagle asks Etana to describe the earth. At the third league, Etana, unable to see the earth or sea, loses his nerve and demands to be taken back down. After a gap, Etana recounts a dream of heaven to the eagle, which he interprets as a favorable omen.[84] The two take off again for heaven. And they make it! They enter through the gates of the high gods Anu, Enlil, and Ea and then those of Sîn (the moon god), Adad

81. For more on Shamash (Sumerian, Utu), see briefly Black and Green 1992, 182–84.

82. The netherworld imagery is clear but some scholars also see the eagle's time in the pit as a kind of gestation period (e.g., Koubková 2016, 380–81).

83. Unlike the OB and MA versions, the SB version does not tell how the eagle gets out of the pit.

84. Novotny places the very broken MS c in the gap (2001, xviii, 39). Haul prefers to suspend judgment on its placement (2000, 208–9). The fragment describes Etana's arrival at home and a conversation with his wife that includes the words *šammu ša alādi*, "plant of birth." See Foster 2005, 553 for a partial English translation.

(a storm god), and Ishtar, just as the dream predicted. Frustratingly, it is at this point that the text breaks off.

Nergal and Ereshkigal

This narrative poem is known in a couple of different versions: a short version (almost 90 lines) from a MB el-Amarna tablet and a longer one (about 430 lines), attested in a NA tablet from Sultantepe and a Hellenistic tablet from Uruk.[85] The older version is probably a shortened form of a fuller story.[86] There are fragmentary sections in both versions and they differ significantly in details and thematic emphasis. As Neal Walls succinctly states: "the violence of the Amarna text is replaced by deception and seduction" in the first millennium version.[87] Still, their main plot point is the same, namely, how it happened that Nergal, god of plague and destruction, married Ereshkigal, the queen of the netherworld, and assumed that dreary realm's throne.[88] Although not explicit in the actual text, scholars have suggested that the narrative may be summarized by a pun between the Akkadian words for death (*mūtu*) and husband (*mutu*): Nergal avoids death and instead becomes Ereshkigal's husband.[89] According to Gwendolyn Leick, the myth "is in fact the only Mesopotamian text that could be described as a love-story."[90]

Both versions of the story begin with the gods in the heavens holding a feast. The sky god Anu sends his messenger Kakka to tell Ereshkigal to send a messenger up to heaven to fetch her portion of the meal. (The later version is significantly expanded here, due especially to repetition.) When Ereshkigal's messenger Namtar arrives, Nergal does not honor him appropriately. Why he

---

85. The most recent edition of all versions is Ponchia and Luukko 2013, which includes a lengthy introduction and commentary on the text. For the MB version from el-Amarna, see also Izre'el 1997, 51–61 with pls. XXIII–XXX. (The el-Amarna tablet comprises two parts indirectly joined to one another. One part is housed at the British Museum in London (BM 29865 = Bu. 88-10-13, 69), the other at the Vorderasiatisches Museum in Berlin (composed of fragments VAT 1611 + 1613 + 1614 + 2710). See https://cdli.ucla.edu/dl/photo/P270856_d.jpg for an image of the two tablets together.) For a recent English translation with notes and references, see Foster 2005, 506–24. Other translations include Dalley 2000, 163–81; Bottéro and Kramer 1989, 437–64; Müller 1994c. For a monographic treatment of the literary and religious character of the text (and a German translation), see Hutter 1985. Reiner 1985, 50–60 offers a brief literary reading. Walls 2001, 127–82 provides a lengthier interpretation, informed by feminist literary theory, with references to much secondary literature. A synoptic outline of the different versions' contents is presented in Ponchia and Luukko 2013, x–xi. See also Foster 2005, 506–8.

86. See Gurney 1960, 107; Foster 2005, 209, with other references.

87. Walls 2001, 131.

88. For more on Nergal, see Wiggermann 1998–2000. For more on Ereshkigal, see briefly Black and Green 1992, 77.

89. As argued by Bottéro 1992, 245. See also, e.g., Walls 2001, 128, 173 n. 4; Foster 2005, 506.

90. Leick 1994, 250.

acts in such a disrespectful manner is unclear. Walls suggests, "it may be chauvinistic pride, disrespect for the realm of the dead, or unthinking hubris." But, as he recognizes, neither version specifies Nergal's motivations.[91] At this point the two versions diverge in plot.

In the older version, when Namtar reports the slight to Ereshkigal, she demands the celestial gods hand over Nergal for execution. But when Namtar returns to the heavens to make the arrest, he cannot find Nergal among the gods. Although escaping judgment for the moment, Nergal weeps before Ea about his imminent fate. Ea, being the god of wisdom, devises a clever plan to deliver Nergal. Ea gives Nergal a chair/throne and arms him with fourteen diseases. With these in hand Nergal heads off to the netherworld and demands entry. Namtar reports to Ereshkigal that the dishonoring god has appeared at her gates. She tells Namtar to let him in so she can kill him. As Namtar enters through the fourteen gates of the netherworld, he stations a disease at each and then rushes into Ereshkigal's court. He seizes her by the hair and positions her for decapitation. Ereshkigal cries out for mercy and offers to make him her husband and king of the netherworld. Nergal is moved with compassion and suddenly turns tender toward the chthonic queen. He kisses her, wipes away her tears, and presumably accepts her proposal with a rather opaque final statement, whose translation and signficance to the story is disputed.[92]

In the later version, there is a gap after Namtar's arrival in heaven to receive Ereshkigal's portion of the feast. When the text resumes, Ea is scolding Nergal for not honoring Namtar, and Nergal seems to have decided to go to the netherworld for some reason. The passage is unclear as is Nergal's motivation.[93] Ea then instructs Nergal to build a throne, which only imitates precious stones and metals, to take with him. The purpose of this throne is disputed among interpreters, with some scholars suggesting it is a gift, a ritual object to escape the netherworld, or a foreshadowing of Nergal's rule in the netherworld.[94] Ea also warns Nergal about accepting any hospitality while in the netherworld, even if the queen tempts him with her own body. As with Nergal's motivations, interpreters are divided about what to make of Ea's willingness to help. Is he being genuine, as most assume, or deceitful?[95]

---

91. Walls 2001, 135.

92. Scholars also disagree about what to do with the last line on the tablet (rev. 46), which reads *a-du ki-na-an-na*. Are these words part of the myth's text, to be read as the completion of the sentence begun in line 45? Or, are they simply a scribal note about the composition's completion. See Ponchia and Luukko 2013, xcvii–xcviii for interpretive alternatives and references to the literature.

93. Compare Foster 2005, 514–15 (lines ii 17'–22'), e.g., with Ponchia and Luukko 2013, 25 (lines 99–104) and their commentary on pp. 39–41. See also Walls 2001, 136–37 on Nergal's motivation.

94. See, e.g., Reiner 1985, 52; Dalley 2000, 163; Ponchia and Luukko 2013, 40; Walls 2001, 177 n. 27.

95. For the interpretation that Ea acts with deceit in this context, see Bottéro 1992, 244–45.

When Nergal arrives, he is welcomed into court through seven gates, despite being recognized as the dishonoring god of the opening scene. Nergal kneels and kisses the ground before the queen and is then offered all the hospitality that Ea warned him about, including the pleasure of Ereshkigal's amorous company. At first, Nergal does not accept any of the hospitality. But after a break in the text, Ereshkigal is again making herself available to Nergal, and he gives in to his desire. The two gods embrace.

After six days of making love, Nergal decides to leave—his reasoning is unclear—and deceives Namtar to let him out.[96] The gods, surprised to see Nergal returned, have Ea disfigure him as a means of disguise. (Apparently, they are anticipating a search party.) When Ereshkigal awakens to find Nergal missing, and learns from Namtar of Nergal's deceptive escape, she mourns uncontrollably until Namtar volunteers to make her lover return. Ereshkigal sends a message with Namtar, in which she vulnerably (or pathetically?) explains her lonely, loveless life as judge in the netherworld and then menacingly threatens to release the dead to consume the living if the gods do not return her lover.[97] Namtar repeats the message to the gods in heaven but cannot find Nergal among them. When Namtar reports back to his lady and mentions a disfigured god among them, she sees through Ea's deceit and demands that Namtar seize that god and return him to her. But Namtar again cannot find Nergal. The text is fragmentary at this point. In a rather broken section, it seems that Ea is advising Nergal to take a throne and six other items as he returns to the netherworld. Nergal enters all seven gates again, seizes Ereshkigal by the hair, and pulls her from the throne.[98] They embrace and again go off to bed—this time for a full seven days. The final preserved scene has Anu sending Kakka to the netherworld again (just as at the beginning) in what seems to be an official proclamation of Nergal's new role as ruler of the netherworld. The last dozen or so lines are lost.

Despite a general agreement about the purpose of the myth, to enthrone Nergal as the king of the netherworld, interpreters remain divided on a number

96. Six rather than seven days of lovemaking (as at the myth's conclusion) seem significant but precisely what that significance is remains unclear. It may be that the seventh day would mark the completion of Nergal's transformation into a denizen of the netherworld's realm as seven nights of lovemaking with Shamhat marked the completion of Enkidu's alienation from his animal herd (see SB Epic of Gilgamesh I 194–202, cited on page 114, below). See similarly Walls 2001, 146.

97. In the midst of this speech, Ereshkigal also states *mus[uk]kā[kū]-ma ul ebbēk ul adâni dinī ša ilī rabûti* (See Ponchia and Luukko 2013, 19, line 313), which most translate as declarative sentences: "I am unclean. I am impure. I cannot judge the cases of the great gods" (see, e.g., Ponchia and Luukko 2013, 29; Walls 2001, 154; Dalley 2000, 173; Leick 1994, 252; Bottéro and Kramer 1989, 450). Thus, she is refusing to perform her job. A minority of scholars translate the line as a series of questions: "Am I unclean? Am I impure? Can I not (still) judge the cases of the great gods?" (so, e.g., Foster 2005, 520, citing Edzard 1989, 126–27 in a review of Hutter 1985).

98. What he does at each gate is unclear due to the fragmentary state of the witnesses. See Ponchia and Luukko 2013, 62–63 for various suggestions, the two most popular of which seem to be that Nergal left one of his items at each gate or he did something violent.

of details in the myth due to gaps in the text and various obscurities in our understanding, for example, of various actors' motives and the meaning of key objects or features in the story. The summary has introduced several of these issues already. At the broad interpretive level, another matter that has garnered considerable attention is the dynamics in the relationship between Ereshkigal and Nergal. Drawing on feminist critical theory, some scholars have found in the myth an important opportunity to interrogate the politics of gender and sexuality in Mesopotamian society. Rivkah Harris, for example, sees a kind of charter myth for gender, wherein the two deities are "emblematic, possessing what the ancients considered to be feminine and masculine human traits and characteristics." These traits are not simply descriptive; the myth "reveals," rather, in Harris's interpretation, "how gender relations *ought* to have been structured, according to the androcentric perspective of Mesopotamian literature."[99] Nergal's aggression and Ereshkigal's ultimate submission both reflect what is expected of Mesopotamian men and women.[100] Building on this idea, Walls notes in his rich interpretive study that "a feminist analysis of power relations in 'Nergal and Ereshkigal' reveals the supernal gods' conspiracy to limit Ereshkigal's freedom and power. As an autonomous woman, Ereshkigal threatens first Nergal's life and then the entire cosmos with the release of the dead upon the earth. This dissolution of cosmic boundaries illustrates the chaos of feminine power in ancient Mesopotamian discourse."[101] Yet, as Walls shows, Ereshkigal's power is circumscribed in the myth by common patriarchal tropes: Ereshkigal is the wily temptress, the nude seductress, the naïve victim, the scorned demon-lover, and ultimately the domesticated wife. "The myth implies," concludes Walls, "that Ereshkigal, like all unruly women, can be pacified through sex and controlled through masculine intimidation. Ereshkigal thus models women's complicity with patriarchal authority rather than resistance to masculine domination."[102]

Descent of Ishtar

Descent of Ishtar is another narrative poem about a deity knocking on the gates of the netherworld. In this case, the deity is Ishtar, goddess of sex and war, who decides to invade the netherworld, where her sister Ereshkigal is queen.[103]

99. Harris 2000, 129, 132, emphasis added.

100. See esp. Harris 2000, 139–42.

101. Walls 2001, 172. Tiamat in Enuma Elish is another example of controlled and subjugated feminine chaos (see page 85, above).

102. Walls 2001, 173.

103. Lapinkivi 2010 is the most recent edition, which offers the text, a translation, and commentary. Foster 2005, 498–50; Dalley 2000, 154–62; Bottéro and Kramer 1989, 318–31; Müller 1994a all provide translations—the last also includes a discussion of the text in light of the Sumerian poem. (Lapinkivi 2010, xii–xiii provides a very long list of translations not noted here.) Reiner 1985, 29–49

The Akkadian poem is a shortened version (138 lines) of the much older and more fully developed Sumerian poem (412 lines). It comes down to us in only a few manuscripts from first millennium Assyria (i.e., Nineveh and Assur).[104] Interestingly, several of the passages in the poem occur in slightly altered form in Nergal and Ereshkigal and the SB Epic of Gilgamesh.[105]

The myth begins rather abruptly with Ishtar setting her mind on a visit to the netherworld. Within a dozen lines she is demanding the gatekeeper to open up or, repeating Ereshkigal's words from the previously discussed myth, she will break the gates down and release the dead to consume the living. Ereshikigal laments the situation but lets her in with the stipulation that she must subject herself to the ancient rites, which commence in the following lines. The rites consist of the gatekeeper removing an article of clothing or piece of jewelry from Ishtar at each of the seven gates, causing her to enter the netherworld completely naked.[106]

What Ishtar does upon entering the netherworld is unclear. What is manifestly clear, however, is Ereshkigal's anger and subsequent command for Namtar to release sixty diseases upon Ishtar, who succumbs to their effects. Ishtar's demise has cosmic significance; immediately, sexual activity among the living ceases.[107] A vizier of the gods named Papsukkal, in mourning, goes to petition the moon god Sîn and Ea on Ishtar's behalf, repeating the effect her demise has had upon the land of the living. Ea, drawing on his creative wisdom, comes to the rescue. He makes a being named Atsushunamir, which means "His Appearance is Bright."[108] Ea advises him how to trick Ereshkigal into making an oath and granting him a request. Atsushunamir is to request a drink from a water skin, which seems to be the key to the entire rescue operation. The significance

---

offers a close reading of the Akkadian version. Lambert 1990 edits a fragmentary Akkadian tablet from OB Ur that presents a similar descent story centered on Ningishzida.

104. An appendix on a MA tablet (LKA 62, rev. 10–20) contains the opening eleven lines of a version of the myth that "deviates considerably from the Neo-Assyrian version" (Lapinkivi 2010, xi; see p. 23 for the text). For more on LKA 62, see Hurowitz and Westenholz 1990, 46–49, who describe the tablet as a school exercise. The main text on the tablet, according to Hurowitz and Westenholz, is "a fascinating and unusual allegorical tale of an Assyrian king fighting his enemies in the guise of a hunter dealing with an insolent pack of wild asses" (1990, 46). They identify the king as Tiglath-pileser I (likewise, Foster 2005, 336–37, who provides a translation). Others see the text quite differently: as a parody of an Assyrian royal inscription (Edzard 2004b, who provides an edition of the text) and "a Neo-Assyrian scribal experiment in counterdiscoursiveness" (Finn 2017, 151–54, here 152).

105. These are cited in Foster 2005, 24; Lapinkivi 2010, xi.

106. For more about this enigmatic rite, see Lapinkivi 2010, 55–59.

107. Bottéro and Kramer 1989, 327.

108. This being is called an *assinnu* and *kulu'u* in the Nineveh and Assur manuscripts, respectively. For a discussion of these terms, see Lapinkivi 2010, 72–79 (disregarding the gnostic references).

of the water skin is unclear. Many interpreters believe it is the goddess herself or it could simply contain the water of life necessary for reviving Ishtar [109]

Ereshkigal is outraged at the request and curses Atsushunamir with the same curse Enkidu lays upon Shamhat in the SB Epic of Gilgamesh.[110] Still, Ereshkigal respects the request, which seems to have implied the release of Ishtar. The goddess is sprinkled with water of life (from the water skin?) and brought to Ereshkigal, who orders her release, provided she finds a substitute (who must be Tammuz).[111] She is then led out through (and reclothed at) the seven gates. The last dozen lines suddenly and laconically introduce Tammuz, who seems to be ritually purified (prepared for burial), and his sister Belili, who mourns her brother's loss.

Scholars have frequently interpreted Ishtar's descent to and rise from the netherworld as a Mesopotamian etiology for the changing seasons. According to this interpretation, when the goddess (Akk. Ishtar; Sum. Inana), who is closely associated with fertility, died and descended to the netherworld, certain aspects of fertility and reproduction came to an end. When she rose again, having been replaced in the netherworld by Tammuz/Dumuzi (Akk./Sum.), who is associated with *different* elements of fertility, those attributed to Ishtar (or Inana) return while those attributed to the other deity diminish.[112] (Incidentally, scholars do not always agree on what each deity represents in this seasonal scheme.) But there is a problem: To find support for this seasonal interpretation in the Akkadian version of the story one must assume a good bit of content from the *Sumerian* version, which is much fuller and as much as a millennium older. Many scholars would prefer to interpret the first millennium Akkadian version of the story in its own right and on its own terms. When considered in this manner, the Akkadian version does not support the seasonal interpretation; it seems rather to provide an etiology for the obscure ritual implied at the end of the text.[113]

Other Netherworld Myths

In keeping with the theme of visiting the netherworld, there are two other texts worthy of brief mention. The first is the twelfth tablet of the SB Epic of

109. For the former view, see, e.g., Lapinkivi 2010, 83; for the latter, Reiner 1985, 43.

110. See page 117, below.

111. So the version from Assur. The Ninevite version introduces the idea of a substitute rather abruptly after Ishtar has exited the final gate.

112. Viewing the myth (through the lens of the fuller Sumerian version) as an example of dying and rising gods who cause seasonal change has been a popular though disputed interpretation. See, e.g., Jacobsen 1976, 55–63, whose interpretation is more complicated than described here, and Lambert 1990, 290; to the contrary, Foster 2007, 58. On dying and rising gods in the ancient Near East, see Mettinger 2001.

113. Thus, e.g., Foster 2005, 504 n. 2; Dalley 2000, 154; Reiner 1985, 47–48.

Gilgamesh, widely seen as an appendix to the main epic (tablets I–XI, for which see page 109, below).[114] Tablet XII, written in prose, is a partial translation of the Sumerian tale called Bilgames and the Netherworld and preserves the part of the story in which Enkidu, Gilgamesh's servant, volunteers to fetch Gilgamesh's *pukku* (probably a ball) and *mekkû* (a stick or mallet) from the netherworld, where they had fallen during the men's play. (In the previous eleven tablets of the epic, Enkidu is called Gilgamesh's friend.)[115] Gilgamesh advises Enkidu on how to behave in the netherworld so as not to be counted among its residents but Enkidu does not listen. Having become entrapped in the deadly realm permanently, Gilgamesh goes to three high gods successively, Enlil, Sîn, and then Ea, seeking help (with the same words each time) for his imprisoned friend. Only Ea, the god associated with wisdom, subterranean water, and magic, offers help by explaining how Gilgamesh could conjure Enkidu's ghost from the grave.[116] When his ghost appears, the two greet one another briefly. The remainder of the text is occupied with Gilgamesh's questions about the fate of various kinds of people in the netherworld (e.g., the man with one, two, three, etc. sons, the man killed in battle, the person without funerary offerings, etc.), which Enkidu describes briefly.

The other netherworld-related text, The Netherworld Vision of an Assyrian Prince, is attested on a single, poorly preserved tablet from Assur. Given its fragmentary text and enigmatic subject matter, the composition is quite difficult to describe let alone interpret, as the following will attest.[117] The prince in the text is usually identified as Assurbanipal, though this remains uncertain.[118]

The text (probably) begins with a description of a previous king's misdeeds and greed (obv. 1–15)—perhaps to be identified with the crown prince's father (thus, Esarhaddon)—and then a description of the same king—though this is uncertain since the text is quite fragmentary—in great distress and mourning (obv. 16–27). In the midst of this latter description appears a son of a scribe (obv. 17), perhaps related to or the very same scribe that is mentioned at the end of the text. In obv. 27 a certain Kumaya, "son of [. . .]," appears, who is likely the

114. See, e.g., George 1999, 100; 2003, 1:47–54 for full discussion. Foster (2001, 129) and Maul (2005, 40–42) decide to leave the twelfth tablet out of their translations altogether. The critical edition is available in George 2003, 1:726–34; for his earlier translation, see 1999, 191–95.

115. The first eleven tablets of the poem are poetic, which is one reason this last tablet is considered an appendix. See George 2003, 1:48. For the translation of *pukku* and *mekkû*, see George 2003, 2:898–900. Enkidu's different role is another reason for seeing tablet XII as an appendix.

116. For necromancy in Mesopotamia, see, e.g., Finkel 1983–1984

117. See Livingstone 1989, 68–76 for an edition; Foster 2005, 832–39 for an introduction (also Foster 2007, 97–98) and translation. The various studies cited below provide entry points into the extensive secondary literature this strange text has generated.

118. See, e.g., Kvanvig 1988, 432; Livingstone 1989, xxviii; Foster 2005, 833; 2007, 97; Sanders 2009, 161; Finn 2017, 107. The initial suggestion for this identification goes back to von Soden 1936.

same person as the crown prince (rev. 13 and 32; Assurbanipal). Kumaya intends to go to the netherworld (obv. 28), it seems, and incubates a dream via a prayer to the netherworld's queen, the goddess Ereshkigal, to do so. Ereshkigal grants the dream to him, though in it she refuses to give Kumaya what he was seeking to learn (the day of his death [?], as mentioned in obv. 33), perhaps due to an earlier offense hinted at in obv. 29 (he "angered the heart of the god, while he kept uttering blessings").[119]

Although Kumaya repeatedly curses his first dream, he prays again to Ereshkigal for a revelation and receives a dream of the netherworld. The text switches to the first-person voice suddenly (rev. 1–29) as Kumaya describes fifteen hybrid (*Mischwesen*) divine beings.[120] Kumaya also sees Nergal, the king of the netherworld, who threatens to kill him (rev. 11–15). He narrowly escapes death thanks to the intervention of Nergal's vizier, Ishum (rev. 16–17).[121] Nergal delivers a foreboding threat of violence and distress for Kumaya's future that will leave him without rest (rev. 19–20). The deity then describes the visionary's interred royal predecessor (designated *zārûka*, "your father" or "your ancestor" in rev. 26), whose reign serves as a sign to the visionary (rev. 22–28).[122] Scholars identify this king variously as Esarhaddon (Assurbanipal's father), Sennacherib (Assurbanipal's grandfather), or both in sequence (Sennacherib in rev. 22–25, Esarhaddon in rev. 26–27).[123]

Kumaya wakes up in terror (rev. 29), which the text, returning to the narrator's third-person voice, describes as something of a panic attack (rev. 29–31). In a final statement about Kumaya, the narrator writes: "He cried, 'Why have you decreed this for me?,' and in his pain he praised before the peoples of Assyria the mighty deeds of Nergal and Ereshkigal, who had come to the aid of the prince" (rev. 32).[124]

---

119. The translation follows Livingstone 1989, 70. See Sanders 2009, 158 for Kumaya's offense.

120. On *Mischwesen* in ancient Mesopotamia, see Wiggermann 1993–1995; Wiggermann 1992 is a study of the ritual texts that used figurines of these monsters for prophylactic ritual purposes. For a fascinating reading of rev. 2–10 in light of the so-called *Göttertypentext*, the Epic of Gilgamesh, and the "poetic mechanics" (84) and epistemic mode of modern science fiction, see Bach 2018. (The *Göttertypentext* was edited by Köcher 1953, who describes the text as "a description of twenty-seven statues or images of Babylonian gods and *Mischwesen* ["eine Beschribung von 27 Statuen oder Abbildungen von babylonischen Göttern und Mischwesen," 59]. Wiggermann 2018 provides references to additional relevant textual material, bibliography, and a new interpretation.)

121. As Foster notes, there are clear echoes of the myth of Erra and Ishum in this scene (2007, 97), for which see the following page.

122. How one identifies the referent of *zārûka* will dictate how one translates the term.

123. For Esarhaddon, see, e.g., Foster 2005, 833. For Sennacherib, see Sanders 2009, 160. For both in sequence, see, e.g., Finn 2017, 105–6; Kvanvig 1988, 430–34, both of whom translate the text slightly differently than, e.g., Foster and Livingstone.

124. Livingstone 1989, 76.

The text suddenly switches focus to a scribe (rev. 33–35), who, like the prince, has taken the professional position of his father and had previously been unjust in his professional dealings. The scribe takes the message of the vision to heart and, in the text's final self-referential line that provides its etiology, goes to tell the palace about the vision, which he believes will be an expiation for his previous sins.[125] Given the text's apparent criticism of the palace, as Foster writes, "it is certainly hard to see how its author could have expected royal gratitude for his effort."[126]

Although many scholars find political implications in the story, the details of such interpretations vary considerably.[127] This is due not only to the gaps in the text but also, as the above description shows, to the disagreements about the specific identity of the main actors in the story. Unfortunately, this interpretive uncertainty is unlikely to change without the discovery of more textual evidence.

Erra and Ishum

This long narrative poem from the early first millennium describes the destructive power of the god Erra, a personification of war and plague.[128] (Although originally a separate deity, Erra was conflated with the god Nergal, king of the

125. See Sanders 2009, 160–61 for this interpretation. He calls the scribe "a double of the crown prince: like the prince a sinner who occupies the post of his father" (160).

126. Foster 2007, 98.

127. E.g., Sanders 2009 offers an interesting religio-political interpretation of the text, situating it within the reign of Assurbanipal (the text's prince). Finn 2017, 104–9 interprets the text as a counterdiscourse against royal prerogatives. Kvanvig's older study is primarily concerned with the vision on the reverse of the tablet, though he too offers a political interpretation of the text (1988, 389–441).

128. The poem's incipit is *Šar gimir dadmē*, "king of all the habitations," which recalls the incipit to the Epic of Anzu. Both poems were written on a tablet found in a temple to Nergal in Tarbisu; see Saggs 1986; Annus 2001, xxv for his interpretation of the significance of this fact. See also Machinist 2005, who sees a conscious and deliberate development from Anzu to Enuma Elish to Erra and Ishum, an idea that is significantly developed in Wisnom 2014. The most recent critical edition is Cagni 1969. Several more witnesses have been found since his work, mentioned by Müller 1994b, 781; George 2013b, 66 n. 4; Foster 2005, 911, the last of whom also provides the most recent English translation (880–911) with many references to the literature. Other translations include Cagni 1977 (with extensive notes); Dalley 2000, 282–315; Bottéro and Kramer 1989, 680–727 (with discussion; see also Bottéro 1985, 221–78); Müller 1994b. Thematic studies of importance include Machinist 1983 (on rest and violence); Cooley 2008 (on the role of celestial divinatory language in the poem); George 2013b (on the poem's view of war); Ponchia 2013–2014 (on intertextuality, interpretive strategies, and the scholarly participation in the production of revelation). More briefly, Frahm 2011, 347–49 (earlier, 2010, 6–8) argues the poem is a countertext to Enuma Elish. Noegel 2011 finds alliterations, puns, and several other rhetorical devices used in the poem. Polentz 1989 is a monographic treatment of the literary features of the poem and includes a translation. Wisnom 2014 finds allusions in the poem to the Epic of Anzu, Enuma Elish, Atram-hasis, the Epic of Gilgamesh, and the Sumerian Lugal-e (208–61). Finally, she provocatively suggests a close structural affinity between the poem and the Sumerian Lamentation over the Destruction of Sumer and Ur (262–303). The precise dating of the poem is disputed, though many scholars think the poem was composed in the early first millennium. See Cagni 1969, 37–45; 1977, 20–21 for older views; George 2013b, 47 for

netherworld.) Sensing that he is held in contempt, Erra sets off on a rampage of violence depicted in the text as the grim and hellish consequences of total war in the land and its human cost in misery and death.[129] Unlike the other narrative poems discussed here, *Erra and Ishum* hardly uses direct narration of events to convey its plot. Instead, the poem is mostly composed of long monologues spoken by Erra or his vizier Ishum, in which they describe the atrocities of war, even as, apparently at one point in the poem, Erra is committing them. The narrator, after introducing the poem, appears between speeches only briefly. Thus, as George notes, "the speeches serve to tell the story and thus function as narrative."[130] As Foster has demonstrated, the poem is strikingly original and experimental, proving that first millennium scribes were quite capable of producing sophisticated literature.[131] The poem probably consisted of almost eight hundred lines originally over five tablets but is presently rather fragmentary in tablets II and III.[132] Determining who speaks when and for how long is sometimes difficult; scholars disagree in some passages. The following description follows Foster's translation by and large.[133]

Although Erra is the main protagonist of the poem, the prologue (lines 1–22) is framed by a focus on Ishum (lines 1–5, 19–22), Erra's vizier and the voice of reason and restraint in the poem.[134] Within this *inclusio*, lines 6–18 describe Erra lounging in bed, lethargic but restless for action, debating about what he should do. Erra's heart muses within him, encouraging him, his seven weapons, and Ishum all to ready themselves for battle. But Erra ultimately decides to stay in bed and make love to his wife Mami.[135] The poem then turns to Erra's seven personified weapons, which the high god Anu had given him. They address their master and taunt him for his effete decision. They praise the soldier's life on campaign and claim his lethargy has bred contempt for his divinity, noise among humans, and an overabundance of wild animals. The weapons also complain that they have grown lethargic and *need* a battle to set themselves right. Finally,

---

a brief discussion with a few recent references (to which add Cole 1994, 252, who offers tentative support for an eighth-century date).

129. For Erra sensing he is held in contempt, see I 77, I 120–121, III D 15, and IV 103 in Foster 2005, 884, 886, 901, and 906, respectively.

130. George 2013b, 47.

131. See Foster 2007, 106–9.

132. See George 2013b, 66 n. 4, who revises the most recent edition's line count based on a photograph of an unpublished tablet in Mosul, Iraq.

133. Foster 2005, 880–911.

134. For Ishum's role as a restrainer of Erra's irrational and indiscriminate violence, see recently George 2013b. The understanding of the prologue presented here depends on his treatment (48–52), which builds on Müller's translation (1994c) and interpretation of who speaks when in the opening lines (1995). The latter work provides references to alternative understandings, to which add Farber 2008. For Ishum's role as protector of humans, see Weiershäuser 2010; for Ishum's role as watchman and illuminator of city streets, see George 2015.

135. This may be the first attestation of "make love not war" in world literature.

Erra is roused to fight, despite Ishum's attempt to dissuade him, and sets out to remove Marduk, the high god of the pantheon and maintainer of cosmic order, from his heavenly seat.

When Erra sees Marduk, Erra asks him why his divine image is so lackluster, which is perhaps a pretext to get Marduk to remove himself from the throne while his image is repaired.[136] But Marduk already knows Erra's plan and will have nothing of it because the last time he left his seat, chaos broke out over the entire creation. Erra offers to maintain order this time while Marduk is away. Pleased with the idea, Marduk agrees to step down temporarily to allow his cult image to be refurbished.

Tablet II is fragmentary and the details of the narrative are difficult to understand. It begins with the description of the disarray that befalls the cosmos in Marduk's absence. Then, after a gap, the gods are debating Marduk's decision, and Ea describes how human craftsmen have restored Marduk's image. When Marduk returns, Erra seems to take offense. After another gap, the radiance of the Fox star—identified with Erra—is a harbinger of Erra's wrath.[137] The gods worry. The goddess Ishtar asks Erra to relent, but, as Ishum reports, when Erra is angry, no one can pacify him. Erra then launches into a long monologue (that continues into tablet III), in which Erra's description of his destructive abilities seems to blend into a description of his actual destructive actions. As Foster astutely notes, this speech is unique in Akkadian because "Erra narrates his own actions" in "an attempt to fuse narrative and the narrated, discourse and event."[138]

Ishum reports that Enlil has left Nippur as a result of Erra's rampage. Unsatisfied, Erra speaks to his seven weapons, encouraging them to go out and wreak more harm. Ishum questions Erra about his actions, but Erra seems to feel entitled to the mayhem, citing the fact that Marduk had abandoned his post previously. "It seems," George suggests, "that his earlier absence from his temple has produced an instability in the cosmos which has repercussions even after he reoccupied it."[139] Two more speeches from Ishum end tablet III. The first reveals the earthshaking might of Erra's destruction; the second, separated from the previous by a break, reports his conquest of Babylon, home to Marduk's temple.

Tablet IV opens with another long speech from Ishum reporting more of Erra's war atrocities. The language is graphic and brutal, conveying clearly the author's

---

136. Tablets I and II of the poem contain much lore surrounding the divine image, its origins, construction, and repair. For more about divine images and the Mesopotamian concepts of deity, see, e.g., Berlejung 1998 (more briefly, 1997); Dick 1999; Walker and Dick 2001; Krebernik 2002; and various articles in Porter 2009; Pongratz-Leisten 2011.

137. For an exposition of this and other celestial features in the poem, see Cooley 2008.

138. Foster 2005, 880.

139. George 2013b, 54.

view that war is indeed hell.[140] Ishum describes the destruction of one Babylonian city after another: Babylon, Sippar, Uruk, and Der, all the while inserting quotations within his speech from others. He cites Marduk's lament over Babylon, the deity Ishtaran's over Der, and a city mayor's remorse of the day of his birth. Ishum even quotes Erra himself as the deity carries out his killing spree with relish. Ishum's speech continues until Erra interrupts and decrees universal civil war. After listing eight different peoples and the social structures of land, city, house, man, and brother, he proclaims, they "must not spare (one another), let them kill each other! Then, afterward, let the Akkadian, arise to slay them all, to rule them, every one" (IV 135–136).[141] This enigmatic Akkadian (*Akkadû*) may be the Babylonian people or an individual; the matter is disputed among scholars.[142]

Finally, Erra sends Ishum out to fight the only sensible battle in the poem, that is, one against the traditional enemies of Babylonia.

The final tablet, tablet V, begins with Erra addressing the gods. He says,

"No doubt I intended evil in the bygone lapse,
"I was angry and wanted to lay waste the people.
"Like a hireling, I took the lead ram from the flock,
"Like one who did not plant an orchard, I was quick to cut it down,
"Like a scorcher of the earth, I slew indiscriminately good and evil.
    (V 6–10)
. . . .
"So too no one can reason where one is in a frenzy.
"Were it not for Ishum my vanguard, what might have happened?"
    (V 12–13)[143]

Ishum responds in a terse three-line speech, in the middle of which he exclaims, "No doubt this is true, now calm down, let us serve you!" (V 18).[144] A happy Erra now utters a blessing on Babylonia, after which the voice of the long-silent narrator breaks into the text. He praises Erra (called Nergal here) and Ishum, summarizes the poem, and then mentions how the author received the text in a dream and wrote it down faithfully. Tablet V concludes with Erra's words blessing all those who honor the poem, including a promise of safety for any house that possesses a copy of it.

---

140. This is in stark contrast to, e.g., the Neo-Assyrian royal inscriptions where the king's military exploits and humiliating defeats of the enemy are celebrated. For the poem's depiction of war, see George 2013b, noting esp. p. 56.

141. Foster 2005, 907–8.

142. For the former, see, e.g., Cagni 1977, 57 n. 151; and Müller 1994b, 798 n. 136a; for the latter, e.g., Dalley 2000, 315 n. 52; George 2013b, 57.

143. Foster 2005, 908–9.

144. Foster 2005, 909.

Interpreters largely agree that the most explicit concerns of the poem center on the destructive personality of Erra and the hellish nature of war. Within this broad sphere of agreement, however, interpretations differ significantly. Does the poem depict a particular historical event (i.e., military disaster) in Babylonian history? And if so, which event?[145] Should we interpret the poem, rather, as a vivid and gruesome depiction of the chaos that ensues with civil war or armed rebellion against the established order of things?[146] Or, as George suggests, is the poem a kind of allegory against "war's incomparable horror and irresistible force"?[147] "If we remove the cloak of allegory," George writes, "what Kabti-ilāni-Marduk wants of his poem is that it open the eyes of people—everywhere and at all times—to Erra as the most violent power in the world, that is to the terrible reality of war . . . ; and that it serve as a warning not to hold Erra 'in contempt', that is not to go to war lightly."[148] In his view, the poem repudiates Erra's style of warfare—indiscriminate, aggressive, and offensive—and upholds Ishum's, which is justified, measured, and defensive.[149] In contrast to this philosophical interpretation, Cagni, though admitting the poem's didactic potential, prefers to interpret Erra and Ishum as a kind of cultic hymn, intended for use in the temple veneration of Erra.[150]

Despite the difficulty adjudicating between competing modern interpretations of the poem, there is one *ancient* interpretation of the text for which there is compelling evidence. This ancient interpretation stems from the last lines of the poem, save three, which read:

> The house in which this tablet is placed,
> though Erra be angry and the Seven be murderous,
> The sword of pestilence shall not approach it,
> safety abides upon it. (V 57–59)[151]

Apparently, some ancient readers took these lines literally as there are several amulets inscribed with excerpts of the poem (fig. 12).[152]

---

145. See Müller 1994b, 781–82 for a roundup of suggestions, which range from the eleventh to the seventh century BCE, with literature.

146. See, e.g., Foster 2007, 67; Müller 1994b, 782.

147. For the poem as allegory, see George 2013b, 47, 65; see also Cagni 1977, 14. Quotation from George 2013b, 48.

148. George 2013b, 65.

149. George 2013b, esp. 61–63, developing an idea in Bottéro 1985. For an interpretation of Erra and Ishum as contrasting and balancing characters in a cycle of rest and violence, see Machinist 1983, esp. 223–26.

150. Cagni 1977, 14.

151. Foster 2005, 911.

152. See, e.g., Reiner 1960. In light of this, note, also, Machinist 1983, who develops the provocative idea that Erra and Ishum as a whole may be understood "as a kind of incantation—that form of literature where, one might argue, the power of language is most explicitly recognized and

FIGURE 12. A stone amulet inscribed
with an excerpt from Erra and Ishum.
Photo © Trustees of the British Museum,
London.

Epic of Gilgamesh

The final narrative poem to be considered here is the most famous of them all,
a story well-known outside of the esoteric circles of Assyriology and ancient
Near Eastern Studies.[153] Its existential appeal to modern readers, no doubt, is due

---

celebrated, and put to use, as here, both to expose a problem of potentially cosmic dimensions to its
source and to offer a means for its resolution or neutralization" (226).

153. The most recent critical edition is George 2003, which provides extensive and indispensable
introductions to various facets of the epic and matters related to its history and reconstruction, a full
treatment of all known tablets relating to any stage of the epic in Akkadian, a synopsis and exegesis
of the SB version, a critical edition of the Sumerian Bilgames and the Netherworld, lines 172–end,
translations and critical philological notes of all the edited material, a very rich bibliography of past
studies, editions, and translations, and finally hand copies of various cuneiform tablets used in the
edition. (For reflections on the editing process [modern and ancient], see George 2008.) Wasserman 2011a and Streck 2007a offer quite substantial reviews of this important work. Wasserman also
offers reflections on the circulation of the epic in ancient times as well as its "resonances" with other
texts. Tigay 1982, though now dated, retains its usefulness for understanding the literary evolution
of the Epic (also discussed in George 2003, 1:3–70). Translations based on George's critical edition
include George 1999; Foster 2001 (updated in Foster 2019); Maul 2005 (among others), all of which
include brief introductions and/or other materials (e.g., George and Foster also include the related
Sumerian tales; Maul offers brief commentary). Since 2003, more tablets belonging to the epic have
been published or identified. See, e.g., Maul 2005, 11; Arnaud 2007, nos. 42–45 (with George 2007d);
George 2007b; 2009, no. 6; Al-Rawi and George 2014; Jiménez 2014, 99–102; George 2018. For brief
introductions to the epic, see George 2010b and more imaginatively George 2007c. A longer introduction intended for general readers (in German) is available in Sallaberger 2013. For reflections on
the genre of the epic, see George 2005a. Two classic literary critical essays in English remain useful: Moran 1995; Jacobsen 1976, 195–217, both of which are reprinted in Foster's translation (2001,
171–207). Abusch 2015b offers a collection of critical essays addressing various aspects of the epic.
North and Worthington 2012 provide a comparative reading of the epic alongside Beowulf. For the

to the humanity of its protagonist, who undergoes profound personal growth—
from cocksure warrior to weary sage. His unrealistic search for immortality
leads him on a desperate journey; his utter failure to achieve his goal moves
him in the end to acquiesce, frustrated and in tears, to his mortality. Gilgamesh
returns from his journey and, as the epic tells us from its very beginning, records
all that he had learned on a stela for posterity. The poem invites its audience to
find this stela and read it to learn from his hard-won wisdom. In this way, the
epic affirms that Gilgamesh's absurd failure was in fact a kind of spiritual victory, worthy of attentive reflection, which it receives the world over to this day.[154]

The literary history of the epic is rather long and well-studied. Gilgamesh,
or rather, Bilgames, as he is called, appears in five Sumerian episodic tales, the
earliest of which dates back to the Ur III period (2112–2004 BCE). Three of these
episodes, adapted for their new setting, make their way into the Akkadian epic
at various points in its prolonged evolution.[155] The Akkadian epic itself is first
attested in about sixteen OB tablets.[156] Unfortunately, the evidence is still too
fragmentary to determine the full outline of the OB version, though it is clear
that the essential outline of the story, as compared with the SB version summarized below, is already in place by this time.[157] George, the most recent editor
of the epic materials, describes the tablets from the next period of available
evidence, the mid- to late second millennium, as "a disparate group of tablets
that hold little in common," hailing from Nippur, Ur, Emar, Ugarit, Megiddo,
and Hattusa.[158] One or other of these tablets provides a glimpse at the civilizing
of Enkidu, the journey to the cedar forest, the incident with Ishtar and the bull of
heaven, and Enkidu's demise, but again the full extent of the epic (in its various
editions) in this period is not entirely known. That must await the material that

modern literary history and reception of the epic, see Ziolkowski 2011. For an account of its loss
and rediscovery, see Damrosch 2006. Many other studies, too numerous to list here, have appeared
since the new critical edition. The bibliographies attached to the various works cited in this section
provide points of entry to this literature. For discussions of the epic outside Assyriology and ancient
Near Eastern studies, see, e.g., Maier 1997 and esp. Ziolkowski 2011.

154. Gilgamesh has been translated into a great many modern languages. I know of no published
exhaustive listing.

155. For the relationship between the Sumerian tales and the OB Epic of Gilgamesh in Akkadian, see George 2003, 1:7–22; Tigay 1982, 21–38; with a focus on the Huwawa narrative, Fleming
and Milstein 2010.

156. See George 2003, 1:159–286 for an edition of the OB material; add now George 2009,
no. 6; 2018.

157. For the most up-to-date sketch of what is present and what is missing, see George 2003,
1:23–24. Note, however, the recent implications of a new OB tablet for the episodes involving
Enkidu and the harlot (George 2018).

158. George 2003, 1:24. See George 2003, 1:287–347; now also Arnaud 2007, nos. 42–45; with
George 2007d for editions of this material. George identifies six tablets from the Neo-Assyrian
period as probably related to some MB recension of the poem. See George 2003, 1:26 and the editions on pp. 348–75.

comprises the SB version from the many first millennium libraries, the editing together of which is attributed to the famed scholar Sin-leqi-unninni.[159]

According to George's recent reconstruction, Sin-leqi-unninni's SB version of the poem originally had nearly 3000 lines distributed over 11 tablets.[160] In his estimation, the preserved sources, now more than 116 tablet pieces comprising at least 73 manuscripts, provide about 2400 of these original lines.[161] Since many of these lines included in the count are still fragmentary, George believes that we still only possess about two-thirds of the original poem.[162] Appended to these 11 tablets is tablet XII, a prose addition and partial Akkadian translation of an earlier Sumerian tale in which the ghost of Enkidu, whom Gilgamesh now calls "my servant" rather than "my friend," describes to Gilgamesh what he has seen in the netherworld (see page 101, above). The reason for this addition is unclear. It may have been added, as George notes, "to round off the Series of Gilgameš with a sermon that leaves no uncertainty about the fate of each and every mortal."[163] If this is the case, the final tablet makes explicit the wisdom Gilgamesh learned in his impetuous journey.

The epic begins with two prologues, which together illustrate, as William Moran notes, how "Gilgamesh not only has *emūqān*, physical strength, but *nēmēqu*, wisdom."[164] The first prologue, added for the SB redaction, is retrospective in character and sapiential in tone, commending a mode of reading that elevates thoughtful reflection over royal celebration.[165] It describes Gilgamesh as

[He who saw the Deep, the] foundation of the country,
[who knew ...,] was wise in everything!
. . . .
He saw the secret and uncovered the hidden,

---

159. For more about this important figure in Mesopotamian literary and scholarly tradition, see Beaulieu 2000.

160. See George 2003, 1:379–741 for an edition of the SB material.

161. The numbers are from George 2003, 1:379, which are now too low since new pieces have been identified, some of which remain unpublished.

162. George 2003, 1:418–19.

163. George 2003, 1:32. See also his survey of other opinions on pp. 49–52 and his own further speculations (as he calls them) on pp. 52–54.

164. Moran 1995, 2331.

165. See likewise Tigay 1982, 143–46, 149; George 2003, 1:29, 32–33, where he notes, "In so far as we know it, the Old Babylonian poem was a hymn to heroism and kingly might, bursting with the confident exuberance of a young literature in a period of cultural rebirth. Sîn-lēqi-unninni's sombre meditation is less confident and more introspective, and brings the same despondent resignation to its consideration of the human lot that is displayed in other meditative works of the mid- to late second millennium, especially the Poem of the Righteous Sufferer [i.e., Ludlul bel nemeqi] and the Babylonian Theodicy. The reworking of the poem was consequently a modernization in thought as well as in language and style. The result was a text that holds much in common with what we call 'wisdom literature.'" For so-called "wisdom literature," see page 172.

he brought back a message from the antediluvian age.
He came a distant road and was weary but granted rest,
[he] set down on a stele all (his) labours. (I 1–2, 7–10)[166]

And at its conclusion, the first prologue issues this call to the reader, which emulates the opening lines of the Cuthean Legend of Naram-Sin:[167]

[*Find*] the tablet-box of cedar,
[*release*] its clasp of bronze!
[*Open*] the lid of its secret,
[*lift*] *up* the tablet of lapis lazuli and read out
all the misfortunes, all that Gilgameš went through! (I 24–28)[168]

Gilgamesh, this prologue claims, learned great wisdom in his travails and brought back secret knowledge from before the flood. He inscribed this hard-won wisdom on a stela and interred it in a foundation. Although on one level the foundation deposit trope establishes future kings as the implied audience of the poem (since only future kings would discover such deposits), on another it provides an etiology for the poem, since the inscribed stela must be none other than the lapis lazuli tablet in the tablet box.[169] The poem is therefore *not* hidden away for an exclusive, future royal audience but openly available to all who hear or read its text.[170]

This first prologue also celebrates the majestic walls and city plan of Uruk as a shining example of Gilgamesh's royal achievements.

He built the wall of Uruk-the-Sheepfold,
of holy Eanna, the pure storehouse.
See its wall which is like a *strand of wool*,
view its parapet which nobody can replicate!
Take the stairway that has been there since ancient times,

166. George 2003, 1:539.
167. See page 125, below, for a treatment of this text.
168. George 2003, 1:539.
169. On kings as future audience, see Pongratz-Leisten 1999b. As for etiologies, the epic contains several folk explanations for items within a Mesopotamian cultural purview, including the existence of a spring and fall New Year's (II 268–269 and see George 2003, 1:457–58), the marking of inducted temple-slaves (III 124; George 2003, 2:816), the rift between the Lebanon and Anti-Lebanon ranges (V 133–134; George 1990), the various fates of Ishtar's lovers in tablet VI, the use of the thigh portion in Ishtar's cult (VI 154–159; George 2003, 1:476), the prostitute's ambiguous social position (VII 102–123, 151–61; George 2003, 1:481), the use of sails (X 180–183; George 2003, 1:502–3), the habits of particular bird species (XI 148–156; George 2003, 1:517), the use of cultic jewelry (XI 165–167; George 2003, 1:518), sea bed diving (XI 287–293; George 2003, 1: 524), and the molting of snakes (XI 305–307; George 2003, 1:525). For the stela being the lapis lazuli tablet, see also George 2003, 1:446; Tigay 1982, 144.
170. For an interpretation of the secrecy motif in the epic, see Lenzi 2014.

and draw near to Eanna, the seat of Ištar,
that no later king can replicate, nor any man.
Go up on to the wall of Uruk and walk around,
survey the foundation platform, inspect the brickwork!
(See) if its brickwork is not kiln-fired brick,
and if the Seven Sages did not lay its foundations!
[One *šār* is] city, [one *šār*] date-grove, one *šār* is clay-pit, half a *šār* the
    temple of Ištar:
[three *šār*] and a half (is) Uruk, (its) measurement. (I 11–23)[171]

A portion of these lines appear again at the conclusion of tablet XI (I 18–23 //
XI 323–328) after Gilgamesh's failed attempts to achieve immortality.[172] Framing the poem in this way may imply a kind of existential interpretation: the
city is the only enduring monument to Gilgamesh's unique reign; it will be his
legacy long after his own biological demise.[173] Or, following George's recent
interpretation, the frame intends to communicate that, although mortal individuals come and go—no matter how mighty they are or how stubbornly they resist
their inevitable fate, the collective destiny of humankind, represented by the
ever-enduring city, is immortalty.[174]

   In contrast to the reflective first prologue, the second prologue, beginning in
I 29, which we know was the opening line to the OB version of the epic, focuses
on the young, inexperienced Gilgamesh, the warrior-king, whose extraordinary
characteristics (one-third human, two-thirds divine) and royal accomplishments
set him apart from all others.[175] The expected celebration of his physical features
and martial prowess comes to the fore here, which leads into the first conflict
of the poem: Gilgamesh is a tyrant. He does not allow the men and women of
Uruk any rest. The former he tires out with sport and the latter with his sexual
advances. When the women finally cry out to heaven for redress, the high god
Anu commissions the goddess Aruru to fashion Gilgamesh's equal, a wild man
of the steppe named Enkidu, who runs with the animals and undermines the
success of an unnamed hunter.[176]

   Terrified and dismayed by Enkidu, the hunter seeks his father's and then Gilgamesh's advice about what to do. Both advise the hunter to engage the services

---

171. George 2003, 1:539.

172. George 2003, 1:725.

173. So, e.g., Jacobsen 1976, 208. George characterizes this view as the conventional one (2012, 234).

174. George 2003, 1:527–28; in a fuller manner George 2012.

175. What is now the first cola of tablet I, line 29 in the SB recension of the epic (*šūtur eli šarrī*) is cited as the incipit in the colophon of the Pennsylvania tablet, which bears an OB version of the epic (see George 2003, 1:180–181).

176. For Enkidu's role in the epic as Gilgamesh's double, see Hawthorn 2015.

of the prostitute Shamhat, who can tame the wild man with her sexual charms and turn the animals against him. The next time Enkidu comes to the watering hole, the hunter is waiting for him with Shamhat, who seduces Enkidu.

> For six days and seven nights Enkidu, erect, did couple with Šamḫat.
> After he was sated with her delights,
> he turned his face toward his herd.
> The gazelles saw Enkidu and they started running,
> the animals of the wild moved away from his person.
> Enkidu had defiled his body so pure,
> his legs stood still, though his herd was on the move.
> Enkidu was diminished, his running was not as before,
> but he had *reason*, he [was] wide of understanding. (I 194–202)[177]

Abandoned by his herd, Enkidu looks to Shamhat for direction. She encourages him to find a place at Uruk, where Gilgamesh, she confides, has already had dreams about Enkidu and about how Gilgamesh will find in him an intimate friend who is his equal.[178] But Enkidu entertains the idea of entering Uruk to challenge Gilgamesh, an idea Shamhat discourages.

At the start of the imperfectly preserved tablet II Shamhat clothes Enkidu and leads him to a shepherd's outpost, a place in between the wilds of the steppe and the civilization of Uruk, where they introduce Enkidu to the staples of Mesopotamian diet: bread and beer.[179] After a substantial break in the text, we find Enkidu in Uruk blocking Gilgamesh from entering the bride's chamber

177. George 2003, 1:549–51.

178. Several times in the epic Gilgamesh's love for Enkidu or his treatment of him is likened to or is suggestive of the love or treatment of a wife/woman. The significance of this idea varies among interpreters, with some seeing a sexual relationship between Gilgamesh and Enkidu (see esp. Walls 2001 in the chapter entitled "The Allure of Gilgamesh: The Construction of Desire in the Gilgamesh Epic") and others seeing this as a means to express the tight emotional bond between friends (e.g., Foster 2009, 178–79). With regard to the dreams, the literature on dreams in the epic is extensive. See Noegel 2007, 58–82; Böck 2014 for recent discussions with previous literature.

179. The OB version in the Pennsylvania tablet preserves a fuller account of this episode, which makes the civilizing intent of the passage quite clear:

> The harlot opened her mouth,
> saying to Enkidu:
> "Eat the bread, Enkidu, the thing proper to life;
> drink the ale, the lot of the land."
> Enkidu ate the bread until he was sated,
> he drank the ale, seven jugs (full).
> His mood became free, he was singing,
> his heart became merry and his face shone bright.
> The barber treated his body so hairy,
> he anointed himself with oil and became a man. (iii 94–108; George 2003, 1:177)

to exercise the right of *jus primae noctis*, that is, Gilgamesh was about to enter the bride's bedroom to have sexual relations with her before the groom. A great fight ensues. Another break interrupts the SB narrative; in the continuation of the story, in which Gilgamesh introduces Enkidu to his mother, Gilgamesh and Enkidu have become close friends. Shortly after that rather poorly preserved episode Gilgamesh proposes that the two of them journey to the cedar forest and defeat the terrifying monster-guardian Humbaba. Enkidu and the city elders counsel against the rash and dangerous journey, but Gilgamesh is determined to go through with it.

At the beginning of tablet III the elders encourage Gilgamesh to trust the experience of his new-found friend and charge Enkidu to bring Gilgamesh back safely. The two heroes then visit Ninsun, the mother of Gilgamesh, to receive her blessing for the journey. The news of their adventure saddens Ninsun, who goes before Shamash, the sun god and god of justice, to ask him to protect her son on this journey and in battle against the mighty Humbaba.[180] She then calls Enkidu before her and announces her intention to adopt him as her own. After some broken sections the tablet ends as it began: with the elders encouraging Gilgamesh to trust the experience of his new-found friend and charging Enkidu to bring Gilgamesh back to them safely.

The journey to the cedar forest that Gilgamesh and Enkidu undertake in tablet IV is narrated in five highly repetitive cycles. It begins with the two heroes covering a distance in three days that would take a normal person a month and a half to travel. At the end of each three-day journey, Gilgamesh and Enkidu set up a ritual assemblage to incubate a dream. Gilgamesh falls asleep. And then in the middle of the night he awakens with a start, frightened by a foreboding nightmare. In each case, he tells Enkidu about the nightmare, who then rather unconvincingly interprets it—the prerogative of Gilgamesh's mother earlier in the epic—in a favorable way. Throughout the five iterations of this cycle only the lines describing the five dreams and their interpretations differ substantially, though in most cases the dreams and interpretations are poorly preserved. The tablet concludes with a conversation between Gilgamesh and Enkidu, in which Gilgamesh encourages his friend, who is apparently having second thoughts about their attack, to be strong and continue on to their anticipated fight.

Tablet V opens with Gilgamesh and Enkidu standing at the edge of the cedar forest. After a break and a rather broken passage of dialogue, we find the two heroes confronting Humbaba. Humbaba insults Enkidu. Gilgamesh seems to be losing his nerve, but Enkidu encourages his friend to press on. When another break in the text ends, the three are already in the throes of battle. Shamash

---

180. For Shamash as protector of travelers, see the Great Hymn to Shamash, lines 65–72 (Foster 2005, 630; Lambert 1960, 130–31).

sends the winds against Humbaba, and Gilgamesh gets the better of the monster. Humbaba pleads for his life before the king, promising to deliver as much cedar as Gilgamesh could ever want. Enkidu encourages Gilgamesh to ignore these pleas. And then Humbaba appeals to Enkidu to intercede for him, initiating a repetitive exchange between the two (that is incompletely recovered and separated by a long break), in which Enkidu worries that killing Humbaba will anger Enlil, the high god of the pantheon. After another short lacuna, Humbaba curses Gilgamesh and Enkidu and then the two dispatch him. The tablet concludes with the two heroes felling cedars in the forest and sending them downstream. Enkidu also fashions a door to take back to Nippur as a votive offering to its resident deity, Enlil, perhaps to appease his anger for Humbaba's murder.

As tablet VI opens Gilgamesh is cleaning himself up. Ishtar, the goddess of sex and war, takes notice and proposes they wed: "Come, Gilgameš, you be the bridegroom! Grant me your fruits, I insist! You shall be my husband and I will be your wife!" (VI 7–9).[181] Her proposal comes with a promise of power, honor, and prosperity. But Gilgamesh will have none of it. Rather than offering a simple rejection, however, he bitterly spurns her. Marrying her, he claims, would be the death of him.[182] And then in what seems to be a condensation of a rich but mostly lost mythology Gilgamesh recites the litany of lovers that Ishtar has taken and broken.[183] Angered at these insults, Ishtar goes before her father, Anu, god of the heavens, and insists he give her the Bull of Heaven to bring drought upon Uruk.[184] As the bull is wreaking havoc on the inhabitants, Enkidu and Gilgamesh attack and slay the bull. They strip the animal of its massive horns, which Gilgamesh dedicates to Lugalbanda, his father. The people of Uruk, in contrast to their previous complaints about Gilgamesh, now honor and celebrate the heroes for their salvific feat. Gilgamesh and Enkidu make merry at a feast, where the latter falls asleep. Enkidu awakens just as the tablet is concluding to reveal a foreboding dream.

The dream must have been recounted at the beginning of tablet VII, which is not yet recovered in the SB version. Assuming it was similar to the contents of the Hittite paraphrase of the episode, Enkidu learns in his dream that the gods are angry at Gilgamesh and Enkidu for killing Humbaba and the Bull of Heaven. They decide that one of them must die, and Enkidu is the one selected.[185] When the SB text is available again, Enkidu is expressing regret, directed at the cedar

181. George 2003, 1:619.

182. For a close reading of this episode in light of the broader epic and its construction of desire, see Walls 2001, 34–50.

183. See George 2003, 1:473–74; Abusch 1986.

184. Her threat consists of raising the dead to consume the living, just as she threatens in Descent of Ishtar and Ereshkigal does in the myth Nergal and Ereshkigal.

185. See George 2003, 1:478.

door he made earlier, about the trouble he spent making it and dedicating it to Enlil at Nippur. Apparently, Enkidu believes this pious act has not granted him the favor he sought. Instead, he thinks now that he should have given it to Shamash, the god that had come to their aid. Gilgamesh, saddened by the announcement of his friend's impending death, tries to comfort Enkidu and promises to intercede with the gods on his behalf. But Enkidu discourages him from wasting his time; Enlil's decree is unchangeable.

At dawn of the following day, Enkidu launches into a lengthy curse against the hunter and then Shamhat the prostitute.[186] Shamash scolds Enkidu for his bitter curses, reminding him that without the prostitute he would never have met his friend Gilgamesh, who, according to Shamash, "[will make] weep for you the people of Uruk, he will make them sob for you.... [And] he, after you are gone he will have himself bear the matted hair of mourning, [he will don] the skin of a lion and go roaming the [wild]" (VII 144–147).[187] Thus, Enkidu turns to bless her and then recounts to Gilgamesh yet another dream he had had. In this final dream Enkidu recounts how he was dragged off to the netherworld, where he saw the shades of great kings and priests.[188] Foreshadowing the lesson Gilgamesh will learn by the epic's end, the poem implies here that no one can cheat mortality; everyone, no matter how great, comes to the same shadowy end. The fragmentary remainder of the tablet describes Enkidu's final days. Presumably he dies with Gilgamesh standing beside him, though these lines are still lost.

Lament and funerary preparations fill tablet VIII, which unfolds over a four-day period. The day after Enkidu's death, Gilgamesh takes up a long lament (nearly sixty lines), which concludes with these poignant words:

Hear me, O young men, hear [me!]
Hear me, O elders [of the populous city, Uruk,] hear me!
I shall mourn Enkidu, my friend,
like a professional mourning woman I shall lament bitterly.
The axe at my side, in which my arm trusted,
the sword of my belt, the shield in front of me,
my festive garment, the girdle of my delight:
a wicked wind has risen up against me and robbed me.
O my friend, a mule on the run, donkey of the uplands, panther of the
    wild,

186. The curse on the latter parallels the curse against Atsushunamir in Descent of Ishtar (see George 2003, 1:479–80).

187. George 2003, 1:641–43. Gilgamesh also mentions the donning of a lion's pelt and roaming the wild in tablet VIII, lines 90–91 (see George 2003, 1:657).

188. The description of the netherworld is similar to the ones given in both Descent of Ishtar and Nergal and Ereshkigal (see George 2003, 1:481–82).

my friend Enkidu, a mule on the run, donkey of the uplands, panther of
   the wild!
We (it was) who joined forces and climbed the [uplands,]
seized the Bull of Heaven and [killed it,]
destroyed Ḫumbaba, who [dwelt in the Cedar] Forest.
Now what sleep is it that has seized [you?]
You have become unconscious and cannot hear [me!] (VIII 42–56)[189]

The next day Gilgamesh begins the funerary preparations, calling on artisans
to make a statue of his friend.[190] After a brief break in the text, Gilgamesh is
speaking to his deceased friend, assuring him that he will honor him with a public funeral, after which Gilgamesh will "don the skin of a [lion] and [go roaming
the wild]" (VIII 91).[191] On the third day Gilgamesh chooses an opulent funerary
offering—a very wide array of expensive items, the listing of which occupies
nearly forty lines—that will accompany Enkidu to the netherworld. Meat is prepared to offer to the netherworld gods during a funerary banquet. And then in a
long, formulaic passage (about seventy lines in the incompletely recovered text)
Gilgamesh dedicates a litany of the grave goods to various netherworld deities.
It seems that Gilgamesh continues the ritual activities surrounding Enkidu's
funeral on the fourth day. The significance of these actions is unclear, since the
tablet breaks off some two dozen lines before its end.[192]

   Tablet IX begins with the sorrowful musings of a weeping Gilgamesh. Dev-
astated by the loss of his friend and confronted by the inevitability of death,
he laments: "I shall die, and shall I not then be like Enkidu? Sorrow has entered
my heart. I became afraid of death, so go roaming the wild, to Ūta-napišti, son
of Ubār-Tutu, I am on the road and travelling swiftly" (IX 3–7).[193] The decision
to visit Uta-napishti, the immortal flood hero, whom the gods settled at the
end of the world, brings the major theme of the epic to the fore: Gilgamesh is
determined to resist and to undo his mortality. After a cryptic dream episode
and a harrowing run-in with lions, Gilgamesh arrives at a distant mountain
in the East named Mashu, which is guarded by a couple of scorpion-human
hybrid beings (*Mischwesen*).[194] They recognize Gilgamesh immediately as a

   189. George 2003, 1:655.
   190. As George explains, "the purpose of the statue was apparently to represent the deceased
at the funerary banquet and, after the interment of the body, either to act as the focus for the regular
post mortem rites through which the Babylonians paid their respects to the dead or, as part of the
interment, to provide a home for the deceased's ghost" (2003, 1:487).
   191. George 2003, 1:657.
   192. See George 2003, 1:664–65.
   193. George 2003, 1:667.
   194. See George 2003, 1:491–92 for a discussion of the run-in with lions. On *Mischwesen* in
ancient Mesopotamia, see note 120, above.

king with a semidivine pedigree and question him about how he had arrived at such a distant locale. A break interrupts. When the text begins again Gilgamesh is telling the scorpion-people that he is seeking Uta-napishti and the key to immortality. The scorpion-people warn Gilgamesh that the journey, which no one had ever undertaken before, would require traveling twelve double hours through thick darkness on a path that is associated with the sun.[195] Another gap of some thirty-five lines occurs here. When the text resumes, the scorpion-man allows Gilgamesh to pass. In a highly repetitive passage of some thirty lines Gilgamesh races through the path of the sun and comes out before the sun (*lām šamši*) catches up with him. What he sees when he emerges is a fantastical forest of trees made from precious stones. Watching Gilgamesh as he walks through this forest of wonders is presumably Shiduri, the ale-wife Gilgamesh will meet in tablet X.

Seeing Gilgamesh coming from a distance, Shiduri bars her door and takes refuge on her roof. After a broken exchange, Gilgamesh briefly describes his exploits with Enkidu (X 31–34); Shiduri questions his unkempt appearance, deep sorrow, and aimless wandering (X 40–45); and then Gilgamesh asks why he should *not* be in this condition, since Enkidu's death has overwhelmed him (X 47–71). In the conclusion of his reply, Gilgamesh says:

> The case of [my friend] Enkidu [was *too much* for] me to bear,
> [so on a distant path] I roam the wild.
> (For) I, [how could I stay silent?] How could I stay quiet?
> [My friend, whom I love, has turned] to clay,
> my friend Enkidu, whom I love, has [turned to] clay.
> [Shall not I be like] him and also lie down,
> [never to rise] again, through all eternity? (X 65–71)[196]

This conversation, with a small variation, is repeated when Gilgamesh comes upon both Ur-shanabi, the boatman Gilgamesh will meet next, and Uta-napishti, the flood hero he seeks.[197]

After describing his condition, Gilgamesh asks Shiduri about the way to Uta-napishti.[198] She explains that no one but Shamash, the sun god, can cross

---

195. For various interpretations of this difficult geographical detail, see George 2003, 1:494–97.
196. George 2003, 1:683.
197. Shiduri's questions in tablet X 40–45 are repeated by Ur-Shanabi and Uta-napishti in X 113–118 and 213–218, respectively. Gilgamesh's reply in X 47–71 to Shiduri is then repeated in X 120–148 to Ur-Shanabi and again in X 220–248 to Uta-Napishti, but in these two cases they also include the insertion of the same four lines that Gilgamesh speaks to Shiduri in X 31–34 (prior to her questions) in lines 128–131 and 228–231.
198. These lines are also repeated after Gilgamesh's exchange with Ur-shanabi (see X 150–154).

FIGURE 13. A two-column tablet bearing part of the flood story in the Epic of Gilgamesh, identified by George Smith in 1872. Photo © Trustees of the British Museum, London.

the ocean, which includes the Waters of Death and separates their location from Uta-napishti's distant shore. Then she mentions Ur-shanabi, Uta-napishti's boatman, who presumably ferries supplies to him. Impulsively, Gilgamesh, thinking he could force the boatman to ferry him to Uta-napishti, rushes to ambush Ur-shanabi and destroy the "stone ones," who are apparently his crew. After the repetitive exchange mentioned above, Ur-shanabi explains to Gilgamesh that he himself has destroyed the crew who were providing the punting poles necessary for the crossing. Now Gilgamesh must cut the three hundred poles they will need, the boatman says. No sooner as said, Gilgamesh has cut them, and the two have shoved off for Uta-napishti's shore. When they run out of punting poles, Gilgamesh fashions a sail out of their clothing—an etiology for the technology, it seems—to propel them the rest of the way.

After Gilgamesh greets Uta-napishti and they go through the same exchange as when he met Shiduri and Ur-shanabi, Gilgamesh describes his long, arduous journey. But Uta-napishti seems unsympathetic to his hardship. In a long speech that runs to the end of the tablet Uta-napishti scolds Gilgamesh for his fool's errand and then, after a gap, explains to him the inevitability of death and its unknowable schedule.

> [*You,*] you kept toiling sleepless (and) what did you get?
> You are exhausting [*yourself with*] ceaseless toil,
> you are filling your sinews with pain,
> bringing nearer the end of your life.
> Man is one whose progeny is snapped off like a reed in the canebrake:
> the comely young man, the pretty young woman,
> *all* [*too soon in*] their very [*prime*] death abducts (them).
> No one sees death,
> no one sees the face [of death,]
> no one [hears] the voice of death:
> (yet) savage death is the one who hacks man down. (X 297–307)[199]

The gods, Uta-napishti explains in the last couplet of the tablet, have decreed life and death for humanity. But they did not reveal the day of a person's death. Uta-napishti's long speech here, as George has noted, encapsulates "the essence of the poet's message."[200] But Gilgamesh apparently does not yet grasp its meaning.[201]

At the start of tablet XI Gilgamesh seems disappointed by the normal appearance of Uta-napishti ("your form is not different, you are just like me," XI 3) and puts aside the idea of assaulting him, apparently to wrest from him the secret of immortality ("I was fully intent on doing battle with you, [*but*] in your presence my hand is stayed," XI 5–6).[202] Instead, Gilgamesh asks how Uta-napishti managed to secure immortality for himself ("How was it you attended the gods' assembly, and found life?" XI 7), which introduces the long story of the flood (198 lines in XI 9–206).[203] Uta-napishti presents this antediluvian tale, which is probably based on some version of the same flood story as is found

---

199. George 2003, 1:697.
200. George 2003, 1:504.
201. For a close reading of Uta-Napishti's discourse on death in X 301–321, see Helle 2017.
202. George 2003, 1:703 for both quotations.
203. Translation from George 2003, 1:703.

in Atram-hasis, as the first of two secrets he tells Gilgamesh (recall I 7–8).[204] At the conclusion of the story Uta-Napishti asks Gilgamesh a very similar question to the one that had prompted the diluvian digression: "But now, who will bring the gods to assembly for you, so you can find the life you search for?" (XI 207–208).[205] The question is rhetorical; no one can assemble the gods for Gilgamesh. The implication: Gilgamesh cannot find the immortality that he was looking to acquire from Uta-napishti. "The difference" between the two men, writes literary historian David Damrosch, "is not one of character but of era: the day is past when the gods would convene in assembly to change a man's destiny on earth. . . . When Gilgamesh visits Utnapishtim, history visits the world of myth, to learn from it and at the same time to measure the distance of [Gilgamesh's] modern times from the days of Utnapishtim the Distant."[206]

As if to prove to Gilgamesh that achieving immortality is impossible, Uta-napishti challenges the road-worn king to stay awake for seven days. But Gilgamesh falls asleep immediately and remains so for a full week. Uta-napishti and his wife mark each day's passing with a baked loaf set out alongside Gilgamesh. When he awakens, he protests that he had only just fallen asleep, though the loaves in various states of decomposition prove otherwise. Despairing, Gilgamesh asks Uta-napishti:

> "How should I go on, Ūta-napisti? Where should I go?
> The Thief has taken hold of my [*flesh.*]
> In my bed-chamber Death abides,
> and wherever I might turn [*my face*], there too will be Death."
>   (XI 243–246)[207]

The flood hero offers no reply. Instead he commands the boatmen to bathe Gilgamesh and clothe him with fresh garments. The two then set off for their return journey. Just as they have left, Uta-napishti's wife implores her husband to grant Gilgamesh a parting gift, something for his toil and hardship. While the boat is still near to shore, Uta-napishti reveals to Gilgamesh a second secret, the location of a rejuvenating plant in the Apsu, the subterranean home of Ea, god of water and wisdom. Once Gilgamesh obtains the plant, he tells Ur-shanabi his plan to test it on an old man in Uruk. But on the return trip to Uruk a snake steals the plant while Gilgamesh is bathing. Adding insult to injury, the snake

---

204. For Atram-hasis, see page 80, above; George 2003, 1:18; Tigay 1982, 214–18. For notes on this flood account and comparisons with others preserved from ancient Mesopotamia, see George 2003, 1:509–21. For the flood tradition more broadly, see Chen 2013; Finkel 2014.

205. George 2003, 1;717.

206. Damrosch 2003, 73–74.

207. George 2003, 1:719.

demonstrates the effectiveness of the plant by sloughing off its skin as it slithers away, an obvious etiology for why snakes molt. Frustrated by the loss, Gilgamesh weeps and laments the bankruptcy of his efforts. He has utterly failed.

Gilgamesh and Ur-shanabi return to Uruk, where Gilgamesh, in a final speech, encourages Ur-shanabi to examine the walls of Uruk. The walls, the poem seems to imply, are permanent and exist in contrast to the impermanence of human life. It is only with these last seven lines, repeating the lines from Sin-leqi-unninni's prologue, that Gilgamesh learns the lesson his journey was to instill: no amount of effort can alter the fact that humans are mortal.

Legends of Akkadian Kings

In the late twenty-fourth century BCE a king by the name of Sargon (Akk. *Šarru-kīn*, "the king is true, legitimate") came to power and established the first empire in Mesopotamian history by way of a series of military victories in northern Mesopotamia, Syria, and western Iran.[208] He and his dynasty are called the Akkadians because the imperial capital was Akkade, a city which is still lost to us but probably lay near the confluence of the Diyala and Tigris rivers. Sargon reigned from 2334–2279 BCE; the ten kings comprising his dynasty ruled until the mid twenty-second century (2279–2154 BCE). Although political unity was under constant threat as the old, independent city-states chafed under the novelty of central rule, sources indicate that arts and crafts flourished under the Sargonic dynasty as did trade, which brought merchants from as far away as Bahrain and the Indus River Valley. Many Old Akkadian Sargonic royal inscriptions have come down to us in OB copies, which scribes made, apparently, by copying actual inscriptions from votive statues that had been placed in the sanctuary at Nippur, a city of great religious significance in early Mesopotamian history as it was the home of the high god Enlil.[209]

Sargon was remembered throughout Mesopotamian history as conqueror par excellence; in fact, he became something of a model or measure for other would-be royal greats. For this reason, several later kings adopted Sargon as their own name, including the important Neo-Assyrian usurper who ruled from 721–705 BCE and founded the Neo-Assyrian Sargonid dynasty, which included kings Esarhaddon, Sennacherib, and Assurbanipal after him. The most

---

208. For a discussion of the use of the term "legend" as opposed to "saga" and "epic," see Haul 2009, 9–13.

209. For an overview of the Akkadian kings in history and literature, see Franke 1995a. A brief survey of the political history is presented in Van De Mieroop 2007, 63–73; Kuhrt 1995, 44–55. Their royal inscriptions are edited in Frayne 1993; studied by Franke 1995b. The definitive study of the Akkadian empire in its many facets is Foster 2016.

memorable among (the first) Sargon's successors was his grandson Naram-Sin (2254–2218 BCE), who centralized and organized the empire, successfully defended it from multiple enemy attacks, and declared himself a god while still living—an act unheard of among earlier Mesopotamian kings. Despite Naram-Sin's brilliant military successes and savvy administrative skills, later tradition remembers him mostly in negative terms: he is the king who overstepped and suffered at the hands of the disciplining gods. The Sumerian text Curse of Akkade already bears witness to this negative memory, which was perpetuated in several Akkadian compositions as well. The later tradition seems therefore to fall into a kind of symmetry, one king, Sargon, became a positive model and the other, Naram-Sin, a negative one for kings of later times.[210]

Aside from references in the so-called historical omens and chronicles, there are about two dozen compositions that describe the exploits of these great kings of the Akkadian Empire distributed unevenly throughout Mesopotamian history.[211] The earliest witness for one of the compositions is an Old Akkadian school tablet describing the great revolt against Naram-Sin, known also from historical inscriptions.[212] The latest witnesses are among tablets from the great archives of the first millennium. The compositions are also found in the Akkadian language on tablets from el-Amarna in Egypt, the Hittite capital of Hattusa (in modern Turkey), which also includes some compositions translated into Hittite, and the Old Assyrian trading colony at Kanesh (also in modern Turkey).[213] All of these textual witnesses taken as a whole present clear evidence for the texts' widespread appeal. The overwhelming majority of the compositions, however, are known from tablets found at Old Babylonian sites. Unfortunately, most of

210. So Foster 2007, 17. Franke has captured the literary treatment of the two kings in relation to what we know about them from their royal inscriptions well when she writes, "in narratives, Sargon is always praised as a radiant hero, a master of difficulties, a discoverer of the new. He thus bears characterizations that are lacking from his own inscriptions but that are readily found in those of Naram-Sin. Almost opposite is the image we gather of Naram-Sin from narratives about him. Although we occasionally meet with lines that applaud Naram-Sin's deeds and strength, the most consistent portrait drawn of him is that of a king who chooses wrongly when faced with difficult decisions" (1995a, 838).

211. The number is approximate due to uncertainty about how some tablets relate to one another, whether slightly deviating duplicates of the same composition or a discrete composition (see Haul 2009, 15). Most recently, all of the pertinent texts have been cataloged with publication information and references to secondary literature in Haul 2009, 15–31. Most of the texts are edited in J. Westenholz 1997a, who also includes a couple of related letters (see her catalog on pp. 4–5). Haul 2009 studies a selection in more detail (with updated editions). Several of the texts are translated in Foster 2005, inter alia. The titles of some of these compositions vary from scholar to scholar.

212. For an edition of this text, see Haul 2009, 313–17; J. Westenholz 1997a, 221–29 (with related OB texts edited on 230–61). Haul 2009, 33–94 discusses the text in detail and its relationship to the authentic royal inscriptions.

213. For the most recent edition of this text (which is not included in J. Westenholz 1997a), see Haul 2009, 339–54; note also Alster and Oshima 2007. See Foster 2005, 71–75 for a translation.

the compositions are still imperfectly recovered due to the fragmentary nature of the various witnesses.

Just as the compositions' geographical and chronological distribution varies so too does their tone, which, as Joan Westenholz summarizes, runs the gamut "from panegyric poetry to narrative poetry to prose, with monologues and dialogues more prevalent than third-person narratives."[214] Despite this variation, one constant theme is the military action of the two great kings.

According to Michael Haul, nine of the compositions are to be categorized as pseudepigraphic fictional *narû*s ("stelae"). That is, these texts adopt a literary conceit in which the composition is presented as the king's very own words, spoken retrospectively in the first-person, even though in fact the texts were composed by someone else. The author has adopted the voice of the king and placed words in his mouth. Thus the labels pseudepigraphic and fictional. Also, the compositions read as though they were actually inscribed on a stone monument—a *narû*, a stela—and erected for posterity to read.[215] Two texts of this type, The Cuthean Legend of Naram-Sin and The Birth Legend of Sargon, are treated here as important representatives of the Akkadian royal legends; other pseudepigraphic fictional *narû*s are treated later in the book.[216]

The Cuthean Legend of Naram-Sin is a well-known and well-studied legend about Naram-Sin's hubris.[217] The text of this fictional poem is preserved in several editions.[218] The OB edition is known from two manuscripts from Sippar. The MB edition comes to us from at least one, perhaps two tablets from the archives of the Hittite capital, Hattusa, attesting to the poem's far-flung popularity. The SB edition is the best attested with six tablets from Nineveh, one from Sultantepe, and one from Kish.[219] The discussion here focuses on the 180 lines of the SB edition, which seems to be a truncated version of what must have been a much longer poem in earlier centuries.

---

214. J. Westenholz 1997a, 6.

215. For a thorough review of the debate about the existence, definition, and population of this category of texts, see Haul 2009, 95–187, who lists ten of the Akkadian legends as *narû* texts on p. 168, one of which is not in the first-person voice and not certainly fictional (see pp. 33–57 for full discussion).

216. See page 145, below.

217. The most recent edition is J. Westenholz 1997a, 263–368. More recent studies include an essay from Pongratz-Leisten 2001, an interpretive summary with literature in Foster 2007, 15–17, a monograph on the Akkadian royal legends by Haul (2009), and Finn's treatment of the text in her study of compositions critical of royalty in the first millennium (2017, 61–69).

218. For reasons to consider this text a fiction, see Haul 2009, 186. For examples of verse structure and poetic features in the text, see Haul 2009, 176–85, who has a higher opinion of the composition's literary artistry than does J. Westenholz (1997a, 299).

219. See J. Westenholz 1997a, 263, 269, 281, 296–97. In addition, the composition is attested in several tablets written in Hittite; see the references provided for text 21B in J. Westenholz 1997a, 3–15.

The text begins with an exhortation to its audience to "[o]pen the tablet-box and read out the stela [*narû*], [which I, Naram-Sin], son of Sargon, [have inscribed and left for] future days."[220] This language establishes Naram-Sin as the narrator, who has left his story behind on a stela for his audience to read and glean wisdom, much like Gilgamesh in the SB prologue of that epic. The opening lines therefore also provide the text's etiology and indicate a didactic purpose.[221] The conclusion to the text in even clearer terms reiterates Naram-Sin's exhortation to read from the stela he has erected in the hometown of the god Nergal, king of the underworld. That is, the stela was erected in the city of Cutha, which gives the poem its name: the "Cuthean Legend." The lines read:

> You, whoever you are, be it governor or prince or anyone else,
> whom the gods will call to perform kingship,
> I made a tablet-box for you and inscribed a stela for you.
> In Cutha, in the Emeslam,
> in the cella of Nergal, I left (it) for you.
> Read this stela!
> Hearken unto the words of this stela![222] (149–155)

After the three-line introduction, Naram-Sin begins his retrospective account with a brief review of the fate of king Enmerkar, an early Mesopotamian king of great renown and subject of Sumerian epic poems.[223] Just as Naram-Sin does later in the text, Enmerkar queries the gods via extispicy, that is, via the examination of animal entrails for a favorable omen from the gods. The oracular reply is somewhat broken, but the consequences are rather clear: Enmerkar receives a harsh judgment—why is not clear, though it may have been for disobeying the omens; he dies—his corpse is mentioned twice in broken lines; and his ghost as well as those of his descendants are condemned to drink muddied water in the netherworld.[224] As a result of this ignoble death, Enmerkar cannot leave behind a stela to instruct subsequent kings about the army that he had defeated. This failure to erect a stela seems to be the most important point of Naram-Sin's

---

220. J. Westenholz 1997a, 301.

221. It also, according to Haul (2009, 172), is a signal that the text is not an actual royal inscription but a fiction.

222. J. Westenholz 1997a, 327. I have changed Westenholz's spelling of Kutha to Cutha for consistency.

223. I am following J. Westenholz's restorations and interpretations of lines 4–30; as she describes in her notes to these lines, there are several difficult issues for the interpreter and thus alternative renderings (1997a, 300–8).

224. J. Westenholz 1997a, 294 believes Enmerkar's harsh judgment was for disobeying the omens.

review. Though this failure might seem of little consequence at this point in the narrative, it takes on much greater significance in light of the poem's conclusion.

The text turns now to introduce Naram-Sin's enemies, who are described as mixed-creatures ("A people with partridge bodies, a race with raven faces" in line 31), created by the gods and raised in the mountains, which are peripheral to Mesopotamia proper and the traditional source of Mesopotamian enemies.[225] Seven kings—a conventional number, all brothers—lead a multitudinous army.[226] For reasons that are unclear, this army moves against a number of locales surrounding the Mesopotamian heartland, devastating several armies in their wake.[227] A concerned Naram-Sin sends out a scout with instructions to prick one of the mountain soldiers with a pin to see whether they bleed, that is, to see whether they are human or demonic. Having learned that the barbarian soldiers are indeed men, he consults the gods via extispicy, the wording of which parallels Enmarkar's own inquiry. In his first of three internal dialogues—an unusual rhetorical strategy in Akkadian materials, Naram-Sin decides to go on campaign without the gods' favorable oracle. His words may be the most defiant assertion of human autonomy in all of Akkadian:

Thus I said to my heart (i.e., to myself), these were my words:
"What lion (ever) performed extispicy,
"What wolf (ever) consulted a dream-interpreter?
"I will go like a brigand according to my own inclination.
"And I will cast aside that (oracle) of the god(s); I will be in control of myself."[228] (79–83)

But his plan does not go well. Over the course of three years his troops sustain incredibly high losses: 120,000, 90,000, and 60,700 men, respectively, after which time Naram-Sin confesses his distress: "I was bewildered, confused,

225. The line about mixed creatures, however, may be corrupt. See J. Westenholz 1997a, 308, whose translation is cited above. In the MB edition Ea, god of wisdom and water, who is often associated with the creation of people, is credited with their creation. He also seems to endow them with the ability to increase all sorts of diseases and evils in the land, where they must roam without the security of a city or the pleasantries of civilized life, such as beer and bread (J. Westenholz 1997a, 286–89).

226. 360,000, the number of enemies stated in the text, is also conventional in the Mesopotamian sexagesimal numbering system, $60 \times 60 \times 10$.

227. The reason seems to be indicated in line 48. When a scout is said to have seized them (*iṣbassunūtī-ma*) in some way (J. Westenholz translates "A scout (tried to) intercept them" [1997a, 313]), the mountain army reacts by striking their thigh (*imḫaṣū šaparšun*). This enigmatic phrase has elicited a variety of interpretations, none of which is more than a contextual guess. As Westenholz writes, "these ad hoc interpretations demonstrate our ignorance of many aspects of the ancient culture of Mesopotamia" (1997a, 312). A few of the locales named in the context are unknown or disputed.

228. J. Westenholz 1997a, 317.

sunk in gloom, desperate, and dejected" (line 88).[229] He again offers his inner musings, which center this time on his reputation and predicament rather than his autonomy:

> Thus I said to my heart, these were my words:
> "What have I left to the dynasty!?
> "I am a king who does not keep his country safe
> "and a shepherd who does not safeguard his people.
> "How shall I ever continue to act so that I can get myself out
>   (of this)!?"[230] (89–93)

All manner of evils had descended upon the land in the train of the enemy horde's successes. Ea, god of wisdom and frequent advocate for humanity, intercedes with the great gods on behalf of Naram-Sin, and the tide turns:

> When the New Year's Festival of the fourth y[ear arri]ved,
> with the fervent prayer which Ea [. . .] of the [great] gods,
> I [sacr]ificed the holy sacrifices of the New Year Festival.
> I sought the holy omens.[231] (104–107)

The second consultation via extispicy again echoes the language used in previous inquiries. And this time, apparently, the gods smile upon Naram-Sin's military endeavors, because he has an immediate success: he captures a dozen enemy combatants. In his final internal dialogue, his words show he had learned his lesson: "Thus I said to my heart, [these were my words]: 'Without omens, I will not bring myself to [impose] punishments'" (124–125).[232] He consults the gods about the fate of the captured men, and the gods decree mercy. In a long explanation (seventeen lines), Ishtar, goddess of sex and war, manifested in her planetary form Dilbat (Venus), explains that the gods themselves will impose their punishment upon the enemy in due time. In the final two lines of his retrospective account, Naram-Sin states, "To the great gods I brought (the captives) as tribute, I did not lay hand on them to kill them."[233] This merciful treatment stands in stark contrast to, for example, Neo-Assyrian annals, which often describe the brutal violence inflicted upon their enemies.

---

229. The OB edition describes the devastation to the land in terms of a flood: "Like the flood (overflowing the banks) of the canal, it transformed the land" (J. Westenholz 1997a, 277). Translation from Westenholz 1997a, 319.

230. J. Westenholz 1997a, 319. See also the OB edition (J. Westenholz 1997a, 273).

231. J. Westenholz 1997a, 321.

232. J. Westenholz 1997a, 323.

233. Foster 2005, 354 (lines 145–146); compare J. Westenholz 1997a, 327 (lines 147–148).

After this scene, the text turns to the audience, as cited above. The advice that Naram-Sin has left on his stela is not what one would expect to hear from a Mesopotamian king. Naram-Sin tells the audience not to fear (their enemies, presumably); rather, they should secure their cities and possessions and then hang up their weapons.

> Tie up your weapons and put (them) into the corners!
> Guard your courage! Take heed of your own person!
> Let him roam through your land! Go not out to him!
> Let him scatter the cattle! Do not go near him!
> Let him consume the flesh of your offspring!
> Let him murder, (and) let him return (unharmed)!
> (But) you be self-controlled, disciplined.
> Answer them, "Here I am, sir!"
> Requite their wickedness with kindness![234] (164–172)

The text concludes with an address to the wise scribe and to the reader once again.

> Wise scribes,
> let them declaim your inscription.
> You who have read my inscription
> and thus have gotten yourself out (of trouble),
> you who have blessed me, may a future (ruler)
> Bless you![235] (175–180)

These last lines may provide the key to understanding the role of Enmerkar at the beginning of the text. Because Enmerkar did not erect a stela describing his travails, Naram-Sin could not learn from him and thereby keep himself from trouble. Naram-Sin therefore wishes his stela will do for his readers (future kings) what Enmerkar could not do for him. And, in turn, just as they will bless Naram-Sin—something he could not do for Enmerkar, a future ruler will bless them.

Although the explicit audience is defined as future rulers, it seems the text is also aware of scribes who would be reading the text and making their own inscriptions. In fact, we know that many scribes did read the text; the composition was used in first-millennium Babylonia during the first stage of scribal education alongside several other literary texts, all of which, as Paul-Alain Beaulieu

---

234. J. Westenholz 1997a, 329.
235. J. Westenholz 1997a, 331.

FIGURE 14. The obverse of a student tablet containing an excerpt of The Sargon Birth Legend in the second of four columns. Photo © Trustees of the British Museum, London.

notes, "present a consistent and distinctive image of the monarchy. They depict the king always in the same role; not as conqueror, administrator, or provider of social justice but as religious leader and teacher of wisdom."[236] Thus, it seems that the latest version of the text, despite its explicit address to a future ruler, was used (along with other texts) to shape perceptions of royal ideology in the minds of scribes who likely would serve the king during their careers.

The Sargon Birth Legend may be treated more briefly. It is a poorly preserved composition, known only from a few Ninevite tablets and one student excerpt

236. For the text's use in scribal education, see Gesche 2000, 148–50. Quotation from Beaulieu 2007a, 142. Finn interprets the scribe at the end of this text as inserting "his value as an agent for the king's memorialization" and thereby implicitly criticizing certain royal behaviors and commending others (2017, 68–69).

from the city of Dilbat, all of which are from the first millennium (fig. 14).[237] The
first part of the composition, a mere thirty-three lines, is universally acknowl-
edged to present a fictional account of Sargon's birth, as told by the king himself
(in the first-person) later in his life. The second part—if it even belongs with the
first—is difficult to understand. It comprises a series of statements and questions
about the behavior of animals. The present treatment is limited to the first part
of the text, which is considered by most scholars to be a clear example of the
pseudepigraphic fictional *narû* genre.

The first eleven lines of the poem convey the story of Sargon's birth under
unusual circumstances.

> Sargon, the mighty king of Akkade, am I.
> My mother was an en-priestess(?), my father I never knew.
> My father's brother inhabits the highlands.
> My city is Azupurānu, which lies on the bank of the Euphrates.
> She conceived me, my en-priestess mother, in concealment she gave me
> birth,
> She set me in a wicker basket, with bitumen she made my opening
> water-tight,
> She cast me down in the river from which I could not ascend.
> The river bore me, to Aqqi the water-drawer it brought me.
> Aqqi the water-drawer, when lowering his bucket, did lift me up,
> Aqqi the water-drawer did raise me as his adopted son,
> Aqqi the water-drawer did set me to his gardening.[238] (1–11)

These lines utilize the well-known folkloric motif of the child in danger at birth,
familiar to many modern readers from the story of Moses's birth in the biblical
book of Exodus, in order to present Sargon as extraordinary from birth.[239]

Without another word about Sargon's childhood, the text moves straight to
his divine election and coming to the throne. While gardening for his father,
Ishtar loved Sargon and, as a result of this love, it is implied, he became king.
He ruled for an uncertain number of years over the "black-headed people,"
a traditional description of Mesopotamians, who were imagined metaphorically

237. The most recent edition is J. Westenholz 1997a, who refers readers to Lewis 1980 for a
fuller treatment of the piece. Other translations include Foster 2005, 912–13; Hecker 2001, 55–57.
238. J. Westenholz 1997a, 39–41.
239. For Moses, see Exod 2. For a thorough study of the folkloric motif, see Lewis 1980. The
lines also contain several words with a double meaning. E.g., the city of Sargon's birth, Azupuranu,
is also the name of an abortifacient used in ancient Mesopotamia (J. Westenholz 1997a, 39); Aqqi,
the name of the water-drawer who found Sargon, means "I poured (water)."

to be sheep; the king was their shepherd.[240] After a brief description of Sargon's military expeditions to far-off and inaccessible places, Sargon offers a challenge to "whatever king will arise after me" to match his feats of valor.[241] In this way, Sargon presents himself as the paradigmatic king, by which all other kings should measure their stature and success.

Historiographical Texts

At the most general level, Akkadian historiographical texts are those texts we identify as containing presentations of historical actors and their actions.[242] These presentations, however, are no less dispassionate or objective than the actors or their actions that populate the texts. Indeed, the texts to be discussed in this section are tendentious documents, mainly concerned with supporting and perpetuating specific aspects of royal ideology. They therefore revolve thematically around the king, his legitimacy, his pious and just acts, and, especially in later Assyria, his military prowess. This thematic focus means, on the one hand, that these documents must be scrutinized carefully when utilized in historical reconstructions and, on the other, that many of them are quite useful evidence for understanding royal ideology as it changed through ancient Mesopotamian history.[243]

Thousands of Akkadian texts have been identified as historiographical, ranging from the late third millennium through the final centuries before the Common Era. These texts are inscribed on a very wide variety of material supports, including clay bricks, tablets, cylinders, and prisms; metal tablets; stone tablets, stelae, statues, and slabs; cylinder seals (and their impressions); weights; beads; a wide variety of votive items; various temple and palace architectural features; rock faces; and even gaming boards. Some were put on public display; some were filed away as copies in temple or palace archives; and some were buried

240. He ruled for possibly fifty-four years, according to the Sumerian King List. See J. Westenholz 1997a, 40.

241. J. Westenholz 1997a, 45.

242. Grayson 1980 is still of fundamental value for its masterful outline and synthesis of Babylonian and Assyrian historiographical texts, though some points are disputed and outdated. (Old Akkadian inscriptions from Sargon of Akkade and his successors [2334–2154 BCE] do not factor significantly in the treatment.) Other overviews include Liverani 1995; Charpin 2010, 215–46, whose research has focused on Neo-Assyrian and Old Babylonian periods, respectively. The value-laden judgments that the above definition of historiographical texts reflects should not be underestimated or the interpretive standpoint of the one making it since historical texts sometimes mythologize history and mythological texts may sound historiographical in some ways. See Pongratz-Leisten 2001, 19.

243. See, e.g., Van De Mieroop 1999, 39–85 for a useful discussion of both aspects.

in foundation deposits, to be discovered by a future king. Through intense cataloging, translation, and critical study of the form and content of these texts,
scholars have organized this mass of data into manageable and useful categories.
The ones used here are based on A. Kirk Grayson's survey.[244] According to his
analysis, there are three main types of texts: royal inscriptions, chronographic
texts, and historical-literary texts.[245]

Royal Inscriptions

Grayson divides these prose texts into four subcategories: Labels, Dedicatory
Inscriptions, Commemorative Inscriptions, and Letters to Gods (from Assyria
only).[246]

244. Grayson 1980. For a slightly different general classification, see Renger 1980–1983.

245. I have followed Grayson in excluding royal letters, some of which (genuine or pseudepi-
graphical) were copied centuries after the kings' deaths and used in the scribal curriculum. For an
overview, see, e.g., Foster 2007, 21–23, 26–27 for the late period; 2009, 201–2 for all periods. See
also Frahm 2005. Mary Frazer has written a dissertation on this corpus at Yale University (see Frazer
2015; 2013, 195 n. 50; the latter article lists several royal letters).

246. Selections of Akkadian royal inscriptions in translation appear in various anthologies,
mentioned on page 77, above. Many Assyrian inscriptions are available in English in Cogan 2008;
Chavalas 2006; Grayson 1972, 1976. A smaller selection appears in German in Hecker 2004 (which
also includes some chronographic texts and treaties); Borger 1984. The creation of editions of all
royal inscriptions is an on-going project, first started at University of Toronto under A. Kirk Grayson, continuing under the direction of Grant Frame (NA inscriptions) at University of Pennsylvania
and Jamie Novotny (NB inscriptions) at University of Munich (see https://www.en.ag.geschichte
.uni-muenchen.de/research/rinbe/index.html). These projects have published the following volumes
of Akkadian royal inscriptions in various series: Frayne 1993, 1990; Frame 1995; Donbaz and Grayson 1984; Grayson 1987, 1991, 1996; Tadmor and Yamada 2011; Leichty 2011; Grayson and Novotny
2012, 2014; Novotny and Jeffers 2018. The remainder of the inscriptions of Assurbanipal are still in
progress (see http://oracc.museum.upenn.edu/rinap/rinap5/). Stein 2000, 127–78 presents the Kassite
inscriptions, some of which may not be authentic (i.e., these inscriptions are only known from copies
made centuries after the kings supposedly lived and the names of these kings are only known from
these late documents [e.g., Agum-kakrime, which is briefly treated with pseudepigraphic fictional
narûs below on page 147]). Langdon 1912 is the last full edition of the NB royal inscription corpus,
which is now woefully outdated. Da Riva 2013 publishes the inscriptions of Nebuchadnezzar, carved
on rock faces in the Biqa' Valley in Lebanon. Schaudig 2001 offers editions of the inscriptions of
Nabonidus, the last NB king, and Cyrus the Great, the first Persian to rule Mesopotamia. Novotny's
project, mentioned above, will publish all of the NB royal inscriptions in new editions. The last royal
inscription, which commemorates the Hellenistic king Antiochus I Soter (281–261 BCE), is edited
in Kuhrt and Sherwin-White 1991; studied in Beaulieu 2014. (Stol and van der Spek offer a new
but preliminary edition at http://www.livius.org/cg-cm/chronicles/antiochus_cylinder/antiochus
_cylinder1.html). As George 2011 shows, the corpus is still growing. The secondary literature on
royal inscriptions is too extensive to list here in full. A few studies must suffice. Franke 1995b is
important for Old Akkadian inscriptions. Fales 1999–2001 provides an update on various aspects of
Neo-Assyrian royal inscriptions (see previously Fales 1981). Da Riva 2008 introduces and surveys
Neo-Babylonian royal inscriptions (see earlier Berger 1973). And Radner 2005 contains much of
general interest related to royal inscriptions, especially with regard to the perpetuation and remem-
brance of the king's name.

Labels

Labels are the most basic of these inscriptions.[247] They are inscribed on a vast array of items throughout Mesopotamian history to denote royal ownership. A representative example, appearing "on a number of bricks, some stone objects, and a bronze sword" from the Assyrian city of Assur during the reign of Adad-narari I (1305–1274 BCE), gives a sense of these simple texts:[248]

> (Property of) the palace of Adad-nārārī, king of the universe, son of Arik-dīn-ili, king of Assyria, son of Enlil-nārārī (who was) also king of Assyria.[249]

Sometimes labels have a commemorative purpose in that they indicate the king's role in building a particular edifice, usually the one in which the object is a part.[250]

Dedicatory Inscriptions

Dedicatory inscriptions, like labels, are also rather straightforward texts and appear on a variety of objects. The two distinguishing features of dedicatory inscriptions are (1) they always appear on objects of a cultic nature, including parts of a temple, and (2) these objects are explicitly dedicated to a deity; thus, they do not belong to the king. Dedicatory inscriptions appear throughout Mesopotamian history in Sumerian as well as Akkadian. Typically, they follow a basic format: the name of the deity to whom the object is dedicated, the name of the king who is dedicating the object, and a verb of dedication. A purpose clause as well as the name of the object being dedicated may also be included.[251] A simple example that appears on a silver bucket from Neo-Assyrian times illustrates the form:

> For the god Adad, who resides in the city Guzana, his lord: Esarhaddon, king of Assyria, son of Sennacherib, king of Assyria, made (this bucket) for his (long) life.[252]

247. Admittedly, it is quite a stretch to consider these labels literature in any meaningful sense of the word. I include them for the sake of completeness.

248. Quotation from Grayson 1987, 172.

249. Grayson 1987, 173. According to Grayson, one brick that bears this inscription provides evidence for the first example of movable type (1987, 172).

250. For this reason Grayson treats them with commemorative inscriptions (1980, 155–56), to be treated below.

251. See Grayson 1980, 157, 162 for details.

252. Leichty 2011, 282.

Commemorative Inscriptions

Commemorative inscriptions are probably the most interesting of those presented so far. In general, they do precisely what the name suggests: they commemorate royal actions. Because these actions are mainly concerned with building activities and military exploits, they are of particular interest to historians.[253] Sometimes these texts were inscribed in both Sumerian and Akkadian, though after the Old Babylonian period, the use of Sumerian becomes increasingly rare. As with Sumerian royal inscriptions, building activities dominate Babylonian commemorative inscriptions from Old Babylonian times down to the last royal inscription in Akkadian under Antiochus I (281–261 BCE). Military exploits, contrary to contemporary Sumerian royal inscriptions, have a prominent place in the Old Akkadian inscriptions and begin to appear in Assyrian royal inscriptions during the Middle Assyrian period (starting with Adad-narari I, 1305–1274 BCE); military exploits come to dominate Assyrian inscriptions until their demise with the Neo-Assyrian Empire in the late seventh century.[254]

When commemorative inscriptions are arranged in chronological order, they are called *Annals*, which only occur among Assyrian texts and are first attested in the inscriptions of Tiglath-Pileser I (1114–1076 BCE; see fig. 15).[255] When military exploits are arranged geographically, they are called *Display Texts*, though this is a misnomer since these were sometimes not displayed at all but interred in buildings as foundation deposits. A good example of a text that was displayed is the Standard Inscription of Assurnasirpal II (883–859 BCE) at Kalhu. As mentioned in the earlier treatment of repetition, this text was inscribed hundreds of times across stone reliefs showing various scenes in his North West Palace.[256] The text's ornamental character is underlined by the fact that scribes often truncated the text to fit the available space on the inscribed object, even abruptly ending in the middle of a sentence at times.[257] (See the palace relief in fig. 10.) The categorical distinction between annals and display texts, though useful,

253. Of course, a wide variety of topics are mentioned in the inscriptions so that they are of interest to scholars of the history of religions (e.g., Vera Chamza 2002), historical geography (e.g., Parpola and Porter 2001), military history (e.g., De Backer 2012), construction of gender (e.g., Chapman 2004), and many other areas of historical inquiry.

254. See Grayson 1987, 128. Babylonian royal inscriptions are not entirely devoid of military exploits. For two inscriptions with military events from the reign of Samsu-iluna, king of Babylon (1749–1712 BCE), see Frayne 1990, 388–91; for another from the little known king Ashduni-iarim of Kish, see Frayne 1990, 654–55.

255. Grayson 1991, 7. Another first in this king's inscriptions is a description of the royal hunt, which continues to appear in Assyrian royal inscriptions thereafter. A striking example appears in an inscription from Assur-bel-kala (1073–1056 BCE) (Grayson 1991, 99, 103–4).

256. See page 60, above.

257. See Russell 1999, 39–40.

FIGURE 15. A tablet bearing a section of Tiglath-Pileser I's annals, showing long lines of prose that stretch across the entire tablet. Photo © Trustees of the British Museum, London.

is not absolute, as the extraordinarily long inscription of Assurnasirpal II in the Ninurta temple at Kalhu demonstrates.[258]

As one would expect, these texts show variations in form throughout the centuries, which cannot be reviewed here in detail, and can vary significantly in length from a handful of lines to several hundred.[259] Their content, although broadly centered on the king's activities mentioned above, may be presented in a monotonous or formulaic fashion or with a creative flair. The following description of Adad-narari II's military might (reigned 911–891 BCE) is an example of a creative moment in the inscriptions, though it will no doubt strike the modern reader as overly indulgent.

> [I scorch] like the god Girru (fire god), [I overwhelm like the deluge, . . .],
> I have no successful opponent; [I am belligerent like a young bull], I strike
> [the wicked like] the fierce [dagger, I constantly blow like the onslaught

258. See Grayson 1991, 191–223.
259. For generalizations, see Grayson 1980, 150–55 and 160–61.

of the wind, I] rage like the gale, I uproot (people) [like hair] of the skin, [I overpower like the net], I enclose [like the trap], at the mention of [my strong] name [the princes of the four quarters] sway like reeds in a storm, [at the onset of my campaign] their weapons [melt] as though in a furnace.[260]

Commemorative texts often conclude with an address to a future king (who may find the inscription) to honor it, with curses for anyone who removes or defaces it, and/or with a prayer/blessing, especially in the Neo-Babylonian period, for the life of the king.[261]

Letters to the Gods

In first-millennium Assyria a particular historiographical text developed in which the king wrote a letter to the god to report his activities.[262] People had been writing prayers in the form of letters to their gods since the third millennium. The Assyrian letters to the gods are different in that they are complex, literary creations that utilize sophisticated language and imagery not found in the very simple letter prayers of earlier times.[263] Like the commemorative inscriptions, these prose texts are written in the first-person voice of the king. Aside from this constant, they are rather heterogeneous in form and content, making a summary of them all but impossible here. The most important (and well-preserved) example of these texts is Sargon's letter to Assur, the chief god of the Assyrian pantheon, concerning the king's eighth campaign, which reports in celebratory fashion the king's military expedition against their northern enemy Urartu.[264] In the following passage Sargon describes his defeat of Rusa I, king of Urartu, in a manner that shows the close connection between royal piety and military victory:

> Assur, my lord, heard my just discourse, it pleased him. To my honest plaidoyer gave he heed, he accepted my plea. He dispatched to my side his furious weapons which, when they appear, crush the disobedient from where the sun rises to where it sets.... With only my single chariot and

---

260. Grayson 1991, 157.
261. For the Neo-Babylonian period, see Da Riva 2008, 97–98.
262. See Grayson 1980, 157–59; Pongratz-Leisten 1999a, 210–65; Foster 2007, 91.
263. See the OB letter prayer cited on page 44, above.
264. Given its good state of preservation, Sargon's letter of his eighth campaign has become the model example or paradigm for our understanding of the genre (so Pongratz-Leisten 1999a, 261). See Foster 2005, 790–813 for a brief introduction and English translation. The most recent monographic treatment is Mayer 2013, who offers an extensive introduction, edition of the text, and German translation. Hurowitz 2008 offers literary observations on the text.

the horsemen who ride with me, who never leave me in hostile or friendly territory, the elite squadron of Sin-ah-usur, I fell upon him like a furious arrow, I defeated him and forced him into retreat. I made a huge carnage of him, spreading out the corpses of his warriors like malt and choking the mountain slope with them. I made the blood flow like river water in chasms and gullies, I stained red the lowlands, foothills, and ridges, as if with anemone-flowers.[265]

Interestingly, letters from the addressed deities (Ninurta, an important warrior god, in one case and Assur in several others) also exist, in which they respond to what the king had reported. The deity speaks in the first-person and addresses the king directly using second-person pronouns. One of the better preserved among these letters, Assur's response to Assurbanipal's report on the civil war with his brother, Shamash-shum-ukin, offers this interesting passage that again illustrates the coincidence of piety and power:

At the command of my great divinity you conquered their cities and took heavy booty as plunder from them to Assyria. By my great support you brought about the defeat of his warriors. The rest you [handed over] to me alive and (later) slew with weapons in Nineveh, city of your lordship. I sent before you my fierce weapons to defeat your enemies. At the mention of your name, which I made great, your troops go victoriously wherever there is fighting with weapons. Because of your in[cessant] prayers and supplications [with which] you beseeched my great divinity, I stood at your side and [poured out the blood] of your enemies.[266]

Over all, we have about eleven letters sent between gods and kings, many of which, unfortunately, are rather fragmentary.[267]

Chronographic Texts: King Lists and Chronicles

Two kinds of texts populate this category, according to Grayson: *King Lists*, which he defines as "a list of royal names with the possible addition of regnal years and filiation," and *Chronicles*, "a prose narration, normally in the third person, of events arranged in chronological order."[268] Despite Grayson's

265. Foster 2005, 798.
266. Livingstone 1989, 111.
267. Pongratz-Leisten 1999a, 262 offers a full listing.
268. Grayson 1975 collects much of the material and is still considered the starting point for the study of chronicles. Glassner 2004 also collects the material. Van der Spek and Finkel are preparing editions of all of the Hellenistic chronicles, including several unpublished ones; preliminary

clear definitions, some texts, as he recognizes, show characteristics of both king lists and chronicles.[269] Moreover, as others have observed, the criteria for establishing "chronicles" as a unified genre within historiographical texts is still insufficiently articulated.[270] Taken as a whole, texts recognized as king lists and chronicles contain information about kings from the Old Akkadian period (as in "Chronicle of Early Kings") down to the second century BCE (as in the "King List of the Hellenistic Period").[271] These data have helped scholars piece together the succession of kings and sometimes the length of their reigns, though such use requires careful scrutiny since the years given in the texts are not always accurate or consistent. Chronicles include information about events during various kings' reigns in a terse, ostensibly dispassionate style and have therefore elicited much interest from historians. The historical events these texts record vary in character. Some chronicles are quite narrow, focusing on one reign or one religious ceremony through time, or tendentious, revealing political and theological agendas. Some are concerned with the remote past, while others are focused on contemporary events as they unfolded. The information they present, it seems, was drawn from a variety of texts—when sources can be identified—such as year names, astronomical diaries, omen collections, or the literary tradition. The reliability of this information must be established on a case-by-case basis. The archival contexts of the Babylonian chronicles, whether found in a private or temple library, suggest these texts originated among scribes with quite learned interests.[272]

Historical-Literary Texts

This somewhat amorphous category is another modern contrivance that subsumes texts, according to Grayson, of "various refined literary forms," whose "content is concerned mainly with historical or natural events rather than with mythological or supernatural occurrences."[273] The label is unfortunate since

---

versions are available at http://www.livius.org/cg-cm/chronicles/chronoo.html. Waerzeggers 2012 is an important article that, among other things, surveys the scholarship on chronicles, reassesses the genre as a whole (rejecting several texts Grayson accepted into the corpus), and reexamines the provenance of the texts. According to Waerzeggers, there are about forty-five *Babylonian* chronicles (2012, 287–88 with references; she does not deal with Assyrian texts), a third of which are from Borsippa and the remainder from Babylon. The king lists are edited in Grayson 1980–1983. The quotations are from Grayson 1980, 172.

269. Grayson gives the Assyrian King List as an example (1980, 172).

270. See Waerzeggers 2012, 287 with other references.

271. For the Chronicle of Early Kings, see Grayson 1975, no. 20. For the King List of the Hellenistic Period, see Grayson 1980–1983, 98–100.

272. Waerzeggers 2012, 294–95. Some of the tablets bearing chronicles also contain excerpts of other scholarly genres. See Leichty and Walker 2004; Waerzeggers 2012, 295.

273. Grayson 1975, 5.

some of the materials discussed in previous historiographical subsections are also of a historical nature and have a literary quality to them. Moreover, the category itself is not settled since scholars differ about which texts should be included in it and how to arrange the texts that are included into meaningful subcategories.[274] The following subsections modify Grayson's and are nothing more than one way to organize this material.[275]

Royal Historical Epics

Royal historical epics narrate the feats and conquests of historical kings.[276] One might speculate that they were used in a victory celebration at court or in a public setting, but we have no evidence for this currently. Though there must have been a great many royal epics lauding the might and military prowess of ancient Mesopotamian kings, only a modest number of these texts have actually survived, and, unfortunately, most of them are poorly preserved. Judging from the fact that many of the textual witnesses to the poems come from late tablet collections, dating sometimes many centuries after the lives of the celebrated kings, these royal epics held the interest of scribes long after the reigns of the renowned kings.

The earliest example of an Akkadian royal historical epic does not come from Mesopotamia proper but from Mari, an important Syrian city on the bend of the Euphrates River. The text of about 170 lines celebrates the city's last king, Zimri-Lim (ca. 1775–1762 BCE), and his military victories over enemies in the Habur and Shubartum regions north of the city.[277] As the tablet bearing the text comes from the Mari archive, the poem may very well have been written shortly

274. Grayson arranges the texts into three subcategories: royal historical epics, pseudoauto-biographies, and literary prophecies (1980, 182–88). Röllig (1987, 52–54, 65) divides the texts into epics, *narû*-literature, pseudoautobiographies, and miscellaneous fragmentary narratives. He places the so-called literary prophecies into a kind of miscellaneous category at the end of his survey. How scholars construct and populate the pseudoautobiography/*narû* category (or categories) is rather varied. For a survey of the issues, see Haul 2009, 95–131. His list of what he calls pseudepigraphic inscriptions is on p. 168, which includes the so-called literary prophecies.

275. For criticism of Grayson's "literary-historical" category, see Haul 2009, 99–101.

276. For the use of the term epic, see the literature cited in note 4, above. Grayson provides introductory discussions in 1975, 41–49; 1980, 184–87. For a list of royal epics, see Röllig 1987, 52, 54; Foster 2007, 19–26, who updates Röllig and provides brief descriptions of texts from the mid-second millennium on (see also Foster 2009, 199–201). Foster includes some texts in his discussion that I do not classify as epics (namely, his 2.2.6.1. [letter], 2.2.6.2. [letter], 2.2.8. [bilingual poem], 2.2.10. [letter], and 2.2.11. [land grant, *kudurru*]). The text edited by Finkel 1983, which he calls the Dream of Kurigalzu, and the newly published and quite fragmentary text entitled Hammurabi's Deeds by its editors (Rutz and Michalowski 2016) may also belong among the royal historical epics.

277. Zimri-Lim's reign (and life, probably) came to an end when Hammurabi, his former ally, conquered Mari ca. 1762 BCE. Guichard 2014 provides the much anticipated *princeps* edition of the poem. See Wasserman 2015 for a substantive review.

after the recounted events.[278] After the introductory praise for the king and two initial victories, the poem tells how the king calls his troops to assemble in order to receive their counsel about the enemy. In response to his call, he receives a rousing speech from one of his officers named Ashmad, who mixes metaphors as he describes the enemy troops:

> Why are you concerned about the Shubaru?
> (I assure you that) the fire of your battle has not be[en tur]ned back.
> [The tr]ees of the forest (are) shive[rs of f]ear (and) shadow,
> As long as (lit. in view of the fact that) the blade of the ax has not (yet)
>   felled [th]eir trun[ks].[279]
> Shubartum is scatte[red] like the sheep of a pasture.
> [Gi]ve or[ders][280] to march! The provisions are ready.
> [O Zimri-L]im, may they see your heroism!
> May [people] praise your name [forev]er![281] (ii 39–46)

After the king's third victory and just before the final battle, Zimri-Lim receives a sign from a prophet (*āpilum*) and a favorable omen from Shamash, the sun god and god of justice. Bolstered by the divine support, he deals a crushing blow to the enemy. The text concludes with the king triumphantly entering the town of Terqa, where as victor he confidently requests life, prosperity, and strength from the god Dagan.

In Mesopotamia proper, there are several royal epics from Assyria. Two of these celebrate the Middle Assyrian kings Adad-nerari I (1305–1274 BCE) and Tukulti-Ninurta I (1243–1207 BCE). Unfortunately, the former is poorly preserved among NA copies and the reconstruction of the latter with NA and at least one MA witnesses remains uncertain, though some 430 lines of the text are known.[282] What is clear throughout the latter work is the author's sophisticated

---

278. Guichard 2014, 70–71.

279. *ḫur[bāš]u ṣillu [iṣṣ]ī qištim / gušūr[īšu]nu azzīm-ma lā ḫerû lišān pāšim.* The point of these two lines is to diminish the fearsomeness of the enemy: the forest (i.e., enemy) looks scary, but that is only because the ax (i.e., Zimri-Lim) has not yet subdued it. I thank Michael P. Streck for discussing these lines with me and suggesting the reading *gu-šu-r[i-šu]-nu* rather than *gu-šu-r[u-šu]-nu*, as in Guichard 2014, 18. Note also Wasserman 2015, 54 n. 14, who discusses the present passage briefly.

280. I use Guichard's alternative reading here: *[šu-up]-ra-[am]* (2014, 49).

281. Guichard 2014, 18–19. The translation is my own. I know of no full English translation of the text. Sasson 2015, 32–35 provides a partial translation.

282. Editions are in Weidner 1963 (see also Wilcke 1977, 187–91); Machinist 1978, respectively. (Some new pieces of the latter epic have been found among the Assur tablets; these will be published by Stefan Jakob, along with many other pieces of similar genre.) Machinist offers a very full discussion of the Tukulti-Ninurta Epic, including an insightful literary analysis, on which the present discussion has drawn. For an accessible translation of the latter poem, see Foster 2005, 298–317.

use of language drawn from treaties, laments, hymns, and building inscriptions. Exchange of messengers and letters and the use of several speeches, including a soliloquy from a doomed Kashtiliash IV (1232–1225 BCE), give the poem a liveliness not found in typical royal inscriptions. The protagonists could not have been presented in greater contrast: the divinely-chosen Tukulti-Ninurta I, the just yet mighty Assyrian king, is set against his impious southern neighbor, Kashtiliash IV, a Kassite king of Babylon, who transgressed his own treaty oath and incited the anger of both the gods and the Assyrian king. Despite the Assyrian's overtures for forgiveness, the Kassite persists in his sin while avoiding battle in a cowardly manner and then retreating. Tukulti-Ninurta I calls upon the sun god Shamash, god of justice, to enforce the oath that Kashtiliash has shirked. In the end, the Assyrian king sacks Babylon with the support of the gods.

Other Assyrian royal epics originate in the courts of the Neo-Assyrian kings, though all are fragmentary and the number of preserved lines, with the exception of Shalmaneser III's (858–824 BCE) Campaign to Urartu, are relatively few.[283] The Shalmaneser text reads in its body very much like a campaign narrative, that is, the Assyrian king is an irresistible military force conquering the fortified cities of Urartu. However, unlike a typical campaign narrative, the text includes the king's speech to one of his officers near its beginning and another shortly thereafter to all of his officers. After the conquest of Urartu (narrated in the first-person, unlike the first and last parts of the text), the poem concludes with the king celebrating a festival before Ishtar in the Assyrian city of Arbela.

Just as Assyrian kings had their epics, several royal historical epics celebrate Babylonian kings, including some who reigned in the late second millennium (e.g., Nebuchadnezzar I [1125–1104 BCE] and Adad-shuma-utsur [1216–1187 BCE]) and a couple from the Neo-Babylonian period (Nabopolassar [625–605 BCE] and Amel-Marduk [561–560 BCE]). Like the Assyrian royal epics, most of these texts are poorly preserved and all are known exclusively from late copies. Yet they yield insights that we might not have otherwise learned without them. For example, the Nabopolassar Epic provides the only surviving account of the enthronement of the Babylonian king.[284] And, as Foster has noted, the Babylonian royal epics do not flinch at showing the Babylonian kings in weakness—fear, defeat, or despair.[285] The positive reflex to this is that

---

283. See Livingstone 1989, nos. 17–24, 50 for all of the Neo-Assyrian royal epic texts. Grayson 1996, 84–87 is the most recent edition of Shalmaneser III's Campaign to Urartu. Grayson does not describe the text as a royal epic; rather, he sees it simply as an Assyrian royal inscription in verse. For another translation of the last text, see Foster 2005, 779–82.

284. See Grayson 1975, 84–85.

285. Foster 2009, 200. It is for these very reasons that Haul believes the so-called autobiography of Nebuchadnezzar I (Foster's "Elamite Attack on Babylonia," 2007, 21; translated in Foster 2005, 381–83) is inauthentic and best considered a pseudepigraph (2009, 165).

the texts also show the kings piously engaging in lament and prayer several times, to which the gods inevitably respond with favor.[286] The brightest star among the celebrated kings is Nebuchadnezzar I, who stood out in his times as the king who defeated Kudur-Nahhunte's Elamite forces and brought about the return of Marduk's divine image after a long captivity in Elam—an act that would be remembered for centuries.[287] Several of the royal epic texts depict Elamite aggression, Nebuchadnezzar I's struggle against their forces, and his eventual victory by order of the gods.[288]

Literary Prophecies/Ex Eventu Texts

Prophecy Text A, The Dynastic Prophecy, The Uruk Prophecy, The Marduk Prophecy, and The Shulgi Prophecy comprise a small group of rather fragmentary prose texts known only from a handful of late manuscripts.[289] They have garnered much attention for their perceived similarities to Jewish apocalyptic literature, though more recent study sees only broad conceptual similarities with that late tradition.[290] As is well-established now, the label "literary prophecies" is in fact a misnomer since none of these texts presents oracles delivered by a prophetic figure, as do the prophecies from Mari and Nineveh.[291] (The traditional titles are maintained here simply to aide identification in other secondary literature.) In fact, these five texts may not properly comprise a genre at all,

286. See, e.g, Grayson 1975, 68–69, 90–91 (on the latter, see now Schaudig 2001, 589–90); Frame 1995, 18, 20–21.
287. On the importance of Nebuchadnezzar's reign to Mesopotamian religious history, see Lambert 1964. For a study of Nebuchadnezzar I in Mesopotamian historical memory (and a reassessment of Lambert's view), see Nielsen 2018.
288. E.g., Lambert 1994b (translated in Foster 2005, 371–74); Frame 1995, 19–21 (Foster 2005, 381–83), 18–19 (Foster 2005, 385), and 31–33.
289. Grayson 1975, 13–22; 1980, 183–84 call these texts "Literary Prophecies." Neujahr 2012 prefers the label "*Ex Eventu* Texts" (8) for reasons noted below. Others categorize them as pseudepigraphs (e.g., Longman 1991, 131–90, 233–41; Haul 2009, 166). Neujahr provides the most recent treatment (2012, 1–118), which includes the Akkadian texts (based on the previously published editions), full translations, notes, extensive citations of secondary literature, discussions of all five texts, and their generic relationship. His comparative study presents these texts as part of a broader category he labels mantic historiography, a primary characteristic of which is its use of *vaticinia ex eventu*, i.e., prophecies after the fact. The present summary draws significantly from his work. Prophecy Text A, The Uruk Prophecy, and The Dynastic Prophecy are each known only from a single first millennium tablet (from Assur, Uruk, and Babylon, respectively). The Marduk Prophecy is preserved in three tablets, two from Nineveh and one from Assur; The Shulgi Prophecy comes to us on two tablets, one each from the same two cities. For details, see the literature cited in the presentation of each text in Neujahr 2012.
290. See Neujahr 2012 for the history of scholarship, a critical assessment of previous views, and a sophisticated treatment that posits the usefulness of a broad conceptual comparison rather than a literary formal or genetic relationship.
291. So, e.g., Foster 2007, 27–28. For these prophecies, see page 158, below.

though they do share a common rhetorical use of *vaticinia ex eventu*, that is, prophecies after the fact.[292] Using the literary facade of predicting events that have in fact already happened, these texts attempt to establish credibility and authority in order to commend to some audience their conclusions, which authorize/valorize some contemporary king or course of action via a statement cast as a prediction (e.g., The Marduk Prophecy) or make a genuine (though failed) prediction of future events (e.g., the end of The Uruk Prophecy).

A brief overview of the texts shows that there are a few similarities among them beyond the use of *vaticinia ex eventu* but also several differences. Marduk and deified Shulgi speak in the first person in the texts named after them whereas the other three texts use a third-person voice, as far as can be determined. The first-person texts recount the protagonists' former days in past tense verbs. In Marduk's case, the text describes three instances when he decided to leave his home in Babylon (i.e., was taken captive by enemy troops) and returned. The text then goes on to predict that "a king will arise"—a phrase found in all five texts at least once—who will return Marduk from Elam to Babylon. This clearly intends to celebrate Nebuchadnezzar I (1125–1104 BCE), who returned Marduk to Babylon from Elam, though he is unnamed—as is every king mentioned in these texts.[293] In The Shulgi Prophecy a series of unfortunate events are predicted to follow Shulgi's reign (2094–2047 BCE) that will devastate the land and its people. Then a king will arise who will restore the cult and, presumably (though the text breaks off), bring back prosperity. As the predictions for this final king are all rather vague, it is impossible to know which king the text intends to support via its "prediction."[294] Prophecy Text A is also opaque. It predicts the successive rise of about ten kings, though this number is incomplete since both the beginning and ending of the text are still missing. The text is unique in that it gives the precise number of years for each predicted king's reign but there are no clearly identifiable events mentioned in the text to help us determine the identity of these kings or the time period the text is describing.[295] The Uruk Prophecy also predicts the rise of a long series of kings over Uruk, one of whom will take the goddess of Uruk (Ishtar) to Babylon and the second to last of whom will restore the cult image to its rightful sanctuary in Uruk (which recalls the ending to The Marduk Prophecy). The final king of the text is predicted to reign like a god. If one follows the original editors of the text and identifies the last two kings as Nebuchadnezzar II (604–562 BCE) and

---

292. Note the full discussion of various alternate generic labels in Neujahr 2012, 103–14 (prophecy, apocalypse, literary predictive text, and fictional Akkadian autobiography with a prophetic ending) and his conclusion on pp. 114–15 that the five texts do not comprise a single genre.

293. See Neujahr 2012, 27–41 for a full discussion.

294. See Neujahr 2012, 41–50 for a full presentation.

295. See Neujahr 2012, 14–27 for a full discussion.

his son Amel-Marduk (561–560 BCE), the last prediction was a genuine one that attempted to commend Nebuchadnezzar's son as the rightful heir. But the prediction failed, as Amel-Marduk had a miserably short reign and was assassinated by a usurper.[296] Finally, The Dynastic Prophecy predicts the successive rise and demise of the Neo-Assyrian, Neo-Babylonian, and Persian Empires. After a few lines that may reflect succession problems within the Persian court, the text then predicts the rise of a Hanaean (i.e., Macedonian) army. This army will enjoy an initial victory against the Persians but then the Hanaean army will be defeated and the land will return to a state of well-being. The text shows a few more extremely fragmentary lines that may describe three more kings before it concludes with a colophon designating the text a secret. The Hanaean and concluding sections of this text are highly disputed. If, however, the Hanaean army is identified with Alexander the Great's, then it seems this text offers a genuine but failed prediction since Alexander was never defeated by the Persians. If that is the case, the continuation of the extremely fragmentary text may be a kind of updating of the text. But this is not at all certain.[297]

In many ways these texts have received an amount of attention disproportionate to their fragmentary state of preservation. This is often the case with texts perceived to be of relevance to some aspect of the Bible or the religions rooted therein. The current state of our knowledge and our assessment of these texts as a genre will no doubt change in the future as scholars recover more of their contents.

Pseudepigraphic Inscriptions

As mentioned above in the discussion of the legends of Akkadian kings, pseudepigraphic fictional stela (*narûs*) are texts that adopt a literary conceit in which the text is presented as though the king's words, spoken in the first person retrospectively, were inscribed on a stela and erected for posterity.[298] They serve an

---

296. See Hunger and Kaufman 1975; also, Neujahr 2012, 50–58. Beaulieu 1993b agrees with these identifications of the kings but argues the text should be read against the backdrop of the third century BCE, at a time when Urukean priests were trying to convince Seleucid rulers to support the establishment of the new Anu cult. According to this understanding of the text, Antiochus I should be seen as a kind of Nebuchadnezzar II *redivivus*.

297. See Neujahr 2012, 58–71 for this viewpoint and a review of alternatives.

298. This section draws upon the work of Haul 2009, 95–187. Haul lists some twenty pseudepigraphic texts (168), which he divides into twelve "fictional" *narûs* (ten of which are legends of Akkadian kings) and nine "fingierte Inschriften," "fabricated inscriptions" (five of which are literary prophecies or *ex eventu* texts treated in the previous section). For his distinction between fictional and fabricated, see pp. 133–35. For other discussions of these texts, see Röllig 1987, 53–54; Foster 2007, 14–18; Reiner 1978, 176–79 (who uses the term autobiographies), all of whom differ slightly with regard to which compositions to include in this subcategory. Reiner and Röllig both prefer to separate texts they label *narû* from those labeled autobiographies or pseudepigraphs. Haul surveys

exemplary function. The parade examples are The Cuthean Legend of Naram-Sin and The Birth Legend of Sargon, summarized earlier, though one might also mention the forged Cruciform Monument of Manishtushu, which purportedly presents the words of another king of the Akkadian dynasty.[299] The Sin of Sargon (II), dating from the Neo-Assyrian period, is yet another example of this kind of text.[300] In this rather broken and thus difficult text about the NA king Sargon II (721–705 BCE), Sennacherib, the deceased king's son and heir to the throne, prayerfully contemplates why his father died in an enemy country so that his body could not be retrieved and properly buried. Sennacherib decides to investigate the matter via extispicy, taking the unusual measure of dividing the diviners into several groups so that they would have to make independent inquiries, a practice that he commends to his successor. Having received an affirmative answer to his inquiry (i.e., that his father did unduly exalt the Assyrian gods over the Babylonian ones and had broken a treaty [perhaps with Babylon]), he seeks to remedy the situation through cultic projects, including the manufacture of a statue for Assur, high god of Assyria, and Marduk, chief deity of Babylon.[301] But Sennacherib is prevented from finishing Marduk's statue, which he leaves for his successor—probably his son Esarhaddon—to complete. Given the text's concern with both the gods of Babylon and Assyria, recent interpreters have emphasized the political propagandistic function of the text, which recasts Sennacherib, who had destroyed Babylon during his reign, as favorably disposed to a more conciliatory attitude toward the city and thus supportive of what was in fact his son's policy.[302] Given the very fragmentary state of the text, however, its interpretation remains tentative.

Several other texts often identified as pseudepigraphic in character read very much like normal royal inscriptions but are of uncertain authenticity. Scholars who doubt their authenticity suggest these texts are fictional, indeed, fabrications written to support some political or cultic agenda.[303] Others who accept them as authentic treat them as royal inscriptions. Their classification here as pseudepigraphs is tentative. Among such texts is The Autobiography of

---

the entire issue and all relevant secondary literature rather thoroughly (2009, 95–131). See also note 274, above, for the position of this subcategory within the so-called historical-literary texts. For the discussion of the legends of the Akkadian kings, see page 123, above.

299. See Sollberger 1968 for an edition. Al-Rawi and George 1994, 139–48 edit a new witness. Longman 1991, 218–21 provides a translation.

300. See Tadmor, Landsberger, and Parpola 1989; Livingstone 1989, no. 33 for editions of the text.

301. The broken treaty with Babylon is suggested by Tadmor, Landsberger, and Parpola 1989, 48–49.

302. See Tadmor, Landsberger, and Parpola 1989; Weaver 2004. For a reading of the text within a study of discourse questioning royalty, see Finn 2017, 97–117.

303. See Haul 2009, 133; Longman 1991. They are not exemplary so much as propagandistic.

Kurigalzu and The Agum-kakrime Inscription.[304] This last mentioned text is of considerable interest for its detailed information about the restoration of Marduk to his temple Esagila in Babylon.[305] After a rather standard introduction, consisting of the king's name, genealogy, and epithets, the text describes the king sending for Marduk in his distant exile, choosing his cella by divination, preparing the divine image and cella for his entry (which includes a long list of expensive raw materials), purifying the newly prepared room, and causing Marduk to reside in it (with great rejoicing). The text then mentions the exemptions the king granted the craftsmen who were involved in this work and ends with a long blessing for the king himself. A kind of postscript is attached to the document—one of the so-called *Geheimwissen* colophons though this postscript is not a colophon proper—forbidding the uninitiated from reading the text.[306] This protective measure may have been attached to the text due to its detailed information about the preparation of divine images.[307]

Other Historical-Literary Texts

There are several other important texts that might be called royal historical-literary texts yet are not easily classified under one of the headings above. Two of these relate to the felicitous reign of Nebuchadnezzar I, which seems to have been or, at least, was remembered as a watershed moment in Mesopotamian history.[308] The first text is a late copy of a bilingual inscription, entitled Seed of Kingship.[309] This poetic text praises divinely elected Nebuchadnezzar, who is presented as a descendant of the antediluvian king Enmeduranki. The text goes on to recount how Marduk grew angry with his land, allowed the Elamites to devastate it, and left for a time. In its conclusion, Marduk heeds the prayers of the king and returns to Babylon amid great celebration from both the people and the gods. The other text from the time of Nebuchadnezzar is a prose land grant (*kudurru*) written during the king's reign. It describes in an elevated style the valiant service of one Shitti-Marduk, a village chieftain, during the king's successful campaign against Elam. As a reward for his valor, his village receives various exemptions.[310]

---

304. The most recent edition of The Autobiography of Kurigalzu is Oshima 2012a, 252–57, 262–64. Translations include Foster 2005, 365–66; Longman 1991, 224–25. See Haul 2009, 162–64 for the fictional status of these texts and their categorization as "fingierte Inschriften," "fabricated inscriptions."

305. Oshima 2012a, 225–52, 258–61 provides the most recent edition. See Foster 2005, 360–64 for a translation; Chavalas 2006, 135–39 for van Koppen's translation and interpretation.

306. See Lenzi 2008, 168–219 for these colophons.

307. Lenzi 2008, 211.

308. See note 287, above.

309. See Frame 1995, 23–31; Foster 2005, 376–80.

310. See Paulus 2014, 503–10 for the most recent edition. Also, Frame 1995, 33–35. Foster 2005, 383–84 offers a translation; Hurowitz 1992 assesses the literary qualities of the text.

Three other texts may be mentioned, hailing from the Neo-Babylonian (625–539 BCE) and Achaemenid/Persian (539–331 BCE) periods. The first is a prose composition known under the title The King of Justice.[311] Unfortunately, the composition's only witness has lost both its beginning and ending. The first preserved lines tell of the miserable past conditions, a time when injustice went unchecked and corruption was rampant. Then, the king, presumably named in the lost beginning (probably Nebuchadnezzar II [604–562 BCE] or Nabonidus [555–539 BCE]), is introduced as a tireless advocate of justice and a reformer of the legal system.[312] Several anecdotes follow, providing evidence of the king's unmatched legal wisdom. In one of these, the king decapitates a man who attempted to circumvent justice and has a likeness of his head mounted near the court's gate as a deterrent to such crimes. In another, the king reinstitutes the ancient river ordeal. In recounting this ancient method of determining guilt or innocence, the text provides the fullest account of this harrowing trial-by-ordeal.[313] The last section of preserved text (before breaking off) describes the king rebuilding a temple and lists his abundant food offerings before the gods.

The Verse Account of Nabonidus is another significant composition dating from the early Achaemenid period.[314] The poetic text is preserved on only one damaged tablet. Aside from a number of textual gaps among its damaged lines, the text is also very likely missing two full columns of material in its midsection (the last column on the obverse and thus the first on the reverse). Of great interest in this learned text is the critical stance toward Nabonidus, the last king of the Neo-Babylonian Empire, his devotion to the cult of the moon god Sîn, and his neglect of the *proper* Babylonian rites in Marduk's Esagil temple.[315] Nabonidus's religious predilection is considered an aberration, the result of divine abandonment and human hubris, which the text establishes through a long quotation from the Babylonian king himself. The text disapproves of the king's long stay in the Arabian town of Teima, where he oppresses the local population, and it ridicules his pseudo-intellectual incompetence.[316] Nabonidus's ruinous reign is reversed by the Persian king Cyrus (538–530 BCE), who is

311. The most recent edition is Schaudig 2001, 579–88. Foster 2005, 870–74 offers an English translation.

312. The first editor argued for Nebuchadnezzar II (Lambert 1965, 2–3); several others suggest Nabonidus (e.g., Foster 2005, 870; Schaudig 2001, 579–80; Finn 2017, 190–93).

313. For more on decapitation, see Dolce 2018; on the river ordeal, see Heimpel 1996; Barrabee 2011.

314. The most recent edition is Schaudig 2001, 563–78. See Pritchard 1969, 312–15 for Oppenheim's translation.

315. Schaudig believes the poem is directed at learned readers because of the use of poetic parallelism, the citations of other learned works, and the inclusion of word plays that require knowledge of writing and literature (2001, 564). See the fuller analysis by Beaulieu 2007a and Finn 2017, 172–90.

316. Scholars continue to debate why Nabonidus went to Teima and why he stayed there for so long. See Finkel and Kinnier Wilson 2006 for a survey of opinions and a new suggestion.

welcomed as a liberator and restorer of the proper rites to Babylon, bringing joy to the beleaguered city. Obviously, the text is a pro-Persian piece of propaganda intended to savage Nabonidus's reign. However, as Beaulieu points out, the so-called sins of Nabonidus were not at all unique among Mesopotamian kings.[317] What seems to be at issue is a certain resentment of the king's religious innovations that would have deemphasized Marduk (and his home city of Babylon).

The final text is rather unique in that it is a funerary stela from Nabonidus's mother, Adad-guppi, found (in two copies) in the Syrian city of Harran.[318] The Neo-Babylonian text describes Adad-guppi's devotion to the moon god Sîn in the first-person.[319] After noting how the deity had become angry and abandoned Harran (i.e., the Babylonians and Medes destroyed the site at the time of the destruction of the Neo-Assyrian Empire in the late seventh century BCE), Adad-guppi recounts how she denied herself material comforts and prayed for his return night and day—for ninety-five years, according to the text. Sîn answered her prayer in a dream, revealing that her son, recently ascended to the throne of Babylon, would restore the abandoned temple. Having seen the promise fulfilled, she then describes the blessings she received for her devotion: a good reputation, long life (104 years!), and good health. She offers a prayer-blessing for her son, and then there is a small gap in the text. In the final column, the text, now in the third-person, notes Adad-guppi's death and the days of mourning people observed for her throughout Nabonidus's kingdom. The final paragraph exhorts the reader of the inscription to venerate Sîn and the other gods. As Foster notes, the text "perhaps belonged to a long tradition of first-person narratives on funerary inscriptions in that region."[320]

Legal and Political Documents

Law Collections

As insurers of justice and protectors of the people, kings throughout ancient Near Eastern history issued laws and sealed treaties.[321] The laws attested in Akkadian

317. Beaulieu 2007a, 139–40.
318. The most recent edition is Schaudig 2001, 500–513. Hecker 1988; Longman 1991, 225–28; Longman in Hallo and Younger 2003–2016, 1:477–78 (excerpt); Melville in Chavalas 2006, 389–93 provide translations. Some classify the text as a pseudepigraph (e.g., Longman 1991, 101–2). Reasons for accepting its authenticity are briefly laid out in Haul 2009, 161–62.
319. There is still no solid evidence that she was in fact a priestess dedicated to the god. See Schaudig 2001, 14.
320. See Foster 2007, 48 and Schaudig 2001, 501 for a couple of parallels.
321. We must leave aside here the various decrees, grants, entitlements, and other legal texts originating in the royal sphere as well as any attempt to characterize the many thousands of court

come down to us in only a handful of collections, namely, the laws of Eshnunna (ca. 1770 BCE), the laws of Hammurabi (ca. 1750 BCE), the Middle Assyrian laws (ca. 1076 BCE), the Middle Assyrian palace decrees (ca. 1076 BCE), and the quite brief Neo-Babylonian laws (c. 700 BCE).[322] These are sometimes referred to as codes, but none of these collections is a code strictly speaking, since none presents a body of laws complete enough to encompass the legal needs of the ancient society from which it came.[323] In fact, the Middle Assyrian laws are preserved on fourteen tablets that do not comprise a single composition; the Neo-Babylonian laws are only known from a scribal student's excerpt; and the Middle Assyrian palace decrees topically circumscribe the issue of proper behavior of palace staff, especially women in the royal harem and their male overseers. Modern scholars have divided these legal texts into paragraphs or provisions for ease of reference. For this reason, the laws of Eshnunna are said to contain 60 provisions; the laws of Hammurabi have between 275–300 (the uncertainty is due to damage); source A of the Middle Assyrian laws comprises 59; the Middle Assyrian palace decrees present 23 regulations from the reigns of nine different Assyrian kings who ruled between 1363 and 1076 BCE; and the Neo-Babylonian laws contain only 15 provisions.[324] The topics covered by each corpus differ in detail but also overlap to varying degrees, ranging widely through legal concerns related to agricultural activities, craftsmen and professions, treatment of women, commerce, wages, theft, bodily injury, manslaughter and homicide, marriage, divorce, sexual offenses, adoptions, inheritance, and slavery, among others.[325]

Unlike the smaller collections, the laws of Hammurabi are framed by a prologue and epilogue, written in a literary register of Akkadian, that celebrate the king as the divinely elected dispenser of justice, pious ruler, and wise benefactor of the (subdued) lands. In one passage of the epilogue that epitomizes Hammurabi's legal authority, the king (speaking in the first person) refers to the text

---

cases, transactions, contracts, and agreements—all written in various dialects of Akkadian. For a panoramic view of ancient Near Eastern legal sources and history, see Westbrook 2003; for chapters relevant to Mesopotamia, see pp. 141–226, 361–617, and 883–974. Van De Mieroop 2016, 143–81 situates ancient Mesopotamian legal scholarship within a discussion of scribal epistemology.

322. All are introduced and translated in Roth 1997. See also Borger 1982. Borger 2006, 2–50 (German); Richardson 2000, 2008 (English) offer student editions of the laws of Hammurabi, which is typically one of the first real texts students read when learning Akkadian.

323. For a brief presentation of various ideas about the nature and function of the law codes, see Roth 1997, 4–7.

324. For Hammurabi, see Roth 1997, 71, 74–76. Source B in the Middle Assyrian laws has twenty provisions; C+G shows eleven; the other sources all only preserve a single digit number of provisions.

325. The Middle Assyrian laws from source A (see Roth 1997, 155–76) contain legal provisions in which women factor prominently as do the Middle Assyrian palace decrees, as mentioned above. The laws of Hammurabi are the most topically diverse among the texts considered here.

itself and its material support as he directly addresses would-be readers/hearers of his laws. He states:

> Let any wronged man who has a lawsuit come before the statue of me, the king of justice, and let him have my inscribed stela read aloud to him, thus may he hear my precious pronouncements and let my stela reveal the lawsuit for him; may he examine his case, may he calm his (troubled) heart, (and may he praise me), saying ... [326]

The epilogue also includes, as do so many royal inscriptions, an extensive series of divinely enforced curses directed against any future detractors of the laws or defacers of the stela upon which the laws were inscribed.[327] As the quoted passage indicates, Hammurabi originally had his laws inscribed on several large diorite stelae that were erected in various Babylonian cities. Archaeologists discovered one of these statues in the ancient city of Susa, the Elamite capital, now situated in western Iran (fig. 16). An Elamite king, apparently, took it as booty at some point in time when he sacked Babylon.[328]

The laws of Hammurabi long outlived their namesake. Given Hammurabi's posthumous stature as an iconic Mesopotamian king, it should not be surprising that the laws were received into the scribal tradition and copied for more than a thousand years after his death.[329] One such copy bears a colophon in which the scribe states that he had transcribed the text from a statue in Susa.[330] The fact that other first millennium copies of the laws attest the same archaic monumental cuneiform script (see fig. 11) as was used by Hammurabi's scribes suggests we should take such claims seriously.[331] In addition to these many late copies, the laws of Hammurabi were the only legal collection to be the subject of ancient scholarly commentaries.[332]

Treaties

Though treaties and oaths are mentioned in letters from the early second millennium (e.g., from Mari), only a handful of Akkadian-language treaties or oaths

---

326. Roth 1997, 134 (CH xlviii 3–19). As noted earlier, *narî šaṭram lištassī-ma* may be rendered simply as "let him read my inscribed stela." For the relevance of this passage for the issue of the intended audience, see page 74, above.

327. For a study of the literary qualities of the prologue and epilogue, see Hurowitz 1994.

328. French archaeologists took the stela from Elam to Paris, where it is on display in the Louvre.

329. For Hammurabi as an iconic king, see Hurowitz 2005. For the laws in the first millennium scribal tradition, see Lambert 1989. There are more than four dozen available witnesses to the text; see Oelsner 2012.

330. Fadhil 1998, 726.

331. Maul 2012.

332. Frahm 2011, 101.

FIGURE 16. The stela of the laws of Hammurabi. Photo Credit: Erich Lessing/Art Resource, NY.

have actually survived from the period.[333] In contrast, some thirty-three treaties found at the Hittite capital of Hattusa, two from the coastal city of Ugarit in present day Syria, and two from Alalakh (level IV) in the Hatay province of Turkey present a very substantial corpus of Late Bronze Age treaties, dating between the late sixteenth and mid-thirteenth centuries BCE. Eleven of these thirty-seven texts were composed solely in Akkadian (peripheral Middle Babylonian), the international language of diplomacy at the time; six are Hittite-Akkadian bilinguals.[334] From the first millennium, treaties and loyalty oaths number only twenty—many of which are quite short and fragmentary—and date to the Neo-Assyrian period, specifically, 825–625 BCE.[335] All but one were composed in the Neo-Assyrian dialect. These sparse textual remains are probably but a fraction of the number of treaty-texts that once existed.

The treaties may be categorized broadly as either unilateral or bilateral. Unilateral treaties were imposed upon a political inferior by the superior power (e.g., the Hittite or Assyrian king); thus, they are often called vassal treaties. Bilateral treaties were mutual agreements between political powers that considered one another equal; thus, these are sometimes called parity treaties. The vassal treaties are much more numerous; thirteen of the seventeen texts from the Late Bronze Age and nineteen of twenty texts from the Neo-Assyrian period fall into this category.

The Hittite treaties follow a typical structure (with some variation in both what is included and the order in which they occur) that includes the following, as delineated by Gary Beckman: a preamble, which names the Hittite king; a historical introduction, which details the relations between the two involved parties; the provisions of the treaty, which often involve (for vassals) payment of tribute, loyalty to the king, the establishment of frontiers, military cooperation or obligations, and extradition of fugitives, among other things; an account

---

333. We have a scant few treaties from Mari (see, e.g., Charpin 1991 and Joannès 1991), one from Alalakh level VII (Wiseman 1953, no. 1, translated by R. Hess in Hallo and Younger 2003–2016, 2:329), and five from Tell Leilan (Eidem 2011). As one of the latter shows, the Old Assyrian merchants made treaties with local rulers for the right of passage through their territory (see also, e.g., Çeçen and Hecker 1995).

334. All but three of the texts from Hattusa and both texts from Ugarit are introduced and translated in Beckman 1999. The three that are left out are too fragmentary for translation (Beckman 1999, 8 n. 2). Beckman also includes sixteen diplomatic letters written in Akkadian that shed light on the treaties (125–52), several of which are from Ugarit, and a number of Akkadian-language edicts from the Hittite court (153–85 inter alia), most of which were found at Ugarit. For the treaties from early fifteenth-century Alalakh, see Wiseman 1953, nos. 2 and 3. R. Hess in Hallo and Young 2003–2016, 2:329–32 translates both texts; von Dassow in Chavalas 2006, 174–76 translates the latter.

335. See Parpola and Watanabe 1988 for an introduction and translations. Their text no. 6, The Succession Treaty of Esarhaddon, though treated as one text in the edition, in fact comprises eight nearly identically composed treaties imposed on eight different political entities. (Their text no. 14 is not a treaty or loyalty oath.)

of the deposition of the tablet in the temple of the vassal's high god; a list of divine witnesses, who witness and enforce the treaty; and a section of curses and blessings, which will befall the vassal in accordance with his conformity (or lack thereof) to the provisions of the treaty.[336] Since the official treaties that were deposited were inscribed on metal tablets and placed in a temple in the non-Hittite king's domain, the clay tablets from Hattusa (or, in two cases, Ugarit) that have preserved the treaties to this day must have been filed as copies in the royal archives.

Simo Parpola and Kazuko Watanabe have used the major structural features of the longest (about 670 lines) and most complete of the Neo-Assyrian treaties, the Succession Treaty of Esarhaddon, as a model for identifying the structural elements of the shorter and less-well-preserved examples of the genre.[337] This treaty attests a preamble, which identifies the parties involved; cylinder seal impressions, all of which are Assyrian; a list of divine witnesses; an adjuration for the vassal to accept the treaty terms; and a historical statement, which very briefly delineates the parties' relationship. These are followed by a long list of stipulations, which include: an obligation of undivided loyalty; an opposition to rebellion; a commitment to report disobedience, conspiracy, and sedition; a responsibility to protect the royal heir; a prohibition against fomenting strife within the royal family; and an injunction against any attempt to undo the oaths sworn during the treaty ceremony, among other things.[338] A violation clause follows the stipulations and leads directly into a very long series of traditional and ceremonial curses, separated in the Succession Treaty by a brief vow to obey the treaty stipulations.[339] The colophon and date conclude the treaty. Noticeably absent from the Neo-Assyrian treaties are the blessings for the vassal's obedience and the deposition of the document in a temple.

Divination: Deductive and Intuitive

The art of divination included deductive and intuitive forms; that is, deductive divination learned the divine will through investigation of signs in the world. Intuitive divination did the same through messages delivered by individuals

336. Beckman 1999, 2–3.

337. See Parpola and Watanabe 1988, no. 6 for the text and a translation. See Parpola and Watanabe 1988, xxxv–xliii for using it as a model.

338. According to lines 386–387, the inductees into the treaty are not to "swear the oath with your lips only but shall swear it wholeheartedly" (*ina gumurti libbīkunu*)!

339. Traditional curses are "taken over from the Mesopotamian literary tradition and attested in an identical or nearly identical form in several other texts"; ceremonial curses "involve parables or references to symbolic acts actually carried out during the conclusion of the treaties" (Parpola and Watanabe 1988, xlii).

who had received the messages from the gods via a subjective impression or prompting (i.e., they felt inspired to speak the divine will). Textual evidence for both has come down to us, though the number of texts we have of the former far and away outstrips the few we have of the latter.

Deductive Divination

Deductive divination is rooted in the idea that the divinely created world is filled with signs by which the gods revealed their will to human beings.[340] When signs presented themselves, the diviner's job was to interpret them and tell others, often the king, what these signs meant (i.e., what the gods were communicating). Signs could appear in a great variety of places and circumstances (see below) and could be provoked and unprovoked; that is, they could be actively sought by various means (e.g., examining the entrails and organs of a sheep) and passively observed in the course of everyday life (e.g., a lizard running across the wall of a house). Beginning in the second millennium, scribes compiled lists of signs and their meanings in if-then statements very much like the compilations of laws. If sign X appears, then Y. But the omens were not ironclad predications, inevitably fated to occur; rather, they were harbingers of things to come. If a sign was unfavorable, apotropaic rituals could dispel and avert the evil associated with it.[341] Systematic elaboration of signs and meanings, already present in the second millennium but reaching its zenith in the first, indicate that omen compilations were not based on empirical observations; the meaning of signs was not based on coincidental happenings at the time a sign was observed. Rather, making this connection was an intellectual and scholastic undertaking, achieved via a complex system of hermeneutics rooted in the cuneiform writing system, analogy, and word play.[342] These same hermeneutical methods inspired the development of commentary texts (an extensive, extratextual hermeneutical corpus) that ancient scholars used to explore the signs and their meanings in a deeper fashion.[343]

340. Maul 2003 presents an overview with an introduction, a listing of primary texts (and their editions), and bibliography. See also the brief and quite readable overview in George 2013a, xv–xxi. A monographic treatment of several aspects of divination, especially extispicy, is available in Maul 2013, now translated into English (Maul 2018). Koch 2015 provides a comprehensive treatment of the extensive first millennium sources related to divination in all of its diversity. Van De Mieroop 2016, 87–140 situates ancient Mesopotamian omen collections within a discussion of scribal epistemology.

341. See Maul 1994 for the so-called *namburbî* rituals, which were performed to dispel the evil associated with various manifested signs.

342. See briefly above, page 63. Veldhuis 1999; 2006, 492–96; Van De Mieroop 2016, 122–26 provide useful orientations to this aspect of the omen collections.

343. See Frahm 2011 for the commentary tradition and The Yale Cuneiform Commentary Project for a catalog and numerous editions of commentary texts (https://ccp.yale.edu/). See Brown 2000

Several different functionaries used divinatory treatises related to their professional work. The haruspex, a diviner who read the entrails and internal organs (i.e., exta) of animals, had a collection of extispicy omens numbering to about one hundred tablets, which generated many other texts that were intended to help interpret the omen corpus.[344] The liver was the most prominent organ consulted in this method of divination (hepatoscopy), though the lungs and gall bladder were also examined.[345] Divination texts attest to libanomancy (smoke divination), lecanomancy (oil divination), and other lesser-known mantic methods as well (e.g., the flight of birds and strewing meal).[346] Celestial diviners read lunar, solar, planetary, astral, and meteorological signs in the heavens, as demonstrated in the treatise Enuma Anu Enlil ("When Anu, Enlil"; 70 tablets).[347] Terrestrial and teratological (malformed births) signs were also within their purview, as attested by the treatises Shumma alu ("If a city"; at least 107 tablets) and Shumma izbu ("If a malformed birth"; 24 tablets), respectively (fig. 17).[348] In the late fifth century BCE the celestial diviners developed the first true astrological texts, that is, the use of celestial divination to determine the fate of an individual, based on the time and place of birth.[349] The exorcist also consulted omen collections for a number of reasons: to diagnose the ill (using the treatise Sakkiku, "Symptoms"; 40 tablets); to interpret the harbingers of evil announced in dreams (using the treatise Zaqiqu, "O Dream God"; about 11 tablets); and to read what was presaged in a person's physical features (using the physiognomic treatise Shumma alamdimmû, "If a bodily form" with its four subseries; 12 tablets).[350]

---

for the system of interpretation that supported celestial divination. For a study of scholarship and inquiry in the post-OB period that connects divination with much of the intellectual activities of Mesopotamian scholars, see Lenzi 2015b.

344. Maul 2003, 69–82; Koch 2015, 67–134 for overviews of the extispicy texts with references. For the texts intended to assist in interpretation, see Koch 2005; Frahm 2011, 167–91.

345. Koch-Westenholz 2000.

346. Maul 2003, 82–86; Koch 2015, 134–45.

347. See Rochberg 2004, 219–36 for a broad overview of celestial diviners as a professional group. Also, Beaulieu 2006a; Brown 2000, 33–52; Rochberg 1993, 2010. See Brown 2000, 254–56 for an overview of sources, to which add Verderame 2002 and Gehlken 2012. For introductions to celestial divination, see Rochberg 2004 (esp. 66–78 for Enuma Anu Enlil); Koch 1995; 2015, 146–96.

348. For Shumma alu, see Freedman 1998, 2006, 2017; Rochberg 2004, 78–81; Koch 2015, 233–62. The range of signs in this series is quite broad, including things observed in a house, city, field, river, etc., in the behavior of various animals, in sexual activities of people and of animals, in the interaction of people and animals, etc. For a list see Rochberg 2004, 79; in more detail Maul 2003, 59–60; Koch 2015, 242–56. For Shumma izbu, see Leichty 1970; and the updated edition in De Zorzi 2014. Rochberg 2004, 88–92; Koch 2015, 266–73 offer an overview.

349. See Rochberg 1998, 2004; Koch 2015, 197–211.

350. For Sakkiku, see Labat 1951; Heeßel 2000 for the text; Rochberg 2004, 92–96; Koch 2015, 273–82 offer short introductions. Scurlock 2014 provides a translation of the diagnostic series in English. For Zaqiqu, see Oppenheim 1956; with Butler 1998, 99–101 for the series; Rochberg 2004, 81–86 and Koch 2015, 302–11 offer introductory discussions. The subseries of Shumma alamdimmû are Nigdimdimmû ("If the appearance"; two tablets), Kataduggû ("If the utterance"; one tablet),

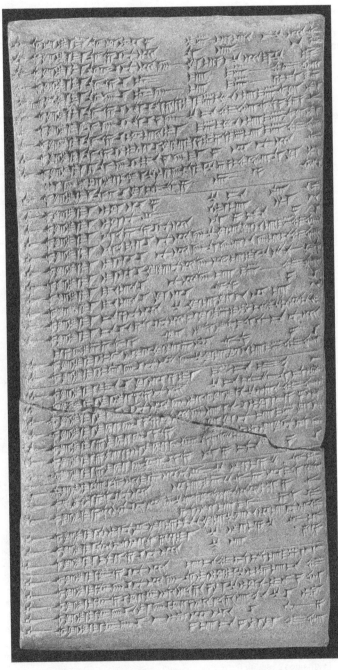

FIGURE 17. A tablet of omens from Shumma izbu. Each line on the tablet presents one omen. Photo © Trustees of the British Museum, London.

The cultural significance of omen texts is well-illustrated by the fact that they are found in very high numbers in first millennium tablet collections, even forming the largest group of texts in the important library of Assurbanipal.[351]

Prophecies (Intuitive Divination)

Unlike omens, which observed signs in the external world, prophecies were intuitively received by prophets and delivered in messenger fashion as the deity's direct speech. As a means of perceiving the divine will, they are correctly considered an aspect of divination. There are two major corpora relating to prophets and their oracles in Akkadian, one originating in Old Babylonian Mari and the other in Neo-Assyrian Nineveh.[352] A number of genres are represented among these texts. The focus here will be on those texts that contain actual oracles and not simply a mention of a prophet (e.g., in a royal inscription, an administrative memo, or lexical list). Texts relating to prophets are known from other locales and in the intervening/subsequent years; but they are not as numerous.[353] The relatively few texts that have come down to us suggest that prophetic oracles were not typically preserved in written form.[354] The mountain of secondary literature that has amassed around these few texts is a clear testament to the intense scholarly interest lavished on Akkadian texts with a perceived connection to the Bible.

In OB Mari we learn the content of prophetic oracles only as they are (re-)presented in letters addressed to the king (who is Zimri-Lim, ca. 1775–1762 BCE, in most cases) by administrative officials or family members (e.g., the queen). The topics treated in these oracles usually relate to the king's military and political situation, both assurances of victory and advice about courses of action, which, interestingly, the king did not always obey.[355] The oracles also include

Shumma sinnishtu qaqqada rabat ("If a woman has a large head"; two tablets), and Shumma liptu ("If the spot"; at least six tablets). See Böck 2000 for text editions. Maul 2003, 66–68, Rochberg 2004, 87–88, and Koch 2015, 282–90 provide brief overviews.

351. See Oppenheim and Reiner 1977, 16.

352. Use of the term "prophets" is a matter of convenience. For a thorough study of the various Akkadian terms for functionaries related to intuitive divination and the place of these functionaries in society, see Stökl 2012.

353. E.g., at OB Uruk and Kish (Dalley 2010). See Nissinen 2003 for a very useful introduction, collection, and translation of nearly all relevant texts with references to the relevant critical editions. Translations of a selection of texts are also available in Hecker 1986, 56–65; Dietrich 1986. Stökl 2012, 29–34 and 104–9 offers the most recent and slightly fuller listing of OB and NA texts (with up-to-date bibliography of critical editions and the numerous studies on the prophetic texts). He estimates the OB corpus comprises about ninety texts relevant to the study of prophets and the later corpus around thirty-six. As he is focused on OB and NA prophets, he excludes some of the later texts in Nissinen's catalog.

354. Nissinen 2003, 13–14, 98.

355. Note, e.g., the defeat of Babylon and victory of Mari in Nissinen 2003, 44. For lack of obedience, see Nissinen 2003, 17 and 30–31.

admonishments concerning city building projects, temple repairs, various cultic matters, and even something as personal as the naming of a child.[356] One oracle, reminiscent of the prophets of the Hebrew Bible, clearly links the king's success with his obedience to the divine will:

> Thus says Adad, "I have given the whole country to Yaḫdun-Lim. Thanks to my weapons, he did not meet his equal. He, however, abandoned my cause, so I g[a]ve to Šamši-Adad the land I had given to him. . . . I restored you to the th[rone of your father's house], and the weapon[s] with which I fought with Sea I handed you.[357] I anointed you with the oil of my luminosity, nobody will offer resistance to you. Now hear a single word of mine: If anyone cries out to <you> for judgment, saying: "I have been wr[ong]ed," be there to decide his case; an[swer him fai]rly. [Th]is is what I de[sire] from you. If you go [off] to the war, never do so [wi]thout consulting an oracle. [W]hen I become manifest in [my] oracle, go to the war. If it does [not] happen, do [not] go out of the city gate."[358]

The NA oracles are mostly preserved on archival tablets from the royal archives in Nineveh, though a few letters also relate the words of prophets.[359] There are only eleven of these archived tablets yielding a total of twenty-nine oracles. Seven tablets contain only one oracle while the others bear several oracles organized into a collection, providing an interesting parallel to the collection of prophetic oracles in the Hebrew Bible.[360] Nearly all of the texts are addressed to either Esarhaddon or Assurbanipal, the two kings that also mention prophets in their royal inscriptions.[361] "Most of the prophecies," as Nissinen has stated, "can be characterized as oracles of well-being (*šulmu*), proclaiming the reconciliation of the king with the gods. This reconciliation guarantees the equilibrium of heaven and earth, as demonstrated by the stable rule of the Assyrian king, his superiority over all enemies and adversaries and the legitimate succession."[362] The goddess Ishtar plays an important role throughout the

356. For the last, see Nissinen 2003, 70.

357. Note the connection here between *Chaoskampf* and kingship, as in Enuma Elish, for which see page 83, above.

358. Nissinen 2003, 21–22.

359. See, e.g., Nissinen 2003, 157–58, 165, 167–75. Nissinen 1998 treats NA references to prophets and prophecies in nonoracular texts.

360. One collection is quite fragmentary (Nissinen 2003, 124). Tablets containing only one oracle are formatted as initial, temporary, and probably disposable reports.

361. A few exceptional cases are addressed to Esarhaddon's mother and one to the entire Assyrian population.

362. Nissinen 2003, 100–101, but see, e.g., 122–23, where the king is scolded for his cultic neglect.

oracles, which utilize both martial and maternal imagery, and the phrase "fear not!," so familiar in biblical contexts, commonly occurs. For example, compare the tenderness conveyed here:

> You whose mother is Mullissu, fear not! You whose nurse is the Lady of Arbela, fear not! Like a nurse I will carry you on my hip. I will put you, a pomegranate, between my breasts. At night I will be awake and guard you; throughout the day I will give you milk, at dawn I will hush you.[363]

with the savagery promised here:

> Like ripe apples your enemies will continually roll before your feet.... I will flay your enemies and deliver them up to you.[364]

Other Scholarly Texts

Ancient Mesopotamian scholars compiled and curated a vast corpus of scholarly materials in Akkadian during the late second and first millennia.[365] The most important materials, after those of deductive divination, were the numerous incantations and incantation-prayers—with attendant ritual instructions—that exorcists collected and sometimes organized into series. These texts and a few series are treated briefly in their place in the next section. Exorcists and physicians also used therapeutic texts to treat various physical maladies. Such medical texts describe procedures and instructions for the production and use of various salves, bandages, poultices, drugs (i.e., plants), amulets, and other paraphernalia.[366] Therapeutic procedures and incantations could be used together to effect healing (see, e.g., *Muššu'u*).[367] Celestial divination, as already mentioned above, was also an important scholarly enterprise. Besides the use of divinatory texts like Enuma Anu Enlil, the celestial diviners (sometimes incorrectly called

363. Nissinen 2003, 127.

364. Nissinen 2003, 102.

365. For a fuller treatment of this material in post-Kassite Mesopotamia, see Lenzi 2015b. For the earlier period (including both Sumerian and Akkadian sources), see Delnero 2015.

366. Thompson 1923; Köcher 1955, 1963–1964, 1971, 1980; Geller 2005; Geller and Panayotov 2019 (unavailable at the time of this writing) provide many relevant medical tablets. Herrero 1984 analyzes therapeutic procedure. Two model studies of particular maladies are Fincke 2000 on eye disease, which will be treated at length in Geller and Panayotov 2019; and Stol 1993 on epilepsy. The relatively new *Journal des médecines cunéiformes* regularly publishes relevant editions, translations, studies, and bibliographies. Scurlock 2014 provides a great many medical sources in translation.

367. Böck 2007.

astrologers) also relied upon hemerologies and menologies, that is, treatises dealing with the nature of the days and months of the year, to determine auspicious and inauspicious times for various activities.[368] Their preoccupation with the heavens led to the creation of a large body of astronomical and calendrical literature that was initially observational but by the mid-first millennium included mathematical schemes to predict celestial phenomena and to regulate the calendar.[369] The regular recording of celestial observations in writing (in astronomical diaries) continued until the very end of the cuneiform tradition in the first century CE.[370]

Prayers, Incantations, Incantation-Prayers, Laments, and Hymns

The labels used in the heading to this section, as in many others, reflect a contemporary categorization.[371] Assigning a text to one or the other category is sometimes a matter of judgment, since evidence for ancient classificatory systems is often absent, incomplete (e.g., due to broken tablets), or otherwise problematic.[372] This is especially pertinent for distinguishing between prayers and hymns, the boundary between which is somewhat porous.

Hundreds of texts belong to the broad categories discussed in this section, spanning the entire history of Akkadian textual evidence.[373] This introductory treatment can by no means do full justice to the great diversity among them.

---

368. See Livingstone 2013 for an introduction, the relevant texts, and discussion; an overview is in Koch 2015, 212–33.

369. "Observational" means the scholars watched the heavens regularly. I do not mean to suggest that celestial (or other) omina were initially empirical or historical in nature. There is no evidence for this idea. See, e.g., Rochberg 2004, 67–68; 2010, 20; Brown 2000, 108–13; Veldhuis 1999, 163–64. See Hunger and Pingree 1999 and Brown 2000 for an introduction to mathematical schemes. Brown 2000, 245–64 offers a bibliography of cuneiform sources (in historical order of appearance) relevant to astronomy and astrology. See Hunger and Pingree 1989 and the now updated edition and study in Hunger and Steele 2018 for another example of a nonmathematical astronomical-astrological text, *MUL.APIN*. Examples of mathematical astronomical texts may be found in Ossendrijver 2012. See Steele 2011 for an introduction to the calendar.

370. For astronomical diaries, see Sachs and Hunger 1988, 1989, 1996; Sachs, Hunger, and Steele 2001; Hunger 2006. Hunger and de Jong 2014 edit the last datable text, written in 79/80 CE.

371. On various proposals for developing categories for these texts, see Foster 2007, 73–74.

372. On some problematic aspects of the ancient evidence relating to prayers, incantations, and incantation-prayers (i.e., scribal superscripts, subscripts, and rubrics as they relate to literary form), see Lenzi 2011, 8–20. Groneberg 2003 discusses hymns, hymnic catalogs, and classification.

373. Von Soden 1957–1971, 1972–1975 provide an overview of prayers and hymns, respectively; for hymns, see also Edzard 1994. For a survey of many texts in these categories from the late period with introductory remarks, see Foster 2007, 42–47, 73–95. The two most important anthologies dedicated to Mesopotamian prayers and hymns are Falkenstein and von Soden 1953 (German) and Seux 1976 (French). Foster 2005 (English) also includes a very generous selection of texts included in this section, as does Farber 1987, 255–81; Hecker 1989. For an important study (with catalog)

Prayers

When some nonhuman benevolent entity, often a deity, is directly addressed and petitioned in a text, modern scholars have been inclined to call the text a prayer.[374] The concluding lines of a text inscribed on a brick from Babylon offer a concise example:

> O Nabu and Marduk, as you go joyfully in procession through these streets, may words favorable of me be upon your lips. As I proceed before you within the(se streets), may I live a life enduring till distant days, in good health and [satisfac]tion forever.[375]

Prayers are rather diverse in terms of length, form, and content. For example, a prayer may be as simple and brief as a personal name (e.g., "Nebuchadnezzar" means "O Nabu, guard my firstborn [Akkadian, *Nabû-kudurrī-uṣur*]), a short letter addressed to a deity (e.g., the OB letter-prayer cited earlier on page 44), or a few lines on a cylinder seal legend directed to a god.[376] But prayers may also be much longer and quite complex, as is a highly artificed, literary prayer to Marduk, which runs to over two hundred lines.[377] And they may display great scribal prowess, as does a double acrostic prayer from the first millennium, in which the first and last signs/syllables of the lines, when read vertically, encode the name, position, and reverence of the scribe who wrote the

---

of all known incantations (Sumerian and Akkadian) from the earliest to OB times, see Cunningham 1997; and the additions in Wasserman 2003b, 185–224 (see esp. 185 n. 5). There is no published catalog of the much larger post-OB incantation corpus. For a catalog of all Akkadian incantation-prayers (almost exclusively first millennium texts), see Mayer 1976, 375–436. Frechette 2012, 249–75 updates Mayer with regard to the incantation-prayers that also bear the *shuila* rubric (see below). Oshima 2011, 83–136 catalogs (and provides extensive references for) all texts relevant to this section directed to Marduk. The remainder of the book offers a sizeable selection of text editions. Lenzi 2011 provides a critical introduction to Mesopotamian prayer, hymns, and ritual speech with introductory discussions of the most important kinds of prayers and twenty-nine annotated, translated examples. Finally, Streck and Wasserman are cataloging and editing all of the OB and MB Akkadian texts relevant to this section online at SEAL (http://www.seal.uni-leipzig.de/).

374. The differentiation between prayer and hymn is not absolute, since many texts that we call prayers open with praise—sometimes at great length—and many of the texts we label hymns, although dominated by praise, also include petitionary statements toward the end. For a discussion of the problem, see Oshima 2011, 33–37.

375. The translation is Foster's (2005, 847).

376. For personal names, see, e.g., Albertz 1978, 102–19. For OB letter-prayers in general, see the introductory remarks in Lenzi 2011, 53–55. For Akkadian and Sumerian examples of prayers on Kassite (MB) cylinder seals, see Limet 1971.

377. See Foster 2005, 611–16 for a translation; Oshima 2011, 137–90 is the most recent edition. For several prayers of similar length, see, e.g., Foster 2007, 78–81; Lambert 1959; Groneberg 1997.

text.[378] Prayers may stand alone, as the first three named groups do.[379] They may be embedded in another literary genre (e.g., a royal inscription, as was the brief prayer inscribed on a brick cited above).[380] They may be collected into a series.[381] And they may be integrated into a larger ritual. Examples of the latter are quite varied. They include, for example, the diviner's *ikribu-* and associated prayers, which were spoken in preparation for and at various stages of an extispicy, and various royal and temple rituals (such as the Assyrian royal coronation; the *takultu*-ritual, in which a divine meal is presented in the temple; and the Akitu festival, i.e., New Year's festival).[382]

Incantations

Scholars have tended to use the label "incantation" for a much broader array of ritual speech than prayer.[383] When a malevolent, undesirable, or dangerous entity/situation is described and/or addressed in a text (e.g., a god, a demon, an illness, a ghost or witch, a screaming baby, a woman giving birth, etc.) to facilitate exorcism, protection, or cessation of the condition at hand, modern scholars usually call such a text an incantation. The label also includes, however, texts that describe and/or address a divine image (being prepared to receive

378. See Lambert 1968, 130–32 for an edition. Translations are in Foster 2005, 704–5; Seux 1976, 264–66. Sweet 1969 recognized the double acrostic.

379. See also Foster 2005, 387 for a brief prayer inscribed on a bronze hatchet belonging to Nebuchadnezzar, "king of the world" (see Frame 1995, 16–17 for an edition).

380. This is especially true in the first millennium. See Foster 2007, 82–87 for other examples.

381. As were the diviner's *tamitu*-queries, which posed specific yes-no questions to the gods of divination (Shamash and Adad) during an extispicy. See Lenzi 2011, 46–49 for introductory remarks and references. The relevant texts are edited in Lambert 2007. All of the texts are preserved in first millennium copies but some probably go back to OB times. For similar texts that are the product of actual NA divinatory practice, see Starr 1990.

382. See Lenzi 2011, 46–49 for introductory remarks and references on extispicy, including several translated examples. The first millennium texts are in need of a modern edition. The most important available materials are surveyed in Lambert 2014. Concerning the royal coronation, see Foster 2005, 334 for a translation of the MA prayer; Müller 1937 for more about the accompanying ritual. Compare the more expansive NA coronation hymn/prayer of Assurbanipal in Livingstone 1989, 26–27 (without ritual context). See Foster 2005, 335 for a translation of the *takultu*-ritual prayer. Frankena 1954 presents a full treatment of the ritual. For the Akitu festival, see, e.g., the Hellenistic Babylonian Akitu-festival text treated in Linssen 2004, 215–37.

383. The translation "incantation" has become traditional in modern Assyriology even though it is problematic in that it reflects an outdated Frazerian-mode of thinking in anthropology and religious studies in which magic and religion are clearly demarcated. "Ritual wording" may be a better choice. Foster (2007, 91–95) provides a brief description of incantations in terms of the dominant taxonomy in the field, according to which there are four kinds: legitimation, prophylactic, Marduk-Ea (which include a brief dialogue between the two gods), and consecration incantations. The last category is sometimes considered under incantation-prayers, about which see the comments by Frechette in Lenzi 2011, 29 n. 75.

the deity), an item of ritual use (e.g., the kiln in the text below), or an animal (e.g., a bull whose hide will be used to make a cultic drum) to effect some ritual transformation. Two brief examples illustrate the kinds of texts included under this label.

An incantation from the first millennium to exorcize a contagious condition marked by fever reads:

> Incantation: Fire, fire!
> Fire seized a lone man.
> It seized (his) insides, (his) temple,
> It spread (to others) the gnawing of (his) insides,
> The stock of the human race was diminished.
> Belet-ili went before Ea the king,
> "O Ea, humankind was created by your spell,
> "Second, you pinched off their clay from the firmament of the depths.
> "By your great command, you determined their capacities.
> "I cast a spell on the . . . -disease, fever, boils,
> "Leprosy(?), jaundice!
> "Rain down like dew,
> "Flow down like tears,
> "Go down to the netherworld!"
> This incantation is an incantation of Belet-ili, the great queen.[384]

Another example of a first millennium incantation, part of a larger ritual to help a woman overcome miscarriage, has some brief ritual instructions before giving the words of the incantation:[385]

> She rises from the river and approaches the potter's kiln. She embraces the kiln and says the following:
> O pure kiln, great daughter of Anu,
> Within whom the fire flares into being,
> Within whom valiant Girra has taken up his dwelling,
> You are sound, your equipment is sound,
> Whether you be empty or full, you are [sound?].
> But when I conceive,
> I cannot bring to term what is within me.

---

384. See Lambert 1970, 39–45 for an edition of the fire incantation texts. The incantation cited above comes from pp. 42–43, lines 20–33, the translation of which is Foster's (2005, 971, which does not include the word "Incantation:" at the beginning).

385. For a study of the ritual, see Couto-Ferreira 2013.

Please give me your soundness,
Take away my distress!
Let no [imperfect vessel] come out from you,
So too for me, may what is within me thrive,
May I see my baby,
May I find acceptance in the house wherein I dwell![386]

As illustrated by the translation of the first text, incantations often bear the word én, Sumerian for "incantation" in a superscript.[387] This marked the beginning of the wording on the tablet (as opposed to ritual directions, which often followed the text of the incantation or occurred elsewhere). The appearance of deities and demons and the inclusion of various mythological narrative components (e.g., the conversation between Marduk and his father Ea or even a creation narrative) are common in these texts, as are various legitimizing techniques at their conclusion (e.g., disowning the incantation and claiming it belongs to a deity).[388] Incantations attempt to affect situational conditions through the use of performative language and other ritual actions. It is therefore not surprising that they often exhibit poetic qualities in their language, use vivid similes and metaphors, and utilize word play and analogies (e.g., the kiln is likened to a pregnant woman) to achieve their desired results.[389] In contrast to most early incantations (Old Akkadian to Old Babylonian), which come down to us in one copy, incantations from the mid-second millennium on are very often found in multiple copies from various sites.

Incantation-Prayers

The word "incantation-prayer" (which translates the German *Gebetsbeschwö-rung*) is used in Assyriology for those texts that do not fit the previous two categories. Like prayers, these texts address a benevolent entity, usually a deity,

386. See von Weiher 1998, 58–65 for the entire text; the citation is obv. 26–32. The translation of the incantation is from Foster 2005, 979. The translation of the ritual instructions is my own. The anxiety expressed in the last line is an important clue to the social ramifications of infertility for women in ancient Mesopotamia.

387. Older incantations often use the superscript én-é-nu-ru (about which, see Cunningham 1997, 9–10).

388. For the inclusion of a creation narrative, see the well-known example in the incantation against toothache in Foster 2005, 995; see similarly the OB incantations translated in Foster 2005, 180–81. For disowning the incantation, see Lenzi 2010.

389. See Reiner 1985, 94–100; Veldhuis 1991 for close readings of Akkadian incantations. See the extensive catalog of similes in OB incantations in Wasserman 2003b, 112–22. There is nothing comparable for the much larger corpus of post-OB incantations. For word play, see, e.g., Ford 2008, who cites previous literature.

but like incantations they also bear the én superscript. There are several hundred incantation-prayers.[390] Referencing Werner Mayer's classic study of the texts, Christopher Frechette summarizes how these texts may be arranged into subgroupings. He writes,

> Mayer distinguished three major subtypes of incantation-prayers: shuillas, namburbis and prayers serving to free a person from malignant powers; beyond these he identified an array of smaller groups, though he stressed that these should not be taken as an exhaustive listing.... The smaller groups concern the dissolution of unclear or bad dreams, the fending off of field pests, shigu-prayers (petitions for absolution from sin), and blessings for houses and buildings.[391]

The incantation-prayers follow a fairly consistent structure, often including the following six elements: (1) invocation/hymnic introduction, (2) self-presentation, (3) lament, (4) description of the supplicant's acts, (5) petition, and (6) concluding praise.[392] The specific ritual purpose of incantation-prayers was often indicated by a one-line rubric placed after the wording of the text and before the prescribed ritual (e.g., nam-búr-bi indicated an incantation-prayer to release the evil announced in an ominous sign; uš$_{11}$.búr-ru-da, the release of witchcraft).[393] One very well-attested rubric classifies over one hundred incantation-prayers as *shuila*-prayers. (Sum. šu-íl-lá [with variations] means "lifted-hand.") These incantation-prayers, as Frechette writes, "emphasized the communicative gesture to which the shuilla-rubric refers, a salutation signaling recognition of a reciprocal but asymmetrical relationship between client and deity.... This gesture would have provided a particularly apt ritual focus for expressing both the *desire* to (re)establish such a relationship with the deity and the *anticipation* of the deity's acceptance of this relationship and favorable response to the petitions presented."[394] The lifted-hand salutation, from which

390. Cataloged in Mayer 1976, 375–436.

391. Frechette in Lenzi 2011, 29 n. 75, who refers to Mayer 1976, 13–18. For a recent edition of two *shigu*-prayers, see Oshima 2011, 296–304.

392. See Mayer, 1976, 34–37; Frechette, 2012, 129–31 for a review and discussion of these elements, which do not occur in every incantation-prayer and vary in length when they do. I am leaving out of present consideration the rubric (see above) and ritual instructions, which occur after the wording of the incantation-prayer.

393. See Mayer 1976, 22–26. Unfortunately, these rubrics (and the rituals that often follow them) are not always translated in the anthologies. For *namburbis*, see Maul 1994. For anti-witchcraft literature, see Abusch and Schwemer 2011, 2016.

394. See Frechette in Lenzi 2011, 35 (emphasis original). For Frechette's full presentation of the evidence, see Frechette 2012. I am currently cataloging, transliterating, and translating into English all known tablets preserving *shuila*-prayers at the following web site: http://www1.pacific.edu/~alenzi/shuilas/catalog.html.

FIGURE 18. A cylinder seal impression depicting a presentation scene. A divine media-
tor leads a supplicant, followed by another god, into the presence of a seated deity,
whom they greet with uplifted hands. © Trustees of the British Museum, London.

this kind of prayer takes its name, appears frequently in so-called presentation scenes on cylinder seals, in which a mediator-deity leads a person into
the presence of a seated deity (see fig. 18). Another kind of incantation-prayer,
whose purpose is designated by a distinctive rubric, is the *dingirshadabba*-
prayer, a prayer to calm the heart of an angry personal god.[395] Unlike the other
incantation-prayers, these do not always follow a clear structure.[396]

Just as prayers could be collected into series and embedded in complex ritual
activities, so too could incantations and incantation-prayers. This is most evident in the first millennium in ritual series such as Lamashtu (to repel the female
demon of the same name), Shurpu ("Incineration," to release the evil consequences—"the curse"—of some transgression), Maqlu ("Burning," to release
witchcraft), and Mis pi (a ritual to "open the mouth" of a divine image), among
many others.[397] Incantations and incantation-prayers could also appear in royal
ritual ceremonies such as Bit sala' me, "The House of Water Sprinkling," and
Bit rimki, "The House of Bathing," which kept the king in proper standing with
the gods.[398]

395. Some scholars will call these texts (along with *shigu*-prayers) penitential prayers or psalms.
So, e.g., van der Toorn 1985; Foster 2007, 78.

396. These incantation-prayers are not included in Mayer's study (1976). For a brief introduction to Akkadian examples, see Lenzi 2011, 40–43. A sample of these prayers was edited in Lambert
1974. A new edition of the prayers, including all those known in Sumerian, Akkadian, and bilingual
versions, is now available in Jaques 2015. On the limited structural homogeneity of these prayers,
see the treatment in Jaques 2015, 134–91.

397. See Farber 2014; Reiner 1958; Abusch 2015a; Walker and Dick 2001, respectively.

398. For Bit sala' me, see Ambos 2013; for Bit rimki, see Læssøe 1955.

Laments

Although incantation-prayers typically include a section of lament or complaint in which the supplicant bemoans their situation and several of the so-called great prayers elaborate on the supplicant's suffering at significant length, some prayers are so thematically dominated by complaint and woe that scholars have dubbed them laments.[399] There is no indication in the texts that they should be separated from other prayers except for the thematic prominence of lamentation.[400] Noteworthy examples include prayers directed to Marduk by, according to its colophon, a son of Nebuchadnezzar II (604–562 BCE); to Assur, chief god of Assyria, by Tukulti-Ninurta I (1243–1207 BCE); to Ishtar by Assurnasirpal I (1049–1031 BCE); and an Assyrian prayer to Nabu, Marduk's son and scribal deity, which Alasdair Livingstone suggests might be associated with Assurbanipal (668–627 BCE).[401]

Hymns

As the above survey shows, a cornucopia of hymnic material exists in a variety of genres in Akkadian literature (e.g., prayers, narrative poems, and royal inscriptions).[402] When an independent text describes some benevolent entity—

---

399. The incantation-prayer (*shuila*) with the longest lament section is the so-called Great Ishtar Prayer, for which see Foster 2005, 599–605; Zernecke in Lenzi 2011, 257–90. See esp. the great prayers to Marduk, mentioned earlier (see note 377), to Nabu (see Foster 2005, 621–26), and to Ishtar (see Foster 2005, 606–10; Ishtar-Baghdad published in Groneberg 1997, 97–108). The lamentations in incantation-prayers, the great prayers, and the prayers registered here as laments may be profitably compared with texts such as OB Man and His God, Ludlul bel nemeqi, and similar compositions (discussed below on page 172). See Foster 2007, 78; Groneberg 1997, 104–5 for the general point; for a detailed comparison of lament material in incantation-prayers with the laments in Ludlul bel nemeqi tablets I and II, see Lenzi 2015a. For a comparison of several features but esp. the lament material in selected Marduk prayers with Ludlul bel nemeqi, see Oshima 2011. For the category of laments, see Foster 2007, 42–44. Obviously, the texts placed in this category will vary by scholar. For example, SEAL categorizes many of the OB great prayers as well as the OB Man and His God as lamentations (their category 3).

400. See, however, Groneberg 2003, 63–64 for a literary catalog (now published in Wasserman 2016, no. 19) that classifies two Akkadian texts, referred to by incipit, under the term *inḫu*, "lament" (see vi 22′–24′). The full text of these laments is not known.

401. On Nebuchadnezzar II's prayer, see Finkel 1999 for the first treatment; Foster 2005, 852–56 for a translation; Oshima 2011, 316–27 for the most recent edition. For a translation of Tukulti-Ninurta I's prayer, see Foster 2005, 318–23. For a translation of Assurnasirpal I's prayer, see Foster 2005, 327–30. For the prayer to Nabu, see Livingstone 1989, xxvi and 30–32. The text is only attested on a tablet from Sultantepe, which may speak against its association with Assurbanipal.

402. This section draws from material in Lenzi 2011, 56–60, which provides more description and references than are provided here. A well-studied example of the hymnic material in a royal inscription is the prologue and epilogue of the laws of Hammurabi (for this text, see page 150, above); see Hurowitz 1994. For translations, see Foster 2005, 126–35; Roth 1997, 76–81, 133–40.

usually a deity, but also a king, temple, or even city—and praise and adulation dominate the content, scholars typically call the text a hymn.[403] The praise may relate to the deity's attributes, position among the gods, relationship to their temple(s), and/or role in the human social world. Petition may occur in hymns, especially toward the end of such texts; but such petition focuses on the well-being of a king rather than on forgiveness of sins or deliverance from some evil, as in many prayers.[404] In any case, petition is not a major motif.[405] Hymns might include mythological narrative, as in the OB Agushaya Poem, which recounts the goddess Ishtar's conflict with Ea, god of wisdom, and his creation of Saltu, "strife."[406] Hymns could also become sites of theological exposition and innovation, as in the several so-called syncretistic hymns from the first millennium, in which a high deity (or parts of the deity) are equated with other deities.[407] Although hymns vary in length, we find some OB examples comprising precisely fourteen quatrains (fig. 19) and other hymns that run to exactly two hundred lines.[408] As in some prayers, scribes displayed their literary prowess in a

403. For the problems and artificiality of distinguishing between praise for deities, kings, temples, and cities, see Edzard 1994. For an example of a hymn to a king, see the OB bilingual hymn to Hammurabi (1792–1750 BCE; Foster 2005, 136–37; Hecker 1989, 726–27) and the MA ode to Tiglath-Pileser I (1114–1076 BCE; Foster 2005, 324–26), though the latter may turn out to be a fragment of a royal epic (see Hurowitz and Westenholz 1990 for a full discussion); for hymns to cities, see Livingstone 1989, 20–26; Foster 2005, 840, 876–77; Hecker 1989, 768–70; Seux 1976, 122–24. Given the way many narrative poems begin and/or end (e.g., Ludlul bel nemeqi begins and ends with praise for Marduk; Epic of Anzu opens with expressions of praise for Ninurta; Atram-hasis ends with praise for Enlil, etc.), we should recognize that our distinctions between texts labeled hymns and some labeled narrative poems are artificial and do not necessarily reflect the ancients' ideas about classification.

404. For petitions at the end of hymns, see, e.g., the OB hymn to Ishtar (see note 408, below) and Assurbanipal's hymn to Marduk and and his wife Zarpanitu, where the acrostic forms the petition (see note 409 below).

405. See Oshima 2011, 34–35.

406. As J. Westenholz has noted, the poem is "a hymn in narrative mode" (1999, 87). See Groneberg 1997, 55–93 for an edition, translation, and commentary; Foster 2005, 96–106; Hecker 1989, 731–40 give translations.

407. See Oshima 2011, 391–95 for a list of various syncretistic texts, including several hymns, and discussion.

408. For fourteen quatrains, see the OB hymn to the goddess Ishtar (fig. 19), edited by Thureau-Dangin 1925 and treated by Edzard 2004a, 510–15, and the one to the goddess Nanaya, edited most recently anew by Streck and Wasserman 2012. Foster 2005, 85–92; Seux 1976, 39–45; Falkenstein and von Soden 1953, 235–39; Hecker 1989, 721–26 offer translations. For examples of two hundred line hymns, see the Hymn of Bullutsa-rabi to Gula, goddess of healing, edited in Lambert 1967 (other translations include Foster 2005, 583–91; partially in Hecker 1989, 759–64), and the Great Hymn to Shamash, sun god and god of justice, edited in Lambert 1960, 121–38, 318–23, 346 with pls. 33–36, 73 (other translations include Foster 2005, 627–35; Seux 1976, 51–63; Falkenstein and von Soden 1953, 240–47). Many new tablets belonging to this hymn have been identified (see, e.g., George and Al-Rawi 1998). Two important studies include Castellino 1976 on structure; and the close reading of Reiner 1985, 68–84.

FIGURE 19. The reverse of an OB tablet containing the last six of fourteen quatrains of a hymn to Ishtar, each separated by a faint rule line. The
final three-line section on the tablet states the hymn is for the life of
Ammiditana, an OB king of Babylon. The last, indented line on the tablet
reads "its refrain," which is an instruction about how the hymn was to be
performed and probably identifies the previous three lines as the content
of the refrain. The signs in the lower right corner are upside down
because they belong to the obverse of the tablet. The scribe ran out of
room and continued writing the line around the edge of the tablet onto the
reverse. Photo Credit: © RMN-Grand Palais/Art Resource, NY.

few hymns through the use of acrostics, in which the first sign of each inscribed line, when read vertically top to bottom, spells out a name or sentence.[409]

Based on the fact that various terms in the semantic domain of music (e.g., *zamāru*, "song") occur in scribal superscripts, subscripts, and rubrics in both the texts themselves and various catalogs of the texts, many of the compositions that we designate as hymns were probably sung or chanted and, at least sometimes, were accompanied by music of some kind.[410] Scholars have not been able to match this scribal information, however, to structural features of the hymns.[411] As with prayers, scholars are again forced to use their own categories to organize the material (e.g., by time period, entity praised, and/or various characteristics that stand out to the modern interpreter).[412]

While the communication that the prayers, incantations, incantation-prayers, laments, and hymns were intended to facilitate was dominated by words to be recited, the communication was not always *limited* to words. What was to be spoken was often accompanied by gestures and other ritual actions.[413] As mentioned above, these actions are sometimes described in the recited text or specified on the tablet or series in which the wording is preserved.[414] Sometimes, however, there is no written information about the accompanying actions, leaving the interpreter quite in the dark about the text's ritual context.

409. See, e.g, Assurbanipal's hymn to Marduk and his wife Zarpanitu in Livingstone 1989, 6–10 for an edition; Foster 2005, 821–26; Seux 1976, 115–21; Falkenstein and von Soden 1953, 249–53 for translations. Another example may be found in the very dated edition of Strong 1898, 154–62. Foster 2005, 849–51; Seux 1976, 124–28 give translations.

410. See Groneberg 2003 for an important study (note esp. her conclusion on p. 70). Also, Oshima 2011, 35; Edzard 1994, 20. Like the hymns, some scholars believe narrative poems (i.e., epics) were also sung or chanted (so, e.g., West 1997a, 181). See the earlier discussion of audience in ch. 1.

411. The fragmentary state of many hymns has not helped matters. Classificatory scribal labels, as Groneberg 2003 shows, do not seem to correspond to textual form. Rather, they may have reflected the text's musical accompaniment, mode of performance, language, ritual function, and/or content.

412. See, e.g., von Soden 1972–1975, 545–48; Foster 2007, 78–91.

413. In fact, nonverbal communication was also possible. E.g., "a votive statue placed in a temple or a cylinder seal depicting a presentation scene may represent a petitioner's attempt to express their concerns or praise to a benevolent being *visually*, a manner completely lacking any linguistic form of communication" (Lenzi 2011, 11, emphasis original). We also know that amulets, plaques, buried figurines, and other ritual paraphernalia could be used to communicate the undesirability of a malevolent being's approach, the result of which is very much like what is expressed in many incantations. See, e.g., the two uninscribed Lamashtu amulets pictured in Farber 2014, 41.

414. E.g., after an incantation-prayer's wording and rubric, the next line on the tablet sometimes has the Sumerian superscript dù-dù-bi or kìd-kìd-bi, "its ritual," which is then followed by instructions. Sometimes whole prayers are embedded in ritual instructions, as is the case, e.g., in a section from the Babylonian Akitu festival (Linssen 2004, 215–37). In other cases, ritual instructions cite the incipit, or opening line, of a prayer, incantation, or incantation-prayer that is to be recited. See, e.g., the ritual tablet for the royal ritual Bit sala' me (Ambos 2013) or the Hellenistic ritual instructions for replacing the head of a ritual drum (Linssen 2004, 270–74). Performance instructions apparently accompany some hymns, as is the case in two OB hymns that have the words "its refrain" at their conclusion (see note 408, above, for the texts, and fig. 19).

Meditations on Human Suffering and the Divine

The texts in this category are sometimes classified as "wisdom literature," a term borrowed from biblical studies and used in Assyriology as a fuzzy category of convenience to classify compositions whose contents resonated (for some early Assyriologists) with those of Proverbs, Ecclesiastes, and Job.[415] This approach is most evident in Lambert's publication in 1960 entitled *Babylonian Wisdom Literature*, which brought together an assortment of sayings, proverbs, instructions, debates, dialogues, fables, and narrative poems, the latter of which deal in various degrees with life's vicissitudes, especially suffering and the role of divinity therein.[416] Most of these texts have been or will be treated under different headings elsewhere in this book. The four poems treated in this section are Man and His God; the Babylonian Theodicy; Ludlul bel nemeqi, "I will praise the lord of wisdom"; and *Ugaritica* 5, no. 162 (which Foster has entitled A Sufferer's Salvation).[417] Each poem deals specifically with the relationship between human suffering and divinity. The first poem is from the Old Babylonian period; the last three are likely from the late second millennium, though dating the texts is difficult. The characteristic that distinguishes these poems from laments or prayers, which also frequently deal with human suffering in relation to divinity, is the putative audience: none of the texts is directed to a deity; all are directed, rather, to fellow mortals.[418] In all but *Ugaritica* 5, no. 162 (which is quite incomplete), human sin is to blame for divinely ordained suffering.

The Old Babylonian composition Man and His God, somewhat similar to a Sumerian composition of the same name, recounts a dialogue of sorts between a man and a deity in sixty-eight lines.[419] The dialogue is framed by an introduction

415. See Lambert 1960, 1–2. For a review of the history of scholarship surrounding the use of this category, see Cohen 2013, 7–19. Against the recent trend among scholars to reject "wisdom literature" as a category, Cohen argues for its continued usefulness. George likewise sees value in grouping texts as "wisdom," "not by virtue of formal characteristics, but because they share moral tone and philosophical attitude" (2005a, 53).

416. Lambert included some hymns as well (see 1960, 118–38).

417. Foster 2005, 410–11. Only Ludlul bel nemeqi and the Babylonian Theodicy are included in Lambert 1960. For the status of all four among other "wisdom literature" texts, see von Soden 1990, 110–57.

418. For this reason, I have excluded several of the so-called great prayers that are directed to deities rather than a human audience, though the issue of human suffering in relation to the deity is treated extensively. *Ugaritica* 5, no. 162 is still incomplete; it is listed here with the other texts tentatively. It may in fact turn out to be a hymn directed to Marduk.

419. See ETCSL 5.2.4 for an English translation of the Sumerian composition. See Lambert 1987 for the most recent edition of Man and His God. I cite from his translation. See also Foster 2005, 148–50; von Soden 1990, 135–40. Oshima briefly summarizes the text and compares it to Ludlul bel nemeqi (Oshima 2014a, 22–24). The only witness to this text often has two poetic lines on one line of the tablet. Thus, Lambert rearranges the tablet's 69 lines into 92 poetic lines in his edition, plus the line containing the copyist's name (line 69 on the tablet). Line numbers here refer to tablet lines, as is the case in Lambert's edition.

(lines I–II) and a pious concluding exhortation (line 68). The introduction characterizes the relationship between the man and his god as an intimate one ("A man weeps to his god like a friend," line I) and the man's condition as one of emotional and physical exhaustion, which has pushed him to lament raucously before the god ("A bull is his speech, [his] voice two lamenters," line 8).[420] In the opening lines of the man's lament he wonders what sin he has committed to deserve the suffering he is enduring. After a fragmentary section in which the sufferer may confess his wrongdoing (see line 26), the man turns to describe his afflictions and punishment that his god has brought upon him. Another fragmentary section follows (where the man's lament probably ends), during which the man seems to have gained the deity's attention (if not in this passage, then certainly just after it; see line 43b, "he raised him to the earth"). The suffering man then receives from his god healing, food, and clothing in lines 44–45 and a reply to his lament, in which the deity speaks comforting words: the man's punishment is complete, his life is restored, and his divine protection is assured. Amid these words is a slight scolding, which may be the reason for the man's suffering: "Your path is straight and compassion is bestowed on you, You who in future days will not forget [your] god,[421] Your creator, and that you are well favoured" (55–57). The deity also connects in his reply divine beneficence and the man's future moral uprightness: "Eternal life I will provide you. As for you, unblenchingly anoint the parched, Feed the hungry, give water to the thirsty to drink" (61–63). Moreover, anyone who opposes the man will suffer (64–65). The final line of the conclusion (68b) seems to imply a didactic intent to the poem: "May the prayer (*unnēnu*) of your servant sink into your mind."[422]

The Babylonian Theodicy is a learned poem known today from ten first-millennium manuscripts and an ancient commentary. The poem consists of twenty-seven stanzas of eleven lines each, though stanzas IX–XI are not yet recovered and many of the 297 lines are still fragmentary.[423] Every line in each stanza begins with the same sign, which varies from stanza to stanza. When the twenty-seven different head signs are strung together (as an acrostic), the resulting sentence reads (with restorations): "I am Saggil-ki[na]m-ubbib, the

420. Indeed, the poem could be categorized with laments (see below), as have some scholars (e.g., see SEAL 3.1.1.1).

421. Lambert (1987, 199) recognizes though does not prefer an alternative translation that understands the line as a kind of oath intended as an exhortation ("You must never, till the end of time, forget [your] god," according to Foster 2005, 149).

422. So Lambert 1987, 201.

423. See Oshima 2013 for a handbook edition; 2014a for the full critical edition with an introduction, transliteration of the composite text, score of all known manuscripts (add now the fragment in Jiménez 2014, 102–3), a translation, critical and philological notes, rich bibliography of secondary literature, and photographs/handcopies of the witnesses. Other translations include Bottéro in Cavigneaux 2014a; Foster 2005, 914–22; von Soden 1990, 143–57; Lambert 1960, 63–89. An Italian translation with commentary will be published in Piccin forthcoming.

mašmašu-priest, who blesses god and king." Saggil-kinam-ubbib probably lived around the eleventh century BCE; thus, the poem may date to that time, if in fact Saggil-kinam-ubbib composed it.[424]

The poem is a dialogue, though debate may be better, between two men, who have been labeled "friend" and "sufferer" by modern scholars.[425] In alternating stanzas, the sufferer complains and the friend rebuts. The sufferer laments his own plight—he was orphaned early in life, he suffers in mind and body, and he is living in poverty—before asserting his piety and decrying the prosperity of the impious in contrast to his own want. After a break, the sufferer threatens to abandon the ways of the gods and "roam about the far outdoors like a bandit" (line 139).[426] Clearly, the sufferer is troubled by the unfair advantages and injustices in society (see stanzas V, XVII, XXIII, XXV), his lack of provision despite his scribal education (XIX) and piety (III, V, VII), and, ultimately, the questionable value of honoring the gods (VII, XIII, XXIII).

The sufferer's personal laments, questioning of traditional values, and threats to go rogue, so to speak, are answered by the friend in turn. Although the friend begins with some sympathy for the orphaned sufferer, noting the inevitability of death (lines 16–17), he quickly turns to the traditional idea that piety begets blessing and prevents adversity: "He who looks to his god has a protector, the humble man who reveres his goddess will garner wealth" (lines 21–22).[427] In response to the sufferer's complaints and in defense of the traditional view of the gods, the friend beats this drum numerous times (IV, VI, XII, XX, XXII) alongside the ideas of divine incomprehensibility (VIII, XXIV) and the untimely demise of the impious wealthy (VI, XVII, XXII).

How to interpret the ending of the poem (stanzas XXVI and XXVII) is a matter of some disagreement. According to Lambert, the friend agrees in stanza XXVI with the sufferer's earlier accusations of human prejudice and injustice (XXV); the gods have indeed made human nature crooked and full of lies. Having garnered some sympathy, the sufferer makes a final statement, which Lambert characterizes as "a plea that his friend contemplate his grief, and that the gods resume their protection." But, according to Lambert, this "pathetic" ending undermines the very issues the two have been arguing throughout the entire poem so that the poem does not (and the author apparently cannot) resolve the antinomies that arise between traditional dogma and the observations of

424. See the brief discussion on page 27, above, treating authorship in Akkadian literature. For more on this famous scholar, his composing the poem, the possibility of pseudonymous authorship, and the date of the poem, see Oshima 2013, xiv–xvii; 2014a, 121–24.
425. See page 184, below, for other debates.
426. The translation is Foster's (2005, 917).
427. Foster 2005, 915.

everyday life.[428] According to Foster, the poem draws to a close more open-endedly. The sufferer, he writes, "concludes by voicing, in effect, a *challenge* to his gods to take better care of him in the future—at least, mercy and a greater sense of divine responsibility are his only hope. The reader is left to judge whether or not he concludes with a vote of no confidence."[429] According to Oshima's recent interpretation, the traditional view is upheld in the end: The friend in his last stanza (XXVI) scolds the sufferer and rather strongly blames the sufferer's impiety for his suffering. The sufferer, realizing his waywardness finally turns to the gods for help (XXVII).[430]

Ludlul bel nemeqi, "I will praise the lord of wisdom," is the Akkadian name of a narrative poem that retrospectively recounts in a first-person voice the divinely imposed suffering and divinely enacted restoration of the poem's pro-tagonist, a notable figure named Shubshi-meshre-Shakkan. The poem probably comprised some six hundred lines originally, written over five tablets (according to Oshima's recent edition), though just over 70 percent of the poem is presently preserved.[431] The poem is attested on more than five dozen manuscripts, all of which come from major first millennium libraries and archives. Fifteen of the known manuscripts are school exercise tablets. The poem was also the subject of an ancient commentary.[432] Many scholars believe the poem was composed in the last quarter of the second millennium, but there is currently no solid proof

---

428. Lambert 1960, 65. Oppenheim is harsher in his assessement, writing "[t]he argument is without vigor and cogency, the end contrived and lame" (Oppenheim and Reiner 1977, 273).

429. Foster 2005, 914 (emphasis added). See also Foster 2007, 35, where he writes: "The suf-ferer concludes by saying that he has lived decently and can only hope that the gods will finally treat him as he deserves."

430. Oshima 2013, xxxi–xxxiii and 2014a, 140–42. His emphasis on the sufferer's beliefs and his claim that the man makes "a profession of faith" reflect modern ideas about religion more than the ancient Babylonian cultural context.

431. See Annus and Lenzi 2010 for a handbook edition; Oshima 2014a for the most recent critical edition with an introduction, transliteration of the composite text, score of all known manuscripts, a translation, critical and philological notes, rich bibliography of secondary literature, and photo-graphs/handcopies of the witnesses. There is some uncertainty about the number of tablets in the poem and its length. Oshima's recent suggestion (2012b and now 2014a, 6–7) that there may have been another tablet between what was previously identified as tablets III and IV (compare Annus and Lenzi 2010; Lambert 1960, who produced an earlier and still valuable critical edition of the poem) is quite reasonable. Future evidence, in my opinion, is likely to confirm the idea. The estimate of the text's current state of recovery is my own, based on five tablets of 120 lines each and a careful collation of all known manuscripts. Other translations of the poem, which vary significantly in the ordering of the final tablet's lines, include Foster 2005, 392–409; von Soden 1990, 110–35; Lambert 1960, 21–62. An Italian translation with commentary will be published in Piccin forthcoming.

432. See Oshima 2014a, 377–79 for the most up-to-date list of manuscripts. My edition of the commentary is available through the Yale Cuneiform Commentary Project (CCP 1.3, https://ccp .yale.edu/P394923).

for this reasonable hypothesis.[433] The poem shows a remarkable familiarity with medical vocabulary, the incantatory and lament traditions, witchcraft and demonology, and learned interpretive techniques.[434] Its anonymous author was very likely a professional exorcist.[435]

After an opening hymn that alternates between praise of Marduk's wrath and his mercy (I 1–40), the remainder of tablet I describes the man's social problems that his punishment brought upon him while tablet II takes up the physical suffering that he endured at Marduk's hand. Tablet III and IV recount his salvation and describe the reversal of his physical suffering while tablet V reintegrates the man into his community and offers concluding praise to Marduk.

The opening hymn establishes the doxological and didactic intent of the poem (see esp. I 39–40) but also underlines thematically the sovereignty and incomprehensibility of Marduk's will in distributing wrath and mercy ("Marduk, he sees everything in the heart of the gods, But no god can learn his counsel," I 31–32; "Without his consent, who could assuage his striking? Apart from his intention, who could stay his hand?" I 35–36).[436] In the lines immediately following the hymn we learn that Marduk's anger toward the protagonist results in the man's loss of divine protection and the establishment of evil or obscure signs and terrifying dreams. Expelled from his house, he loses favor with the king and he suffers professionally from courtiers who scheme against him. Terrified, the man falls further out of social favor among his community, family, and friends, and finds himself completely without help. His possessions are seized, his property ruined, and his office occupied. Utterly grief-stricken, afraid, and without help from his prayers, he hopes for relief in the future.

But at the start of tablet II, the second year of his trials, he is disappointed; he is surrounded by evil and without help from his personal deities and ritual experts.[437] He wonders why he is being treated as though he were impious when in fact he honors the divine rites and the king. This causes the man to lapse temporarily into a deep agnosticism about the knowability of the gods and to muse on the frailty and vacillations of human existence. Turning from his theological doubts, the man recounts a litany of demonically delivered physical ailments that reflect the phraseology of laments in prayers and lists of symptoms

---

433. For introductory issues, see Annus and Lenzi 2010, ix–xxxix; Oshima 2014a, 3–77, who also reviews related texts.

434. For medical vocabulary, see Annus and Lenzi 2010, xxvii. For incantatory and lament traditions, see Lenzi 2015a. For witchcraft and demonology, see Noegel 2016, who also shows numerous instances of the deliberate use of paronomasia for learned and thematic effect. For learned interpretive techniques, see Lenzi 2015d.

435. Lenzi 2012.

436. The translation follows Annus and Lenzi 2010, 32 with a few minor changes. For an interesting treatment of the opening hymn, see Piccin and Worthington 2015.

437. For a literary reading of tablet II, see Reiner 1985, 101–18.

in medical texts. As his condition worsens, he is confined to his bed; he finds no help from the ritual experts; and he receives no mercy from his gods. Burial preparations and lamentation are complete; all that remains is to await death. But salvation is at hand.

In a series of dreams at the beginning of tablet III, several divine beings visit the protagonist; they speak his deliverance and heal him. Marduk's wrath is appeased; he had heard the man's pleas for salvation. In a broken passage, it seems that the man admits to his sins and acts of negligence. The remainder of tablet III, the ending of which is still uncertain, describes the reversal of his physical afflictions, which seems to continue into the very fragmentary and incompletely reconstructed tablet IV. At the opening of tablet V we meet a refreshed Shubshi-meshre-Shakkan, restored to health and praising Marduk's healing powers. He enters the Esagil temple complex—the temple of Marduk in Babylon. As he enters twelve different temple gates, he receives items related to his restoration (e.g., abundance, life, clear signs, release from guilt, relief of lamentation, etc.).[438] After recounting some rites at the temple, the poem offers a crescendo of praise that moves from the citizens of Babylon to all of humanity. The conclusion to the poem is not entirely recovered, but its didactic and doxological ("your [i.e, Marduk's] praise is sweet!" V 120) intentions are again affirmed.

The fundamental question for understanding this text is: What is this unique poem's purpose? The answers scholars have suggested are quite varied. Is Ludlul a fictional narrative poem with sapiential intentions, something like the Epic of Gilgamesh? Is it a narrative philosophical treatment of the issue of theodicy?[439] Is it an attempt (perhaps polemical) to exalt Marduk's cult status or to critique a political dynasty for honoring the wrong gods?[440] Is it a thanksgiving hymn with a more substantive narrative element than is typical of that genre? Was the poem written for a real person named Shubshi-meshre-Shakkan as a thanksgiving hymn and subsequently taken into the scribal curriculum?[441] (Several documents name the man in them.)[442] Is the poem an in-group propagandistic pseudepigraph, written by a learned exorcist to lend ideological support to the institution and worldview of exorcism?[443] These questions—not all

438. The author has utilized learned hermeneutics to connect each gate's name with what the man receives at the gate. See Lenzi 2015d.

439. So, e.g., Jacobsen 1976, 162; Bottéro 1965–1966, 105–11.

440. See Moran 2002, 182–200, who argues that Marduk must become the devotee's personal god; similarly Albertz 1988. Oshima 2014a, 69–73 suggests the poem was at least partly intended to be a theological polemic against the Kassite dynasty.

441. As argued by Oshima 2014a, 18, 28–34.

442. See Oshima 2014a, 16–17 for the most recent roundup of relevant texts.

443. As I have argued (Lenzi 2012). I think the learned quality of the poem and the ritual officials' failures to diagnose the man's problems suggest an origin in intellectual, ideological activity rather than liturgical needs.

of which are mutually exclusive—strike at the heart of the issues surrounding this interesting text. Given the new textual basis for the poem, we are likely to see many new interpretive studies of Ludlul bel nemeqi in the near future.

Ugaritica 5, no. 162 is a broken tablet from Ugarit preserving forty-five lines of a composition—some suggest it is a hymn or prayer—that sounds very much like Ludlul bel nemeqi.[444] Unfortunately, the beginning and ending of the tablet are broken off. Like Ludlul bel nemeqi, the protagonist laments his confused omens and dreams, his preparations for burial and completed lamentation, and his pitiful, afflicted condition. He exhorts the reader/listener to praise Marduk and extols how Marduk, despite bringing the punishment, has had mercy on him. This latter passage is similar to lines at the beginning of Ludlul bel nemeqi V. Absent is any mention of sin. But, given the fragmentary condition of the composition, this is not surprising.

A few examples of other Akkadian texts that lament some human loss but do not direct themselves to deities may also be mentioned here. An OB text preserves a fragment of a lament over a destroyed city, a well-known genre in Sumerian literature.[445] Another OB text entitled Elegy on the Death of Naram-Sin by its editor offers a panygeric to the Old Akkadian king.[446] In a NA royal inscription (K.891), Assurbanipal boasts of his pious acts on the obverse of the tablet and then on the reverse bitterly questions and complains about his ill-treatment, using words and phrases that echo Ludlul bel nemeqi.[447] Finally, there is an Assyrian elegy for a woman who died in childbirth, which is particularly moving. It speaks in the voice of the deceased woman, who vividly describes how her happiness in pregnancy turned to sorrow as death pulled her away from her husband.[448]

444. Oshima 2011, 205–15 offers the most recent edition. See also Foster 2005, 410–11; and the recent translation in Cohen 2013, 165–75, who also discusses the text's loose relationship to Ludlul bel nemeqi. The genetic relationship between Ludlul bel nemeqi and the text is unclear. Oshima (2011, 205 n. 2) reports a verbatim parallel between Ludlul bel nemeqi V 18 and line 43′ of the present text, which he confirms in his edition of the poem (2014a, 319). Oshima 2014a, 25 n. 104 catalogs other turns of phrase that are comparable, though not identical in both compositions.

445. See Wasserman 2003a for an edition; Foster 2005, 153 for translation.

446. See J. Westenholz 1997a, 203–20.

447. See Luckenbill 1927, 376–78 for an older translation, cited in Foster 2007, 43. Finn 2017, 83 notes briefly "the clear thematic parallels with the sufferer in *Ludlul*." See the recent edition and translation by Jamie Novotny and Joshua Jeffers at http://oracc.museum.upenn.edu/rinap/rinap5/Q003771/html. The text will appear in print in the royal inscriptions of Assurbanipal (RINAP 5). I discussed the implications of the use of Ludlul bel nemeqi for the interpretation of this text in Lenzi 2018. The fuller treatment will appear in a chapter of a book I am currently writing, tentatively entitled *Suffering in Babylon*.

448. See Livingstone 1989, 37–39 for an edition; see Foster 2005, 949; Hecker 1989, 780–81 for translations. Reiner 1985, 85–93 offers a literary analysis, as does George 2010a. The latter also publishes the first ever copy of the composition's only textual witness.

Proverbs, Advice, Dialogues, and Debates

Proverbs

Bilingual proverbs (Sumerian-Akkadian, Akkadian-Hittite, and Akkadian-Hurrian) are much better attested than proverbs preserved solely in Akkadian.[449] Akkadian proverbs appear in only a few tablets (mostly fragmentary) and as citations in other texts, especially letters.[450] Their identification as proverbs in the latter contexts is not always clear and simple. Still, what has come down to us is enough to confirm that proverbs, aphorism, and epigrammatic sayings existed among Akkadian speakers and writers. The content and topics of the proverbs that we have are similar to the proverbs found throughout the ancient Near East, touching on interpersonal relationships, success in daily life, religious concerns, financial matters, and general reflections about life, among many others.[451] The terseness of many proverbs makes translation difficult. And even when a translation is clear, the *meaning* of the proverb may remain opaque. What, for example, does this proverb mean? "(It is said), 'the unlearned is a cart, the ignorant his road.'"[452] According to Lambert, it is analogous to the English saying "the blind leading the blind."[453] As is the case with any intercultural attempt at understanding aphorisms, the interpretation of Akkadian proverbial sayings requires a good deal of contextualization and historical imagination.[454] And, despite our best efforts, uncertainty is likely to haunt our understanding.

Instructions/Advice

Several ancient Near Eastern cultures frame proverbial, practical wisdom as the speech of a sage or father to his pupil or son. Well-known examples hail from Egypt and the Bible, including Instructions of Ptahhotep, Instructions of

449. For an introduction to proverbs, Sumerian and Akkadian, see Wasserman 2011b. For a selection of the bilingual material in translation (with references to the editions of Lambert 1960, 222–75; Alster 1997), see Foster 2005, 422–33; also, Cohen, 2013, 199–211.

450. See Lambert 1960, 275–78 (proverbial collections), 280–82 (proverbs in other texts); Cohen 2013, 213–31 (proverbs in letters). See also van Dijk 1976, no. 53; Streck and Wasserman 2016, who publish a new proverbial tablet of OB provenance (BM 13928) and republish the MB tablet CBS 14235, treated previously by Lambert (1960, 276–77).

451. For the even smaller corpus of Akkadian riddles, which are generically related to proverbs, see Cavigneaux 2006–2008, to which add now Streck and Wasserman 2011, 123–24.

452. The Akkadian is *lā lamdum-mi eriqqu, lā mūdû ḫarrā[ššu]*. Note the balance between the two halves of the saying and the consonance of *lā lamdum* and *lā mūdû*.

453. Lambert 1960, 260–62.

454. For a general introduction to paremiology (the study of proverbs), see Mieder 2012. See, e.g., Alster, a major contributor to the scholarship of Mesopotamian proverbial literature, who offers a persuasive interpretation of an Akkadian proverb cited in a letter to an Assyrian king (1989).

Amenemope, and Prov 1:8–19 and 2:1–22, among others. Within Mesopotamia, we have the Sumerian Instructions of Shuruppak alongside a few Akkadian texts, the best representatives of which are Counsels of Wisdom and the Instructions of Shupe-ameli.[455]

Counsels of Wisdom, originally about 150 lines in length, is a series of topical instructions in which a father presumably—the opening lines are fragmentary—offers practical life-advice to a boy addressed as "my son" (see line 81).[456] The composition is known from just over a dozen and a half first-millennium manuscripts from Nineveh, Assur, Babylon, Nippur, Kish, and Sippar. Significantly, about a third of these are school exercise tablets.[457] Lambert, one of the early editors of the text, divided the work into sections by topic, which treat the kind of company one should keep, the kind of girl one should *not* marry (i.e., a slave girl or prostitute), the means to avoid and diffuse conflicts with adversaries, the importance of propriety in one's speech, and the reward of personal piety, among others.[458] Each topic occupies from as few as five to almost twenty lines. Though the order of topics seems to follow no rhyme or reason, I have argued elsewhere that the poem is loosely organized around a "house" *Leitmotif.* There is movement within the text from its opening to closing lines, which describe the young man's household/parents and his future professional patron deity, Ea, god of wisdom, respectively. There is also an anchoring point in the text's central pericope (lines 81–92, cited earlier on page 20), which describes the young man's future professional obligations as a scribal administrator. Around this central passage are arranged moral admonitions pertaining to the young man's personal life. Given these structural and rhetorical features, I suggest:

> the program of Counsels of Wisdom was scribal centered. In its first millennium setting, the text reflected and simultaneously perpetuated within the scribal curriculum the values and social position of the successful scribe, who held a place above the common person but served under those in political and religious power. Counsels of Wisdom advises young men training for the scribal profession in the art of maintaining this precarious

455. Sumerian Instructions of Shuruppak is also attested in a fragmentary Akkadian translation (see Lambert 1960, 92–95; Alster 2005, 48 with pls. 13–15 for another Akkadian translation of the text).

456. See Lambert 1960, 96–107 for an edition; Oshima is preparing a new edition with several unpublished witnesses. I thank him for sharing this edition with me before publication. According to Oshima's reconstruction, Lambert's text may be about fifteen lines too long. Foster 2005, 412–15; von Soden 1990, 163–68 provide translations. I have treated the text in two related essays, one an encyclopedia entry and the other an interpretive essay (Lenzi forthcoming, 2019).

457. For witnesses from Kish, see now Gurney 1989, nos. 50, 51, and 88. Some of the manuscripts from Nineveh, Sippar, and Babylon will be published in Oshima's edition.

458. See Lambert 1960, 96. The very short fragment of a text that Lambert calls Counsels of a Pessimist includes similar practical life-advice (see Lambert 1960, 107–9).

position by moving the young man from his parental house [in the opening lines] through the scribal house [in the closing lines] while educating him about the importance of integrity in the house of his future lord [lines 81–92] and self-control in the maintenance of his own [the surrounding admonitions]. Thus, Counsels of Wisdom offers a distinctive form of managerial wisdom to future literate professionals.[459]

The Instructions of Shupe-ameli is a similar text covering many of the same kinds of topics, that is, practical concerns related to personal and professional success in life.[460] Presently, the Akkadian text comprises about 150 lines and is known only via fragmentary tablets from Ugarit, Emar, and Hattusa. Despite the discovery of these witnesses at sites peripheral to Mesopotamia, the composition probably originated in Mesopotamia during the Old Babylonian period since its title appears in an OB literary catalog.[461] What sets this text apart from the previous one is the fact that the son answers the father's positive advice with negative statements, "that expose the uselessness of the father's instructions," as Yoram Cohen writes. "The father's instructions are in fact pointless because death is fast approaching. Although one may possess wealth, as the son concludes, it will not hinder death's arrival."[462]

The same pessimistic sentiment expressed by Shupe-ameli's son appears in a number of other Akkadian texts that convey advice. Among these are lines 9–10 of a very fragmentary text Lambert called Counsels of a Pessimist: "[Whatever] men do does not last for ever, Mankind and their achievements alike come to an end."[463] This "negative wisdom" comes through strongly in The Ballad of Early Rulers, which asks the whereabouts of several well-known but dead ancient luminaries as a foil for reflecting on the transitory character of life.[464] It also finds expression in Enlil and Namzitarra, which is translated into Akkadian in tablets from Emar and Ugarit and augmented with proverbs from a father to his son; in fragmentary dialogic texts; and in many other passages of larger works (e.g., Epic of Gilgamesh).[465]

459. Lenzi 2019, 69.

460. The ancient title of the text is *Shima milka*. Cohen 2013, 81–128 is the most recent treatment and translation; he includes extensive references to the secondary literature.

461. See Cohen 2013, 115.

462. Cohen 2013, 121.

463. Lambert 1960, 109.

464. For the phrase "negative wisdom," see Cohen 2013, 14–16, who has borrowed the label from biblical studies. See Cohen 2013, 129–50 for the most recent treatment of The Ballad of Early Rulers. See also Foster 2005, 769–80, who refers to the poem as a drinking song, for another translation.

465. For Enlil and Namzitarra, see Cohen 2013, 151–63. For the fragmentary dialogic texts, see Streck and Wasserman 2014; 2011, 117–23. For larger works, see the Yale tablet of OB Gilgamesh

A rather unique admonitory text, entitled Advice to a Prince (also referred to as the Babylonian *Fürstenspiegel*), offers counsel to a domestic king about royal success via a series of conditional statements. The if-clause (protasis) mentions the king's behavior; the then-clause (apodosis) states the resulting effect(s).[466] For example, the text begins:

> If a king does not heed justice, his people will fall into anarchy, and his land will become a waste. If he does not heed the justice of his land, Ea, king of destinies, will change his destiny so that misfortune constantly hounds (him). If he does not heed his princes, his days will be cut short. If he does not heed the scholars, his land will rebel against him. If he heeds the scoundrel, the land will defect. If he heeds the craftiness of Ea, (it will mean) the defeat of the national army, (and) among the great gods they will constantly hound him in deliberate and righteous ways.[467]

The text goes on to offer warnings against violating various rights of the citizens of Sippar, Babylon, and Nippur, prompting Lambert to write, "the aim of the text is clearly to protect the rights of the citizens of Sippar, Nippur, and Babylon from taxation, forced labour, and misappropriation of their property."[468] The identity of the king—if there was a single king in mind at the time of writing—is uncertain as is the precise identity of the person(s) or group behind the text's composition. As Lambert notes, the conditional sentence syntax and the use of certain phrases in the apodoses recall omen literature, which "was well suited for warnings to a king.[469] The completely general protasis, 'If a king ...', avoided any insinuations against him."[470] Despite the composition's interest in three southern cities, the text was initially known only from a tablet in Assurbanipal's library. A duplicate, however, has turned up in Nippur.[471] The authoritative invocation of the text in a Neo-Babylonian letter from a scholar to

---

iv 140–143 (George 2003, 1:200–201), the Meissner tablet cols. i–iii (perhaps from Sippar) of the same (George 2003, 1:276–79), and SB Gilgamesh X 297–322 (George 2003, 1:696–99); see also, e.g., Ludlul bel nemeqi II 33–48 (Annus and Lenzi 2010, 20, 35–36; Oshima 2014, 88–89).

466. Lambert 1960, 110–15 offers an edition (with earlier literature) on the basis of one Ninevite tablet. Cole 1996, no. 128, the most recent edition, includes a duplicate from Nippur. Lambert's introduction was not replaced by Cole. Recent translations include Foster 2005, 867–69; von Soden 1990, 170–73. Hurowitz 1998 gives a literary reading that highlights the role of the god Ea in the text. Biggs 2004 argues that the text is deliberately archaizing in an attempt to create the appearance of greater antiquity and thus greater authority for its political claims. For the text as evidence within a discussion of civic institutions and the limitations of Mesopotamian royal power in Babylonia, see Kuhrt 2014. Finn 2017, 85–95, 200–202 treats the text within a study of discourse questioning royalty.

467. Cole 1996, 273.

468. Lambert 1960, 111.

469. Note, however, that the sentences lack the Akkadian conditional particle *šumma*, "if."

470. Lambert 1960, 110.

471. See note 466, above.

the Assyrian king and the text's inclusion in a literary catalog indicate the piece was rather well-known among literate individuals in the first millennium.[472]

Dialogues

In a similar vein to the above texts is The Dialogue of Pessimism, a unique text from the first millennium that presents the vacillations of a master and the obsequious agreements of his servant.[473] The master decides on some course of action, to which the servant offers his support and reasons. But the master then immediately changes his mind and decides against the proposed action, to which, again, the servant offers his support and reasons. For example:

"Servant, listen to me."
"Yes, master, yes."
"I will make loans."
"So make them, master, [make them]. The man who makes loans, his grain is (still) his grain while his interest is profit."
"No, servant, I will certainly not make loans."
"Do not make them, master, do not make them. Loaning is [swee]t(?) as falling in love, getting back as pain[ful] as giving birth. They will consume your grain, be always abusing you, and finally they will swindle you out of the interest on your grain."[474]

The master vacillates on ten different actions: to visit the palace, to take a meal, to roam[475] the countryside, to start a family, to commit fraud, to love a woman, to sacrifice to his god, to make a loan, and to do a public good, according to the Assyrian version.

How to read this rather odd dialogue, that is, whether to read it as humorous satire or something more serious (i.e., a commentary on all human action), will turn on one's interpretation of the final cryptic exchange:

472. For the NB letter, see Reiner 1982. The letter is now published as SAA 18, no. 124 (see Reynolds 2003, 101). The citation is in rev. 2–6. For the literary catalog, see Lambert 1989, 95–96.

473. The poem is known from a handful of first millennium manuscripts and probably dates around the same time since its text mentions an iron dagger in line 52. For an edition, see Lambert 1960, 139–49; Saporetti 2004. Foster 2005, 923–26; Livingstone in Hallo and Younger 2003–2016, 1:495-96; von Soden 1990, 157–63 offer translations. For other translations and secondary literature on the poem's meaning, see Foster 2007, 35–36; more recently, Samet 2008; Minunno 2010; Metcalf 2013.

474. Foster 2005, 925.

475. Identifying the topic turns on our understanding of the rare word *muttaprassidu*, "roaming, roving one," which Lambert, e.g., understands as the activity of a hunter (1960, 145) while others see the activity as aimless wandering (e.g., Foster 2005, 923).

"Servant, listen to me."
"Yes, master, yes."
"What, then, is good?"
"To break my neck and your neck and throw (us) in the river is good.
Who is so tall as to reach to heaven? Who is so broad as to encompass
the netherworld?"
"No, servant, I will kill you and let you go first."
"Then my master will certainly not outlive me even three days!"[476]

As is widely recognized, the servant draws on a traditional proverbial saying
("Who is so tall as to reach to heaven? Who is so broad as to encompass the
netherworld?") to underline human limitation. And the master's response to the
servant's suggestion along with the servant's retort exposes an ironic reversal of
roles, of which the master is blind: he is in fact dependent on his servant. Putting
these pieces together, Christopher Metcalf has recently suggested an interesting
philosophical interpretation of the poem:

> Death is an absolute fact of human existence that offers us release from
> the decisions that we are constantly forced to take and that offer us no
> absolute certainty.... The final reversal shows that those who enjoy the
> freedom to make such choices are incapable of taking them (the master),
> while those who would be sufficiently experienced to make an intelligent
> choice lack the power to do so in practice (the slave).[477]

Debates/Disputations

In the Sumerian and Akkadian compositions modern scholars have labeled
debates or disputations, two personified entities, including animals (e.g., horse
vs. ox; bird vs. fish), plants (e.g., tamarisk vs. palm), tools (hoe vs. plow), and
seasons (winter vs. summer), argue about which of the two of them is of more
worth.[478] The argument centers on the debaters' inherent properties, which are,

476. Foster 2005, 925–26.
477. Metcalf 2013, 261, 264. Helle 2017, 216–19 responds to Metcalf's reading and argues that
the last passage of the text implies that suicide empowers humans to overcome the uncertainty of
the time and cause of their death.
478. For a general overview of both Sumerian and Akkadian disputation poems, see Volk 2012.
The Akkadian disputations have been treated briefly in Vogelzang 1991; exhaustively by Jiménez
2017, who also discusses the Sumerian ones briefly (13–26). Jiménez presents new editions of three of
the eight disputations in Akkadian (The Series of the Poplar [167–227], The Series of the Spider [291–
323], and for the first time Palm and Vine [221–87]) as well as possibly related fragments (396–99) and
an edition and study of a previously poorly known fable, which he calls The Story of the Poor, Forlorn
Wren (325–73). See Lambert 1960, 175–85, 168–75, and 210 for editions of Ox and Horse, Nisaba and

as Vanstiphout has suggested, "the starting point, or the material basis, or both, of the argument. . . . The Dispute *explicitly* lists them, compares them, discusses them, eventually points out their consequences and counterpoints. The point is that in this type of composition the natural properties are turned into *values*. . . . The inanimate contenders stand for something which can best be described as *sets of values*."[479] Although important, the utility of each protagonist to humans is not the sole point of the debate since most sparring partners are, on the face of things, equally valuable; rather, in keeping with the texts' uses in the scribal curriculum, the participants' rhetorical skills and the ethical values they embody or exemplify are the central matters and, in the Sumerian texts, decide the victor.[480]

Although disputations are best known from the Sumerian literary corpora, there are presently eight examples of the genre preserved in Akkadian: The Tamarisk and the Palm, The Series of the Willow/Poplar, Nisaba and Wheat, The Ox and the Horse, The Tale of the Donkey, The Series of the Fox, The Series of the Spider, and the recently discovered Palm and Vine.[481] Most of these texts are attested in only a few tablets and are still rather fragmentarily reconstructed. The Akkadian disputations, like their Sumerian counterparts, probably followed a tripartite structure, though their incomplete recovery does not always bear this structure out explicitly in each text.[482] The disputations begin with a cosmologically oriented prologue, which establishes the place of the two contenders in the created order. For example, The Series of the Spider opens with these lines:

> When the gods in their assembly created [*the universe*],
> Brought into being the [S]ky, put tog[ether *the Netherworld*],

---

Wheat, and The Tale of the Donkey, respectively (with notes on pp. 331–33, 337). The Series of the Fox was edited by Kienst in 2003. Lambert's edition is useful but outdated (1960, 186–209, 333–37). Jiménez can now adduce eleven more fragments; see his introduction to the text with a textual catalog and notes in 2017, 39–57 and his editions of the fragments on pp. 377–95. An excerpt of the text is translated in Foster 2005, 930. The Tamarisk and the Palm is the best-preserved (and most studied) disputation, available in one Sumerian tablet and several Akkadian tablets (two from Old Babylonian Shaduppum—probably indirectly joined, two from Assur—likely of Middle Assyrian origins, and one from late-second-millennium Emar), which show significant textual variation. See Cohen 2013, 178–98; more recently Jiménez 2017, 28–39 for an overview; Wilcke 1989 for the most recent edition (add Cavigneaux 2003), which presents the various Akkadian versions in score fashion on pp. 171–78. (Lambert's edition, 1960, 151–64, 328–30, 346, is now outdated.) Streck 2004 offers an important study of the arboreal realia; Foster 2005, 927–29 gives a translation. Though not offering a new edition for these last five texts, Jiménez 2017, 28–68 provides further notes and secondary literature on them.

479. Vanstiphout 1990, 280 (emphasis original).

480. Vanstiphout 1990, 280–81; see also Vanstiphout 1992c, 342–50. It is likely that the Akkadian disputations ended with a victor, too. The present evidence, however, does not show this feature in the poems clearly (Jiménez 2017, 72).

481. For the Sumerian texts, see the series of articles from Vanstiphout (1990, 1992a, 1992c, and 2014). Some scholars exclude The Series of the Fox from the disputations (e.g., Vanstiphout 1988).

482. See Jiménez 2017, 69–72 for a recent overview.

They brought forth living beings, all creatures,
Wild animals of the steppe, beasts of the steppe, and all creatures of
    civilization.
After t[hey had distribu]ted all sanctuaries to the living beings,
(And) to the wild animals and creatures of civilization had distributed
    the temples.
[Am]ong all the creatures (and) every species, [*Spider*] kept boasting
    extravagantly:
"[. . .] . . . in my kind I am the strongest!"
Ninshiku [saw i]t and (said): "I (hereby) create two pipsqueaks,
"Among the creatures I (hereby) give them splendid names.
"(The first) I (hereby) call '[str]ong *ḫamānīru*',
"I (hereby) proclaim the name (of the second) to be '[. . .] . . . *ešqapīzu*.'"
[Spider,] the *ešqapīzu*, and the *ḫamānīru* started a quarrel.[483]

The disputation proper follows and forms the main part of the poem. Here the
contenders present their case for supremacy, exchanging rhetorical barbs and
attempting to establish their relationship to royalty (the palace and king or their
own) along the way. The following example comes from a well-preserved section of the otherwise only partially known (and recently recovered) Palm and
Vine. The palm is speaking:

Rope is the product of my branches:
The fisherman takes mesh for his net,
The bird hunter plaits strands for his snare.
The builder restores the ruin with the help of my beams.
The *marmaḫḫu*-priest makes splendid his flour oblations with my innards,
The miller brings his regular portions to the table of gods and king.
In the gateway, the entrance of the gods, my doors span wide,
My title—"the king"—surpasses that of all other trees.
How dare you compare yourself with me in a contest?
Conceitedly confronting me, provoking a quarrel?[484]

The disputations likely ended with an adjudication scene in which one of the
contenders is pronounced the winner, though this is currently unattested clearly
in any of the Akkadian texts.

---

483. See Jiménez 2017, 302–5 for the text and translation. The translation of the two named creatures is uncertain, though it is likely that the words designate some kind of small creature, perhaps
insects (Jiménez 2017, 71, 319, 322–23). Tamarisk and Palm begins similarly, see Cohen 2013, 181.
    484. See Jiménez 2017, 250–51 for the text and translation.

Although the disputations exhibit playful, humorous banter (and thus in many respects belong with the texts discussed in the following section), they also likely had a pedagogical role in the scribal curriculum, teaching students vocabulary, rhetoric, and various aspects of material culture. Moreover, as Enrique Jiménez has convincingly shown, these texts parody epic narrative poetry and thus offer "a critical response to the sophisticated language and contents of 'serious' Babylonian literature."[485] Yet the very act of producing a parody demonstrates and perpetuates the importance of the text being parodied.[486] Thus it seems that the disputations were, among their other uses, a subtle medium for the enculturation of young scribes into matters more serious.[487]

Satire, Parody, and Humor

We all know humor when we hear or see it. Satire and parody require a bit more reflection. Although satire and parody are related and may both utilize humor, the two terms are not identical literary phenomena. Satire, according to William Jones, "adopts a critical attitude toward its target with the goal of censuring human folly.... The satirist serves as self-appointed prosecutor, judge, and jury, exposing and condemning the worst excesses of human behavior," utilizing humor, shame, or outrage in the process to bring the wayward and wicked back to moral rectitude.[488] Parody is a "form of ironic imitation," according to Linda Hutcheon and Malcolm Woodland. "In formal terms," they write, "parody is a doubled structure, incorporating backgrounded aspects of the parodied text of the past into the foreground of its present self. The two texts neither merge nor cancel each other out; they work together, while remaining distinct," to effect some rhetorical purpose, which runs the gamut from sharp rebuke through satirical criticism to playful tribute.[489] Because humor, satire, and parody rely on cultural context for their rhetorical success, it is very difficult to identify them in another culture, especially one so far removed in time as is ancient Mesopotamia. We are no doubt missing out on some Mesopotamian fun. This final section of the survey offers a small selection of compositions many Assyriologists suggest were primarily intended as satire, parody, or humor.[490]

485. Jiménez 2017, 99.
486. Jiménez 2017, 107.
487. See Jiménez 2017, 121–24.
488. Jones 2012, 1255–56.
489. Hutcheon and Woodland 2012, 1001, 1002.
490. For general discussions of satire, parody, and humor in Mesopotamian texts, see Foster 1974; 1995; 2007, 37–39; 2009, 209–10; Reiner 1978, 201–2; D'Agostino 1998, 2000. These provide references and treatments to several other texts that are not discussed here. Frahm 1998 centers his discussion on the dark humor of NA royal inscriptions. Worthington 2010 reassesses D'Agostino's

The first is a short piece found in the house of purification priests at OB Ur. It presents a man's condescending lecture on the finer details of laundering to a fuller, who angrily replies in the last third of the text.[491] Although many have seen humor in this text, a recent interpretation suggests it is "a mocking allegory" for the specialized job of ritual purification.[492] According to Michaël Guichard and Lionel Marti, "the lesson would be that purification is a matter for specialists, and more subtly, that this knowledge was not within anyone's reach and, moreover, could not be reduced to a series of technical manipulations, which were in any case completely incomprehensible to the client."[493]

From the NA period come two Assyrian pieces that parody well-established genres in order to lampoon a man named Bel-etir, "who," according to the editor of the texts, "seems to have been involved in rebellious activities against Assyria."[494] One text alludes to the opening lines of The Cuthean Legend of Naram-Sin, thus signaling a farcical use of the *narû* ("stela") genre.[495] Rather than praising the man, as would a stela, it presents a litany of abuses and insults, including the following from the end of the text:

> "This is the stela which the whore set up for the son of Iba, the fart
>   factory,
> (blank space ... [i.e., nothing])[496] she left for the future."
> In the whole of it, in the essence of it,
> there is [   ][497] for the future.
> He praised himself, like a nitwit, a bungler,
> [Bawling] countless obscenities about himself from his own imagination,
> He made his own declaration, he did his own praising,
> he did his own talking, he [did his own bo]asting,
> He made himself a byword and an insult in common speech,
> Yet this man hadn't even enough sense to think straight![498] (24–31)

---

interpretation of the cathartic role of healers in several of the texts discussed in this section. For another possible parody in LKA 62, see note 104.

491. For a recent edition, see Wasserman 2013, 273–75 (= SEAL 7.1.2.1). Foster 2005, 151–52 offers a translation. Both also point to further secondary literature.

492. Among those who find humor, see, e.g., D'Agostino 2000. Wasserman 2013, 257 believes the text may be humorous but its main purpose was "to teach or to test knowledge of different technical terms pertaining to the fuller's work."

493. Guichard and Marti 2013, 56.

494. Livingstone 1989, xxviii; his editions of the text are on pp. 64–66 (nos. 29 and 30). See Foster 2005, 1020–22 for another translation.

495. See page 145, above.

496. See Foster 2005, 1021 n. 1, who interprets the blank space on the tablet as implying "that she had left nothing for the future."

497. Livingstone suggests the gap in the text may have read something along the lines of "this teaching" (1989, 66).

498. Foster 2005, 1021.

The other text opens with the Sumerian superscript én, "incantation," thus implying a parody of that genre. The text invokes the man's name, which is modified by a series of insulting epithets:

> O Bel-etir, you kidnapped catamite, doubly so,
> with runny eyes, doubly so,
> with shifty eyes, doubly so,
> Son of Iba, that missed period, that shit bucket of a fart factory,
> Of a vile family, lackey of a dead god,
> of a house whose star has vanished from the heavens.[499] (1–3)

The text closes with what may be a satirical adjuration.

The Aluzinnu-text probably parodies a number of learned genres that were only meaningful to advanced scribes and scholars, including a contorted god-list, a humorous pseudo-hymn (in which the goddess Ishtar praises herself in a most unflattering manner), a jester-like lampooning of professions (an exorcist burns down the house he is cleansing), ridiculous omens, and a grotesque menology, which commends certain months for eating various dishes loaded with scatological ingredients.[500]

Another example of Mesopotamian humor is The Poor Man of Nippur, known from only a few mid-first millennium tablets.[501] This comic folktale follows a poor man from Nippur named Gimil-Ninurta, who exacts his revenge threefold upon the city's mayor, because the mayor had accepted the poor man's gift (a goat) but slighted the pauper out of the benefits accepting the gift implied (an invitation to the feast). Gimil-Ninurta promises to humiliate the mayor three times for treating him so disgracefully. In each case of revenge, Gimil-Ninurta beats the mayor. In the first two beatings, Gimil-Ninurta disguises himself to gain entrance to the mayor's house (first as a royal courier

---

499. Foster 2005, 1021.

500. Foster 2005, 939–41 provides a provisional translation. Older editions are now outdated; Jiménez is working on a new one that will include many unpublished manuscripts (2017, 102 n. 273). The following is based on Jiménez's comments (2017, 101–3), which cite older studies.

501. Gurney 1956 provides the *princeps* edition of the poem (see also Gurney 1957, 135–36; 1958, 245), which includes two tablets from Sultantepe (STT 38 and 39 in Gurney and Finkelstein 1957; STT 116 was later added to STT 39 in Gurney and Hulin 1964, 1) and a fragment from Assurbanipal's library among the witnesses. A NB fragment from Nippur also contain bits of the story (see de Jong Ellis 1974). George 1993, 75 has a few collations of these tablets. Ottervanger 2016 provides the most recent edition with commentary. See Foster 2005, 931–36; von Soden 1990, 174–80 for translations. Gurney 1972; Jason 1979 adduce folkloric parallels for the story. D'Agostino 2000; Dietrich 2009 provide recent discussions of the text. The latter argues the novel thesis that the poor man is in fact the mayor's predecessor in office. Finally, Ian Worthington, his students, and a number of Assyriological colleagues (some of whose work is cited throughout this book) have created a short film based on the story (https://www.youtube.com/watch?v=pxYoFlnJLoE).

and then as a doctor—the mayor defers to them both). In the last act of revenge, Gimil-Ninurta hires someone to pretend to be him in order to provoke the mayor's household. When they all come running out of the house to chase after the pretender, Gimil-Ninurta springs from his hiding place and beats the now unguarded mayor a third time. The tale is highly structured and rife with puns and other scribal embellishments.[502] Besides the violent humor and ironic situations, the fictional story lampoons bureaucratic corruption.[503] The tablet fragment from Nippur that bears the story proves the tale was used to educate future scribes.[504]

The last comic tale, known from a single NB tablet from a scholar's house at Uruk, mocks a physician's ignorance of basic Sumerian, the language of learning.[505] The physician, a certain Amel-Baba from Isin, where he is a priest of the healing goddess Gula, heals a man from Nippur, a certain Ninurta-paqidat.[506] The latter, wishing to show his gratitude, invites the former to Nippur for a feast. To help the physician find his way to Ninurta-paqidat's house, he gives the physician some directions within Nippur that will lead him to an old woman, who will show him the rest of the way. This sets the stage for the comedy. When the physician finds the old woman in Nippur and asks (in Akkadian) about Ninurta-paqidat, she replies in Sumerian. The learned physician mistakes her basic Sumerian for rudeness and scolds the woman, who then translates her reply for the physician into Akkadian to exonerate herself. The physician asks three questions, the old woman replies three times, the physician takes offense at each, and the woman then translates each reply into Akkadian. After the final translation, the old woman runs out of patience and encourages students to take up their practice tablets as projectiles and run the fool out of town.[507] The last sentence, of course, suggests the tale was used in scribal education.

502. For the structure, see Cooper 1975, who also provides a translation. For puns, see Noegel 1996.

503. For the tale being fictional, see Haul 2009, 148–49. Jiménez considers the story as a possible parody (2017, 101).

504. De Jong Ellis 1974.

505. George 1993 is the most recent edition. Foster 2005, 937–38 (with other references); Reiner 1986 also provide translations. George believes the mockery is in the physician's ignorance of the Nippurean dialect of Babylonian rather than of Sumerian (1993, 71–2).

506. George 1993 has shown that the names are probably to be read as Akkadian rather than Sumerian, as do most translations.

507. The word for such tablets is *imšukku*, which seems to be a homonym of a word for chamber pot (so George 1993, 71). Worthington suggests this scatological double entendre is part of the humor: "Babylonian and Assyrian healers inspected urine for diagnostic and prognostic purposes, so for the unfortunate healer to be driven out of town by a volley of chamber pots is ironic" (2010, 30).

Although the survey in this chapter covers the major kinds of texts available to read in Akkadian and summarizes many of the more important individual works, it offers nothing more than a beginning, a primer. As the notes show rather conspicuously, there is so much more to read and even more to consider when it comes to interpreting these ancient works. In addition, by the time you read this chapter the catalog of Akkadian literary material will have grown, a characteristic likely to continue as long as archaeologists are pulling tablets from the ground and philologists are deciphering the massive backlog of tablets in museums.

Here at the conclusion to what there is to read in Akkadian it may be worth taking a moment to identify also some of the things that are absent from the textual record, what there is *not* to read. What did the ancient scribes not write? Although the scribes wrote myths, legends, narrative poems, commentaries, and even humorous vignettes, they did not produce anything like our modern novels, nonfiction books, biographies, magazines, or newspapers; and they did not write literary criticism or anything like a poetics. The scribes wrote law collections, treaties, and royal inscriptions, nearly all of which advanced or served in some way the king's position in society and his political agenda, yet they authored no critical histories about themselves or other societies, no legal textbooks, and no works dedicated to political theory. The scribes made lists—seemingly endless lists—of all kinds of things in their world (i.e., of words, of cuneiform signs, of names, of prices, of celestial movements, of gods, of omens, of temples, etc.) but nothing that explains or defends their organizing principles explicitly. Rituals, prayers, hymns, incantations, and omen collections abound in the ancient textual record while we have no overt reflections on the nature of their religious devotion, no systematic theologies, no polemical works arguing for the truth of Mesopotamian religious ideas or practices over those of other peoples, and no philosophical investigations into the existence of the gods or the reliability of their revelations.[508] This is only a sample of what the scribes did not write, but it is enough to substantiate the following point that has implications for us as modern readers of this ancient corpus: Considering what is missing in the Akkadian textual record provides an opportunity to recognize how sharply their ancient textual record contrasts with our own modern ones. And this recognition, I suggest, should raise our self-awareness, our literary guard, if you will,

---

508. One may have noticed the lack of abstract or theoretical works in the list here. Some have concluded from such an observation that the ancient scribes were unable to formulate or think with abstract or theoretical principles. Recent scholarship has shown, however, that this absence in the textual record is not evidence for the absence of abstract thinking or the existence of theoretical principles in the scribes' intellectual activities (see page 37 in the discussion of genre). For a study in Mesopotamian scribal epistemology, as viewed through the lexical lists, the omen collections, and the law collections (that is, scholarly texts), see Van De Mieroop 2016.

about how our own literary expectations could, if not tempered by historical study and close attention to the texts, easily distort our understanding as readers and interpreters of Akkadian literature.[509] I conclude this second part of the book then as I began the first. Alongside developing an understanding of the content of Akkadian literature, a reader of Akkadian literature must also develop literary competence to read the material in an informed manner. The two do not develop in sequence, as this book presents them; rather, they develop simultaneously in an ongoing, mutually reinforcing manner.

509. I do not intend this statement to downplay or treat in a facile manner the complicated theoretical relationships between author, reader, text, and the two cultural horizons between textual production, anchored in history, and its consumption, which is ever-changing as new readers come to a text. These critical issues are much too complicated to address here in any substantive manner. A useful beginning in critical theory is Tyson 2015.

Conclusion: The Future of Akkadian Literature

The success that scholars have achieved to date in reconstructing and interpreting the Akkadian textual record may be one of the best-kept secrets of humanistic scholarship. Yet there is still much work to be done. Museums house tens of thousands of tablets in need of decipherment and translation, and archaeological sites throughout Mesopotamia, Syria, and beyond have yet to give up all of their subterranean holdings. There is certainly no shortage of material to work on. And as the workers are relatively few, a motivated individual can make her or his mark on the field. New discoveries will no doubt make many of the statements and ideas presented in this book outdated in short order. Indeed, the future of the field is dynamic and exciting.

Yet, as exciting as the future is for the study of Akkadian literature, there are also many challenges ahead, the gravest of which are on the ground in Mesopotamia itself. In addition to the immeasurable loss of human life and health, the decades of war in Iraq have also led to a great deal of cultural destruction: museums have been looted and many archaeological sites have suffered illicit digging and/or deliberate, ideologically motivated destruction. Sadly, it is likely that much evidence relevant to Akkadian literature has perished. Alongside this challenge at the source of the evidence is the challenge to secure institutional support. Assyriologists—the few who are lucky enough to have an academic post—find themselves currently working for universities with diminishing budgets and increasing pressure from governing bodies to work on something that is relevant to "the real world." Like many other fields in the Humanities, Assyriology (and ancient Near Eastern studies in general) will have to justify its existence and make compelling cases to replace retiring professors.

Despite these difficulties, there is reason to be encouraged. The Akkadian textual record that currently exists, with a history that spans two and a half millennia, offers a panoply of perspectives on a significant chapter of human civilization. As long as there are people curious about the human past, there will be readers of Akkadian literature.

In the Prologue to this book I asked you to consider: Why study this arcane literary corpus? What is there to gain, collectively and individually, from looking to the past and reading these long dead voices? These questions deserve further consideration as we look to the future of the field.

Personal reasons for studying Akkadian literature, if we were to conduct a survey, would be as varied as the people providing them. And exploring collective interests, that is, the broader cultural reasons for studying Akkadian literature, if such an exploration gave specific contexts their full due, would require a separate investigation for each of the nation-states, cultures, and sub-cultures across the globe that have taken an interest in the ancient Near East since the mid-nineteenth century CE, when archaeological excavations revealed previously unknown and nearly unimaginable materials for its historical reconstruction. The conclusions to these studies would be as varied as the cultures investigated; and the resulting books would fill a small library. On top of the volume of data involved in all of this is the artificiality of the division between the collective and the individual, the cultural and the personal. It is a truism that a person is a product of their people, place, and time. With these things in mind, I circumscribe the following reflections to consider a couple of reasons for why some of us study Akkadian literature within a North American, European, Israeli, and Australian academic setting in the first quarter of the twenty-first century CE. One reason is religious, the other genealogical in nature. These reasons are not identical to my personal reasons for studying Akkadian literature, which would include such admissions as I like studying ancient languages and am a history nerd. Rather, they are broad cultural and historical factors within a particular context to which some—though hopefully not all—of you will have a connection.[1] As these reasons show, reading Akkadian literature is not simply about understanding an ancient literary corpus; it is also, among other things, about understanding ourselves.

The first major factor that has influenced and given reason to the North American, European, Israeli, and Australian academic study of the ancient Near East and thus also Akkadian literature is a religious interest or rather a religious *necessity*, given the intellectual currents since the Enlightenment, to explore the historical milieus that produced the scriptures of our dominant religions, Christianity and Judaism—with the evaluation of their truth claims or distinctiveness often an irresistible component. Although the roles are variously embraced or resisted by individuals to differing degrees, we ancient Near Eastern scholars

---

1. These very broad generalizations form important elements in the discourses that surround the study of the ancient Near East within a North American, European, Israeli, and Australian context. Nonetheless, identifying these generalizations as such does not intend to simplify or ignore the complexities of the people involved, whose demographic composition, specific motivations, individual and national interests, and interpretive perspectives, are not at all monolithic.

in the identified contexts as a whole have become custodians, curators, and/ or critics of our religions' cultural nativities, even when we are not personally religious.[2] (Clearly, this religious factor also affects many other scholars and students of the ancient Near East in South America, Asia, and Africa.) The second factor is genealogical; that is, we ancient Near Eastern scholars have a propensity to trace our institutional and intellectual genealogies—cultural, political, literary, artistic, scientific, and so on—back through the classical cultures of Greece and Rome to the "original" societies of the Near East, the so-called cradle of civilization—and largely ignore in the process, it should be added, that cluster of other, later societies dominated by Islam in the same locale. Again, although embraced or resisted by individuals to differing degrees, we ancient Near Eastern scholars in the identified contexts have often considered our cultures to be heirs to the ancient Near East.[3]

Although my personal reasons for studying Akkadian literature are not identical to or comprehended by these broader reasons, they are certainly imbricated in them. Both factors have shaped my scholarship as well as the specific institutional setting of my professional life, which directly affects my personal material well-being. I began my scholarly career with a dissertation comparing features of Mesopotamian and biblical scribal cultures (Lenzi 2008). Institutionally, my faculty appointment is in a Religious Studies department and was explicitly created in 2005 (when I applied to it) to bridge between Religious Studies and Classics, that field of Ancient Studies that so heavily influenced

2. A bibliography of the secondary literature on this issue could easily fill a very large volume. Given the purpose of this book, Younger's brief history of ancient Near Eastern text anthologies (2006) and Chavalas's survey of the comparative use of ancient Near Eastern texts for the study of the Hebrew Bible (2011) make for good entry points. On the problemtic issue of scholars as caretakers rather than critics of a religious tradition, see McCutcheon 2001.

3. Two prominent examples illustrate the point: the book by the late Yale Assyriologist William Hallo entitled *Origins: The Ancient Near Eastern Background of Some Modern Western Institutions* (1996) and a chapter in French Assyriologist Jean Bottéro's popular book *Mesopotamia: Writing, Reasoning, and the Gods*, entitled "Assyriology and Our History" (1992, 26–40). Many other, less-obviously titled examples could be cited. (Classicists, it should be noted, were not always enthusiastic about the efforts to find earlier, ancient Near Eastern precedents for Western cultural features. Pertinent to ancient literature, see, e.g., Haubold 2013, 1–17, who, incidentally, offers an exemplary literary study that is self-conscious of what I am calling the genealogical factor—and his fellow Classicists' resistance to it—while bringing ancient Greek and Akkadian literatures into a fruitful comparative dialogue. His book is an excellent entry into this burgeoning area of comparative literary work.) The propensity to use the ancient Near Eastern past to understand the present is not unique to academics in the identified contexts. See, e.g., Bernhardsson 2005 for the role of ancient Near Eastern archaeology in the creation and early years of the modern nation of Iraq, including the obstacles that the young nation faced in the twentieth century from the imperial powers' interests in Iraq's archaeological exploration. Note also the attempts of a few mid-twentieth-century Chinese scholars to connect the Chinese script to cuneiform and Egyptian hieroglyphs, as described briefly in Wang, Piccin, and Günther forthcoming.

Enlightenment-era intellectuals, who paved the way for our modern democracies.[4] The cultural and the personal are not easily separated.

These broad cultural and historical reasons for studying Akkadian literature are not wrong or bad. We are trying to understand the origins of our dominant religions and our historical connections to the past. However, given how both the genealogical and religious factors developed alongside and contributed to Western imperialist projects in the Near East starting in the nineteenth century CE, and given how religious and political ideology can often strongly motivate research interests and outcomes, it is extremely important to name these factors that inevitably affect those of us in the identified contexts and develop a self-awareness about them so that *why* we study this literature does not determine or unduly influence the *results* of our study or inappropriately steer the implications we draw from such results.[5] Moreover, and more importantly for the purpose of this book with regard to the future directions of the field, we need to remain self-aware about these cultural and historical factors in order to encourage efforts—in a diversity of contexts—to move beyond them; the reasons that some of us have come to study Akkadian literature should not constrain the demographic of its students or the directions of its study.[6] And this brings me back to you, the reader of this book, for whom I reprise, following the example of Sin-leqi-unninni, the close of my Prologue as a kind of epilogue here.

Whoever you are and on whatever continent you find yourself living, ask yourself as you engage in the cross-cultural, cross-temporal activity of reading ancient Akkadian literature: How does this literature affect me, my understanding of the society I live in, my place in it, and my broader outlook on the world? Although such questions have a peculiarly contemporary orientation, we fool ourselves if we believe our interest in the ancient world is simply a dispassionate antiquarianism or a rationalistic quest for knowledge. Part of understanding Akkadian literature—and ensuring the vitality of its future study—is coming to terms with why you and I have any interest in it at all.

---

4. See Gay 1966, 1969.

5. A good starting point for the early years is Larsen 1996 and Kuklick 1996, who focuses on the Americans. For a brief case study—at a comfortable historical distance—of how biblical, national, and Classical interests and Orientalist prejudice coincided in and influenced the writings of an early interpreter of Akkadian literature, see Damrosch's treatment of George Smith (1840–1876), the first person to find a flood story in Akkadian literature (2003, 51–65, note esp. 64; for more detail about Smith's part in the discovery of the Epic of Gilgamesh, see Damrosch 2006, 9–80).

6. Or the range of literatures with which Akkadian literature is compared!

BIBLIOGRAPHY

Abusch, Tzvi. 1986. "Ishtar's Proposal and Gilgamesh's Refusal: An Interpretation of *The Gilgamesh Epic*, Tablet 6, Lines 1–79." *HR* 26:143–87. Repr., pages 11–57 in *Male and Female in the Epic of Gilgamesh: Encounters, Literary History, and Interpretation*. Winona Lake, IN: Eisenbrauns, 2015.

———. 1998. "Ghost and God: Some Observations on a Babylonian Understanding of Human Nature." Pages 363–83 in *Self, Soul and Body in Religious Experience*. Edited by Albert I. Baumgarten, Jan Assman, and Guy G. Stroumsa. SHR 78. Leiden: Brill.

———. 2002. "Water into Fire: The Formation of Some Witchcraft Incantations." Pages 197–216 in *Mesopotamian Witchcraft: Toward a History and Understanding of Babylonian Witchcraft Beliefs and Literature*. AMD 5. Leiden: Brill.

———. 2015a. *The Magical Ceremony Maqlû: A Critical Edition*. AMD 10. Leiden: Brill.

———. 2015b. *Male and Female in the Epic of Gilgamesh: Encounters, Literary History, and Interpretation*. Winona Lake, IN: Eisenbrauns.

Abusch, Tzvi, and Daniel Schwemer. 2011. *Corpus of Mesopotamian Anti-witchcraft Rituals: Volume One*. AMD 8/1. Leiden: Brill.

———. 2016. *Corpus of Mesopotamian Anti-witchcraft Rituals: Volume Two*. AMD 8/2. Leiden: Brill.

Albertz, Rainer. 1978. *Persönliche Frömmigkeit und Offizielle Religion: Religionsinterner Pluralismus in Israel und Babylon*. CThM 9. Stuttgart: Calwer. Repr., Atlanta: Society of Biblical Literature, 2005.

———. 1988. "Ludlul bēl nēmeqi—eine Lehrdichtung zur Ausbreitung und Vertiefung der persönlichen Mardukfrömmigkeit." Pages 25–53 in *Ad bene et fideliter seminandum: Festgabe für Karlheinz Deller zum 21 Februar 1987*. Edited by Gerlinde Mauer and Ursula Magen. AOAT 220. Kevelaer: Butzon & Bercker. Repr., pages 85–105 in *Geschichte und Theologie: Studien zur Exegese des Alten Testaments und zur Religionsgeschichte Israels*. BZAW 326. Berlin: de Gruyter, 2003.

Al-Rawi, F. N. H., and Jeremy A. Black. 1994. "A New Manuscript of Enūma Eliš, Tablet VI." *Iraq* 46:131–39.

Al-Rawi, F. N. H., and Andrew R. George. 1994. "Tablets from the Sippar Library III: Two Royal Counterfeits." *Iraq* 56:135–48.

———. 2014. "Back to the Cedar Forest: The Beginning and End of Tablet V of the Standard Babylonian Epic of Gilgameš." *JCS* 66:69–90.

Alster, Bendt. 1989. "An Akkadian Animal Proverb and the Assyrian Letter ABL 555." *JCS* 41:187–93.

———. 1992. "Interaction of Oral and Written Poetry in Early Mesopotamian Literature." Pages 23–69 in *Mesopotamian Epic Literature: Oral or Aural?* Edited by Marianna E. Vogelzang and Herman L. J. Vanstiphout. Lewiston, NY: Mellon.

———. 1997. *Proverbs of Ancient Sumer: The World's Earliest Proverb Collections.* 2 vols. Bethesda, MD: CDL.

———. 2005. *Wisdom of Ancient Sumer.* Bethesda, MD: CDL.

Alster, Bendt, and Takayoshi Oshima. 2007. "Sargonic Dinner at Kaneš: The Old Assyrian Sargon Legend." *Iraq* 69:1–20.

Ambos, Claus. 2013. *Der König im Gefängnis und das Neujahrsfest im Herbst: Mechanismen der Legitimation des babylonischen Herrschers im 1. Jahrtausend v. Chr. und ihre Geschichte.* Dresden: Islet.

Annus, Amar. 2001. *The Standard Babylonian Epic of Anzu: Cuneiform Text, Translation, Score, Glossary, Indices and Sign List.* SAACT 3. Helsinki: Neo-Assyrian Text Corpus Project.

———. 2002. *The God Ninurta in the Mythology and Royal Ideology of Ancient Mesopotamia.* SAAS 14. Helsinki: Neo-Assyrian Text Corpus Project.

———. 2016. *The Overturned Boat: Intertextuality of the Adapa Myth and Exorcist Literature.* SAAS 24. Helsinki: Neo-Assyrian Text Corpus Project.

Annus, Amar, and Alan Lenzi. 2010. *Ludlul Bēl Nēmeqi: The Standard Babylonian Poem of the Righteous Sufferer.* SAACT 7. Helsinki: Neo-Assyrian Text Corpus Project.

Arnaud, Daniel. 2007. *Corpus des textes de bibliothèque de Ras Shamra-Ougarit (1936–2000) en sumérien, babylonien et assyrien.* AuOrSup 23. Barcelona: AUSA.

Bach, Johannes. 2018. "A Transtextual View on the 'Underworld Vision of an Assyrian Prince.'" Pages 69–92 in *Mesopotamian Medicine and Magic: Studies in Honor of Markham J. Geller.* Edited by Strahil V. Panayotov and Luděk Vacín. AMD 14. Leiden: Brill.

Baker, Heather, and Laurie Pearce. 2001. "Nabû-zuqup-kēnu." Pages 912–13 in *The Prosopography of the Neo-Assyrian Empire 2/2 (L–N).* Edited by Heather Baker. Helsinki: Neo-Assyrian Text Corpus Project.

Barrabee, Janice. 2011. "The King of Justice: A Reconsideration of the River Ordeal in BM 45690." Pages 1–18 in *A Common Cultural Heritage: Studies on Mesopotamia and the Biblical World in Honor of Barry L. Eichler.* Edited by Grant Frame, Erle Leichty, Karen Sonik, Jeffrey H. Tigay, and Steve Tinney. Bethesda, MD: CDL.

Bateman, C. A. 1966. *Preservation and Reproduction of Clay Tablets and the Conservation of Wall Paintings.* Colt Archaeological Institute 3. London: Quaritch.

Batto, Bernard F. 1987. "The Sleeping God: An Ancient Near Eastern Motif of Divine Sovereignty." *Bib* 68:153–77.

Beaulieu, Paul-Alain. 1993a. "Divine Hymns as Royal Inscriptions." *NABU*, no. 84.

———. 1993b. "The Historical Background of the Uruk Policy." Pages 41–52 in *The Tablet and the Scroll: Near Eastern Studies in Honor of William W. Hallo.* Edited by Mark Cohen, Daniel C. Snell, and David B. Weisberg. Bethesda, MD: CDL.

———. 2000. "The Descendants of Sîn-lēqi-unninni." Pages 1–16 in *Assyriologica et Semitica: Festschrift für Joachim Oelsner anlässlich seines 65. Geburtstag am 18. Februar 1997.* Edited by Joachim Marzahn and Hans Neumann. AOAT 252. Münster: Ugarit-Verlag.

————. 2006a. "The Astronomers of the Esagil Temple in the Fourth Century BC." Pages 5–22 in *If a Man Builds a Joyful House: Assyriological Studies in Honor of Erle Verdun Leichty*. Edited by Ann K. Guinan et al. CM 31. Leiden: Brill.

————. 2006b. "Official and Vernacular Languages: The Shifting Sands of Imperial and Cultural Identities in First-millennium B. C. Mesopotamia." Pages 187–216 in *Margins of Writing, Origins of Cultures*. Edited by Seth L. Sanders. OIS 2. Chicago: Oriental Institute of the University of Chicago.

————. 2007a. "Nabonidus the Mad King: A Reconsideration of His Steles from Harran and Babylon." Pages 137–66 in *Representations of Political Power: Case Histories from Times of Change and Dissolving Order in the Ancient Near East*. Edited by Marlies Heinz and Marian H. Feldman. Winona Lake, IN: Eisenbrauns.

————. 2007b. "The Social and Intellectual Setting of Babylonian Wisdom Literature." Pages 3–19 in *Wisdom Literature in Mesopotamia and Israel*. Edited by Richard J. Clifford. SymS 36. Atlanta: Society of Biblical Literature.

————. 2010. "The Afterlife of Assyrian Scholarship in Hellenistic Babylonia." Pages 1–18 in *Gazing on the Deep: Ancient Near Eastern, Biblical, and Jewish Studies in Honor of Tzvi Abusch*. Edited by Jeffrey Stackert, Barbara Nevling Porter, and David P. Wright. Bethesda, MD: CDL.

————. 2014. "Nabû and Apollo: The Two Faces of Seleucid Religious Policy." Pages 13–30 in *Orient und Okzident in hellenistischer Zeit: Beiträge zur Tagung "Orient und Okzident—Antagonismus oder Konstrukt? Machtstrukturen, Ideologien und Kulturtransfer in hellenistischer Zeit."* Edited by Friedhelm Hoffmann und Karin Stella Schmidt. Munich: Brose.

Beckman, Gary. 1999. *Hittite Diplomatic Texts*. 2nd ed. WAW 7. Atlanta: Scholars Press.

Berger, Paul-Richard. 1973. *Die neubabylonischen Königsinschriften: Königsinschriften des ausgehenden babylonischen Reiches (626–539 a. Chr.)*. AOAT 4/1. Kevelaer: Butzon & Bercker; Neukirchen-Vluyn: Neukirchener Verlag.

Berlejung, Angelika. 1997. "Washing the Mouth: The Consecration of Divine Images in Mesopotamia." Pages 45–72 in *The Image and the Book: Iconic Cults, Aniconism, and the Rise of Book Religion in Israel and the Ancient Near East*. Edited by Karel van der Toorn. CBET 21. Leuven: Peeters.

————. 1998. *Die Theologie der Bilder: Das Kultbild in Mesopotamien und die alttestamentliche Bilderpolemik*. OBO 162. Göttingen: Vandenhoeck & Ruprecht; Fribourg: Universitätsverlag.

Berlin, Adele. 1985. *The Dynamics of Biblical Parallelism*. Bloomington: Indiana University Press. Repr., Grand Rapids: Eerdmans, 2008.

Bernhardsson, Magnus T. 2005. *Reclaiming a Plundered Past: Archaeology and Nation Building in Modern Iraq*. Austin: University of Texas Press.

Bezold, Carl. 1886. *Kurzgefasster Überblick über die babylonisch-assyrische Literatur*. Leipzig: Schulze.

Biggs, Robert. 2004. "The Babylonian Fürstenspiegel as a Political Forgery." Pages 1–5 in *From the Upper Sea to the Lower Sea: Studies on the History of Assyria and Babylonia in Honour of A. K. Grayson*. Edited by Grant Frame with Linda S. Wilding. PIHANS 101. Leiden: Nederlands Instituut voor het Nabije Oosten.

Black, Jeremy A. 1990. "A Recent Study of Babylonian Grammar." *JRAS* 1:95–104.

————. 1992. "Some Structural Features of Sumerian Narrative Poetry." In *Mesopotamian Epic Literature: Oral or Aural?* Edited by Marianna E. Vogelzang and Herman L. J. Vanstiphout. Lewiston, NY: Mellon.

Black, Jeremy, Andrew George, and J. Nicholas Postgate. 1999. *A Concise Dictionary of Akkadian*. SANTAG 5. Wiesbaden: Harrassowitz.

Black, Jeremy A., and Anthony Green. 1992. *Gods, Demons and Symbols of Ancient Mesopotamia: An Illustrated Dictionary*. Austin: University of Texas Press.

Böck, Barbara. 2000. *Die babylonisch-assyrische Morphoskopie*. AfOB 27. Vienna: Institut für Orientalistick der Universität Wien.

———. 2007. *Das Handbuch Muššu'u "Einreibung": Eine Serie sumerischer und akkadischer Beschwörungen aus dem 1. Jt. vor Chr.* BPOA 3. Madrid: Consejo Superior de Investigaciones Científicas.

———. 2014. "Gilgamesh's Dreams of Enkidu." *BO* 71:664–72.

Böck, Barbara, and Ignacio Márquez Rowe. 1999–2000. "M M 818: A New LB Fragment of Atra-hasis I." *AuOr* 17–18:167–77.

Bongenaar, A. C. V. M. 1997. *The Neo-Babylonian Ebabbar Temple at Sippar: Its Administration and Its Prosopography*. Istanbul: Nederlands Historisch-Archaeologisch Instituut.

Borger, Rykle. 1982. "Akkadische Rechtsbücher." *TUAT* 1:32–95.

———. 1984. "Historische Texte in akkadischer Sprache aus Babylonien und Assyrien." *TUAT* 1:354–410.

———. 2006. *Babylonisch-assyrische Lesestücke: Vol. 1, Die Texte im Umschrift.* 3rd ed. AnOr 54/1. Rome: Pontifical Biblical Institute.

———. 2010. *Mesopotamisches Zeichenlexikon*. 2nd ed. AOAT 305. Münster: Ugarit-Verlag.

Bottéro, Jean. 1965–1966. "Antiquités Assyro-babyloniennes." *AEPHE.HP* 48:89–111.

———. 1977. "Les noms de Marduk, l'écriture et la 'logique' en Mésopotamie ancienne." Pages 5–28 in *Essays on the Ancient Near East in Memory of Jacob Joel Finkelstein*. Edited by Maria de Jong Ellis. Memoirs of the Connecticut Academy of Arts and Sciences 19. Hamden: Archon.

———. 1985. *Myths et Rites de Babylone*. EPHE.PH 328. Paris: Champion.

———. 1992. *Mesopotamia: Writing, Reasoning, and the Gods*. Translated by Zainab Bahrani and Marc Van De Mieroop. Chicago: University of Chicago Press.

———. 1995. "Akkadian Literature: An Overview." *CANE* 4:2293–2303.

———. 2001. *Religion in Ancient Mesopotamia*. Translated by Teresa Lavender Fagan. Chicago: University of Chicago Press.

Bottéro, Jean, and Samuel Noah Kramer. 1989. *Lorsque les dieux faisaient l'homme: Mythologie mésopotamienne*. Bibliothèque des Histoires. Paris: Galliamard.

Brogan, T. V. F., A. W. Halsall, and W. Hunter. 2012. "Chiasmus." Pages 225–26 in *The Princeton Encyclopedia of Poetry and Poetics*. Edited by Roland Green. 4th ed. Princeton: Princeton University Press.

Brogan, T. V. F., C. Scott, and S. Monte. 2012. "Enjambment." Pages 435–36 in *The Princeton Encyclopedia of Poetry and Poetics*. Edited by Roland Green. 4th ed. Princeton: Princeton University Press.

Brown, David. 2000. *Mesopotamian Planetary Astronomy-Astrology*. CM 18. Groningen: Styx.

Buccellati, Giorgio. 1990. "On Poetry—Theirs and Ours." Pages 105–34 in *Lingering over Words: Studies in Ancient Near Eastern Literature in Honor of William L. Moran*. Edited by Tzvi Abusch, John Huehnergard, and Piotr Steinkeller. HSS 37. Atlanta: Scholars Press.

———. 1993. "Through a Tablet Darkly: A Reconstruction of Old Akkadian Monuments Described in Old Babylonian Copies." Pages 58–71 in *The Tablet and the Scroll: Near Eastern Studies in Honor of William W. Hallo*. Edited by Mark Cohen, Daniel C. Snell, and David B. Weisberg. Bethesda, MD: CDL.

———. 1996. *A Structural Grammar of Babylonian*. Wiesbaden: Harrassowitz.

Butler, Sally A. L. 1998. *Mesopotamian Conceptions of Dreams and Dream Rituals*. AOAT 258. Münster: Ugarit-Verlag.

Cagni, Luigi. 1969. *L'Epopea di Erra*. StSem 34. Roma: Istituto di Studi del Vicino Oriente.

———. 1977. *The Poem of Erra*. SANE 1/3. Malibu, CA: Undena.

Castellino, G. R. 1976. "The Šamaš Hymn: A Note on Its Structure." Pages 71–74 in *Kramer Anniversary Volume: Cuneiform Studies in Honor of Samuel Noah Kramer*. Edited by Barry Eichler. AOAT 25. Neukirchen-Vluyn: Neukirchener Verlag; Kevelaer: Butzon & Bercker.

Cavigneaux, Antoine. 2003. "Fragments littéraires susiens." Pages 53–62 in *Literatur, Politik und Recht in Mesopotamien: Festschrift für Claus Wilcke*. Edited by Walther Sallaberger, Konrad Volk, and Annette Zgoll. OBC 14. Wiesbaden: Harrassowitz.

———. 2006–2008. "Rätsel." *RlA* 11:224.

———. 2014a. "La Théodicée babylonienne d'après les traductions posthumes de Jean Bottéro." *Asdiwal* 9:107–24.

———. 2014b. "Une version sumérienne de la légende d'Adapa." *ZA* 104:1–41.

Cavigneaux, Antoine, and F. N. H. Al-Rawi. 1993. "New Sumerian Literary Texts from Tell Haddad (Ancient Meturan): A First Survey." *Iraq* 55:91–105.

Çeçen, Salih, and Karl Hecker. 1995. "*ina mātīka eblum*: Zu einem neuen Text zum Wegerecht in der Kültepe-Zeit." Pages 31–42 in *Vom Alten Orient zum Alten Testament: Festschrift für Wolfram Freiherrn von Soden*. Edited by Manfried Dietrich and Oswald Loretz. AOAT 240. Neukirchen-Vluyn: Neukirchener Verlag; Kevelaer: Butzon & Bercker.

Chapman, Cynthia R. 2004. *The Gendered Language of Warfare in the Israelite-Assyrian Encounter*. HSM 62. Winona Lake, IN: Eisenbrauns.

Charpin, Dominique. 1986. *Le Clergé d'Ur au Siècle d'Hammurabi (XIXe–XVIIIe Siècles av. J.-C.)*. EPHE.PH 22. Geneva: Droz.

———. 1991. "Une traité entre Zimri-Lim de Mari et Ibâl-pî-El II d'Ešnunna." Pages 139–66 in *Marchands, Diplomates et Empereurs: Études sur la civilisation mésopotamienne offertes à Paul Garelli*. Edited by Dominique Charpin and Francis Joannès. Paris: Éditions Recherche sur les Civilisations.

———. 2010. *Reading and Writing in Babylon*. Translated by Jane Marie Todd. Cambridge: Harvard University Press.

Chavalas, Mark, ed. 2006. *The Ancient Near East: Historical Sources in Translation*. BSAH. Malden, MA: Blackwell.

———. 2011. "The Comparative Use of Ancient Near Eastern Texts in the Study of the Hebrew Bible." *RC* 5.5:150–65.

Chen, Y. S. 2013. *The Primeval Flood Catastrophe: Origins and Early Development in Mesopotamian Traditions*. Oxford: Oxford University Press.

Civil, Miguel. 1975. "Lexicography." Pages 123–57 in *Sumerological Studies in Honor of Thorkild Jacobsen on His Seventieth Birthday June 7, 1974*. Edited by Stephen J. Lieberman. AS 20. Chicago: University of Chicago Press.

Clancier, Philippe. 2011. "Cuneiform Culture's Last Guardians: The Old Urban Nota-
bility of Hellenistic Uruk." *OHCC*, 752–73.

Cogan, Mordechai. 2008. *The Raging Torrent: Historical Inscriptions from Assyria
and Babylonia Relating to Ancient Israel*. Carta Handbook. Jerusalem: Carta.

Cohen, Yoram. 2009. *The Scribes and Scholars of the City of Emar in the Late Bronze
Age*. HSM 59. Winona Lake, IN: Eisenbrauns.

———. 2013. *Wisdom from the Late Bronze Age*. WAW 34. Atlanta: Society of Biblical
Literature.

Cohen, Yoram, and Sivan Kedar. 2011. "Teacher-Student Relationships: Two Case
Studies." *OHCC*, 229–47.

Cole, Steven. 1994. "The Crimes and Sacrileges of Nabû-šuma-iškun." *ZA* 84:220–52.

———. 1996. *Nippur IV: The Early Neo-Babylonian Governor's Archive from Nippur*.
OIP 114. Chicago: Oriental Institute of the University of Chicago.

Collon, Dominique. 1990. *Near Eastern Seals*. Berkeley: University of California
Press.

Cook, E. 2012. "Paronomasia." Pages 1003–4 in *The Princeton Encyclopedia of Poetry
and Poetics*. Edited by Roland Green. 4th ed. Princeton: Princeton University
Press.

Cooley, Jeffrey. 2008. "'I Want to Dim the Brilliance of Šulpae!' Mesopotamian Celestial Divination and the Poem of Erra and Išum." *Iraq* 70:179–88.

Cooper, Jerrold. 1975. "Structure, Humor, and Satire in the Poor Man of Nippur." *JCS*
27:163–74.

———. 1992. "Babbling on: Recovering Mesopotamian Orality." Pages 103–22 in
Mesopotamian Epic Literature: Oral or Aural? Edited by Marianna E. Vogelzang
and Herman L. J. Vanstiphout. Lewiston, NY: Mellon.

Couto-Ferreira, M. Erica. 2013. "The River, The Oven, The Garden: The Female Body
and Fertility in a Late Babylonian Ritual Text." Pages 97–116 in *Approaching Rituals in Ancient Cultures*. Edited by Claus Ambos and Lorenzo Verderame. Studi
Orientali 86. Rome: Serra.

Cunningham, Graham. 1997. *'Deliver Me From Evil': Mesopotamian Incantations
2500–1500 BC*. StPohlSM 17. Rome: Pontifical Biblical Institute.

Curtis, John. 2013. *The Cyrus Cylinder and Ancient Persia: A New Beginning for the
Middle East*. London: British Museum.

D'Agostino, Franco. 1998. "Some Considerations on Humour in Mesopotamia." *RSO*
72:273–78.

———. 2000. *Testi umoristici babilonesi e assiri*. Testi del Vicino Oriente antico 2.
Letterature mesopotamiche 4. Brescia: Paideia.

Dalley, Stephanie. 2000. *Myths from Mesopotamia: Creation, the Flood, Gilgamesh,
and Others*. Rev. ed. Oxford: Oxford University Press.

———. 2010. "Old Babylonian Prophecies at Uruk and Kish." Pages 85–97 in *Opening
the Tablet Box: Near Eastern Studies in Honor of Benjamin R. Foster*. Edited by
Sarah C. Melville and Alice L. Slotsky. CHANE 42. Leiden: Brill.

Damrosch, David. 2003. *What is World Literature?* Princeton: Princeton University
Press.

———. 2006. *The Buried Book: The Loss and Rediscovery of the Great Epic of Gilgamesh*. New York: Holt.

Dandamayev, M. A. 1983. *Babylonian Scribes in the First Millennium B.C.* Moscow:
Izdat Nauka. [Russian]

Daniels, Peter and William Bright. 1996. *The World's Writing Systems.* Oxford: Oxford University Press.

Danzig, David. 2013. "Name Word Play and Marduk's Fifty Names in *Enūma Eliš.*" MA thesis, Yale University.

Da Riva, Rocío. 2008. *The Neo-Babylonian Royal Inscriptions: An Introduction.* GMTR 4. Münster: Ugarit-Verlag.

———. 2013. *The Inscriptions of Nabopolassar, Amel-Marduk and Neriglissar.* SANER 3. Berlin: de Gruyter.

De Backer, Fabrice. 2012. *L'art du siège néo-assyrian.* CHANE 61. Leiden: Brill.

Delnero, Paul. 2010. "Sumerian Extract Tablets and Scribal Education." *JCS* 62:53–69.

———. 2015. "Scholarship and Inquiry in Early Mesopotamia." *Journal of Ancient Near Eastern History* 2:109–43.

———. 2016. "Literature and Identity in Mesopotamia during the Old Babylonian Period." Pages 19–50 in *Problems of Canonicity and Identity Formation in Ancient Egypt and Mesopotamia.* Edited by Kim Ryholt and Gojko Barjamovic. CNIP 43. Copenhagen: Museum Tusculanum.

De Zorzi, Nicla. 2011. "The Omen Series *Šumma Izbu*: Internal Structure and Hermeneutic Strategies." *KASKAL* 8:43–75.

———. 2014. *La Serie Teratomantica Šumma Izbu: Testo, Tradizione, Orizzonti Culturali.* 2 vols. Padua: S.A.R.G.O.N.

Dhorme, Édouard. 1937. *La Littérature Babylonienne et Assyrienne.* Paris: Presses Universitaires de France.

Dick, Michael, ed. 1999. *Born in Heaven, Made on Earth: The Making of the Cult Image in the Ancient Near East.* Winona Lake, IN: Eisenbrauns.

Dietrich, Manfried. 1986. "Prophetenbriefe aus Mari." *TUAT* 2:83–93.

———. 2009. "'Armer Mann von Nippur': Ein Werk der Krisenliteratur des 8. Jh. v. Chr." Pages 333–52 in *Of God(s), Trees, Kings, and Scholars: Neo-Assyrian and Related Studies in Honour of Simo Parpola.* Edited by Mikko Luukko, Saana Svärd, and Raija Mattila. StOr 106. Helsinki: Finnish Oriental Society.

Dijk, Jan van. 1976. *Texts in the Iraq Museum: Vol. 9.* Leiden: Brill.

Dolce, Rita. 2018. *"Losing One's Head" in the Ancient Near East: Interpretation and Meaning of Decapitation.* Studies in the History of the Ancient Near East. New York: Routledge.

Donbaz, Veysel, and A. Kirk Grayson. 1984. *Royal Inscriptions on Clay Cones from Ashur Now in Istanbul.* RIMS 1. Toronto: University of Toronto Press.

Durand, Jean-Marie. 1993. "Le mythologème du combat entre le Dieu de l'Orage et la Mer en Mésopotamie." *MARI* 7:41–61.

Edzard, Dietz Otto. 1965. "Mesopotamien: Die Mythologie der Sumerer und Akkader." Pages 17–140 in *Götter und Mythen in Vorderen Orient.* Edited by Hans Wilhelm Haussig. Wörterbuch der Mythologie I. Alten Kulturvölker 1. Stuttgart: Klett.

———. 1989. Review of *Altorientalische Vorstellungen von der Unterwelt: Literar- und religionsgeschichtliche Überlegungen zu "Nergal und Ereškigal,"* by M. Hutter. *ZA* 79:124–27.

———. 1990. "Selbstgespräch und Monolog in der akkadischen Literatur." Pages 149–62 in *Lingering over Words: Studies in Ancient Near Eastern Literature in Honor of William L. Moran.* Edited by Tzvi Abusch, John Huehnergard, and Piotr Steinkeller. HSS 37. Atlanta: Scholars Press.

———. 1993–1995. "Metrik." *RlA* 8:148–49.

————. 1994. "Sumerische und akkadische Hymnen." Pages 19–31 in *Hymnen der Alten Welt im Kulturvergleich*. Edited by Walter Burkert and Fritz Stolz. OBO 131. Göttingen: Vandenhoeck & Ruprecht; Fribourg: Universitätsverlag.

————. 2004a. "Altbabylonische Literatur und Religion." Pages 485–572 in *Mesopotamiens: Die altbabylonische Zeit*. Edited by Dominique Charpin, Dietz Otto Edzard, and Marten Stol. OBO 160/4. Göttingen: Vandenhoeck & Ruprecht; Fribourg: Academic Press.

————. 2004b. "*LKA* 62: Parodie eines assyrischen Feldzugsberichts." Pages 81–87 in *From the Upper Sea to the Lower Sea: Studies on the History of Assyria and Babylonia in Honour of A. K. Grayson*. Edited by Grant Frame and Linda S. Wilding. PIHANS 101. Leiden: Nederlands Instituut voor het Nabije Oosten.

Eidem, J. 2011. *The Royal Archives from Tell Leilan: Old Babylonian Letters and Treaties from the Eastern Lower Town Palace*. PIHANS 117. Leiden: Nederlands Instituut voor het Nabije Oosten.

Ellis, Maria de Jong. 1974. "A New Fragment of the Tale of the Poor Man of Nippur." *JCS* 26:88–89.

Elman, Yaakov. 1975. "Authoritative Oral Tradition in Neo-Assyrian Scribal Circles." *JANESCU* 7:19–32.

Fadhil, Abdulillah. 1998. "Der Prolog des Codex Hammurapi in einer Abschrift aus Sippar." Pages 717–29 in *Relations Between Anatolia and Mesopotamia: XXXIVème Rencontre Assyriologique Internationale, Istanbul, 1987*. Edited by Hayat Erkanal, Veysel Donbaz, and Ayşegül Uğuroğlu. Ankara: Türk Tarih Kurumu Basımevi.

Fales, Mario, ed. 1981. *Assyrian Royal Inscriptions: New Horizons in Literary, Ideological, and Historical Analysis*. OAC 17. Rome: Instituto per L'Oriente.

————. 1999–2001. "Assyrian Royal Inscriptions: Newer Horizons." *SAAB* 13:115–44.

Falkenstein, Adam. 1968. "Der sumerische und der akkadische Mythos von Inannas Gang zur Unterwelt." Pages 96–110 in *Festschrift Werner Caskel zum siebzigsten Geburtstag 5. März 1966 gewidmet von Freunden und Schülern*. Edited by Erwin Gräf. Leiden: Brill.

Falkenstein, Adam, and Wolfram von Soden. 1953. *Sumerische und akkadische Hymnen und Gebete*. BAW. Stuttgart: Artemis-Verlag.

Farber, Walter. 1987. "Rituale und Beschwörungen in akkadischer Sprache." *TUAT* 2:212–81.

————. 2008. "Die einleitende Episode des Erra-Epos." *AoF* 35:262–67.

————. 2014. *Lamaštu: An Edition of the Canonical Series of Lamaštu Incantations and Rituals and Related Texts from the Second and First Millennia B.C.* MC 17. Winona Lake, IN: Eisenbrauns.

Feldt, Laura. 2013. "Myths and Narratology: Narrative Form, Meaning, and Function in the Standard-Babylonian *Epic of Anzû*." *BSR* 42:22–29.

Fincke, Jeanette. 2000. *Augenleiden nach keilschriftlichen Quellen: Untersuchungen zur altorientalischen Medizin*. Würzburger medizinhistorische Forschungen 70. Würzburg: Königshausen & Neumann.

————. 2004. "The British Museum's Ashurbanipal Library Project." *Iraq* 66:55–60.

Finet, André. 1974. "Citations littéraires dans la Correspondance de Mari." *RA* 68:35–47.

————. 1986. "Allusions et Reminiscences comme source d'Information sur la Diffusion de la Littérature." Pages 13–17 in *Keilschriftliche Literaturen: Ausgewählte*

Vorträge der XXXII. Recontre Assyriologique Internationale Münster, 8.–12.7.1985. Edited by Karl Hecker and Walter Sommerfeld. BBVO 6. Berlin: Reimer.

Finkel, Irving. 1983. "The Dream of Kurigalzu and the Tablet of Sins." *AnSt* 33:75–80.

———. 1983–1984. "Necromancy in Ancient Mesopotamia." *AfO* 29–30:1–17.

———. 1988. "Adad-apla-iddina, Esagil-kīn-apli, and the Series SA.GIG." Pages 143–59 in *A Scientific Humanist: Studies in Memory of Abraham Sachs.* Edited by Erle Leichty, Maria de Jong Ellis, and Pamela Gerardi. Occasional Publications of the Samuel Noah Kramer Fund 9. Philadelphia: University Museum.

———. 1999. "The Lament of Nabû-šuma-ukîn." Pages 323–42 in *Babylon: Focus mesopotamischer Geschichte, Wiege früher Gelehrsamkeit, Mythos in der Moderne; 2. Internationales Colloquium der Deutschen Orient-Gesellschaft 24.–26. März 1998 in Berlin.* Edited by Johannes Renger. CDOG 2. Berlin: SDV Saarbrücker.

———. 2014. *The Ark Before Noah: Decoding the Story of the Flood.* New York: Doubleday.

Finkel, Irving, and J. V. Kinnier Wilson. 2006. "On *būšāna* and *diʾu*, or Why Nabonidus Went to Tema." *Le Journal des médecines cuneiformes* 9:16–22.

Finkelstein, J. J. 1961. "Ammiṣaduqa's Edict and the Babylonian 'Law Codes.'" *JCS* 15:91–104.

Finn, Jennifer. 2017. *Much Ado About Marduk: Questioning Discourses of Royalty in First Millennium Mesopotamian Literature.* SANER 16. Berlin: de Gruyter.

Fleming, Daniel, and Sara Milstein. 2010. *The Buried Foundation of the Gilgamesh Epic: The Akkadian Huwawa Narrative.* CM 39. Leiden: Brill.

Foley, J. M. 2012. "Oral-Formulaic Theory." Pages 976–78 in *The Princeton Encyclopedia of Poetry and Poetics.* Edited by Roland Green. 4th ed. Princeton: Princeton University Press.

Ford, J. N. 2008. "Wordplay in the Lamaštu Incantations." Pages 585–95 in *Birkat Shalom: Studies in the Bible, Ancient Near Eastern Literature, and Postbiblical Judaism Presented to Shalom M. Paul on the Occasion of His Seventieth Birthday.* Edited by Chaim Cohen, Victor Avigdor Hurowitz, Avi M. Hurvitz, Yochanan Muffs, Baruch J. Schwartz, and Jeffrey H. Tigay. Winona Lake, IN: Eisenbrauns.

Foster, Benjamin. 1974. "Humor and Cuneiform Literature." *JANESCU* 6:69–85.

———. 1991. "On Authorship in Akkadian Literature." *AION* 51:17–32.

———. 1993. *Before the Muses: An Anthology of Akkadian Literature.* 2 vols. Bethesda, MD: CDL.

———. 1994. Review of *Mesopotamian Epic Literature: Oral or Aural?*, by M. Vogelzang and H. Vanstiphout. *BO* 51:587–90.

———. 1995. "Humor and Wit in the Ancient Near East." *CANE* 4:2459–69.

———. 2001. *The Epic of Gilgamesh: A New Translation, Analogues, Criticism.* A Norton Critical Edition. New York: Norton.

———. 2005. *Before the Muses: An Anthology of Akkadian Literature.* 3rd ed. Bethesda, MD: CDL.

———. 2007. *Akkadian Literature of the Late Period.* GMTR 2. Münster: Ugarit-Verlag.

———. 2009. "Akkadian Literature." Pages 137–217 in *From an Antique Land: An Introduction to Ancient Near Eastern Literature.* Edited by Carl S. Ehrlich. Lanham: Rowman & Littlefield.

———. 2010. "Similes in the Gilgamesh Epic." Pages 313–21 in *Language in the Ancient Near East.* Vol. 1 of *Proceedings of the 53e Rencontre Assyriologique*

Internationale. Edited by Leonid E. Kogan, Natalia Koslova, Sergey Loesov, and Serguei Tishchenko. Babel & Bibel 4/1. Winona Lake, IN: Eisenbrauns.

———. 2016. *The Age of Agade: Inventing Empire in Ancient Mesopotamia*. New York: Routledge.

———. 2019. *The Epic of Gilgamesh: A New Translation, Analogues, Criticism*. 2nd ed. A Norton Critical Edition. New York: Norton.

———. Forthcoming. "Assyriology: 1850–1970." In *Handbook of Ancient Mesopotamia*. Edited by Gonzalo Rubio. Berlin: de Gruyter.

Frahm, Eckart. 1997. *Einleitung in die Sanherib-Inschriften*. AfOB 26. Vienna: Institut für Orientalistik der Universität.

———. 1998. "Humor in assyrischen Königsinschriften." Pages 147–62 in *Intellectual Life of the Ancient Near East: Papers Presented at the 43rd Rencontre Assyriologique Internationale, Prague, July 1–5, 1996*. Edited by Jiří Prosecký. Prague: Oriental Institute.

———. 2005. "On Some Recently Published Late Babylonian Copies of Royal Letters." *NABU*, no. 43.

———. 2010. "Counter-Texts, Commentaries, and Adaptations: Politically Motivated Responses to the Babylonian Epic of Creation in Mesopotamia, the Biblical World, and Elsewhere." *Orient* 45:3–33.

———. 2011. *Babylonian and Assyrian Text Commentaries: Origins of Interpretation*. GMTR 5. Münster: Ugarit-Verlag.

Frame, Grant. 1995. *Rulers of Babylonia: From the Second Dynasty of Isin to the End of Assyrian Domination (1157–612 BC)*. RIMB 2. Toronto: University of Toronto Press.

Franke, S. 1995a. "Kings of Akkad: Sargon and Naram-Sin." *CANE* 2:831–41.

———. 1995b. *Königsinschriften und Königsideologie: Die Könige von Akkade zwischen Tradition und Neuerung*. Altorientalistik 1. Münster: LIT.

Frankena, R. 1954. *Tākultu de sacrale maaltijd in het assyrische ritueel: Met een overzicht de in Assur vereerde goden*. Commentationes Orientales 2. Leiden: Brill.

Frayne, Douglas. 1990. *Old Babylonian Period (2003–1595 BC)*. RIME 4. Toronto: University of Toronto Press.

———. 1993. *Sargonic and Gutian Periods (2334–2113 BC)*. RIME 2. Toronto: University of Toronto Press.

Frazer, Mary. 2013. "Nazi-Maruttaš in Later Mesopotamian Tradition." *KASKAL* 10:187–220.

———. 2015. "Akkadian Royal Letters in Later Mesopotamian Tradition." PhD diss., Yale University.

Frechette, Christopher. 2012. *Mesopotamian Ritual-prayers of "Hand-lifting" (Akkadian Šuillas): An Investigation of Function in Light of the Idiomatic Meaning of the Rubric*. AOAT 379. Münster: Ugarit-Verlag.

Freedman, Sally M. 1998. *If a City Is Set on a Height: The Akkadian Omen Series* Šumma Alu ina mēlê Šakin, *Vol. 1; Tablets 1–21*. Occasional Publications of the Samuel Noah Kramer Fund 17. Philadelphia: University Museum.

———. 2006. *If a City Is Set on a Height: The Akkadian Omen Series* Šumma Alu ina mēlê Šakin, *Vol. 2; Tablets 22–40*. Occasional Publications of the Samuel Noah Kramer Fund 19. Philadelphia: University Museum.

———. 2017. *If a City Is Set on a Height: The Akkadian Omen Series* Šumma Alu ina Mele Šakin, *Vol. 3; Tablets 41–63*. Occasional Publications of the Samuel Noah Kramer Fund 20. Winona Lake, IN: Eisenbrauns.

Gabbay, Uri. 2012. "Akkadian Commentaries from Ancient Mesopotamia and Their Relation to Early Hebrew Exegesis." *DSD* 19:267–312.

Gabriel, Gösta. 2014. Enūma eliš: *Weg zu einer globalen Weltordnung.* ORA 12. Tübingen: Mohr Siebeck.

Gay, Peter. 1966. *The Rise of Modern Paganism.* Vol. 1 of *The Enlightenment: An Interpretation.* New York: Knopf.

———. 1969. *The Science of Freedom.* Vol. 2 of *The Enlightenment: An Interpretation.* New York: Knopf.

Gehlken, Erlend. 2012. *Weather Omens of* Enūma Anu Enlil: *Thunderstorms, Wind and Rain (Tablets 44–49).* CM 43. Leiden: Brill.

Geller, Markham J. 1997. "The Last Wedge." *ZA* 86:43–95.

———. 2005. *Renal and Rectal Disease Texts.* BAM 7. Berlin: de Gruyter.

Geller, Markham J., and Strahil V. Panayotov. 2019. *Mesopotamian Eye Disease Texts: The Nineveh Treatise.* BAM 10. Berlin: de Gruyter.

George, Andrew R. 1986. "Sennacherib and the Tablet of Destinies." *Iraq* 48:133–46.

———. 1990. "The Day the Earth Divided: A Geological Aetiology in the Babylonian Gilgamesh Epic." *ZA* 80: 214–19.

———. 1992. *Babylonian Topographical Texts.* OLA 40. Leuven: Peeters.

———. 1993. "Ninurta-Pāqidat's Dog Bite, and Notes on Other Comic Tales." *Iraq* 55:63–75.

———. 1999. *The Epic of Gilgamesh: A New Translation.* London: Penguin.

———. 2003. *The Babylonian Gilgamesh Epic: Introduction, Critical Edition and Cuneiform Text.* 2 vols. Oxford: Oxford University Press.

———. 2005a. "The Epic of Gilgamesh: Thoughts on Genre and Meaning." Pages 37–66 in *Gilgamesh and the World of Assyria: Proceedings of the Conference Held at the Mandelbaum House, the University of Sydney, 21–23 July 2004.* Edited by J. Azize and N. Weeks. ANESSup 21. Leuven: Peeters.

———. 2005b. "In Search of the é.dub.ba.a: The Ancient Mesopotamian School in Literature and Reality." Pages 127–37 in *An Experienced Scribe Who Neglects Nothing: Ancient Near Eastern Studies in Honor of Jacob Klein.* Edited by Yitzhak Sefati, Pinhas Artzi, Chaim Cohen, Barry L. Eichler, and Victor Avigdor Hurowitz. Bethesda, MD: CDL.

———. 2007a. "Babylonian and Assyrian: A History of Akkadian." Pages 31–71 in *Languages of Iraq: Ancient and Modern.* Edited by J. Nicholas Postgate. London: British School of Archaeology in Iraq.

———. 2007b. "The Civilizing of Enkidu: An Unusual Tablet of the Babylonian Gilgamesh Epic." *RA* 101:59–80.

———. 2007c. "Gilgamesh and the Literary Traditions of Ancient Mesopotamia." Pages 447–59 in *The Babylonian World.* Edited by Gwedolyn Leick. New York: Routledge.

———. 2007d. "The Gilgamesh Epic at Ugarit." *AuOr* 25:237–54.

———. 2008. "Shattered Tablets and Tangled Threads: Editing Gilgamesh, Then and Now." *Aramazd* 3:7–30.

———. 2009. *Babylonian Literary Texts in the Schøyen Collection.* CUSAS 10. Bethesda, MD: CDL.

———. 2010a. "The Assyrian Elegy: Form and Meaning." Pages 203–16 in *Opening the Tablet Box: Near Eastern Studies in Honor of Benjamin R. Foster.* Edited by Sarah Melville and Alice Slotsky. CHANE 42. Leiden: Brill.

———. 2010b. "The Epic of Gilgamesh." Pages 1–12 in *The Cambridge Companion to the Epic*. Edited by Catherine Bates. Cambridge: Cambridge University Press.

———. 2011. *Cuneiform Royal Inscriptions and Related Texts in the Schøyen Collection*. CUSAS 17. Bethesda, MD: CDL.

———. 2012. "The Mayfly on the River: Individual and Collective Destiny in the Epic of Gilgamesh." *KASKAL* 9:227–42.

———. 2013a. *Babylonian Divinatory Texts Chiefly in the Schøyen Collection*. CUSAS 18. Bethesda, MD: CDL.

———. 2013b. "The Poem of Erra and Ishum: A Babylonian Poet's View of War." Pages 39–71 in *Warfare and Poetry in the Middle East*. Edited by Hugh N. Kennedy. London: Tauris.

———. 2015. "The Gods Išum and Ḫendursanga: Night Watchmen and Street-lighting in Babylonia." *JNES* 74:1–8.

———. 2018. "Enkidu and the Harlot: Another Fragment of Old Babylonian Gilgameš." *ZA* 108:10–21.

George, Andrew R., and F. N. H. Al-Rawi. 1996. "Tablets from the Sippar Library VI: Atra-ḫasīs." *Iraq* 58:147–90.

———. 1998. "Tablets from the Sippar Library VII: Three Wisdom Texts." *Iraq* 60:187–206.

Gesche, Petra D. 2000. *Schulunterricht in Babylonien im ersten Jahrtausend v. Chr.* AOAT 275. Münster: Ugarit-Verlag.

Gill, Sam. 1987. "Prayer." Pages 489–94 in vol. 11 of *Encyclopedia of Religion*. Edited by Mircea Eliade. 16 vols. New York: Macmillan.

Glassner, Jean-Jacques. 2004. *Mesopotamian Chronicles*. WAW 19. Atlanta: Society of Biblical Literature.

Grayson, A. Kirk. 1972, 1976. *Assyrian Royal Inscriptions*. 2 vols. RANE 1–2. Wiesbaden: Harrassowitz.

———. 1975. *Assyrian and Babylonian Chronicles*. TCS 5. Locust Valley, NY: Augustin. Repr., Winona Lake, IN: Eisenbrauns, 2000.

———. 1976. *Babylonian Historical-Literary Texts*. Toronto Semitic Texts and Studies. Toronto: University of Toronto Press.

———. 1980. "Histories and Historians of the Ancient Near East: Assyria and Babylonia." *Or* 49:140–94.

———. 1980–1983. "Königslisten und Chroniken." *RlA* 6:86–135.

———. 1987. *Assyrian Rulers of the Third and Second Millennia BC (to 1115 BC)*. RIMA 1. Toronto: University of Toronto Press.

———. 1991. *Assyrian Rulers of the Early First Millennium BC I (1114–859 BC)*. RIMA 2. Toronto: University of Toronto Press.

———. 1996. *Assyrian Rulers of the Early First Millennium BC II (858–745 BC)*. RIMA 3. Toronto: University of Toronto Press.

Grayson, A. Kirk, and Jamie Novotny. 2012. *The Royal Inscriptions of Sennacherib, King of Assyria (704–681 BC), Part 1*. RINAP 3/1. Winona Lake, IN: Eisenbrauns.

———. 2014. *The Royal Inscriptions of Sennacherib, King of Assyria (704–681 BC), Part 2*. RINAP 3/2. Winona Lake, IN: Eisenbrauns.

Greaves, Sheldon. 1996. "The Power of the Word in the Ancient Near East." PhD diss., University of California, Berkeley.

Groneberg, Brigitte. 1971. *Untersuchungen zum hymnisch-epischen Dialekt der altbabylonischen literarischen Texte*. Münster: Westfälischen Wilhelm-Universität.

———. 1987. *Syntax, Morphologie und Stil der jungbabylonischen hymnischen Literatur*. 2 vols. Stuttgart: Steiner.

———. 1991. "Atramḫasīs. Tafel II iv–v." Pages 397–410 in *Marchands, Diplomates et Empereurs: Études sur la civilisation mésopotamienne offertes à Paul Garelli*. Edited by Dominique Charpin and Francis Joannès. Paris: Éditions Recherche sur les Civilisations.

———. 1996. "Towards a Definition of Literariness as Applied to Akkadian Literature." Pages 59–84 in *Mesopotamian Poetic Language: Sumerian and Akkadian*. Edited by Marianna E. Vogelzang and Herman L. J. Vanstiphout. CM 6. Proceedings of the Groningen Group for the Study of Mesopotamian Literature 2. Groningen: Styx.

———. 1997. *Lob der Ištar: Gebet und Ritual an die altbabylonische Venusgöttin*. CM 8. Groningen: Styx.

———. 2003. "Searching for Akkadian Lyrics: From Old Babylonian to the 'Liederkatalog' KAR 158." *JCS* 55:55–74.

———. 2008. "Anzû stiehlt die Schicksalstafeln: Vorherbestimmung im Alten Orient." Pages 23–39 in *Vorsehung, Schicksal und göttliche Macht: Antike Stimmen zu einem aktuellen Thema*. Edited by Reinhard G. Kratz and Hermann Spieckermann. Tübingen: Mohr Siebeck.

Guichard, Michaël. 2014. *L'épopée de Zimrī-Lîm*. Florilegium marianum 14. Mémoires de NABU 16. Paris: Société pour l'Étude du Proche-Orient Ancien.

Guichard, Michaël, and Lionel Marti. 2013. "Purity in Ancient Mesopotamia: The Paleo-Babylonian and Neo-Assyrian Periods." Pages 47–113 in *Purity and the Forming of Religious Traditions in the Ancient Mediterranean World and Ancient Judaism*. Edited by Christian Frevel and Christophe Nihan. Dynamics in the History of Religion 3. Leiden: Brill.

Guinan, Ann K. 1989. "The Perils of High Living: Divinatory Rhetoric in *Šumma Ālu*." Pages 227–35 in *DUMU-E₂-DUB-BA-A: Studies in Honor of Åke W. Söjberg*. Edited by Hermann Behrens, Darlene Loding, and Martha T. Roth. Occasional Publications of the Samuel Noah Kramer Fund 11. Philadelphia: University Museum.

Gurney, O. R. 1956. "The Sultantepe Tablets (Continued). V: The Tale of the Poor Man of Nippur." *AnSt* 6:145–64.

———. 1957. "The Sultantepe Tablets VI: A Letter of Gilgamesh." *AnSt* 7:127–36.

———. 1958. "The Sultantepe Tablets I (Occasional Publications No. 3): Corrigenda." *AnSt* 8:245–46.

———. 1960. "The Sultantepe Tablets (Continued) VII: The Myth of Nergal and Ereshkigal." *AnSt* 10:105–31.

———. 1972. "The Tale of the Poor Man of Nippur and Its Folktale Parallels." *AnSt* 22:149–58.

———. 1989. *Literary and Miscellaneous Texts in the Ashmolean Museum*. OCuT 11. Oxford: Clarendon.

Gurney, O. R., and J. J. Finkelstein. 1957. *The Sultantepe Tablets: Volume 1*. Occasional Publications of the British Institute of Archaeology at Ankara 3. London: British Institute of Archaeology at Ankara.

Gurney, O. R., and Peter Hulin. 1964. *The Sultantepe Tablets: Volume 2*. Occasional Publications of the British Institute of Archaeology at Ankara 7. London: British Institute of Archaeology at Ankara.

Hallo, William. 1990. "Proverbs Quoted in Epic." Pages 203–17 in *Lingering over Words: Studies in Ancient Near Eastern Literature in Honor of William L. Moran*.

Edited by Tzvi Abusch, John Huehnergard, and Piotr Steinkeller. HSS 37. Atlanta: Scholars Press. Repr., pages 607–23 in *The World's Oldest Literature: Studies in Sumerian Belles-Lettres*. CHANE 35. Leiden: Brill, 2010.

———. 1996. *Origins: The Ancient Near Eastern Background of Some Modern Western Institutions*. CHANE 6. Leiden: Brill.

Hallo, William, and K. Lawson Younger Jr. 2003–2016. *The Context of Scripture*. 4 vols. Leiden: Brill.

Halton, Charles. 2009. "Allusions to the Stream of Tradition in Neo-Assyrian Oracles." *ANES* 46:50–61.

Halton, Charles, and Saana Svärd. 2018. *Women's Writing of Ancient Mesopotamia: An Anthology of the Earliest Female Authors*. Cambridge: Cambridge University Press.

Harper, Robert Francis. 1904. *The Code of Hammurabi King of Babylon*. 2 vols. 2nd ed. Chicago: University of Chicago Press.

Harris, Rivkah. 2000. *Gender and Aging in Mesopotamia: The Gilgamesh Epic and Other Ancient Literature*. Norman: University of Oklahoma Press.

Haubold, Johannes. 2013. *Greece and Mesopotamia: Dialogues in Literature*. Cambridge: Cambridge University Press.

———. 2017. "From Text to Reading in *Enūma Eliš*." *JCS* 69:221–46.

Haul, Michael. 2000. *Das Etana-Epos: Ein Mythos von der Himmelfahrt des Königs von Kiš*. GAAL 1. Göttingen: Seminar für Keilschriftforschung.

———. 2009. *Stele und Legende: Untersuchungen zu den keilschriftlichen Erzählwerken über die Könige von Akkade*. GAAL 4. Göttingen: Universitätsverlag.

Hawthorn, Ainsley. 2015. "'You Are Just Like Me': The Motif of the Double in the Epic of Gilgamesh and the Agushaya Poem." *KASKAL* 12:451–66.

Hays, Christopher. 2008. "Echoes of the Ancient Near East? Intertextuality and the Comparative Study of the Old Testament." Pages 20–43 in *The Word Leaps the Gap: Essays on Scripture and Theology in Honor of Richard B. Hays*. Edited by J. Ross Wagner, C. Kavin Rowe, and A. Katherine Grieb. Grand Rapids: Eerdmans.

Hecker, Karl. 1974. *Untersuchungen zur akkadischen Epik*. AOAT Sonderreihe. Kevelaer: Butzon & Bercker; Neukirchen-Vluyn: Neukirchener Verlag.

———. 1986. "Zukunftsdeutungen in akkadischen Texten." *TUAT* 2:56–82.

———. 1988. "Akkadische Grab-, Bau- und Votivinschriften." *TUAT* 2:479–85.

———. 1989. "Akkadische Hymnen und Gebete." *TUAT* 2:718–83.

———. 1994. "Das Anzu-Epos." *TUAT* 3:745–59.

———. 2001. "Akkadische Mythen und Epen." *TUAT* Supp.:34–60.

———. 2004. "Akkadische Texte." *TUAT* 2:27–93.

Heimpel, Wolfgang. 1993–1995. "Mythologie. A. I." *RlA* 8:537–64.

———. 1996. "The River Ordeal in Hit." *RA* 90:7–18.

Helle, Sophus. 2014. "Rhythm and Expression in Akkadian Poetry." *ZA* 104:56–73.

———. 2017. "Babylonian Perspectives on the Uncertainty of Death: SB *Gilgamesh* X 301–21." *KASKAL* 14:211–19.

———. 2018. "The Role of Authors in the 'Uruk List of Kings and Sages': Canonization and Cultural Contact." *JNES* 77:219–34.

———. Forthcoming. "A Narrative Device in Akkadian Epics? The Two-Act Structure." *JANER*.

Herrero, Pablo. 1984. *Le Thérapeutique Mésopotamienne*. Paris: Editions Recherche sur les Civilisations.

Hess, Christian W. 2010. "Towards the Origins of the Hymnic Epic Dialect." *KASKAL* 7:101–22.

———. 2015. "Songs of Clay: Materiality and Poetics in Early Akkadian Epic." Pages 251–84 in *Texts and Contexts: The Circulation and Transmission of Cuneiform Texts in Social Space*. Edited by Paul Delnero and Jacob Lauinger. SANER 9. Berlin: de Gruyter.

Hess, Richard. 1993. "Smitten Ant Bites Back: Rhetorical Forms in the Amarna Correspondence from Shechem." Pages 95–111 in *Verse in Ancient Near Eastern Prose*. Edited by J. C. de Moor and W. G. E. Watson. AOAT 42. Kevelaer: Butzon & Bercker/Neukirchen-Vluyn: Neukirchener Verlag.

Heeßel, Nils. 2000. *Babylonisch-assyrische Diagnostik*. AOAT 43. Münster: Ugarit-Verlag.

———. 2011. "'Sieben Tafeln aus sieben Städten': Überlegungen zum Prozess der Serialisierung von Texten in Babylonien in der zweiten Hälfte des zweiten Jahrtausends v.Chr." Pages 171–95 in *Babylon: Wissenskultur in Orient und Okzident/Science Culture Between Orient and Occident*. Edited by Eva Cancik-Kirschbaum, Margarete van Ess, and Joachim Marzahn. Topoi 1. Berlin: de Gruyter.

Horowitz, Wayne. 1998. *Mesopotamian Cosmic Geography*. MC 8. Winona Lake, IN: Eisenbrauns.

Hrouda, Barthel. 1996. "Zur Darstellung des Etana-Epos in der Glyptik." *WZKM* 86:157–60.

Hrůša, Ivan. 2015. *Ancient Mesopotamian Religion: A Descriptive Introduction*. Münster: Ugarit-Verlag.

Huehnergard, John. 2011. *A Grammar of Akkadian*. 3rd ed. HSS 45. Winona Lake, IN: Eisenbrauns.

Huehnergard, John, and Christopher Woods. 2004. "Akkadian and Eblaite." Pages 218–87 in *The Cambridge Encyclopedia of the World's Ancient Languages*. Edited by Roger D. Woodard. Cambridge: Cambridge University Press. Repr., pages 83–152 in *The Ancient Languages of Syria-Palestine and Arabia*. Edited by Roger D. Woodard. Cambridge: Cambridge University Press, 2008.

Hunger, Hermann. 1968. *Babylonische und assyrische Kolophone*. AOAT 2. Neukirchen-Vluyn: Neukirchener Verlag; Kevelaer: Butzon & Bercker.

———. 1992. *Astrological Reports to Assyrian Kings*. SAA 8. Helsinki: Helsinki University Press.

———. 2006. *Astronomical Diaries and Related Texts from Babylonia, VI*. Vienna: Österreichischen Akademie der Wissenschaften.

Hunger, Hermann, and Teije de Jong. 2014. "Almanac W22340a from Uruk: The Latest Datable Cuneiform Tablet." *ZA* 104:182–94.

Hunger, Hermann, and Stephen A. Kaufman. 1975. "A New Akkadian Prophecy Text." *JAOS* 95:371–75.

Hunger, Hermann, and David Pingree. 1989. *MUL.APIN: An Astronomical Compendium in Cuneiform*. AfOB 24. Horn: Berger.

———. 1999. *Astral Sciences in Mesopotamia*. HdO 44. Leiden: Brill.

Hunger, Hermann, and John Steele. 2018. *The Babylonian Astronomical Compendium MUL.APIN*. Scientific Writings from the Ancient and Medieval World. New York: Routledge.

Hurowitz, Victor. 1992. "Some Literary Observations on the Šitti-Marduk Kudurru (BBSt. 6)." *ZA 82:*39–59.

————. 1994. Inu Anum ṣīrum: *Literary Structures in the Non-Juridical Sections of Codex Hammurabi*. Occasional Publications of the Samuel Noah Kramer Fund 15. Philadelphia: University Museum.

————. 1998. "Advice to a Prince: A Message from Ea." *SAAB* 12:39–53.

————. 1999. "Canon and Canonization in Mesopotamia—Assyriological Models or Ancient Realities?" Pages 1*–12* in *Proceedings of the Twelfth World Congress of Jewish Studies, Jerusalem, July 29–August 5, 1997, Division A: The Bible and Its World*. Edited by Ron Margolin. Jerusalem: World Union of Jewish Studies.

————. 2002–2005. "An Overlooked Allusion to *Ludlul* in Urad-Gula's Letter to Assurbanipal." *SAAB* 14:129–32.

————. 2005. "Hammurabi in Mesopotamian Tradition." Pages 497–532 in *An Experienced Scribe Who Neglects Nothing: Ancient Near Eastern Studies in Honor of Jacob Klein*. Edited by Yitzhak Sefati, Pinhas Artzi, Chaim Cohen, Barry L. Eichler, and Victor Avigdor Hurowitz. Bethesda, MD: CDL.

————. 2008. "Shutting Up the Enemy: Literary Gleanings from Sargon's Eighth Campaign." Pages 104–20 in *Treasures on Camel's Humps: Historical and Literary Studies from the Ancient Near East Presented to Israel Eph'al*. Edited by Mordechai Cogan and Dan'el Kahn. Jerusalem: Magnes.

Hurowitz, Victor, and Joan Goodnick Westenholz. 1990. "LKA 63: A Heroic Poem in Celebration of Tiglath-Pileser I's Muṣru-Qumanu Campaign." *JCS* 42:1–49.

Hutcheon, Linda, and Malcolm Woodland. 2012. "Parody." Pages 1001–3 in *The Princeton Encyclopedia of Poetry and Poetics*. Edited by Roland Green. 4th ed. Princeton: Princeton University Press.

Hutter, Manfred. 1985. *Altorientalische Vorstellungen von der Unterwelt: Literar- und religionsgeschichtliche Überlegungen zu "Nergal und Ereškigal."* OBO 63. Fribourg: Presses Universitaires; Göttingen: Vandenhoeck & Ruprecht.

Izre'el, Shlomo. 1992. "The Study of Oral Poetry: Reflections of a Neophyte." Pages 155–225 in *Mesopotamian Epic Literature: Oral or Aural?* Edited by Marianna E. Vogelzang and Herman L. J. Vanstiphout. Lewiston, NY: Mellon.

————. 1996. "Mesopotamian Literature in Contemporary Setting: Translating Akkadian Myths." Pages 85–125 in *Mesopotamian Poetic Language: Sumerian and Akkadian*. Edited by Marianna E. Vogelzang and Herman L. J. Vanstiphout. CM 6. Proceedings of the Groningen Group for the Study of Mesopotamian Literature 2. Groningen: Styx.

————. 1997. *The Amarna Scholarly Tablets*. CM 9. Groningen: Styx.

————. 2001. *Adapa and the South Wind: Language Has the Power of Life and Death*. MC 10. Winona Lake, IN: Eisenbrauns.

Izre'el, Shlomo, and Eran Cohen. 2004. *Literary Old Babylonian*. Languages of the World/Materials 81. Munich: Lincom Europa.

Jacobsen, Thorkild. 1976. *Treasures of Darkness: A History of Mesopotamian Religion*. New Haven: Yale University Press.

Jaques, Margaret. 2015. *Mon dieu qu'ai-je fait? Les diĝir-šà-dab(5)-ba et la piété privée en Mésopotamie*. OBO 273. Fribourg: Academic Press; Göttingen: Vandenhoeck & Ruprecht.

Jason, Heda. 1979. "The Poor Man of Nippur: An Ethnopoetic Analysis." *JCS* 31:189–215.

Jean, Charles-François. 1924. *La Littérature des Bayloniens et des Assyriens*. Librairie Orientaliste. Paris: Geuthner.

Jean, Cynthia. 2006. *La Magie Néo-Assyrienne en Contexte: Recherches sur le Métier d'Exorciste et le Concept d'ashiputu*. SAAS 17. Helsinki: Neo-Assyrian Text Corpus Project.

Jeyes, Ulla. 2000. "A Compendium of Gall-Bladder Omens Extant in Middle Babylonian, Nineveh, and Seleucid Versions." Pages 345–73 in *Wisdom, Gods and Literature: Studies in Assyriology in Honour of W. G. Lambert*. Edited by Andrew R. George and Irving L. Finkel. Winona Lake, IN: Eisenbrauns.

Jiménez, Enrique. 2014. "New Fragments of Gilgameš and Other Literary Texts from Kuyunjik." *Iraq* 76:99–121.

———. 2017. *The Babylonian Disputation Poems: With Editions of the* Series of the Poplar, Palm and Vine, *the* Series of the Spider, *and the* Story of the Poor, Forlorn Wren. CHANE 87. Leiden: Brill.

Joannès, Francis. 1991. "Le traité de vassalité d'Atamrum d'Andarig envers Zimri-Lim de Mari." Pages 167–77 in *Marchands, Diplomates et Empereurs: Études sur la civilisation mésopotamienne offertes à Paul Garelli*. Edited by Dominique Charpin and Francis Joannès. Paris: Éditions Recherche sur les Civilisations.

Jones, William. 2012. "Satire." Pages 1255–58 in *The Princeton Encyclopedia of Poetry and Poetics*. Edited by Roland Green. 4th ed. Princeton: Princeton University Press.

Kämmerer, Thomas R., and Kai A. Metzler. 2012. *Das babylonische Weltschöpfungsepos* Enūma elîš. AOAT 375. Münster: Ugarit-Verlag.

Kienst, Burkhart. 2003. iškar šēlebi: *Die Serie vom Fuchs*. FAOS 22. Stuttgart: Steiner.

Kilmer, Anne Draffkorn. 1972. "The Mesopotamian Concept of Overpopulation and Its Solution as Reflected in the Mythology." *Or* 41:160–77.

Kinnier Wilson, J. V. 1985. *The Legend of Etana: A New Edition*. Warminster: Aris & Phillips.

———. 2007. *Studia Etanaica: New Texts and Discussions*. AOAT 338. Münster: Ugarit-Verlag.

Koch, Ulla Susanne. 1995. *Mesopotamian Astrology: An Introduction to Babylonian and Assyrian Celestial Divination*. CNIP 19. Copenhagen: Museum Tusculanum.

———. 2005. *Secrets of Extispicy: The Chapter* Multābiltu *of the Babylonian Extispicy Series and* Niṣirti bārûti *Texts Mainly from Aššurbanipal's Library*. AOAT 326. Münster: Ugarit-Verlag.

———. 2015. *Mesopotamian Divination Texts: Conversing with the Gods: Sources from the First Millennium BCE*. GMTR 7. Münster: Ugarit-Verlag.

Köcher, Franz. 1953. "Der babylonische Göttertypentext." *MIOF* 1:57–107.

———. 1955. *Keilschrifttexte zur assyrisch-babylonischen Drogen- und Pflanzenkunde: Texte der Serien* uru.an.na : maltakal, Ḫar. ra : ḫubullu *und* Ú Gar-šú. Berlin: Akademie.

———. 1963–1964. *Keilschrifttexte aus Assur 1–3*. BAM 1–3. Berlin: de Gruyter.

———. 1971. *Keilschrifttexte aus Assur 4, Babylon, Nippur, Sippar, Uruk und unbekannter Herkunft*. BAM 4. Berlin: de Gruyter.

———. 1980. *Keilschrifttexte aus Ninive 1 und 2*. BAM 5–6. Berlin: de Gruyter.

Koch-Westenholz, Ulla. 1999. "The Astrological Commentary Šumma Sîn ina Tamartišu Tablet 1." Pages 149–65 in *La science des cieux: Sages, mages, astrologues*. Edited by Rika Gyselen. ResOr 12. Bures-sur-Yvette: Groupe pour l'étude de la civilisation du Moyen-Orient.

————. 2000. *Babylonian Liver Omens: The Chapters* Manzāzu, Padānu *and* Pān Tākalti *of the Babylonian Extispicy Series Mainly from Aššurbanipal's Library.* CNIP 25. Copenhagen: Museum Tusculanum.

Komoróczy, Géza. 1975. "Akkadian Epic Poetry and Its Sumerian Sources." *ActAnt* 23:41–63.

Koppen, Frans van. 2011. "The Scribe of the Flood Story and His Circle." *OHCC*, 140–66.

Koubková, Evelyne. 2016. "Fortune and Misfortune of the Eagle in the Myth of Etana." Pages 371–82 in *Fortune and Misfortune in the Ancient Near East: Proceedings of the 60th Rencontre Assyriologique Internationale at Warsaw 21–25 July 2014.* Edited by Olga Drewnowska and Małgorzata Sandowicz. Winona Lake, IN: Eisenbrauns.

Kouwenberg, N. J. C. 2011. "Akkadian in General." Pages 330–40 in *The Semitic Languages: An International Handbook.* Edited by Stefan Weniger. Handbücher zur Sprach- und Kommunikationswissenschaft 36. Berlin: de Gruyter Mouton.

————. 2012. "Diachrony in Akkadian and the Dating of Literary Texts." Pages 433–51 in *Diachrony in Biblical Hebrew.* Edited by Cynthia L. Miller-Naudé and Ziony Zevit. LSAWS 8. Winona Lake, IN: Eisenbrauns.

Krebernik, Manfred. 2002. "Vielzahl und Einheit im altmesopotamischen Pantheon." Pages 33–51 in *Polytheismus und Monotheismus in den Religionen des Vorderen Orients.* Edited by Manfred Krebernik and Jürgen van Oorschot. AOAT 298. Münster: Ugarit-Verlag.

————. 2006–2008. "Qingu." *RlA* 11:178–79.

Kuhrt, Amélie. 1995. *The Ancient Near East: c. 3000–330 BC.* 2 vols. Routledge History of the Ancient World. New York: Routledge.

————. 2014. "'Even a Dog in Babylon is Free.'" Pages 77–87 in *The Legacy of Arnaldo Momigliano.* Edited by Tim Cornell and Oswyn Murray. Warburg Institute Colloquia 25. London: Warburg Institute; Turin: Aragno.

Kuhrt, Amélie, and Susan Sherwin-White. 1991. "The Cylinder of Antiochus I from Borsippa: Aspects of Seleucid Royal Ideology." *JHS* 111: 71–86.

Kuklick, Bruce. 1996. *Puritans in Babylon: The Ancient Near East and American Intellectual Life, 1880–1930.* Princeton: Princeton University Press.

Kümmel, Hans Martin. 1979. *Familie, Beruf und Amt im spätbabylonischen Uruk: Prosopographische Untersuchungen zu Berufsgruppen des 6. Jahrhunderts v. Chr. in Uruk.* ADOG 20. Berlin: Mann.

Kvanvig, Helge S. 1988. *Roots of Apocalyptic: The Mesopotamian Background of the Enoch Figure and of the Son of Man.* WMANT 61. Neuchichen-Vluyn: Neukirchener Verlag.

Labat, René. 1951. *Traité Akkadien de Diagnostics et Pronostics Médicaux. I: Transcription et Traduction; II: Planches.* Collection de Travaux de l'Academie Internationale d'Histoire des Sciences 7. Leiden: Brill.

Læssøe, Jørgen. 1955. *Studies on the Assyrian Ritual and Series* bît rimki. Copenhagen: Munksgaard.

Lambert, W. G. 1957. "Ancestors, Authors, and Canonicity." *JCS* 11:1–14.

————. 1959. "Three Literary Prayers of the Babylonians." *AfO* 19:47–66.

————. 1960. *Babylonian Wisdom Literature.* Oxford: Oxford University Press. Repr., Winona Lake, IN: Eisenbrauns, 1996.

————. 1962. "A Catalogue of Texts and Authors." *JCS* 16:59–77.

————. 1964. "The Reign of Nebuchadnezzar I: A Turning Point in the History of Ancient Mesopotamian Religion." Pages 3–13 in *The Seed of Wisdom: Essays in Honour of T. J. Meek*. Edited by W. S. McCullough. Toronto: University of Toronto Press.

————. 1965. "Nebuchadnezzar King of Justice." *Iraq* 27:1–11.

————. 1967. "The Gula Hymn of Bulluṭsa-rabi." *Or* 36:105–32.

————. 1968. "Literary Style in First Millennium Mesopotamia." *JAOS* 88:123–32.

————. 1970. "Fire Incantations." *AfO* 23:39–45.

————. 1974. "Dingir.šà.dib.ba Incantations." *JNES* 33:267–322.

————. 1980a. "New Fragments of Babylonian Epics." *AfO* 27:71–82.

————. 1980b. "The Theology of Death." Pages 53–66 in *Death in Mesopotamia: Papers Read at the XXVIe Recontre assyriologique international*. Edited by Bendt Alster. Mesopotamia 8. Copenhagen: Akademisk Forlag.

————. 1986. "Ninurta Mythology in the Babylonian Epic of Creation." Pages 55–60 in *Keilschriftliche Literaturen: Ausgewählte Vorträge der XXXII. Recontre Assyriologique Internationale Münster, 8.–12.7.1985*. Edited by Karl Hecker and Walter Sommerfeld. Berlin: Reimer.

————. 1987. "A Further Attempt at the Babylonian 'Man and His God.'" Pages 187–202 in *Language, Literature, and History: Philological and Historical Studies Presented to Erica Reiner*. Edited by Francesca Rochberg-Halton. AOS 67. New Haven: American Oriental Society.

————. 1989. "The Laws of Hammurabi in the First Millennium." Pages 95–98 in *Reflets des deux fleuves: Volume de mélanges offerts à André Finet*. Edited by Marc Lebeau and Philippe Talon. Leuven: Peeters.

————. 1990. "A New Babylonian Descent to the Netherworld." Pages 289–300 in *Lingering over Words: Studies in Ancient Near Eastern Literature in Honor of William L. Moran*. Edited by Tzvi Abusch, John Huehnergard, and Piotr Steinkeller. HSS 37. Atlanta: Scholars Press.

————. 1991. "Three New Pieces of Atra-hasīs." Pages 411–14 in *Marchands, Diplomates et Empereurs: Études sur la civilisation mésopotamienne offertes à Paul Garelli*. Edited by Dominique Charpin and Francis Joannès. Paris: Éditions Recherche sur les Civilisations.

————. 1994a. "Enuma Elisch." *TUAT* 3:565–602.

————. 1994b. "The Fall of the Cassite Dynasty to the Elamites: An Historical Epic." Pages 67–72 in *Cinquante-deux Reflexions sur le Proche-Orient Ancient offertes en homage à Léon De Meyer*. Edited by Hermann Gasche, M. Tanret, C. Janssen, and A. Degraeve. Mesopotamian History and Environment Occasional Publications 2. Leuven: Peeters.

————. 1997. "The Assyrian Recension of Enūma Eliš." Pages 77–79 in *Assyrien im Wandel der Zeiten: XXXIXe Rencontre Assyriologique Internationale, Heidelberg, 6.–10. Juli 1992*. Edited by Hartmut Waetzoldt and Harald Hauptmann. HSAO 6. Heidelberg: Heidelberger Orientverlag.

————. 2007. *Babylonian Oracle Questions*. MC 13. Winona Lake, IN: Eisenbrauns.

————. 2008. "Mesopotamian Creation Stories." Pages 15–59 in *Imagining Creation*. Edited by Markham J. Geller and Mineke Schipper. IJS Studies in Judaica 5. Leiden: Brill.

————. 2013. *Babylonian Creation Myths*. MC 16. Winona Lake, IN: Eisenbrauns.

————. 2014. "The Babylonian *ikribs*." Pages 53–55 in *Divination in the Ancient Near East: A Workshop on Divination Conducted During the 54th Rencontre assyriologique internationale, Würzburg, 2008*. Edited by Jeanette Fincke. Winona Lake, IN: Eisenbrauns.

Lambert, W. G., and Alan Millard. 1969. *Atra-Ḫasīs: The Babylonian Story of the Flood*. Oxford: Oxford University Press. Repr., Winona Lake, IN: Eisenbrauns, 1999.

Landsberger, Benno. 1926. "Die Eigenbegrifflichkeit der babylonischen Welt." *Islamica* 2:355–72.

———. 1976. *The Conceptual Autonomy of the Babylonian World*. Sources and Monographs: Monographs on the Ancient Near East 1/4. Malibu, CA: Udena.

Langdon, Stephen. 1912. *Die neubabylonischen Königsinschriften*. VAB 4. Leipzig: Hinrichs.

Lapinkivi, Pirjo. 2010. *The Neo-Assyrian Myth of Ištar's Descent and Resurrection*. SAACT 6. Helsinki: Neo-Assyrian Text Corpus Project.

Larsen, Mogens Trolle. 1976 *The Old Assyrian City State and Its Colonies*. Mesopotamia 4. Copenhagen: Akademisk Forlag.

———. 1996. *The Conquest of Assyria: Excavations in an Antique Land, 1840–1860*. New York: Routledge.

Lauinger, Jacob. 2004. "A New Fragment of the Epic of Anzû in the Antakya Museum." *ZA* 94:80–84.

Leichty, Erle. 1970. *The Omen Series* Šumma Izbu. TCS 4. Locust Valley, NY: Augustin.

———. 2011. *The Royal Inscriptions of Esarhaddon, King of Assyria (680–669 BC)*. RINAP 4. Winona Lake, IN: Eisenbrauns.

Leichty, Erle, and C. B. F. Walker. 2004. "Three Babylonian Chronicle and Scientific Texts." Pages 203–12 in *From the Upper Sea to the Lower Sea: Studies on the History of Assyria and Babylonia in Honour of A. K. Grayson*. Edited by Grant Frame with Linda S. Wilding. PIHANS 101. Leiden: Nederlands Instituut voor het Nabije Oosten.

Leick, Gwendolyn. 1991. *A Dictionary of Ancient Near Eastern Mythology*. New York: Routledge.

———. 1994. *Sex and Eroticism in Mesopotamian Literature*. New York: Routledge.

Lenzi, Alan. 2008. *Secrecy and the Gods: Secret Knowledge in Ancient Mesopotamia and Biblical Israel*. SAAS 19. Helsinki: Neo-Assyrian Text Corpus Project.

———. 2010. "*Šiptu ul Yuttun*: Some Reflections on a Closing Formula in Akkadian Incantations." Pages 131–66 in *Gazing on the Deep: Ancient Near Eastern and Other Studies in Honor of Tzvi Abusch*. Edited by Jeffrey Stackert, Barbara Nevling Porter, and David P. Wright. Bethesda, MD: CDL.

———, ed. 2011. *Reading Akkadian Prayers and Hymns: An Introduction*. ANEM 3. Atlanta: Society of Biblical Literature.

———. 2012. "The Curious Case of Failed Revelation in *Ludlul Bēl Nēmeqi*: A New Suggestion for the Poem's Scholarly Purpose." Pages 33–66 in *Mediating Between Heaven and Earth: Communication with the Divine in the Ancient Near East*. Edited by Carly L. Crouch, Jonathan Stökl, and Anna Elise Zernecke. LHBOTS 566. London: T&T Clark.

———. 2014. "Advertising Secrecy, Creating Power in Ancient Mesopotamia: How Scholars Used Secrecy in Scribal Education to Bolster and Perpetuate Their Social Prestige and Power." *Antiguo Oriente* 11:13–42.

————. 2015a. "The Language of Akkadian Prayers in *Ludlul Bēl Nēmeqi* and Its Significance Within and Beyond Mesopotamia." Pages 67–105 in *Mesopotamia in the Ancient World: Impact, Continuities, Parallels.* Edited by Robert Rollinger and Erik van Dongen. Melammu Symposia 7. Münster: Ugarit-Verlag.

————. 2015b. "Mesopotamian Scholarship: Kassite to Late Babylonian Periods." *Journal of Ancient Near Eastern History* 2:145–201.

————. 2015c. Review of *The Primeval Flood Catastrophe: Origins and Early Development in Mesopotamian Traditions*, by Y. S. Chen. *HR* 55:367–70.

————. 2015d. "Scribal Hermeneutics and the Twelve Gates of *Ludlul bēl nēmeqi*." *JAOS* 135:733–49.

————. 2016. "Scribal Revision and Textual Variation in Akkadian *Šuila*-Prayers: Two Case Studies in Ritual Adaptation." Pages 63–108 in *Empirical Models Challenging Biblical Criticism.* Edited by Robert Rezetko and Ray Person Jr. AIL. Atlanta: SBL Press.

————. 2018. "'Learn from My Example': The Reception of Ludlul Bel Nemeqi." Paper presented at the International Meeting of the Society of Biblical Literature. Helsinki, Finland, 31 July, 2018.

————. 2019. "'Counsels of Wisdom' as 'White-Collar' Wisdom in First Millennium Ancient Mesopotamia." Pages 60–69 in *Teaching Morality in Antiquity: Wisdom Texts, Oral Traditions, and Images.* Edited by Takayoshi Oshima with Susanne Kohlhaas. ORA 29. Tübingen: Mohr Siebeck.

————. Forthcoming. "Counsels of Wisdom." In *The Library of Wisdom: An Encyclopedia of Ancient Sayings Collections.* Edited by Walter Wilson. Atlanta: SBL Press.

Lewis, Brian. 1980. *The Sargon Legend: A Study of the Akkadian Text and the Tale of the Hero Who Was Exposed at Birth.* ASOR Dissertation Series 5. Cambridge: American Schools of Oriental Research.

Lieberman, Stephen J. 1977. *The Sumerian Loanwords in Old-Babylonian Akkadian, Volume One: Prolegomena and Evidence.* HSS 22. Missoula, MT: Scholars Press.

Limet, Henri. 1971. *Les legendes de sceaux cassites.* Académie royale de Belgique, Classe des letters: Mémoires 60/2. Bruxelles: Palais des Académies.

Linssen, Marc J. H. 2004. *The Cults of Uruk and Babylon: The Temple Ritual Texts as Evidence for Hellenistic Cult Practices.* CM 25. Leiden: Brill-Styx.

Lion, Brigitte. 2008. "Les femmes et l'écrit en Mésopotamie: auteurs, commanditaires d'inscriptions et scribes." Pages 53–68 in *Las culturas del Próximo Oriente Antiguo y su expansión mediterránea.* Edited by J. J. Justel, Juan-Pablo Vita, and José-Ángel Zamora. Zaragoza: Instituto de Estudios Islámicos y del Oriente Próximo.

————. 2011. "Literacy and Gender." *OHCC*, 90–112.

Litke, Richard L. 1998. *A Reconstruction of the Assyro-Babylonian God-Lists*, AN : ^da-nu-um *and* AN : anu ša amēli. Texts from the Babylonian Collection 3. New Haven: Yale Babylonian Collection.

Liverani, Mario. 1979. "The Ideology of the Assyrian Empire." Pages 297–317 in *Power and Propaganda: A Symposium on Ancient Empires.* Edited by Mogens Trolle Larsen. Mesopotamia 7. Copenhagen: Akademisk Forlag.

————. 1995. "The Deeds of Ancient Mesopotamian Kings." *CANE* 4:2353–66.

————. 2004. *Myth and Politics in Ancient Near Eastern Historiography.* Translated by Zainab Bahrani and Marc Van De Mieroop. Ithaca, NY: Cornell University Press.

Livingstone, Alasdair. 1986. *Mystical and Mythological Explanatory Works of Assyrian and Babylonian Scholars.* Oxford: Clarendon. Repr., Winona Lake, IN: Eisenbrauns, 2007.

———. 1989. *Court Poetry and Literary Miscellanea.* SAA 3. Helsinki: Helsinki University Press.

———. 2007. "Ashurbanipal: Literate or Not?" *ZA* 97:98–118.

———. 2013. *Hemerologies of Assyrian and Babylonian Scholars.* CUSAS 25. Bethesda, MD: CDL.

Lloyd, Seton. 1980. *Foundations in the Dust: A Story of Mesopotamian Exploration.* Rev. and enl. ed. London: Thames & Hudson.

Longman, Tremper, III. 1991. *Fictional Akkadian Autobiography: A Generic and Comparative Study.* Winona Lake, IN: Eisenbrauns.

Luckenbill, Daniel David. 1927. *Ancient Records of Assyria and Babylonia: Volume II, Historical Records of Assyria from Sargon to the End.* Chicago: University of Chicago Press.

Luukko, Mikko. 2007. "The Administrative Roles of the 'Chief Scribe' and the 'Palace Scribe' in the Neo-Assyrian Period." *SAAB* 16:227–56.

Luukko, Mikko, and Greta Van Buylaere. 2002. *The Political Correspondence of Esarhaddon.* SAA 16. Helsinki: Helsinki University Press.

Machinist, Peter. 1978. "The Epic of Tukulti-Ninurta I: A Study in Middle Assyrian Literature." PhD diss., Yale University.

———. 1983. "Rest and Violence in the Poem of Erra." *JAOS* 103:221–26.

———. 2005. "Order and Disorder: Some Mesopotamian Reflections." Pages 31–61 in *Genesis and Regeneration: Essays on Conceptions of Origins.* Edited by Shaul Shaked. Jerusalem: Israel Academy of Sciences and Humanities.

Maier, John. 1997. *Gilgamesh: A Reader.* Wauconda, IL: Bolchazy-Carducci Publishers.

Marcus, David. 1977. "Animal Similes in Assyrian Royal Inscriptions." *Or* 46:86–106.

Maul, Stefan M. 1988. *Herzberuhigungsklagen: Die sumerisch-akkadischen Eršaḫunga-Gebete.* Wiesbaden: Harrassowitz.

———. 1994. *Zukunftsbewältigung: Eine Untersuchung altorientalischen Denkens anhand der babylonish-assyrisches Löserituale (Namburbi).* BaF 18. Mainz: von Zabern.

———. 1999. "Der assyrische König—Hüter der Weltordnung." Pages 201–14 in *Priests and Officials in the Ancient Near East: Papers of the Second Colloquium on the Ancient Near East; the City and Its Life held at the Middle Eastern Culture Center in Japan (Mitaka, Tokyo), March 22–24, 1996.* Edited by Kazuko Watanabe. Heidelberg: Winter.

———. 2003. "Omina und Orakel. A. Mesopotamien." *RlA* 10:45–88.

———. 2005. *Das Gilgamesch-Epos.* Munich: Beck.

———. 2012. "Tontafelabschriften des 'Kodex Hammurapi' in altbabylonischer Monumentalschrift." *ZA* 102:76–99.

———. 2013. *Die Wahrsagekunst im Alten Orient: Zeichen des Himmels und der Erde.* Munich: Beck.

———. 2018. *The Art of Divination in the Ancient Near East: Reading the Signs of Heaven and Earth.* Translated by Brian McNeil and Alexander Johannes Edmonds. Waco, TX: Baylor University Press.

Mayer, Werner. 1976. *Untersuchungen zur Formensprache der babylonischen "Gebetsbeschwörungen."* StPohlSM 5. Rome: Biblical Institute Press.

———. 2013. *Assyrien und Urarṭu, I: Der Achte Feldzug Sargons II. im Jahr 714 v. Chr.* AOAT 395/1. Münster: Ugarit-Verlag.

McCall, Henrietta. 1990. *Mesopotamian Myths.* London: British Museum; Austin: University of Texas Press.

McCutcheon, Russell. 2001. *Critics Not Caretakers: Redescribing the Public Study of Religion.* Issues in the Study of Religion. Albany: State University of New York Press.

Meissner, Bruno. 1927. *Die babylonisch-assyrische Literatur.* Potsdam: "Athenaion."

Metcalf, Christopher. 2013. "Babylonian Perspectives on the Certainty of Death." *KASKAL* 10:255–267.

Mettinger, Tryggve N. D. 2001. *The Riddle of Resurrection: "Dying and Rising Gods" in the Ancient Near East.* ConBOT 50. Stockholm: Almquist & Wiksell. Repr., Winona Lake, IN: Eisenbrauns, 2013.

Metzler, Kai A. 2002. *Tempora in altbabylonischen literarischen Texten.* AOAT 279. Münster: Ugarit-Verlag.

Meyers, Eric, ed. 1997. *The Oxford Encyclopedia of Archaeology in the Near East.* 5 vols. New York: Oxford.

Michalowski, Piotr. 1980. "Adapa and the Ritual Process." *Rocznik orientalistyczny* 41:77–82.

———. 1990. "Early Mesopotamian Communicative Systems: Art, Literature, and Writing." Pages 53–69 in *Investigating Artistic Environments in the Ancient Near East.* Edited by Ann C. Gunter. Washington, DC: Smithsonian Institution.

———. 1992. "Orality, Literacy, and Early Mesopotamian Literature." Pages 227–245 in *Mesopotamian Epic Literature: Oral or Aural?* Edited by Marianna E. Vogelzang and Herman L. J. Vanstiphout. Lewiston, NY: Mellon.

———. 1994. "Writing and Literacy in Early States: A Mesopotamianist Perspective." Pages 49–70 in *Literacy: Interdisciplinary Conversations.* Edited by Deborah Keller-Cohen. Cresskill, NJ: Hampton.

———. 1996. "Ancient Poetics." Pages 141–52 in *Mesopotamian Poetic Language: Sumerian and Akkadian.* Edited by Marianna E. Vogelzang and Herman L. J. Vanstiphout. CM 6. Proceedings of the Groningen Group for the Study of Mesopotamian Literature 2. Groningen: Styx.

———. 2005. "The Life and Death of the Sumerian Language in Comparative Perspective." *ASJ* 22:177–202.

Mieder, Wolfgang. 2012. *Proverbs: A Handbook.* International Folkloristics 8. New York: Lang.

Milstein, Sara. 2015a. "The 'Magic' of Adapa." Pages 191–213 in *Texts and Contexts: The Circulation and Transmission of Cuneiform Texts in Social Space.* Edited by Paul Delnero and Jacob Lauinger. SANER 9. Berlin: de Gruyter.

———. 2015b. "The Origins of Adapa." *ZA* 105:30–41.

Minunno, Giuseppe. 2010. "Sull' *Arad Mitanguranni* come Documento Storico-Religioso." *SEL* 27:9–17.

Moran, William. 1971. "Atraḫasīs: The Babylonian Story of the Flood." *Bib* 52:51–61. Repr., pages 33–45 in *The Most Magic Word: Essays on Babylonian and Biblical Literature.* CBQMS 35. Washington, DC: Catholic Biblical Association of America, 2002.

———. 1987. "Some Considerations of Form and Interpretation in Atra-ḫasīs." pages 245–55 in *Language, Literature, and History: Philological and Historical Studies*

Presented to Erica Reiner. Edited by Francesca Rochberg-Halton. AOS 67. New Haven, CT: American Oriental Society. Repr., pages 46–58 in *The Most Magic Word: Essays on Babylonian and Biblical Literature.* CBQMS 35. Washington, DC: Catholic Biblical Association of America, 2002.

———. 1995. "The Gilgamesh Epic: A Masterpiece from Ancient Mesopotamia." *CANE* 4:2327–36.

———. 2002. *The Most Magic Word: Essays on Babylonian and Biblical Literature.* CBQMS 35. Washington, DC: Catholical Biblical Association of America.

Müller, Gerfrid G. W. 1994a. "Ischtars Höllenfahrt." *TUAT* 3:760–66.

———. 1994b. "Ischum und Erra." *TUAT* 3:781–801.

———. 1994c. "Nergal und Ereschkigal." *TUAT* 3:766–80.

———. 1995. "Wer spricht? Bemerkungen zu 'Išum und Erra." Pages 349–60 in *Vom Alten Orient zum Alten Testament: Festschrift für Wolfram Freiherrn von Soden.* Edited by Manfried Dietrich and Oswald Loretz. AOAT 240. Neukirchen-Vluyn: Neukirchener Verlag; Kevelaer: Butzon & Bercker.

Müller, Karl Friedrich. 1937. *Das assyrische Ritual, Teil 1: Texte zum assyrischen Königsritual.* MVAG 41/3. Leipzig: Hinrichs.

Nadali, Davide. 2009. "Sieges and Similes of Sieges in the Royal Annals: The Conquest of Damascus by Tiglath-Pileser III." *KASKAL* 6:137–49.

Neujahr, Matthew. 2012. *Predicting the Past in the Ancient Near East: Mantic Historiography in Ancient Mesopotamia, Judah, and the Mediterranean World.* BJS 354. Providence, RI: Brown University Press.

Nielsen, John. 2018. *The Reign of Nebuchadnezzar I in History and Historical Memory.* SHANE. New York: Routledge.

Nissinen, Martti. 1998. *References to Prophecy in Neo-Assyrian Sources.* SAAS 7. Helsinki: Neo-Assyrian Text Corpus Project.

———. 2003. *Prophets and Prophecy in the Ancient Near East.* WAW 12. Atlanta: Society of Biblical Literature.

Noegel, Scott. 1996. "Word Play in the Tale of the Poor Man of Nippur." *ASJ* 19:169–86.

———. 1997. "Raining Terror: Another Wordplay Cluster in Gilgamesh Tablet XI (Assyrian Version, ll. 45-47)." *NABU,* no. 42.

———. 2000. *Puns and Pundits: Word Play in the Hebrew Bible and Ancient Near Eastern Literature.* Bethesda, MD: CDL.

———. 2005. "Mesopotamian Epic." Pages 233–45 in *The Blackwell Companion to Ancient Epic.* Edited by John Miles Foley. Malden, MA: Blackwell.

———. 2007. *Nocturnal Ciphers: The Punning Language of Dreams in the Ancient Near East.* AOS 89. New Haven: American Oriental Society.

———. 2010. "'Sign, Sign, Everywhere a Sign': Script, Power, and Interpretation in the Ancient Near East." Pages 143–62 in *Divination and Interpretation of Signs in the Ancient World.* Edited by Amar Annus. OIS 6. Chicago: Oriental Institute of the University of Chicago.

———. 2011. "'Word Play' in the Song of Erra." Pages 162–93 in *Strings and Threads: A Celebration of the Work of Anne Draffkorn Kilmer.* Edited by Wolfgang Heimpel and Gabriella Frantz-Szabó. Winona Lake, IN: Eisenbrauns.

———. 2016. "Suffering Ambiguity in *Ludlul Bēl Nēmeqi*: On Erudition, Ideology, and Theology in Tablet I." *BO* 73:613–36.

North, Richard, and Martin Worthington. 2012. "*Gilgamesh* and *Beowulf*: Foundations of a Comparison." *KASKAL* 9:177–217.

Novotny, Jamie. 2001. *The Standard Babylonian Etana Epic: Cuneiform Text, Translation, Score, Glossary, Indices and Sign List.* SAACT 2. Helsinki: Neo-Assyrian Text Corpus Project.

Novotny, Jamie, and Joshua Jeffers. 2018. *The Royal Inscriptions of Ashurbanipal (668–631 BC), Aššur-etel-ilāni (630–627 BC), and Sîn-šarra-iškun (626–612 BC), Kings of Assyria, Part 1.* RINAP 5/1. University Park, PA: Eisenbrauns.

Oates, Joan. 1986. *Babylon.* Rev. ed. London: Thames & Hudson.

Oelsner, Joachim. 2012. "Zur Einteilung des Kodex Hammu-rāpi im Altertum." *ZABR* 18:79–126.

———. 2014. "Überlegungen zu den Graeco-Babyloniaca." Pages 147–64 in *He Has Opened Nisaba's House of Learning: Studies in Honor of Åke Waldemar Sjöberg on the Occasion of His 89th Birthday on August 1st 2013.* Edited by Leonhard Sassmannshausen. CM 46. Leiden: Brill.

Oppenheim, A. Leo. 1956. *The Interpretation of Dreams in the Ancient Near East with a Translation of an Assyrian Dream Book.* TAPS 46.3. Philadelphia: American Philosophical Society.

———. 1960. "The City of Assur in 714 B.C." *JNES* 19:133–47.

Oppenheim, A. Leo, and Erica Reiner. 1977. *Ancient Mesopotamia: Portrait of a Dead Civilization.* Rev. and completed by Erica Reiner. Chicago: University of Chicago Press.

Oshima, Takayoshi. 2010. "'Damkianna Shall Not Bring Back Her Burden in the Future!' A New Mythological Text of Marduk, Enlil and Damkianna." Pages 145–61 in *A Woman of Valor: Jerusalem Ancient Near Eastern Studies in Honor of Joan Goodnick Westenholz.* Edited by Wayne Horowitz, Uri Gabbay, and Filip Vukosavović. BPOA 8. Madrid: Consejo Superior de Investigaciones Científicas.

———. 2011. *Babylonian Prayers to Marduk.* ORA 7. Tübingen: Mohr Siebeck.

———. 2012a. "Another Attempt at Two Kassite Royal Inscriptions: The Agum-Kakrime Inscription and the Inscription of Kurigalzu the Son of Kadashmanharbe." *Babel und Bibel* 6:225–68.

———. 2012b. "How Many Tablets Did Ludlul Bēl Nēmeqi Consist Of?" *NABU*, no. 22.

———. 2013. *The Babylonian Theodicy.* SAACT 9. Helsinki: Neo-Assyrian Text Corpus Project.

———. 2014a. *Babylonian Poems of Pious Sufferers:* Ludlul Bēl Nēmeqi *and the* Babylonian Theodicy. ORA 14. Tübingen: Mohr Siebeck.

———. 2014b. "'Let Us Sleep!' The Motif of Disturbing Resting Deities in Cuneiform Texts." *Studia Mesopotamica: Jahrbuch für altorientalische Geschichte und Kultur* 1:271–89.

Ossendrijver, Mathieu. 2012. *Babylonian Mathematical Astronomy: Procedure Texts.* Sources and Studies in the History of Mathematics and Physical Sciences. New York: Springer.

Ottervanger, Baruch. 2016. *The Tale of the Poor Man of Nippur.* SAACT 12. Helsinki: Neo-Assyrian Text Corpus Project.

Pallis, Svend Aage. 1956. *The Antiquity of Iraq: A Handbook of Assyriology.* Copenhagen: Munksgaard.

Parpola, Simo. 1983. *Letters from Assyrian Scholars to the Kings Esarhaddon and Assurbanipal: Part II: Commentary and Appendices.* AOAT 5.2. Neukirchen-Vluyn: Neukirchener Verlag; Kevelaer: Butzon & Bercker. Repr., Winona Lake, IN: Eisenbrauns, 2007.

————. 1987. "The Forlorn Scholar." Pages 257–78 in *Language, Literature, and History: Philological and Historical Studies Presented to Erica Reiner.* Edited by Francesca Rochberg-Halton. AOS 67. New Haven: American Oriental Society.

————. 1993. *Letters from Assyrian and Babylonian Scholars.* SAA 10. Helsinki: Helsinki University Press. Repr., Winona Lake, IN: Eisenbrauns, 2015.

————. 1997. "The Man Without a Scribe and the Question of Literacy in the Assyrian Empire." Pages 315–24 in *Ana šadî Labāni lū allik: Beiträge zu altorientalischen und mittelmeerischen Kulturen; Festschrift für Wolfgang Röllig.* Edited by Beate Pongratz-Leisten, Hartmut Kühne, and Paolo Xella. AOAT 247. Neukirchen-Vluyn: Neukirchener Verlag; Kevelaer: Butzon & Bercker.

Parpola, Simo, and Michael Porter. 2001. *The Helsinki Atlas of the Near East in the Neo-Assyrian Period.* Helsinki: Neo-Assyrian Text Corpus Project; Chebeague Island, ME: Casco Bay Assyriological Institute.

Parpola, Simo, and Kazuko Watanabe. 1988. *Neo-Assyrian Treaties and Loyalty Oaths.* SAA 2. Helsinki: Helsinki University Press. Repr., Winona Lake, IN: Eisenbrauns, 2014.

Paulus, Susanne. 2014. *Die babylonischen Kudurru-Inschriften von der kassitischen bis zur frühneubabylonischen Zeit: Untersucht unter besonderer Berücksichtigung gesellschafts- und rechtshistorischer Fragestellungen.* AOAT 51. Münster: Ugarit-Verlag.

Pearce, Laurie. 1995. "The Scribes and Scholars of Ancient Mesopotamia." *CANE* 4:2265–78.

Pease, D. H. 1995. "Author." Pages 105–17 in *Critical Terms for Literary Study.* Edited by Frank Lentricchia and Thomas McLaughlin. 2nd ed. Chicago: University of Chicago Press.

Pedersén, Olof. 1985, 1986. *Archives and Libraries in the City of Assur: A Survey of the Material from the German Excavations, Parts I & II.* Acta Universitatis Upsaliensis, Studia Semitica Upsaliensia 6, 8. Uppsala: Almqvist & Wiksell.

————. 2005. *Archive und Bibliotheken in Babylon: Die Tontafeln der Grabung Robert Koldeweys 1899–1917.* ADOG 25. Berlin: Saarbrücken.

Pettinato, Giovanni. 1971. *Das altorientalische Menschenbild und die sumerischen und akkadischen Schöpfungsmythen.* AHAW. Heidelberg: Winter.

Piccin, Michela. Forthcoming. *Ludlul bēl nēmeqi e Teodicea babilonese: Traduzione e commento.* Claudiana: Paideia.

Piccin, Michela, and Martin Worthington. 2015. "Schizophrenia and the Problem of Suffering in the *Ludlul* Hymn to Marduk." *RA* 109:113–24.

Polentz, Bernhard. 1989. *Die Eigenbegrifflichkeit babylonischer Redeformen: Dargestellt am Musterbeispiel des Erra-Epos.* Theorie und Forschung 99. Regensburg: Roderer.

Polinger Foster, Karen. 1991. "Ceramic Imagery in Ancient Near Eastern Literature." Pages 389–413 in *Material Issues in Art and Archaeology II: Symposium Held April 17–21, San Francisco, California, U.S.A.* Edited by Pamela B. Vandiver, James R. Druzik, and George Segan Wheeler. Materials Research Society Symposium Proceedings 185. Pittsburgh: Materials Research Society.

Ponchia, Simonetta. 1987. "Analogie, metafore e similitudini nelle iscrizioni reali assire: semantica e ideologia." *OrAnt* 26:223–55.

———. 2013–2014. "Hermeneutical Strategies and Innovative Interpretation in Assyro-Babylonian Texts: The Case of Erra and Išum." *SAAB* 20:61–72.

Ponchia, Simonetta, and Mikko Luukko. 2013. *The Standard Babylonian Myth of Nergal and Ereškigal*. SAACT 8. Helsinki: Neo-Assyrian Text Corpus Project.

Pongratz-Leisten, Beate. 1994. Ina šulmi īrub: *Die kulttopographische und ideologische Programmatik der* akītu-*Prozession in Babylonien und Assyrien im 1. Jahrtausend v. Chr.* BaF 16. Mainz: von Zabern.

———. 1999a. *Herrschaftswissen in Mesopotamien: Formen der Kommunikation zwischen Gott und König im 2. und 1. Jahrtausend v. Chr.* SAAS 10. Helsinki: Neo-Assyrian Text Corpus Project.

———. 1999b. " 'Öffne den Tafelbehälter und lies . . .' Neue Ansätze zum Verständnis des Literaturkonzeptes in Mesopotamien." *WO* 30:67–90.

———. 2001. "Überlegungen zum Epos in Mesopotamien am Beispiel der Kutha-Legende." Pages 12–41 in *Von Göttern und Menschen Erzählen: Formkonstanzen und Funktionswandel moderner Epik*. Edited by Jörg Rüpke. Potsdamer Altertumswissenschaftliche Beiträge 4. Stuttgart: Steiner.

———, ed. 2011. *Reconsidering the Concept of Revolutionary Monotheism*. Winona Lake, IN: Eisenbrauns.

———. 2015. *Religion and Ideology in Assyria*. SANER 6. Berlin: de Gruyter.

Porter, Barbara N. 1993. *Images, Power, and Politics: Figurative Aspects of Esarhaddon's Babylonian Policy*. Philadelphia: American Philosophical Society.

———. 1995. "Language, Audience, and Impact in Imperial Assyria." Pages 51–72 in *Language and Culture in the Near East: Diglossia, Bilingualism, Registers*. Edited by Shlomo Izre'el and Rina Drory. IOS 15. Leiden: Brill.

———. 2009. *What Is a God? Anthropomorphic and Non-Anthropomorphic Aspects of Deity in Ancient Mesopotamia*. Transactions of the Casco Bay Assyriological Institute 2. Winona Lake, IN: Eisenbrauns.

Pritchard, James. 1969. *Ancient Near Eastern Texts Relating to the Old Testament*. 3rd ed. with supplement. Princeton: Princeton University Press.

Radner, Karen. 2005. *Die Macht des Namens: Altorientalische Strategien zur Selbsterhaltung*. SANTAG 8. Wiesbaden: Harrassowitz Verlag.

Radner, Karen, and Eleanor Robson. 2011. *The Oxford Handbook of Cuneiform Cultures*. New York: Oxford University Press.

Reiner, Erica. 1958. *Šurpu: A Collection of Sumerian and Akkadian Incantations*. AfOB 11. Graz: Weidner.

———. 1960. "Plague Amulets and House Blessings." *JNES* 19:148–55.

———. 1978. "Die akkadische Literatur." Pages 151–210 in *Neues Handbuch der Literaturwissenschaft, Altorientalische Literaturen*. Edited by Wolfgang Röllig. Wiesbaden: Harrassowitz.

———. 1982. "The Babylonian Fürstenspiegel in Practice." Pages 320–26 in *Societies and Languages of the Ancient Near East: Studies in Honour of I. M. Diakonoff*. Edited by M. A. Dandamayev, J. Nicholas Postgate, and Mogens T. Larsen. Warminster: Aris & Phillips.

———. 1985. *Your Thwarts in Pieces, Your Mooring Rope Cut: Poetry from Babylonia and Assyria*. Michigan Studies in the Humanities 5. Ann Arbor: Horace H. Rackham School of Graduate Studies at the University of Michigan.

————. 1986. "Why Do You Cuss Me?" *Proceedings of the American Philosophical Society* 120:1–6.

————. 1991. "First Millennium Babylonian Literature." Pages 293–321 in *The Assyrian and Babylonian Empires and Other States of the Near East, from the Eighth to the Sixth Centuries B.C.* Edited John Boardman, I. E. S. Edwards, E. Sollberger, and N. G. L. Hammond. 2nd ed. CAH 3/2. Cambridge: Cambridge University Press.

Reiner, Erica, and Walter Farber. 2012. "Assyrian and Babylonian, Poetry of." Pages 95–97 in *The Princeton Encyclopedia of Poetry and Poetics*. Edited by Roland Green. 4th ed. Princeton: Princeton University Press.

Renger, J. 1980–1983. "Königsinschriften B. Akkadisch." *RlA* 6:65–77.

Rensburg, J. F. J. van. 1990. "Characterizing a Poetic Line in Young Babylonian: A Metrical and Grammatical Approach." *Journal for Semitics* 2:90–99.

Reynolds, Frances. 2003. *The Babylonian Correspondence of Esarhaddon*. SAA 18. Helsinki: Helsinki University Press.

Richardson, M. E. J. 2000. *Hammurabi's Laws: Text, Translation and Glossary*. BibSem 73. Semitic Texts and Studies 2. Sheffield: Sheffield Academic.

————. 2008. *A Comprehensive Grammar to Hammurabi's Stele*. Gorgias Handbooks 8. Piscataway, NJ: Gorgias.

Rivaroli, Marta, and Lorenzo Verderame. 2005. "To Be a Non-Assyrian." Pages 290–305 in *Ethnicity in Ancient Mesopotamia: Papers Read at the 48th Rencontre Assyriologique Internationale Leiden, 1–4 July 2002*. Edited by W. H. van Soldt, R. Kalvelagen, and Dina Katz. PIHANS 102. Leiden: Nederlands Instituut voor het Nabije Oosten.

Robson, Eleanor. 2001. "The Tablet House: A Scribal School in Old Babylonian Nippur." *RA* 95:39–66.

————. 2008. "Mesopotamian Medicine and Religion: Current Debates, New Perspectives." *RC* 2:455–83.

————. 2011. "The Production and Dissemination of Scholarly Knowledge." *OHCC*, 557–76.

Rochberg, Francesca. 1993. "The Cultural Locus of Astronomy in Late Babylonia." Pages 31–46 in *Die Rolle der Astronomie in den Kulturen Mesopotamiens: Beiträge zum 3. Grazer Morgenländischen Symposium (23–27 September 1991)*. Edited by Hannes D. Galter. Grazer Morgenländische Studien 3. Graz: RM Druck & Verlagsgesellschaft.

————. 1998. *Babylonian Horoscopes*. TAPS 88/1. Philadelphia: American Philosophical Society.

————. 2004. *The Heavenly Writing: Divination, Horoscopy, and Astronomy in Mesopotamian Culture*. Cambridge: Cambridge University Press.

————. 2009. "Conditionals, Inference, and Possibility in Ancient Mesopotamian Science." *Science in Context* 22:5–25. Repr., pages 373–97 in *In The Path of the Moon: Babylonian Celestial Divination and Its Legacy*. AMD 6. Leiden: Brill, 2010.

————. 2010. *In The Path of the Moon: Babylonian Celestial Divination and Its Legacy*. AMD 6. Leiden: Brill.

————. 2016. "Canon and Power in Cuneiform Scribal Scholarship." Pages 217–29 in *Problems of Canonicity and Identity Formation in Ancient Egypt and Mesopotamia*. Edited by Kim Ryholt and Gojko Barjamovic. CNIP 43. Copenhagen: Museum Tusculanum.

Rochberg-Halton, Francesca. 1984. "Canonicity in Cuneiform Texts." *JCS* 36:127–44. Repr., pages 65–83 in *In The Path of the Moon: Babylonian Celestial Divination and Its Legacy*. AMD 6. Leiden: Brill, 2010.

———. 1987. "The Assumed 29th *Aḫû* Tablet of *Enūma Anu Enlil*." In *Language, Literature, and History: Philological and Historical Studies Presented to Erica Reiner*. Edited by Francesca Rochberg-Halton. AOS 67. New Haven: American Oriental Society. Repr., pages 85–111 in *In The Path of the Moon: Babylonian Celestial Divination and Its Legacy*. AMD 6. Leiden: Brill, 2010.

———. 1988. *Aspects of Babylonian Celestial Divination: The Lunar Eclipse Tablets of Enuma Anu Enlil*. AfOB 22. Horn: Berger.

Rogers, Robert William. 1901. *A History of Babylonia and Assyria*. 2nd ed. 2 vols. New York: Eaton & Mains.

Röllig, W. 1987. "Literatur. A. Akkadisch." *RlA* 7:48–66.

Roth, Martha. 1997. *Law Collections from Mesopotamia and Asia Minor*. 2nd ed. WAW 6. Atlanta: Scholars Press.

Rubio, Gonzalo. 2009. "Sumerian Literature." Pages 11–75 in *From an Antique Land: An Introduction to Ancient Near Eastern Literature*. Edited by Carl S. Ehrlich. Lanham: Rowman & Littlefield.

Russell, John Malcolm. 1991. *Sennacherib's Palace Without Rival at Nineveh*. Chicago: University of Chicago Press.

———. 1999. *The Writing on the Wall: Studies in the Architectural Context of Late Assyrian Palace Inscriptions*. MC 9. Winona Lake, IN: Eisenbrauns.

Rutz, Matthew, and Piotr Michalowski. 2016. "The Flooding of Ešnunna, the Fall of Mari: Hammurabi's Deeds in Babylonian Literature and History." *JCS* 68:15–43.

Sachs, Abraham, and Hermann Hunger. 1988, 1989, 1996. *Astronomical Diaries and Related Texts from Babylonia, I–III*. Vienna: Österreichischen Akademie der Wissenschaften.

Sachs, Abraham, Hermann Hunger, and John Steele. 2001. *Astronomical Diaries and Related Texts from Babylonia, V: Lunar and Planetary Texts*. Vienna: Österreichischen Akademie der Wissenschaften.

Saggs, H. W. F. 1984. *The Might That Was Assyria*. London: Sidgwick & Jackson.

———. 1986. "Additions to Anzu." *AfO* 33:1–29.

Sallaberger, Walther. 2013. *Das Gilgamesch-Epos: Mythos, Werk und Tradition*. 2nd ed. Munich: Beck.

Samet, Nili. 2008. "The Babylonian Dialogue Between a Master and His Slave: A New Literary Analysis." *Shnaton: An Annual for Biblical and Near Eastern Studies* 23:99–130. [Hebrew]

Sanders, Seth L. 2009. "The First Tour of Hell: From Neo-Assyrian Propaganda to Early Jewish Revelation." *JANER* 9:151–69.

———. 2017. *From Adapa to Enoch: Scribal Culture and Religious Vision in Judea and Babylon*. TSAJ 167. Tübingen: Mohr Siebeck.

Saporetti, Claudio. 1990. *Etana*. Prisma 124. Palermo: Sellerio.

———. 2004. *Arad mitanguranni: Dialogo fra schiavo e padrone nell'antica Mesopotamia*. 2nd ed. Pisa: Servicio editoriale universitario.

Sassmannshausen, Leonhard. 2008. "Babylonische Schriftkultur des 2. Jahrtausends v. Chr. in den Nachbarländern und im östlichen Mittelmeerraum." *AuOr* 26:263–93.

Sasson, Jack. 1995. "Water Beneath Straw: Adventures of a Prophetic Phrase in the Mari Archives." In *Solving Riddles and Untying Knots: Biblical, Epigraphic, and*

Semitic Studies in Honor of Jonas C. Greenfield. Edited by Ziony Zevit, Seymour Gitin, Michael Sokoloff. Winona Lake, IN: Eisenbrauns.

———. 2015. *From the Mari Archives: An Anthology of Old Babylonian Letters.* Winona Lake, IN: Eisenbrauns.

Schaudig, Hanspeter. 2001. *Die Inschriften Nabonids von Babylon und Kyros' des Großen samt den in ihrem Umfeld entstandenen Tendenzschriften: Textausgabe und Grammatik.* AOAT 256. Münster: Ugarit-Verlag.

Scurlock, Jo Ann. 2014. *Sourcebook for Ancient Mesopotamian Medicine.* WAW 36. Atlanta: Society of Biblical Literature.

Seri, Andrea. 2006. "The Fifty Names of Marduk in *Enūma eliš.*" *JAOS* 126:507–19.

———. 2012. "The Role of Creation in Enūma eliš." *JANER* 12:4–29.

———. 2014. "Borrowings to Create Anew: Intertextuality in the Babylonian Poem of 'Creation' (Enūma eliš)." *JAOS* 134:89–106.

Seux, Marie-Joseph. 1976. *Hymnes et Prieres aux Dieux de Babylonie et d'Assyrie.* Paris: Cerf.

Shehata, Dahlia. 2001. *Annotierte Bibliographie zum altbabylonischen Atramḫasīs-Mythos.* GAAL 3. Göttingen: Seminar für Keilschriftforschung.

Sjöberg, Åke. 1972. "In Praise of the Scribal Art." *JCS* 24:126–31.

———. 1975. "The Old Babylonian Eduba." Pages 159–79 in *Sumerological Studies in Honor of Thorkild Jacobsen on His Seventieth Birthday June 7, 1974.* Edited by Stephen J. Lieberman. AS 20. Chicago: University of Chicago Press.

Slanski, Kathryn E. 2003. *The Babylonian Entitlement Narûs (Kudurrus): A Study in Their Form and Function.* ASOR Books 9. Boston: American Schools of Oriental Research.

———. 2012. "The Law of Hammurabi and Its Audience." *Yale Journal of Law and the Humanities* 24:97–110.

Soden, Wolfram von. 1931. "Der hymnisch-epische Dialekt des Akkadischen." *ZA* 40:163–227.

———. 1933, "Der hymnisch-epische Dialekt des Akkadischen (Schluß)." *ZA* 41:90–183.

———. 1936. "Die Unterweltsvision eines assyrischen Kronprinzen." *ZA* 43:1–31.

———. 1957–1971. "Gebet II. (babylonisch und assyrisch)." *RlA* 3:160–70.

———. 1972–1975. "Hymne. B. Nach akkadischen Quellen." *RlA* 4:344–548.

———. 1978. "Die erste Tafel des altbabylonischen Atramhasis-Mythus: Haupttext und Parallelversionen." *ZA* 68:50–94.

———. 1981. "Untersuchungen zur babylonischen Metrik, Teil I." *ZA* 71:161–204.

———. 1984. "Untersuchungen zur babylonischen Metrik, Teil II." *ZA* 74:213–34.

———. 1990. "Weisheitstexte in akkadischer Sprache." *TUAT* 3:110–57.

———. 1994. "Der altbabylonische Atramchasis-Mythos." *TUAT* 3:612–45.

———. 1995. *Grundriss der Akkadischen Grammatik.* 3rd ed. AnOr 33. Rome: Pontificial Biblical Institute.

Soldt, W. H. van. 1994. *Letters in the British Museum, Part 2.* AbB 13. Leiden: Brill.

———. 1995. "Babylonian Lexical, Religious and Literary Texts and Scribal Education at Ugarit and Its Implications for the Alphabetic Literary Texts." Pages 171–212 in *Ugarit: Ein ostmediterranes Kulturzentrum in Alten Orient: Ergebnisse und Perspektiven der Forschung.* Edited by Manfried Dietrich and Oswald Loretz. ALASP 7. Münster: Ugarit-Verlag.

———. 2011. "The Role of Babylon in Western Peripheral Education." Pages 197–212 in *Babylon: Wissenskultur in Orient und Okzident/Science Culture Between Orient and Occident*. Edited by Eva Cancik-Kirschbaum, Margarete van Ess, and Joachim Marzahn. Topoi 1. Berlin: de Gruyter.

Sollberger, E. 1968. "The Cruciform Monument." *JEOL* 20:50–70.

Sommer, Benjamin. 1998. *A Prophet Reads Scripture: Allusion in Isaiah 40–66*. Contraversions. Stanford: Stanford University Press.

Sommerfeld, Walter. 1982. *Der Aufstieg Marduks: Die Stellung Marduks in der babylonischen Religion des zweiten Jahrtausends v.Chr*. AOAT 213. Kevelaer: Butzon & Bercker; Neukirchen-Vluyn: Neukirchener Verlag.

———. 1987–1990. "Marduk. A. Philologisch. I. In Mesopotamien." *RlA* 7:360–70.

Sonik, Karen. 2009. "Gender Matters in *Enūma Eliš*." Pages 85–101 in *In the Wake of Tikva Frymer-Kensky*. Edited by Steven Holloway, JoAnn Scurlock, and Richard H. Beal. Gorgias Précis Portfolios 4. Piscataway, NJ: Gorgias Press.

———. 2012. "The Tablet of Destinies and the Transmission of Power in Enūma eliš." Pages 387–95 in *Organization, Representation, and Symbols of Power in the Ancient Near East: Proceedings of the 54th Rencontre Assyriologique Internationale at Würzburg 20–25 July 2008*. Edited by Gernot Wilhelm. Winona Lake, IN: Eisenbrauns.

Sonnek, Franz. 1940. "Die Einführung der direkten Rede in den epischen Texten." *ZA* 46:225–35.

Spar, Ira, and W. G. Lambert. 2005. *Literary and Scholastic Texts of the First Millennium B.C.* Cuneiform Texts in the Metropolitan Museum of Art 2. New York: Metropolitan Museum of Art.

Starr, Ivan. 1990. *Queries to the Sungod: Divination and Politics in Sargonid Assyria*. SAA 4. Helsinki: Helsinki University Press.

Steele, John M. 2011. "Making Sense of Time: Observational and Theoretical Calendars." *OHCC*, 470–85.

Steele, Timothy. 2012. "Verse and Prose." Pages 1507–13 in *The Princeton Encyclopedia of Poetry and Poetics*. Edited by Roland Green. 4th ed. Princeton: Princeton University Press.

Stein, Peter. 2000. *Die mittel- und neubabylonischen Königsinschriften bis zum Ende der Assyrerherrschaft: Grammatische Untersuchungen*. Jenaer Beitrage zum Vorderen Orient 3. Wiesbaden: Harrassowitz.

Steinert, Ulrike. 2012. *Aspekte des Menschseins im Alten Mesopotamien: Eine Studie zu Person und Identität im 2. und 1. Jt. v. Chr.* CM 44. Leiden: Brill.

———, ed. 2018. *Assyrian and Babylonian Scholarly Text Catalogues: Medicine, Magic and Divination*. BAM 9. Berlin: de Gruyter.

Steinkeller, Piotr. 1992. "Early Semitic Literature and Third Millennium Seals with Mythological Motifs." Pages 243–83 in *Literature and Literary Language at Ebla*. Edited by Pelio Fronzaroli. Quaderni di Semitistica 18. Firenze: Dipartimento di Linguistica Università di Firenze.

Stökl, Jonathan. 2012. *Prophecy in the Ancient Near East: A Philological and Sociological Comparison*. CHANE 56. Leiden: Brill.

Stol, M. 1993. *Epilepsy in Babylonia*. CM 2. Groningen: Styx.

Streck, Michael P. 1999. *Die Bildersprache der akkadischen Epik*. AOAT 264. Münster: Ugarit-Verlag.

———. 2004. "Dattelpalme und Tamariske in Mesopotamien nach dem akkadischen Streitgespräch." *ZA* 94:250–90.

———. 2007a. "Beiträge zum akkadischen Gilgameš-Epos." *Or* 76:404–23.

———. 2007b. "Der *Parallelismus Membrorum* in den altbabylonischen Hymnen." Pages 167–81 in *Parallelismus Membrorum*. Edited by Andreas Wagner. OBO 224. Göttingen: Vandenhoeck & Ruprecht; Fribourg: Academic Press.

———. 2009. "Notes on the Old Babylonian Epics of Anzu and Etana." *JAOS* 129:477–86.

———. 2014. Review of *The Assyrian Dictionary of the University of Chicago*, Vol. 20: U/W. *ZA* 104:104–7.

Streck, Michael P., and Nathan Wasserman. 2011. "Dialogues and Riddles: Three Old Babylonian Wisdom Texts." *Iraq* 73:117–25.

———. 2012. "More Light on Nanāya." *ZA* 102:183–201.

———. 2014. "Mankind's Bitter Fate: The Wisdom Dialog BM 79111+." *JCS* 66:39–47.

———. 2016. "On Wolves and Kings: Two Tablets with Akkadian Wisdom Texts from the Second Millennium B.C." *Iraq* 78:241–52.

———. Forthcoming. "Akkadian Literature." In *Handbook of Ancient Mesopotamia*. Edited by Gonzalo Rubio. Berlin: de Gruyter.

Strong, S. A. 1898. "A Hymn of Nebuchadnezzar." *Proceedings of the Society of Biblical Archaeology* 20:154–62.

Studevent-Hickman, Benjamin. 2010. "Language, Speech, and the Death of Anzu." Pages 273–92 in *Gazing on the Deep: Ancient Near Eastern, Biblical, and Jewish Studies in Honor of Tzvi Abusch*. Edited by Jeffrey Stackert, Barbara Nevling Porter, and David P. Wright. Bethesda, MD: CDL.

Svärd, Saana. 2013. "Female Agency and Authorship in Mesopotamian Texts." *KASKAL* 10:269–80.

Sweet, Ronald F. G. 1969. "A Pair of Double Acrostics in Akkadian." *Or* 38:459–60.

Tadmor, Hayim, and Shigeo Yamada. 2011. *The Royal Inscriptions of Tiglath-Pileser III (744–727 BC) and Shalmaneser V (726–722 BC), Kings of Assyria*. RINAP 1. Winona Lake, IN: Eisenbrauns.

Tadmor, Hayim, Benno Landsberger, and Simo Parpola. 1989. "The Sin of Sargon and Sennacherib's Last Will." *SAAB* 3:3–51.

Tallqvist, Knut. 1938. *Akkadische Götterepitheta*. StOr 7. Helsinki: Societas Orientalis Fennica.

Talon, Philippe. 2005. *The Standard Babylonian Creation Myth: Enūma Eliš*. SAACT 4. Helsinki: Neo-Assyrian Text Corpus Project.

Tanret, Michel. 2002. *Per aspera ad astra: L'apprentissage du cunéiforme à Sippar-Amnānum pendant la période paléobabylonienne tardive*. Mesopotamian History and Environment, Series III, Texts. Volume I: Sippar-Amnānum; The Ur-Utu Archive, Tome 2. Ghent: University of Ghent.

———. 2004. "The Works and the Days ... On Scribal Activity in Old Babylonian Sippar-Amnānum." *RA* 98:33–62.

Taylor, Jonathan. 2011. "Tablets as Artefacts, Scribes as Artisans." *OHCC*, 5–31.

Thickett, D., M. Odlyha, and D. Ling. 2002. "An Improved Firing Treatment for Cuneiform Tablets." *Studies in Conservation* 47:1–11.

Thompson, R. Campbell. 1923. *Assyrian Medical Texts from Originals in the British Museum*. London: Milford; Oxford University Press. Repr., Osnabrück: Zeller, 1983.

Thureau-Dangin, F. 1925. "Une hymn à Ištar de la haute époque Babylonienne." *RA* 22:169–77.

Tigay, Jeffrey. 1982. *The Evolution of the Gilgamesh Epic*. Philadelphia: University of Pennsylvania Press.

Tinney, Steve. 1999. "On the Curricular Setting of Sumerian Literature." *Iraq* 61:159–72.

———. 2011. "Tablets of Schools and Scholars: A Portrait of the Old Babylonian Corpus." *OHCC*, 577–96.

Toorn, Karel van der. 1985. *Sin and Sanction in Israel and Mesopotamia: A Comparative Study*. SSN 21. Assen: Van Gorcum.

———. 2007. *Scribal Culture and the Making of the Hebrew Bible*. Cambridge: Harvard University Press.

Tropper, Josef. 2012. "Alternierende Metrik in der akkadischen Poesie." Pages 433–42 in *Language and Nature: Papers Presented to John Huehnergard on the Occasion of His 60th Birthday*. Edited by Rebecca Hasselbach and Na'ama Pat-El. SAOC 67. Chicago: Oriental Institute of the University of Chicago.

Tyson, Lois. 2015. *Critical Theory Today: A User-Friendly Guide*. 3rd ed. New York: Routledge.

Van De Mieroop, Marc. 1999. *Cuneiform Texts and the Writing of History*. Approaching the Ancient World. New York: Routledge.

———. 2007. *A History of the Ancient Near East, ca. 3000–323*. 2nd ed. Blackwell History of the Ancient World. Malden, MA: Blackwell.

———. 2015. "Metaphors of Massacre in Assyrian Royal Inscriptions." *KASKAL* 12:291–317.

———. 2016. *Philosophy Before the Greeks: The Pursuit of Truth in Ancient Babylonia*. Princeton: Princeton University Press.

Vanstiphout, Herman L. J. 1986. "Some Thoughts on Genre in Mesopotamian Literature." Pages 1–11 in *Keilschriftliche Literaturen: Ausgewählte Vorträge der XXXII. Recontre Assyriologique Internationale Münster, 8.–12.7.1985*. Edited by Karl Hecker and Walter Sommerfeld. BBVO 6. Berlin: Reimer.

———. 1988. "The Importance of 'The Tale of the Fox.'" *ASJ* 10:191–227.

———. 1990. "The Mesopotamian Debate Poems: A General Presentation (Part I)." *ASJ* 12:271–318.

———. 1992a. "The Banquet Scene in the Mesopotamian Debate Poems." Pages 9–22 in *Banquets d'Orient*. Edited by Rika Gyselen. ResOr 4. Bures-sur-Yvette: Groupe D'études pour la civilisation du Moyent-Orient.

———. 1992b. "Enuma Elish as a Systematic Creed: An Essay." *OLP* 23:37-61.

———. 1992c. "The Mesopotamian Debate Poems: A General Presentation; Part II, The Subject." *ASJ* 14:339–367.

———. 1992d. "Repetition and Structure in the Aratta Cycle: Their Relevance for the Orality Debate." Pages 247–64 in *Mesopotamian Epic Literature: Oral or Aural?* Edited by Marianna E. Vogelzang and Herman L. J. Vanstiphout. Lewiston, NY: Mellon.

———. 1999a. "I Can Put Anything in Its Right Place: Generic and Typological Studies as Strategies for the Analysis and Evaluation of Mankind's Oldest Literature." Pages 79–99 in *Aspects of Genre and Type in Pre-Modern Literary Cultures*. Edited by Bert Roest and Fernand de Varennes. COMERS Communications 1. Groningen: Styx.

———. 1999b. "The Use(s) of Genre in Mesopotamian Literature: An Afterthought." *ArOr* 67:703–17.

———. 2014. "The Sumerian Debate Poems: A General Presentation; Part III." Pages 229–40 in *He Has Opened Nisaba's House of Learning: Studies in Honor of Åke Waldemar Sjöberg on the Occasion of His 89th Birthday on August 1st 2013*. Edited by Leonhard Sassmannshausen. CM 46. Leiden: Brill.

Veldhuis, Niek. 1991. *A Cow of Sîn*. Library of Oriental Texts 2. Groningen: Styx.

———. 1997. *Elementary Education at Nippur: The Lists of Trees and Wooden Objects*. Groningen: Rijksuniversiteit.

———. 1999. "Reading the Signs." Pages 161–74 in *All Those Nations . . . : Cultural Encounters within and with the Near East: Studies Presented to Han Drijvers at the Occasion of His Sixty-fifth Birthday by Colleagues and Students*. Edited by Herman L. J. Vanstiphout, Wout Jac van Bekkum, G. J. H. van Gelder, and G. J. Reinink. COMERS/ICOG Communications 2. Groningen: Styx.

———. 2000. "Kassite Exercises: Literary and Lexical Extracts." *JCS* 52:67–94.

———. 2003a. "Mesopotamian Canons." Pages 9–28 in *Homer, the Bible, and Beyond: Literary and Religious Canons in the Ancient World*. Edited by Margalit Finkelberg and Guy Stroumsa. Jerusalem Studies in Religion and Culture 2. Leiden: Brill.

———. 2003b. Review of *Schulunterricht in Babylonien im ersten Jahrtausend v. Chr.*, by P. Gesche. *JAOS* 123:627–33.

———. 2004. *Religion, Literature, and Scholarship: The Sumerian Composition Nanše and the Birds; with a Catalogue of Sumerian Bird Names*. CM 22. Leiden: Brill.

———. 2006. "Divination: Theory and Use." Pages 487–97 in *If a Man Builds a Joyful House: Assyriological Studies in Honor of Erle Verdun Leichty*. Edited by Ann K. Guinan et al. CM 31. Leiden: Brill.

———. 2010. "The Theory of Knowledge and the Practice of Celestial Divination." Pages 77–91 in *Divination and Interpretation of Signs in the Ancient World*. Edited by Amar Annus. OIS 6. Chicago: Oriental Institute of the University of Chicago.

———. 2011. "Levels of Literacy." *OHCC*, 68–89.

———. 2012. "Prestige: Divergent Receptions of Babylonian Scholarship." Pages 83–103 in *Ansehenssache: Formen von Prestige in Kulturen des Altertums*. Edited by Birgit Christiansen and Ulrich Thaler. Münchner Studien zur Alten Welt 9. Munich: Utz.

———. 2014. *History of the Cuneiform Lexical Tradition*. GMTR 6. Münster: Ugarit-Verlag.

———. Forthcoming. "School and Curriculum." In *Handbook of Ancient Mesopotamia*. Edited by Gonzalo Rubio. Berlin: de Gruyter.

Vera Chamza, Galo W. 2002. *Die Omnipotenz Aššurs: Entwicklungen in der Aššur-Theologie unter den Sargoniden Sargon II, Sanherib und Asarhaddon*. AOAT 295. Münster: Ugarit-Verlag.

Verderame, Lorenzo. 2002. *Le Tavole I–VI della serie astrologica Enūma Anu Enlil*. Nisaba 2. Rome: Di.Sc.A.M.

Visicato, Giuseppe. 2000. *The Power and the Writing: The Early Scribes of Mesopotamia*. Bethesda, MD: CDL.

Vogelzang, Marianna E. 1986. "Kill Anzu! On a Point of Literary Evolution." Pages 61–70 in *Mesopotamien und seine Nachbarn: Politische und kulturelle*

Wechselbeziehungen im Alten Vorderasien vom 4. bis 1. Jahrtausend v. Chr. Edited by Hans-Jörg Nissen and Johannes Renger. BBVO 1. Berlin: Reimer.

———. 1988. *Bin Šar Dadmē: Edition and Analysis of the Akkadian Anzu Poem.* Groningen: Styx.

———. 1990. "Patterns Introducing Direct Speech in Akkadian Literary Texts." *JCS* 42:50–70.

———. 1991. "Some Questions About the Akkadian Disputes." Pages 47–57 in *Dispute Poems and Dialogues in the Ancient and Medieval Near East: Forms and Types of Literary Debates in Semitic and Related Literatures.* Edited by G. J. Reinink and Herman L. J. Vanstiphout. OLA 42. Leuven: Peeters.

———. 1992. "Some Aspects of Oral and Written Tradition in Akkadian." Pages 265–78 in *Mesopotamian Epic Literature: Oral or Aural?* Edited by Marianna E. Vogelzang and Herman L. J. Vanstiphout. Lewiston, NY: Mellon.

———. 1996. "Repetition as a Poetic Device in Akkadian." Pages 167–82 in *Mesopotamian Poetic Language: Sumerian and Akkadian.* Edited by Marianna E. Vogelzang and Herman L. J. Vanstiphout. CM 6. Proceedings of the Groningen Group for the Study of Mesopotamian Literature 2. Groningen: Styx.

Vogelzang, Marianna E., and Herman L. J. Vanstiphout, eds. 1992. *Mesopotamian Epic Literature: Oral or Aural?* Lewiston, NY: Mellon.

———, eds. 1996. *Mesopotamian Poetic Language: Sumerian and Akkadian.* CM 6. Proceedings of the Groningen Group for the Study of Mesopotamian Literature 2. Groningen: Styx.

Volk, Konrad. 2000. "Edubba'a und Edubba'a-Literatur: Rätsel und Lösungen." *ZA* 90:1–30.

———. 2012. "Streitgespräch." *RlA* 13:214–222.

Waerzeggers, Caroline. 2012. "The Babylonian Chronicles: Classification and Provenance." *JNES* 71:285–98.

Walker, C. B. F. 1987a. *Cuneiform.* Reading the Past. Berkeley: University of California Press.

———. 1987b. "The Kouyunjik Collection of Cuneiform Texts: Formation, Problems, and Prospects." Pages 183–93 in *Austen Henry Layard: Tra l'Oriente e Venezia: Venezia, 26–28 ottobre 1983.* Edited by F. M. Fales and B. J. Hickey. Fenice 8. Roma: "l'Erma" di Bretschneider.

Walker, Christopher, and Michael Dick. 2001. *The Induction of the Cult Image in Ancient Mesopotamia: The Mesopotamian Mis Pî Ritual.* SAALT 1. Helsinki: Neo-Assyrian Text Corpus Project.

Walls, Neal. 2001. *Desire, Discord and Death: Approaches to Ancient Near Eastern Myth.* ASOR Books 8. Boston: American Schools of Oriental Research.

Wang, Guangsheng, Michela Piccin, and Sven Günther. Forthcoming. "Alternative Perspectives from the Far East: Ancient Near Eastern Studies (including Egypt) in China." In *Towards a History of Assyriology.* Edited by Sebastian Fink and Hans Neumann. Investigatio Orientis. Münster: Zaphon.

Wasserman, Nathan. 2003a. "A Forgotten Old-Babylonian Lament over a City's Destruction: UET 6/2, 403 and Its Possible Literary Content." *Eretz-Israel* 27:127–32. [Hebrew]

———. 2003b. *Style and Form in Old Babylonian Literary Texts.* CM 27. Köln: Styx; Leiden: Brill.

———. 2011a. "The Distant Voice of Gilgameš: The Circulation and Reception of the Babylonian Gilgameš Epic in Ancient Mesopotamia." *AfO* 52:1–14.

———. 2011b. "Sprichwort (proverb)." *RlA* 13:19–23.

———. 2013. "Treating Garments in the Old Babylonian Period: 'At the Cleaners' in a Comparative View." *Iraq* 75:255–77.

———. 2015. "On the Authorship of the Epic of Zimrī-Līm and Its Literary Context." *AfO* 53:52–56.

———. 2016. *Akkadian Love Literature of the Third and Second Millennium BCE.* LAOS 4. Wiesbaden: Harrassowitz.

Watanabe, Kazuko. 1984. "Rekonstruktion von VTE 438 auf Grund von Erra III A 17." *Assur* 3:164–66.

Waxler, Robert P. 2014. *The Risk of Reading: How Literature Helps Us to Understand Ourselves and the World.* New York: Bloomsbury.

Weaver, Ann M. 2004. "The 'Sin of Sargon' and Esarhaddon's Reconception of Sennacherib: A Study in Divine Will, Human Politics and Royal Ideology." *Iraq* 66:61–66.

Weber, O. 1907. *Die Literatur der Babylonier und Assyrer: Ein Überblick.* Leipzig: Hinrichs.

Weidner, Ernst. 1963. "Assyrische Epen über die Kassiten-Kämpfe." *AfO* 20:113–16.

Weiershäuser, Frauke. 2010. "Weiser Išum, der du den Göttern vorangehst." Pages 351–76 in *Von Göttern und Menschen: Beiträge zu Literatur und Geschichte des Alten Orients; Festschrift für Brigitte Groneberg.* Edited by Dahlia Shehata, Frauke Weiershäuser, and Kamran V. Zand. CM 41. Leiden: Brill.

Weiher, Egbert von. 1998. *Uruk: Spätbabylonische Texte aus dem Planquadrat U 18, Teil V.* Ausgrabungen in Uruk-Warka 13. Mainz: von Zabern.

Weinfeld, Moshe. 1988. "Reed-wall! Hear Me: Leak of Information from the Divine Council." Pages 63–68 in *Linguistic Studies in Memory of Moshe Held.* Edited by Mordechai Cogan. Studies by the Department of Bible and Ancient Near East 3. Beer Sheva: Ben-Gurion University of the Negev Press. [Hebrew]

———. 1997–1998. "'Partition, Partition; Wall, Wall, Listen': "Leaking" the Divine Secret to Someone Behind the Curtain." *AfO* 44/45:222–25.

Weissert, Elnathan. 1997. "Creating a Political Climate: Literary Allusions to *Enūma Eliš* in Sennacherib's Account of the Battle of Halule." Pages 191–202 in *Assyrien im Wandel der Zeiten: XXXIXe Rencontre Assyriologique Internationale, Heidelberg, 6.–10. Juli 1992.* Edited by Hartmut Waetzoldt and Harald Hauptmann. HSAO 6. Heidelberg: Heidelberger Orientverlag.

Weniger, Stefan, ed. 2011. *The Semitic Languages: An International Handbook.* Handbücher zur Sprach- und Kommunikationswissenschaft 36. Berlin: de Gruyter.

West, M. L. 1997a. "Akkadian Poetry: Metre and Performance." *Iraq* 59:175–87.

———. 1997b. *The East Face of Helicon: West Asiatic Elements in Greek Poetry and Myth.* Oxford: Clarendon.

Westbrook, Raymond, ed. 2003. *A History of Ancient Near Eastern Law.* 2 vols. HdO 72. Leiden: Brill.

Westenholz, Aage. 1974/1977. "Old Akkadian School Texts: Some Goals of Sargonic Scribal Education." *AfO* 25:95–110.

———. 2007. "The Graeco-Babyloniaca Once Again." *ZA* 97:262–313.

Westenholz, Joan Goodnick. 1992. "Oral Traditions and Written Texts in the Cycle of Akkade." Pages 123–54 in *Mesopotamian Epic Literature: Oral or Aural?* Edited by Marianna E. Vogelzang and Herman L. J. Vanstiphout. Lewiston, NY: Mellon.

———. 1997a. *Legends of the Kings of Akkade*. MC 7. Winona Lake, IN: Eisenbrauns.

———. 1997b. "Studying Poetic·Language." *Or* 66:181–95.

———. 1999. "In the Shadow of the Muses: A View of Akkadian Literature." *JAOS* 119:80–87.

Wiggermann, F. A. M. 1992. *Mesopotamian Protective Spirits: The Ritual Texts*. CM 1. Groningen: Styx.

———. 1993–1995. "Mischwesen. A. Philologisch. Mesopotamien." *RlA* 8:222–46.

———. 1998–2000. "Nergal. A. Philologisch." *RlA* 9:215–23.

———. 2008. "A Babylonian Scholar in Assur." Pages 203–34 in *Studies in Ancient Near Eastern World View and Society: Presented to Marten Stol on the Occasion of His 65th Birthday, 10 November 2005, and His Retirement from the Vrije Universiteit Amsterdam*. Edited by R. J. van der Spek. Bethesda, MD: CDL.

———. 2018. "The Göttertypentext as a Humanistic Mappa Mundi: An Essay." Pages 351–70 in *Sources of Evil: Studies in Mesopotamian Exorcistic Lore*. Edited by Greta Van Buylaere, Mikko Luukko, Daniel Schwemer, and Avigail Mertens-Wagschal. AMD 15. Leiden: Brill.

Wilcke, Claus. 1977. "Die Anfänge der akkadischen Epen." *ZA* 67:153–216.

———. 1989. "Die Emar-Version von 'Dattelpalme und Tamariske'—ein Rekonstruktionsversuch." *ZA* 79:161–90.

———. 1999. "Weltuntergang als Anfang: Theologische, anthropologische, politisch-historische und ästhetische Ebenen der Interpretation der Sintflutgeschichte im babylonischen *Atram-hasīs*-Epos." Pages 63–112 in *Weltende: Beiträge zur Kultur- und Religionswissenschaft*. Edited by Adam Jones. Wiesbaden: Harrassowitz.

Winter, Irene. 2000. "Babylonian Archaeologists of The(ir) Mesopotamian Past." Pages 1785–89 in *Proceedings of the First International Congress on the Archaeology of the Ancient Near East, Rome, May 18th–23rd 1998*. Edited by Paolo Matthiae. Rome: Università degli studi di Roma "La Sapienza".

Wiseman, Donald J. 1953. *The Alalakh Tablets*. Occasional Publications of the British Institute of Archaeology at Ankara 2. London: British Institute of Archaeology at Ankara.

Wisnom, Laura Selena. 2014. "Intertextuality in Babylonian Narrative Poetry: *Anzû*, *Enūma Elish*, and *Erra and Ishum*." PhD diss., University of Oxford.

———. 2015. "Stress Patterns in *Enūma Eliš*: A Comparative Study." *KASKAL* 12:485–502.

Worthington, Martin. 2010. "Medicine, Comedy, Power and Their Interconnections in Babylonia and Assyria." *Journal des médecines cunéiformes* 15:25–39.

Younger, K. Lawson, Jr. 2006. "The Production of Ancient Near Eastern Text Anthologies from the Earliest to the Latest." Pages 199–219 in *Orientalism, Assyriology and the Bible*. Edited by Steven W. Holloway. HBM 10. Sheffield: Sheffield Phoenix.

Zaccagnini, Carlo. 1978. "The Enemy in the Neo-Assyrian Royal Inscriptions: The Ethnographic Description." Pages 409–24 in *Mesopotamien und seine Nachbarn: Politische und kulturelle Wechselbeziehungen im Alten Vorderasien vom 4. bis 1. Jahrtausend v. Chr.* Edited by Hans-Jörg Nissen and Johannes Renger. BBVO 1. Berlin: Reimer.

Ziegler, Nele. 2016. "Aqba-Hammu et le début du mythe d'Atram-hasis." *RA* 110:107–26.

Zimmern, Heinrich. 1913. *Sumerische Kultlieder aus altbabylonischer Zeit*. VS 10. Leipzig: Hinrichs.

Ziolkowski, Theodore. 2011. *Gilgamesh Among Us: Modern Encounters with the Ancient Epic*. Ithaca: Cornell University Press.

Zólyomi, Gábor. 2011. "Akkadian and Sumerian Language Contact." Pages 396–404 in *The Semitic Languages: An International Handbook*. Edited by Stefan Weniger. Handbücher zur Sprach- und Kommunikationswissenschaft 36. Berlin: de Gruyter.

INDEX

Bold indicates the main treatment of a particular composition or type of text.

abortifacient, 131 n. 239
Abraham (biblical), 94 n. 76
acrostics, 27–28, 162, 171, 173
Adad, 84 n. 27, 89, 95, 134, 159, 163
Adad-guppi, 149
Adapa, Myth of, 41 n. 112, 42, 48 n. 143, 50 n. 156, 67, **91–93**
administrative texts, 5, 9, 15, 22, 26 n. 43, 33, 35 n. 92, 74, 81 n. 14, 149–50 n. 321, 158
Advice to a Prince, **182**
Africa, 195
agnosticism, 176
Agum-kakrime Inscription, 133 n. 246, **147**
Agushaya Hymn, 50 n. 161, 169
Akitu ritual. *See* New Year's ritual
Akkade, 123, 131, 132
Akkadian empire, 3, 123–24, 146
Akkadian language, 1–5, 23; accentuation of, 45 n. 129, 48; dictionaries for, 16; literary dialects of, 4, 33–34, 71, 73; meter in, 49–52; normalization/transcription of, 19; peripheral dialects of, 3; periodization of, 3–4; pronunciation of, 19–20, 47 n. 139; prose/verse in, 44–47, 51; translation of, 16–20; transliteration of, 17–18, 23
Alalakh (Tell Atchana), 10, 153
Alexander the Great, 145
allusion, literary, 64–67, 88 n. 43, 148 n. 315
Aluzinnu-text, 67, **189**
Amenemope, Instructions of, 180

Amorite, 1
amphibrach, 48, 51
amulets, 108, 160, 171 n. 413
Ancient Near East: geography of, 3 map 1; history of (general), 4 n. 16
An-gin₇, 88 n. 43
annals, royal, 135, 136 fig. 15. *See also* royal inscriptions
antediluvian texts, age, xxii, 80 n. 12, 112, 121–22, 147
anthologies, Akkadian, 77, 133 n. 246, 161 n. 373, 195 n. 2
anthropogony, 62, 81, 83, 84–86
Antiochus I Soter, 133 n. 246, 135, 145 n. 296
Anu (Sum. An), 81, 85, 92, 95, 96, 98, 116, 145 n. 296
Anzu, Epic of, 34, 42, 43 n. 120, 66, 71, 80 n. 12, 84, 85 n. 32, **87–91**, 104 n. 128, 169 n. 403
apocalyptic literature, Jewish, 143
apodosis, 63
apotheosis, 124
Apsu, 63, 85, 122
Arabic, 1
Aramaic, 1–2, 5, 73
Arkeoloji Museum (Istanbul), 12
Asia, 195
assonance, 45, 51, 55
Assur (deity), 43, 84, 137, 138, 146, 168
Assur (Qalat Shergat; city), 9, 11, 71 n. 273, 87 n. 41, 100, 101 n. 111, 102, 134, 141 n. 282, 143 n. 289, 180, 185 n. 478
Assurbanipal, 26, 28, 102, 103, 104 n. 127, 123, 133 n. 246, 138, 159, 163 n. 382,